EUROPEAN SOCIETY IN UPHEAVAL

Second Edition

PETER N. STEARNS
CARNEGIE-MELLON UNIVERSITY

EUROPEAN SOCIETY IN UPHEAVAL

SOCIAL HISTORY SINCE 1750

Macmillan Publishing Co., Inc.
NEW YORK

Collier Macmillan Publishers
LONDON

Macmillan Publishing Co., Inc.
866 Third Avenue, New York, New York 10022

Collier-Macmillan Canada, Ltd.

Library of Congress Cataloging in Publication Data

Stearns, Peter N
  European society in upheaval.

  Bibliography: p.
  Includes index.
  1. Europe—Social conditions. I. Title.
HN373.S68   1975   309.1′4   74-6635
ISBN   0-02-416210-8

Printing: 1 2 3 4 5 6 7 8   Year: 5 6 7 8 9 0

For T. E. D., who enhanced my knowledge of the subject

Acknowledgments

I am deeply indebted to Professors Emile Karafiol and Patricia Branca for reading this manuscript and for their many suggestions. I wish also to thank the many students, both graduate and undergraduate, whose questions and research have deepened my understanding of modern social history.

CONTENTS

1
Introduction
                                                                    1

2
Premodern Society in Europe
                                                                    13

5

Mature Industrial Society   179

6

The Consumer Society

7

Conclusion: Modernization Revisited

EUROPEAN SOCIETY IN UPHEAVAL

1
INTRODUCTION

The basic fact of European history since 1750 has been an unprecedented social upheaval. Every age is a time of change, and Europe had not been static in the previous centuries. But in the last two hundred years a new kind of society has been formed, as different from its predecessor as agricultural society was from the hunting culture with which man first began to fight for survival. Beginning in the eighteenth century, demographic, economic, and political forces arose that were truly revolutionary in their intensity. The population of the Continent began to expand rapidly and, in addition, grew exceptionally mobile. Europe became urbanized; for the first time in human history the majority of people lived in cities, and the countryside was partially urbanized as well, as a city economy and culture spread outward. The economy of Europe was transformed. Production expanded greatly, and new methods of marketing and transport arose. Finally, governments gradually adopted new methods and policies, often spurred by pressures from below as new groups gained political consciousness. The result was an increasingly active government that sought change in many areas—in agricultural methods, in the organization of cities, in industry and technology, and in more conventional matters such as police and military structure. Population growth, the industrialization of the economy, and the modernization of the state—here were the most obvious motors for change.

The result was a transformation that touched every aspect of life; and in many ways the less familiar changes were more important. People became sexier. They had intercourse more often, both in and out of marriage. Their bodies changed. Modern European man is taller, is heavier, and has bigger feet than his premodern counterpart. Women are taller as well, but ultimately their physical image, and with a bit of a lag their physical reality, stressed greater slenderness, along with an increase in bust size. The age of puberty declined, ultimately by as much as eight years; in 1700, most lower-class girls began to menstruate only at age eighteen to twenty. These basic biological changes seem an integral part of modernization, and are occurring today in other parts of the world, such as Japan, where a similar social upheaval has been underway for some time. The list of fundamental transformations is lengthy, and this book will cover many of them in detail. Premodern society had a different notion of work from modern society. It had little specific sense of leisure; the notion of vacations and regular, off-the-job recreation was born in the nineteenth century.

There are a number of labels commonly used to describe the social upheaval of the last two centuries. Industrialization is one. It is useful to think of two fundamental economic revolutions in human history, the first, agricultural, bringing men out of the caves and into settled communities, and the second, industrial, creating the urban society we live in today. But a vaguer term, *modernization,* may be better. Modernization includes industrialization and the extension of a profit-making, market mentality to shops, farms, and even individual families to some extent. It embraces political change. A modern political society has an active state (whether totalitarian or democratic) and a population that is conscious of the national political process and insistent on having at least a pro forma voice in it; hence the universality of popular elections in all modern countries. Most of all, modernization involves a change in outlook. Compared to premodern people, modern man is rational, believing that planning and good order are important and possible; secular, with little or no interest in traditional religion; and progressive, holding that change is desirable and that the future is likely to be better than the past. Obviously these values are not absolutes; modern people are not completely rational and they often worry about the future. But as a model that indicates trends in values, the idea of a modernization of outlook has considerable validity.

Any change as great as industrialization and modernization creates a great deal of stress. At every stage of the modernization process large groups of people were fearful of change. Ironically, the same transformation that spread an idea of progress also enhanced a more traditional notion that somehow the past was better. An example: polls in France as late as the 1950s revealed that the majority of the population believed that people lived longer in the past than in modern society, apparently assuming that the stress of modern life, in contrast to the peaceful existence of the countryside, must have reduced longevity. The facts were quite different, for longevity has steadily increased with modernization. But the point is that most people, even today, are ambivalent about change, wanting it in some respects but fearing its consequences in others. Certain groups, throughout the modernization process, have been positively antimodern, specifically attacking the values and institutions of change, and although they have yet to win out they play a consistently important historical role.

Modernization from the first has involved continuing tension between efforts to protest basic changes and efforts to adapt to them. The history of protest itself is divided between attacks against modern society and agitation for gains within its framework. In either case protest is dramatic and has readily drawn the attention of historians. It is easy to assume that great change caused great unrest and that even when people were not taking to the streets they were just waiting for a chance to rise up. In fact, without minimizing the importance of protest, particularly in key stages of the modernization process, the theme of adaptation is more important. People learned to live with change, sometimes surprisingly quickly, although often with a certain amount of tension. One of the basic questions in the history of European modernization is why adaptation was so widespread, for there are areas of the world in which it is still not clear that modernization can take hold at all.

The terms *modernization* and *industrialization* can be loaded ones. When we say that a group was antimodern or that an area was slow to industrialize we do not mean that they were therefore bad. There are eminently good reasons to oppose or delay change. But there is a bias in this book, and it is well to state it frankly at the outset. On the whole I believe that the modernization process has been a liberating one. Not only are modern people richer and healthier than ever before, they are also freer. Premodern society, though by no means completely dismal or static, was stifling for many people, whether they recognized it or not. In both town and countryside close-knit groups regulated the lives of individuals very closely. Modernization steadily weakened these structures, replacing them with more impersonal but also more remote sources of control.

This is not a claim that all is well with modern society. There are immense evils, some of them correctable; in certain areas quite radical change is needed. And the modernization process, in addition to bringing considerable stress to most groups (for the very fact that individual freedom and choice increased caused great confusion), undoubtedly damaged the position of some types of people. The insane are one example, by no means insignificant. It is impossible at this point to compare rates of insanity from premodern to modern society. They have not necessarily gone up. But insanity in modern society is identifiable; it is feared; and from the early stages of modernization its worst victims were institutionalized. In premodern society the insane were normally treated within family and village, for the boundary line between normal and abnormal behavior was less clear. Modern man, more rational, perhaps in some ways more fearful, tries to isolate the deviant. In general one can note a number of types of people whom modernization has hurt, because they cannot mesh easily with its canons of behavior. At an extreme the suicide rate has probably gone up, although we need real caution here, for the rate varies greatly from one modern country to the next, generally along the same lines that one finds in premodern rates. In Europe the countries with the darkest winters, notably in Scandinavia, along with Austria had the highest suicide incidence in the seventeenth century and they still have today. But it is possible to argue that the stress of modernization pushes more people to the brink of despair, or over it, than was true before.

But although many historians would disagree, this is not the case for large groups in the population. It has been argued that modernization reduces the status of women; we will contend that the reverse is true. It has been argued that the elderly are worse off; here the evidence is murkier, particularly for the late nineteenth century, but by the twentieth century the elderly, too, were benefiting from a certain kind of liberation. It is easy to romanticize the past. Very early in the modernization process city dwellers picked up a nostalgia for the countryside that had been part of Europe's literary tradition since ancient times. Many historians and social scientists have followed suit. Certainly there have been some losses; the reader can judge for himself how many. But most European people have clearly come to believe that modern society is better than premodern, which is why they continue to flock to the cities and, with rare exceptions, refuse to leave once there. This study will attempt to show why they make this kind of decision.

We are dealing with the modernization process from the standpoint of social history. It would be possible to concentrate on more specific aspects of modernization, which would bring us closer to the concerns of conventional history. The social historian is concerned with changes in the values and behavior patterns of a whole society or large groups within it. He deals with changes in formal ideas—the Enlightenment, for example—when they affect the thinking of large groups, but not with the ideas in detail. Political processes are interesting as they affect people. A law can be passed whose impact differs greatly from its intent; the social historian is not concerned with the details of its passage (the changes in ministries or even the parliamentary debates), but with this impact. And there are major areas of behavior that have little or no direct political or intellectual significance but are more important for understanding people—family ties, for example, or the development of new recreation patterns.

Social history thus has a rather different focus from other branches of history. It is an approach more than a special set of topics, for the social historian attempts to judge every aspect of society, politics as well as toilet training, in terms of what it reveals about widely held values and behavior.

Every aspect of modern society has a history. Newspapers and other popular media constantly comment on novelty and change in the basic fabric of society, and it is only through social history that we can evaluate what they are talking about. For example, we constantly hear about the decay of family life. This is a historical judgment, yet too few students of the family bother to study its past and too few historians, who do deal with the past, have bothered to study the family. The result leaves vast room for ignorance. In fact the family has not necessarily decayed with modernization; in some ways it has been strengthened, but only a historical perspective reveals this. And complaints that the family is collapsing go back to the beginnings of modernization, which suggests that laments about declining family ties play a major role in anxiety about the whole process of change, perhaps stemming from this kind of concern more than from actual changes in the family. The social history of modernization attempts to give perspective to every major aspect of modern society, so that we can judge what is new and what not new, which is the only way to gain a sense of social trends.

Obviously, the modernization process did not affect each group in the same way, nor did it proceed at a constant pace. To grasp its essentials we will rely heavily on concepts of periodization and social stratification. This involves some major simplifications. Important changes occur within major periods, marking off subsections. Individuals vary greatly within even a carefully defined social group. We will later describe, for example, how the working class around 1900 spent relatively little of any extra income on housing; but individual workers can be found who devoted great attention to improving their living quarters. We deal, inevitably, with averages and general trends, not year-by-year or person-by-person detail.

In 1750 Europe was divided into a number of social groupings. With modernization the nature of the groupings changed, but society remained far from homogeneous. Not only economic position but also family structure and religious life divided the major social classes of every country.

The term *social class* is used very broadly as a descriptive category. It denotes people who have a roughly similar style of life and social status. Some sociologists prefer the word *stratum* to *class,* reserving the latter for groups that sense a common interest and try to act upon it. In 1900 only a minority of workers belonged to class-conscious organizations such as unions or socialist parties. We will deal with this group, but when we discuss the working class a much larger number of people is involved. Some of them disagreed vigorously with others in the same class about political goals, for although there is usually a general relationship between class and political outlook, politics is not the best way to define a class. But workers shared a roughly common employment situation, similar recreational patterns and attitudes toward work, a comparable family life, and so on. And in all these respects they differed from other classes at the time. Finally, although they did not necessarily share a positive sense of class unity, they knew they were different from nonworkers. They would regard both peasants and businessmen as outsiders, whether they felt a sense of class conflict against them or not.

European social classes were defined by several fundamental factors, whose combination tended to change over time. In traditional society, status was the key criterion. Many groups were marked off by law, so that they had different rights, different taxes to pay, even distinctive styles of dress. With modernization legal status was largely erased, but a sense of status continued to define many groups who would try to distinguish themselves by intermarriage and special patterns of consumption. The perpetuation of the old notion of status most obviously differentiates aristocrats from big businessmen in Europe, well into the recent period, for aristocrats tried to set themselves off even when they no longer had legal privileges or unusually high incomes. But similar distinctions mark artisans off from factory workers and, to an extent, professional people, like lawyers, off from businessmen.

Type of work often supplemented descriptions of status. The key traditional distinction was between people who worked with their hands and those who did not, and this remains important today. In particular it came to mark off the lower middle class from the working class, even when levels of earnings were not much different.

Increasingly, in industrial society, money was the great determinant of social class. It also played a role in premodern society, within the status groups. Rich peasants, for example, must be discussed somewhat separately from ordinary peasants, and the latter from landless laborers, even though all were usually in the same legal category. By the nineteenth century earnings and property ownership spoke more loudly, and groups with the same earnings could rarely stay apart too long. Hence aristocrats and big businessmen, artisans and the better-paid factory workers increasingly coalesced into single classes because of shared economic position.

By the twentieth century, stratification became more complex. Not only law but also property ownership had disappeared as the major criteria of social divisions. They still had influence, directly and through tradition. Modernization did not neatly replace one kind of social definition with another. But increasingly job position was the key, not only dividing manual from nonmanual workers but also differentiating the latter in terms of position in a bureaucratic hierarchy. Earnings would usually reflect the main distinctions, but sometimes less sharply than before.

All of these distinctions must be explored more fully as we discuss the major stages of modernization. For now the main point is that we are looking for ways to define groups that shared values and styles of life, for this is the only way to grasp social reality. There were, of course, trends that cut across class lines. Religion or, later, nationalism were shared by many groups. Family patterns, though rarely the same at any one time, could be copied, so that it is possible to talk of trends in family structure quite apart from class. The whole modernization process indeed would ultimately touch society generally, which is why an overall definition is possible. But at any given point, even in the present day, social classes differed in important respects even when they were moving in the same direction. Any effort to label a period's culture usually means that only one or two social classes are being considered, at best. A good example is Victorian England, which has been praised or blamed for its harmony, rigid morality, and optimism. The definition almost completely ignores the lower classes. In fact, as we will see, it distorts the middle and upper classes as well.

For the unfortunate fact is that most historians, although recognizing class lines in principle, have generalized about classes more than they have studied them. When the middle class or bourgeoisie is mentioned, many notions come to mind (depending a bit on what kind of historian has been read most recently): dynamic (the businessman); cruel and exploitative (the businessman again); puritanical and repressed (middle-class women, and possibly the poor old businessman again); fearful and incipiently fascist (the shopkeeper and clerk). Yet the middle class has almost never been examined closely. As for the more inarticulate levels of society, the workers and peasants, they come to attention usually only when they protest, which was not their normal activity. In taking class lines seriously, as the social historian must to understand the impact of modernization, a fresh look is required at the upper levels of society, who are too often known only by a few articulate individuals, and a much more comprehensive survey of the masses of the population.

How many social classes should be considered? In English history there is a longstanding tradition, for the nineteenth and twentieth century, of dividing into threes: upper, middle, and lower. This trinitarian impulse is lazy and inaccurate, taking only the grossest kind of economic divisions into consideration. We will require a more elaborate framework, given the various criteria that set groups off from each other. Moreover, within even more limited social classes there was often a division, admittedly fuzzy, between elements that could basically accept modernization and those that were frightened by it. The lower middle class, for example, has often been seen (particularly in Germany) as a backward-looking unit, terrified by big business and impersonal organization. In fact the group was divided, even though it shared a similar life style in other respects. Here and in other cases social classes constantly tended to pull apart, between those who could adapt and those who could not. Finally, factors of age and sex must be introduced. Age has yet to receive due attention, but we are beginning to know something about the history of key groups like adolescents (a creation of modern society) and the elderly. Sex considerations are more obvious, and special attention needs to be given to women within each major social class.

A society at any given stage of modernization can be understood in terms of certain general trends and institutions, such as technological levels and political structure. Its people, however, must be broken down by class and often by subgroup, by age level, and by sex. A complex array, to be sure, but not indigestible and essential to grasp the way contemporary society came into being.

Periodization, fortunately, can be somewhat simpler. Because it is less concerned with single events and great men, social history does not need a detailed chronology. What happened in a decade is more important than what happened in a year. What follows is based on a fourfold periodization of the development of modern society, after an initial section on the preindustrial setting. It derives from a combination of major changes in demography; key economic changes, in terms ultimately of major stages of industrialization; and related alterations in social structure. It may be that this periodization needs further refinement, for the bases of periodization are not well worked out in social history and the field has long relied on divisions established by political events; but the present divisions constitute a reasonable first step.

It is increasingly recognized that essential aspects of the modernization process were taking shape in Western Europe from about 1750 onward, in the form of population increase and the spread of new forms of manufacturing. From this base flowed industrialization itself, from about 1820 onward (a bit earlier in England). This second phase of modernization saw only a minority of the population touched by the factories directly, but it witnessed the most rapid urbanization. Together the first two stages of modernization, 1750–1820 and 1820–1870, constitute the period in which change was most bewildering and the institutions of society most severely challenged.

From about 1870 onward industrial society matured. Family life stabilized; population growth declined. But stabilization brought new tensions as key social groups defined their interests more clearly, and continued innovation in technology and social organization produced its own strain. In fact the last two decades of this third phase of modernization saw much of European society in disarray. Staggered by World War I, the social structure that had been tossed up by mature industrialization was no longer adequate. Many people viewed the 1920s as a new, and horrible, kind of society. In fact the basic trends were not novel, but cruelly distorted by the impact of the first total war.

Gradually, by around 1950, a fourth phase of modernization emerged. Some have labeled it postindustrial or postmodern, claiming that the very basis of industrial society has been overturned. It is more accurate to view it as a new stage within a basic process, and from the European stand-point, at least to date, a far more successful stage than its predecessor.

Thus in coming to terms with the modernization process, we have a variety of social groups and several key periods. One other ingredient must be tossed into the pot. Europe, a relatively small continent, is bewilderingly diverse in terms of geography, climate, ethnicity, and historical tradition. Many social historians find it difficult to deal with more than a single region or city; this level of detail has a longstanding tradition in French social history, for example, where even a single village can be the focus of a massive monograph. At one level of historical reality the small region has to be isolated. Peasants in the poor, mountainous areas of the Auvergne differed greatly from wheat growers in Normandy. Peasants in vineyard regions are almost always more independent-minded than those who raise grain. Workers in Birmingham, where shops were fairly small and skill levels high, behaved quite differently from textile workers in Manchester; they even voted differently. Distinctions of this sort could be multiplied, but we lack the space to make them. And there are general processes that can be identified across the small regional lines, even if they would need refinement when applied to any given area.

We also take relatively little account of national distinctions. In many respects, for social history, these have far less reality than the internal regional divisions. The processes of modernization and the nature of the key social classes cut across national lines, despite undeniable differences in political structure.

Above the national level, however, certain large regional variations must be consistently noted. The big division is between eastern and western Europe. Germany from the Elbe River eastward, most of the Habsburg monarchy, and Russia constitute the bulk of the eastern zone. With due allowance for special Mediterranean traditions, the southern half of Italy and the southern half of Spain had a similar social framework, with the big qualification that levels of urbanization were far higher. The eastern–southern zone was characterized by large landed estates and, even at the end of the eighteenth century, a tight manorial system. Both peasantry and aristocracy were profoundly different from their western counter-parts as a result. The preindustrial middle class was distinctive as well. Indeed it barely existed in eastern Europe, given the small size of cities, whereas in southern Europe it was highly traditionalist and tied to the aristocracy. Although important parts of this zone had a solid manu-facturing tradition, as was true of Russia and parts of the Balkans, the area was not easily open to modernization. When modernization came it had to be copied from the West. It caused more tension as a result, and in some cases (as in the south) was less successful. Certainly the chronology was different. This area of Europe entered the first phases of modernization only around 1870, so that developments then in many

**Table 1.
European Zones of
Social Development**

		Smooth Industrialization	
		West Britain, Scandi- navia, France *	*West Central* West Germany, Northern Italy, Low Countries, Northern Spain, Czechoslovakia *
	Preindustrial patterns	Early open to eco- nomic and political aristocracy change; parliamentary tra- dition	Strong; big role in bureaucracy; effi- cient; some links to middle class
	peasantry	Independent land tenure; low tradi- tional birth rate; much market pro- duction; relatively wealthy	Independent land tenure; less wealthy
	urban	Relatively large commercial cities; strong middle class; weakened artisan guilds	Less commercial middle class, larger professional element; strong artisan guilds
	Moderniza- tion patterns	Early industrializa- tion; early decline of birth rate; early decline of religion; high level of desire for mobility, rising income; restrained political extremes	More state role in industrialization; more resistance to modernization; more persistence of religion; rise of political extremes (socialism, nation- alism); lower levels of protest based on personal acquisitiveness

* Indicates middling
position, close to
next group over.

ways mirrored those of the west a century before. Industrial maturity was reached only in the mid-twentieth century. Again we can talk of some common processes, but we will have to call attention consistently to differences in stage of development and in the precise form involved.

The game of regional lines can be played almost endlessly, and it is important. The accompanying chart suggests a somewhat more detailed breakdown, based on preindustrial patterns of land tenure and class structure and subsequent distinctions that flowed from them even as modernization took hold. Aside from the big regional gap already outlined, the detailed variations will rarely be insisted upon in the interests of getting at modernization as a process.

Later, Induced Industrialization		Incomplete Modernization	
East Central	*East*	*South*	*Balkans*
Austria, East Germany, Baltic States	Russia, Poland, Rumania, Hungary *	Southern Spain, Southern Italy, Ireland *	
Strong feudal aristocracy	Strong; economically inefficient; linked to state	Urbanized; absentee; inefficient	No large native aristocracy
High birth rate; mainly large estates; some large independent peasants; high traditional poverty	High birth rates; tightly tied to large estates; few large or independent peasants; poverty	Sharecropping; declining economy; poverty	Herding economy; few tools
Middle class dependent on state; small business element; small cities; strong guilds	Essentially no manufacturing cities or independent urban classes	Strong guilds; large professional middle class	No specialized artisanry; small merchant class
Later but successful industrialization; lack of rural protest; strong urban resistance to industrialization; open to fascism	Heavy state role in industrialization; lack of independent middle class, high rural unrest; open to communism and/or authoritarianism	Not open to nineteenth-century industrialization; high levels of rural unrest and/or religious fervor; long-lasting population growth and/or emigration	Not open to nineteenth-century industrialization; gradual growth of nonindustrial cities, more artisanal specialization

For recent European social history gains its real significance from its involvement in this process. It provides a more generalizable set of case studies of modernization than the United States, for example. For in Europe modernization occurred against the backdrop of a rich traditional society. Its development had to contend with a traditional upper class and with a peasantry, both largely absent in North America. In this sense Europe, along with its main regional variants, provides a better way to grasp what modernization involves, what its essential preconditions are, for students of contemporary modernization in Asia, Africa, or Latin America. Europe also offers something of a model for understanding contemporary American society. In many ways modernization has produced a similar product on the two continents. But at some key stages, European modernization was less successful than North American, if only because there were more traditional forces to contend with. More tentatively, it will be argued that Europe in the most recent phase of modernization, the development of a consumer society, has been more successful than its American counterpart, not in terms of world power, obviously, but in terms of the creation of a somewhat more humane, certainly better adapted, style of life.

There is no field of history undergoing more exciting changes than social history over the last decade. Knowledge of family life, work and leisure, as well as demography and social protest, grows each year. New areas are being opened up, as in the study of criminality in the past. Huge gaps remain, of course, for some facets of social history have not been explored at all and others have been studied only for a single country or region. Certain generalizations thus must be based on rather limited examples. Some crucial open questions will be outlined. But all this is part of the excitement of the subject. We need to stimulate further research and ask new questions, yet we can share in the growing understanding of how modern social processes work. The result can shape a better grasp of what our own society is like and where it may be heading than any other approach to social science.

An analytical bibliography at the end of the book offers guidelines for further reading in the major aspects of modern European social history and an indication of the types of material utilized for the essay itself.

2

PREMODERN SOCIETY
IN EUROPE

During the century or so before 1750 European society was not changing very rapidly. Population growth was slight in most areas, though it hit relatively high levels in Russia. Social mobility seems to have been modest, as most people stayed in the station of life into which they were born. The size of cities increased somewhat and urban influence on the economy may have increased. In Holland there were significant improvements in agricultural productivity; in France a few new manufacturing procedures were developed. But these developments had scant significance for most European people.

Discussion of premodern society as of about 1700 can convey a false sense of stability. In England, for example, population growth, economic expansion, and concomitant social tensions had been considerable into the mid-seventeenth century. Here and in other parts of Europe major unrest around 1648 suggested substantial social change. But even in previous centuries change had not been so marked as it was to be from about 1750 onward. Cities had expanded, and with them two crucial new social groups, the artisans and the bourgeoisie. Improvements in agriculture allowed general population increase off and on from the tenth century. In western Europe peasants had freed themselves from the tightest manorial restrictions and had altered their family structure. All of this formed a crucial basis for later modernization; it was no accident that western Europe was the seat of the initial upheaval. But the common image of preindustrial society as relatively stagnant is not wrong, if the modern period is taken as the measurement, for change occurred within an essentially rural, communal structure. In some areas of Europe the basic structure of a premodern society lasted well into the nineteenth century. So although we focus on the early eighteenth century for a definition of the society in western Europe, many themes will carry through to 1850 or beyond for the east and south; our chronological range will thus be considerable.

It is essential to have some notion of the nature of premodern Europe in order to grasp the causes, the impact, and the basic meaning of modernization. Causes will be addressed more directly in the following section, but the main question is obvious: was modernization somehow forced on a reluctant populace by factors beyond their control, disturbing a cherished routine? Or did it flow from a society even though key institutions were unquestionably hostile to change? Determination of the nature of preindustrial society says much about potential reactions to change regardless of cause. If we see preindustrial communities as well integrated, giving their inhabitants an automatic sense of identity, then the impact of urban and industrial growth must have been severe. But if preindustrial communities are seen as impoverished and authoritarian, perhaps many people welcomed the chance to try something new.

Certainly an evaluation of premodern society continues to enter our judgments of our own day. Ironically, it is not only conservatives who display nostalgia for past values lost; many radicals also assume that things were better before industrial capitalism reared its ugly head. Modern impersonality is contrasted with the tight personal relationships of the premodern world. The modern family is seen as loose to the point of anarchy, compared to the embracing family structure of times gone by. Old people, now shunted aside by a utilitarian society, are held to have had an integral place in peasant life. And so it goes. It is generally agreed that premodern society was very different from its successor, and in some aspects of life this is all that can be safely concluded; for it is as anachronistic to measure traditional society by modern values as to judge the direction of modern life by, say, degrees of religious fervor. We can note also some areas of continuity, for many groups tried to preserve traditional values even in quite new settings. But it is difficult to avoid some value judgments about the quality of life in premodern society, for the contrast tells us so much about what we have become.

Agricultural Society

The basis of European society in 1700 was agricultural. Everywhere the leading social class, the aristocracy, depended ultimately on agriculture for its economic support. And everywhere the most numerous class was made up of the peasants and associated rural artisans who lived in small towns, in villages, and sometimes on isolated farms. In 1800, 95 per cent of the Russian population and 80 per cent of the French population was rural. Even in 1850 France was still 75 per cent rural, Germany 65 per cent, and Austria 82 per cent. And as late as 1900 Russia was 88 per cent rural, Greece 85 per cent, and France still over 50 per cent.[1] Throughout the century, then, though in declining proportions, agriculture and activities directly related to agriculture remained the source of support for the majority of people throughout most of Europe. Focus on the industrialization and urbanization of Europe leads naturally to a tendency to neglect the continued importance of rural life. The agricultural basis of society must be understood particularly when considering society before the industrial revolution, before there was any massive inducement to leave the countryside for the city.

Agricultural Methods

In 1800 agriculture was almost everywhere designed primarily to feed the owners and workers of the land on which production took place. Certainly there were outside markets for agricultural production. Cities depended on the possibility of buying food. Even areas in eastern Europe, notably Poland and the Ukraine, exported grain to the more urban West. Obviously, producers near cities had frequent market contacts. Regions with specialties such as wine growing had some local exchanges at least and often sold more widely. Areas on navigable rivers were naturally more exposed to market opportunities than other regions. Finally, some exchanges were necessary even for agricultural communities themselves. Salt and metals had to be brought in. Wealthy peasants in parts of Austria and Germany bought meat imported from Hungary.

Nevertheless, even in comparatively wealthy and urbanized countries most peasants were concerned primarily with production for their own needs. This is why their agriculture is often described as a subsistence economy even though they produced enough extra to support the upper classes and to feed the cities. Even many large estates produced for only a local market, and almost all estates filled most of the consumption needs of the local labor force. In general, only the spread of an urban economy after 1750 created a sufficiently massive market to induce peasants and landowners to concentrate on production for distant sales rather than for local consumption. In eastern, and to a lesser extent south-

---

[1] The term *rural* is not totally accurate here, because in most countries it includes all residents of agglomerations with less than 3,000 inhabitants. Although the bulk of this category was indeed rural, a minority were small-town artisans and bourgeois dependent on rural society only indirectly.

ern, Europe the rise of cities in the west after 1800 did create a potential market for export even before industrialization occurred locally, and agricultural methods were accordingly altered early in the century. But almost everywhere in 1750 agriculture was still intended above all for local consumption.

This fact explains a number of the key features of preindustrial agriculture. Agriculture was not, in 1750 and even after, designed primarily to maximize production. In a predominantly nonmarket situation maximization simply made no sense. The local market was finite, traditionally at least. The number of people to feed in a village or on an estate could not expand rapidly. Undue attention to production would be a waste of time because there would be no way to dispose of a major increase. Efforts had to concentrate primarily on assuring existing standards for the existing population. Agriculture was designed, particularly for the peasants but also to a degree for the aristocracy, to maintain traditional (and often rather low) levels of consumption and to support the structure of rural society more generally. Notions of expansion and progress came hard to the rural producer.

The character of preindustrial agriculture showed most clearly in the methods employed, which were largely traditional and severely limited the productive capacity of agriculture. Even after major improvements in method were developed, beginning in England in the eighteenth century, they were extremely slow to spread, for producers could see no need for them. Farm machinery was nonexistent. Only a few simple tools aided the various processes of planting and harvesting. Sometimes the wooden plow was pushed by hand; even when it was drawn by oxen, women and children followed behind, manually distributing the seed. Harvesting was done by hand with a sickle for cutting. The scythe was known but not widely used despite the fact it would have saved on labor; it cut the grain too low, and peasants wanted to leave stalks for their animals to graze on. Peasants thrashed their grain by flailing it or walking on it.

With such simple methods, the amount of land that any one family could cultivate was obviously very small, and production was low. In a good year the methods did allow production somewhat beyond the needs of the producers themselves. It was on this margin that aristocrats lived and preindustrial cities survived. But the margin was small indeed, and it was curtailed by the traditional practice of leaving much of the land fallow each year. This was the only way known to replenish the fertility of the soil. In most areas one third of the cultivated land was left fallow annually; in some parts of southern Europe half the land was set aside. In the eighteenth century alternative methods of restoring nitrogen to the soil by planting clover or turnips had been developed, but such methods were used by only a few large estates in England and northern France. Similarly, new systems of drainage that allowed the utilization of fields previously too wet for cultivation and improved the yield in existing plots were confined initially to Holland and the British Isles.

Finally, most villages possessed, usually as commons land, substantial tracts regarded as unsuitable for cultivation; at most they were devoted to occasional forestry and scrubby pasture land. Large sections of most countries, particularly on the Continent, had never been opened to agriculture at all. Only developments in the nineteenth century would show that cultivation of many of these areas was possible. In the meantime, agriculture before industralization was characterized not only by simplicity of tools and methods, but also by a real limitation of the amount of land that was used at any one time.

Preindustrial agriculture was also dominated by the need to produce almost all the foods needed locally. Only a few products were brought in from the outside. Most villages were isolated from major markets. Only rutted wagon tracks connected them even to other villages in the neighborhood. Outside merchandise was a rarity and was usually either brought by itinerant peddlers or available on regular but infrequent market days in the area. Actually shops were unknown in most villages. Most goods needed for day-to-day consumption had to be locally produced. Even individual families typically attempted substantial self-sufficiency in what they themselves produced.

Primary attention had to be given to a starchy staple, traditionally one of the cheaper grains, such as rye or oats, which were used for bread. Only in a few wealthy regions, such as parts of northwestern France, was wheat widely cultivated. In addition to the staples, however, a variety of other products were necessary. At least a few animals were kept for fiber, hides, and milk as well as for meat. Many regions raised grapes for wine; in other areas grains were used for beer and liquors. And of course each area sought its fuel in woods nearby. Most families made their own clothes and built or maintained their own housing. Some important activities required a degree of specialization. Shepherds, millers, and sometimes a variety of artisans took charge of work no one family could do for itself, but they too engaged in more general farming of their own. Such specialization remained almost entirely local. Only for a very few products or services did a village or estate have to look beyond its borders.

This was another important deterrent to maximization of agricultural production. Regions failed to specialize fully in the products for which their soil and climate were best suited. Some regions had to attempt production, such as wine growing or meat raising, for which they were ill adapted. Small estates and villages with highly diversified agriculture were inefficient and uneconomical in all their products, resulting in poor quality and high costs even in the villages themselves. And the tendency to self-sufficiency severely limited the consumption standards of most localities. Products that could not be raised in the area, such as coffee and tea, were generally unknown. Areas ill suited to production of a major staple were doomed to poverty regardless of their potential for more specialized production.

The starkest tragedy of rural life was the famine, to which preindustrial agriculture was peculiarly vulnerable. When crops failed even in a single locality, widespread starvation could result, because of the difficulty of importing food from other areas. Those who did not die went hungry. Many had to go into debt to tide themselves over, and because rural loans were risky, the interest rates were high, up to 60 per cent a year. Hatred of the money lender was thus widespread, and because Jews served as lenders in much of eastern Europe, peasant anti-Semitism was widespread. But there was no doing without some help in a crisis, for rural charities or relief programs were almost nonexistent. It has been estimated that a famine of some degree of severity occurred once every four years in the rural world, because of bad weather or other conditions. Its impact was exacerbated by the necessity of saving one seed of every four produced for planting next year's crop, for this was low-yield agriculture. Rural society was thus poor and open to frequent crises. Poverty varied with the region, growing greater as one moves eastward across the map of Europe, but no large group of peasants was immune from potential tragedy. Poor diets, along with various epidemic diseases, kept the average lifespan of the rural population low; half the children born would die before they reached the age of two.

Even in a rich agricultural country like France many peasants lived badly, quite apart from famine years. Their housing was mean and small, with earthen floors, inadequate light and air (the French government taxed cottages by the number of windows they had, which forced even wealthy peasants to do without ventilation in their eagerness to foil the state), and crude construction from clay or logs. Animals frequently shared the small space. Poor chimneys filled the house with smoke in winter, and diseases such as tuberculosis were widespread. Clothing was crude, of rough wool or linen, and lacked variety. Many peasants went barefoot or at most had a pair of wooden shoes. Many ate only starches, drank only water, for meat and wine were too expensive except on the most important feast days. Most peasants had an inadequate diet; some did not even consume enough calories to sustain an active life. In Ireland it was estimated that a quarter of the population starved to some extent every year; here and in other countries much of the peasantry virtually hibernated in winter because their energy was so low. These were the worst conditions, but even richer farmers and members of the local aristocracy lived in circumstances that modern people would judge poverty-stricken.

The conditions of preindustrial agriculture also encouraged a distinctive attitude toward work, on the part of peasant producers and also many landlords. Intense work was not seen as a virtue. Peasants worked hard, in terms of long hours of often heavy physical labor; this was true of women and children as well as men. But there was also a great deal of what a modern economist would call underemployment, for many people clung to existence without enough land to keep them busy all the time. More generally, people mixed what we might see as leisure activities with their work. Agricultural laborers gossiped or sang in the fields together. On cold winter nights peasants in various parts of France gathered to sing and tell stories in a barn, but repaired tools or did sewing all the while. Finally, there were days apart from work altogether. In the Orthodox countries of the east as many as eighty to a hundred days were taken off each year for religious festivals. Catholic areas were only a bit less relaxed, and Protestant peasants, with fewer religious festivals, developed or revived secular holidays such as May Day. This was a distinctive kind of life with an undeniable charm, for sociability relieved what were usually extremely boring jobs. But there was a vicious circle involved as well. Agricultural producers could not work too hard because their diets were typically deficient, particularly in protein. They could afford little meat. Because they did not work intensely they were inhibited from increasing their production. This was a deeply rooted work system that made a great deal of sense, particularly because there was no known way to avoid a natural calamity that could wipe away years of hard labor.

Land Tenure

Nothing better illustrates the character of preindustrial agriculture than the way land was divided and owned. Correspondingly, a change in land tenure patterns was one of the prerequisites for any major alteration of agricultural methods. Hence Great Britain, the one area of Europe in which a rapid rise in agricultural productivity was taking place during the eighteenth century, was also the scene of tremendous changes in landholding. On the Continent substantial changes were also taking place, but usually they confirmed and extended earlier methods. Systems of rural tenure and labor still conformed to the character of preindustrial agriculture.

There were, of course, a variety of systems of tenure. In certain areas, such as parts of central France, land was worked on the basis of individual farms and might even be enclosed by fences; the plots were relatively small and the methods and the tenure itself highly traditional. In general, however, two primary systems of tenure existed in Europe. Both systems could be found in most regions. Both had some support in tradition; even in the most recent cases, such as Russia, several centuries of development had led to the patterns existing in the eighteenth century. The two systems were vastly different, however, and so were the resulting positions of peasantry and aristocracy. Furthermore, each system was dominant in different parts of Europe, and in the second half of the eighteenth century each tended to increase at the expense of the other in its areas of dominance.

Roughly speaking, northwestern Europe was an area of small holdings in which peasants directly controlled at least half of the cultivatable land. Most peasant plots were still part of a large estate, and some dues and services were owed to the lord, and these taxes could take a big chunk of peasant earnings (up to 30 per cent in France, for example). However, peasants could usually buy, sell, and leave the land without difficulty. There were important large holdings as well that depended on peasant labor, but these did not involve the majority of the rural population. From the Elbe River in the east to the Atlantic in the west, from Tuscany and northern Spain to Scandinavia, most rural residents based their life on small plots of land operated as part of a village structure.

In eastern Germany and beyond and in southern Italy and southern Spain large estates dominated. The major exceptions to this were the areas of modern Serbia and Bulgaria, where most peasants were free from noble control of any sort. But around 1800, in eastern Prussia, for example, about 62 per cent of the land was held directly in large units. The rest of the arable land was operated in a village system, over which landlords usually had feudal rights. Even on the large estates, villages often administered the land; this was generally the case in Russia. But ultimate control rested with the landlord, and in many cases he administered the estate directly. Certainly the social and economic character of these regions was determined by the preponderance of large estates.

The older of the two systems was that of village small holding. Many villages and their basic tenure patterns dated from early medieval times. The system was highly traditional and in many ways was a typical expression of peasant agriculture and social structure. It therefore had some importance even outside its stronghold in western Europe. In England, where a rather new organization of agricultural labor was taking shape in the eighteenth century, village tenure had flourished earlier and still hung on in some cases. In eastern Europe, where the system was overlaid by the dominant large estates, small holding had existed earlier and persisted in a minority of cases. In Russia, when the emancipation of the peasants cut down the large estates in 1861, village small holding was resumed under government encouragement. And in France, western Germany, northern Italy, and elsewhere in the northwest the system was clearly dominant by 1700. Furthermore in France and neighboring territories the revolution of 1789 removed the last restrictions on peasant ownership of most of the land. In western Germany, to be sure, many peasants remained under some feudal obligations well into the nineteenth century, but they were imposed over a small-holding system.

The typical holding in the regions of peasant tenure was tiny indeed. The average small holding was only nine acres in France. In Russia, where the climate was far less favorable, the average peasant holding after emancipation was about twenty acres. Holdings of this size were usually manageable by a single peasant family, with some extra help at harvest time. And they were sufficient to support a family, except in regions of low fertility or in years of bad harvests. However, peasant tenures were by no means uniform. Only in a few mountain villages was there anything like equality, and here equal holdings may have resulted from the fact that there was little wealth there to tempt the greedy. In France at the end of the seventeenth century only about a tenth of the peasantry owned the "average" small holding. A smaller number had much larger plots. A village of a hundred families would include one or two big farmers who owned the plows and oxen and employed labor on their land. A larger number had only a plot or two and had to do something else to eke out an existence, most commonly hiring out to the farmers or the aristocracy as laborers. There were few people who were absolutely landless; inequality did not go this far.

In 1800 the most important small-holding regions, such as northern France and western Germany, were characterized not only by small average plots but also by division of holdings into separate strips and by a substantial portion of land held in common. Each village was surrounded by several basic fields, usually three in the areas where one third of the land (that is, one of the basic fields) was left fallow each year. The individual family possessed one or more small strips of land in each of the fields. When peasants left land to each of their sons, the strips were repeatedly divided, leading to the patchwork of several plots characteristic of many parts of France today. Furthermore, another part of the land around the village was owned by no individual but by the village as a whole. In 1800 one sixteenth of all the land in France was thus devoted to village commons. Both the commons and the division of land into individual plots clearly expressed the purposes of village agriculture.

Village agriculture provided some minimal protection for all members of the community. The commons were used for cooperative grazing and, where forested, provided wood for the whole village. The village itself determined the use and organization of the common land. The commons also served to protect the poorer members of the village. Often peasants with only a garden plot scraped out a living by gathering wood, tending flocks, and even cultivating part of the commons. Division of individual plots into strips protected each owner by giving him holdings in different places. If disaster overtook one section, no one family would bear the entire burden. If one section was more fertile than the others, all landowners would share in its fertility. In a few areas this general concern for sharing was extended to periodic redistribution of the land according to need. In Russia after the emancipation a minority of villages redistributed land as often as every ten years according to family size; there was no real private ownership at all. This was, of course, an exceptional development; most village tenure, as we have seen, involved substantial inequality. But universally there remained the desire to offer some collective control and protection.

Finally, division into strips required cooperation. The plots were too small to farm individually, and they could not be fenced in. The village collectively decided times of planting and harvesting. Few peasants could afford their own oxen, so when plowing was to be done it was a joint venture. The plow itself was hard to turn, which was one reason land was laid out in long strips, and the turning, too, required village help. The village, and village tradition, determined what land would be left fallow. Animals in collective flocks were allowed to graze in all the fields after harvest.

The need for joint effort was another reason that village agriculture was not easily adapted to change. Its collective framework allowed little room for individual initiative. The small size of most plots offered scant margin for risk or capital for unusual investment. But there was some collective security for all members of the system. In preindustrial agriculture this had to be the primary goal of small producers.

The other major system of tenure presented many contrasts to the village structure. Most obviously, land holdings in eastern and southern Europe were typically quite large. Junker estates in east Prussia, for example, averaged three hundred acres, and some ranged as high as two thousand. Again, there was great variety and inequality, but the scale was quite different. The estates were capable of significant output, which was above all designed to benefit the owner. The estates usually produced most of what their laborers required for consumption. But production did not end there; estate agriculture made sense only if a significant surplus was available for the profit of the owner. Estates therefore tended to expand in importance in the areas they dominated as market possibilities increased. In the early nineteenth century German and Russian landlords eagerly took advantage of the markets created by a rising population and by the urbanization of western Europe and extended the estate system. They purchased many small peasant holdings and forced other peasants, still legally serfs, to include their land in the lord's domain. Well into the nineteenth century the estate system showed a dynamism that was less evident in the small-holding system.

The methods used on the estates were not greatly different from those used in village agriculture. To be sure, more complex equipment could be employed on these large holdings, and some was introduced by the early nineteenth century. There was experimentation with new specialized crops, such as sugar beets in eastern Germany. Some Junkers even built their own refineries and distilleries to capitalize on their substantial production. But on the whole it was not new equipment or products that gave vitality to the estates of eastern and southern Europe; rather, it was a system of servile labor.

Serfdom was virtually unrelieved in the areas of large estates until 1848 at the earliest. Efforts at reform, as in Prussia during the Napoleonic period, came to little. In fact, many estate owners sought to increase the severity of the impositions on their peasants to provide additional income. Except in Prussia after 1807, landlords continued to control the movements of their labor force so that peasants could not leave the estate without permission. Heavy quotas of work service were required, sometimes as much as two days a week, often backed by floggings and other punishments. The resulting cheap labor was the basis of landlord profits. Aspects of the system were to continue in most areas, except Russia, even after serfdom was abolished. Although increasingly pressed, the large-estate system usually endured unless abolished by political means.

This meant that, with rare exceptions, large-estate agriculture was only a bit less conservative than peasant agriculture. It was so easy to exploit workers that little thought was given to more fundamental economic improvements, even when market opportunities increased. Absentee landlords in southern Italy and southern Spain simply took over half their peasants' produce, under the sharecropping system. Although often poor themselves, maintaining at best a shabby gentility, they could not be bothered with the kind of investment and planning that would have created a new production system. Elsewhere a minority of landlords during the eighteenth century began to talk of agricultural improvements, for the idea of change was in the air. But talk was cheap, and the improvement societies formed in Russia had little impact on practice. Even where the middle classes purchased landed estates, as occurred widely in France and southern Italy during the eighteenth century, they typically imitated the aristocracy, at most trying to increase peasant dues without investing in new equipment. For they saw land less as a way to make more money than as a sign of social prestige, and the aristocratic work ethic that they were imitating did not call for much attention to economic detail.

So both the main systems of land tenure were geared mainly to preservation of the status quo. It would take quite a jolt to prod either the average peasant owner or the average landlord into making major changes.

The Rural Classes: The Aristocracy

The fortunes of the aristocracy were based on agriculture, even when the most prominent members of the class spent their lives in the cities. This was Europe's ruling class. Its wealthiest members overshadowed even the richest businessman. It dominated the political and religious establishments. But its roots were on the land, and ultimately, despite persistent and clever use of its other sources of power, the aristocracy declined as the land lost its economic vitality.

In premodern society, the aristocracy was a legal status group more than an economic class, for as we will see there were really two economic categories within the aristocracy. Legal privileges were extensive. In most countries regional parliaments met to discuss taxation and other measures. Composed of three or four legal estates, each with an equal vote, they gave aristocrats substantial political voice; for the class itself constituted one whole estate, the second, and heavily influenced the first, which was dominated by the upper clergy. In some areas only aristocrats could own land; this was true in East Prussia until 1808. Generally, even in western Europe, the class had special hunting rights, which allowed them to ride roughshod over the peasants' fields in search of game. They had special courts for themselves, and normally ran the local courts that had jurisdiction over crimes committed by peasants. They had privileges of dress; only aristocrats could legally carry swords. At an extreme, this led to the anomaly of an impoverished noble, forced to till his own small estate, proudly wearing his weapon as he pushed the plow.

Legal privilege was linked to a distinctive value system that placed the aristocracy on top of a rigidly hierarchical society. The fact that many other groups, including peasants and businessmen, accepted this hierarchy is another way of saying that the aristocracy was the ruling class, for not only its leaders but also its values predominated. The aristocracy was rooted in a sense of separate and superior status, passed on by birth and recognized in law. This feeling was particularly intense among those aristocrats of ancient vintage, descended from the fighting nobles of the middle ages. But actually most aristocrats were of more recent creation. Many people were ennobled in the seventeenth and eighteenth century for service to the state. In some areas, particularly Russia, this practice continued through the nineteenth century; Lenin's father, for example, was ennobled for state service. Usually these new aristocrats were able to gain some land, though in Russia many were quite poor and dependent on their salaries as state bureaucrats. In France, Prussia, and even Russia the service aristocracy increased its landed holdings in the eighteenth century. But the main point is that, no matter how new, aristocratic families quickly picked up the belief in inherited birthright. One of the great strengths of the class, well into modern times, was its ability to persuade new entrants and even nonmembers of the importance of gentle birth.

The aristocracy viewed the whole of society in terms of inherited status; where a man was born, there he was to remain. The class took pains to enforce its sense of inherited distinctions in society. It rarely intermarried with other groups, particularly in eastern Europe. Occasionally financial need might compel an alliance with a business family, but this was frowned upon; for merchants were seen as tainted by their daily preoccupation with earning money. From the peasants, on whom the class depended for its primary income, great respect was exacted. In the Baltic regions they addressed their lord as "Father." And aristocrats as landlords attempted to take a patriarchal approach to their tenants and serfs. Rarely did they deign to collect dues directly; this was left to middlemen, in England as in southern Italy. And peasant anger was more likely to be directed against these agents than against the owners. For, in addition to the deference that many in the lower classes felt for their social superiors, the aristocracy carefully granted favors to the rural poor. It could give servant jobs to daughters. As local magistrates it could settle peasant disputes. And it gave out periodic favors and tips. Well into the eighteenth century it was able to enforce its view of a society based on inherited status.

Ancestry alone did not, of course, complete the definition of the aristocrat. It was assumed that birth transmitted certain unique virtues. The qualities regarded as aristocratic varied with the region and type of aristocracy, but there were certain common features. The aristocrat was expected to maintain a particular sense of honor. In Prussia aristocratic honor was given legal recognition, and an aristocrat's word was accepted in court without affidavit. In most places sense of honor was expressed in dueling. Aristocratic honor abhorred commercialism and usually commerce itself, although individual aristocrats invested boldly, ran coal and iron mines, and carefully supervised estates.

The aristocrat cultivated physical bravery; everywhere military service and leadership were typical expressions of the aristocratic code. The aristocracy also clung to a belief in noblesse oblige, in a superior aristocratic ability to care for the lower orders of society. This led them to expect, and through the eighteenth century usually to obtain, the leading places in government. It could also lead them, even in areas of great aristocratic exploitation of labor, to claim and even to implement feelings for the poor. In Russia, for example, the nineteenth century saw many aristocrats make efforts to improve the health and education of their peasants while exacting servile dues.

Finally, the aristocracy felt itself to be the bearer of a distinct and superior code of manners and culture. It was a leisured class, devoted to activities inaccessible to the crowd. It strove to maintain a peculiar style of life. This effort took the form of dandyism for the British court aristocracy, of widespread gambling, which provided excitement and showed scorn for money, of the adoption of French language and culture by many Russian nobles, of distinctive homes and clothing in many areas, and of the perpetuation of exclusive hunting rights almost everywhere. In the concepts of distinctive honor, manners, bravery, and public service the aristocracy saw the fulfillment of its superior status.

Structure of the Aristocracy

The special position of the aristocracy rested on several factors. The class was a small one. In Hungary 5 per cent of the Magyar population claimed aristocratic status; a large segment of ethnic Poles were aristocrats. But these were exceptional cases. Generally, reliance on inherited status and the relatively expensive style of life severely limited entry. In 1789 there were only 400,000 French aristocrats, a substantial number but less than 2 per cent of the population. About the same percentage applied in Russia, and in most of Germany less than 1 per cent of the population was aristocratic.

Despite its small size the class was divided into distinct subgroups. There were some impoverished nobles, like the *hobereaux* in France who proudly maintained their titles while serving as gamekeepers or beggars. In Poland and Hungary this type was particularly important, often owning a tiny plot of land; the Polish *golota,* or barefoot nobility, comprised the largest segment of the class.

More generally important were nobles' younger sons. In most parts of Europe the aristocracy carefully maintained a system of primogeniture, whereby the eldest son inherited the main title and estates. This was vital if a family was not to dissipate its wealth, but it left the massive problem of what to do with surplus male children. Some of them could acquire lesser noble titles and enter the government, military, or clergy. Britain was unique in allowing younger sons to go into business without losing their claim to aristocratic status, for the British aristocracy was unusually tolerant of commerce. Elsewhere the problem of placing younger sons was acute, for the aristocracy had a high birth rate.

The two main groups of aristocrats were gentry and magnates. The gentry were small landlords with local rather than national political influence. They named judges and parish church officials. In eastern and southern Europe they made local laws and provided rudimentary police services. In England they served as local judges, the justices of the peace. They received dues and work services from the peasantry on their estates. In western Europe, where servile obligations were relatively low, they used tenants, sharecroppers, or paid labor to work their estates. In any case, revenues were usually sufficient for a distinctive style of life.

The gentry lived simply but well. Their manor houses were plain but solid. They hunted, held lavish feasts and dances, and often gambled. They married among their own kind, although sometimes a match with a merchant's daughter was sought for economic reasons. This was not a cultured group, although some in government service obtained extensive education. But there was no question of the firm position of the gentry. Even the magnates were scorned as urbanized and vain.

At the top of the aristocracy was a handful of magnates of great wealth and sophistication. In Hungary, around 1800, out of a total of 75,000 aristocratic families, there were at most two hundred magnate families. This was an elite group. It had few contacts with lower levels of nobility. Intermarriage between magnates and lesser aristocrats was unlikely. Both groups had more contacts with local middle-class elements of roughly comparable wealth than they had with each other. Despite shared legal status and many common values, the differences within the aristocracy could seem overwhelming.

The magnates were distinguished, basically, by the greater economic power behind them. They were the possessors of the most extensive estates in both eastern and western Europe and, correspondingly, of the most imposing family backgrounds and titles. They left the detailed administration of their estates to paid overseers and spent most of their time in the cities. English aristocrats had a six-month "season" in London, when they sponsored the leading balls and concerts. The Hungarian magnates long preferred to live in Vienna. The income from their estates freed the magnates to devote much time to leading positions in the state, the army, and the church. They traveled extensively; the Continental tour was an accepted part of the education of leading young aristocrats in Russia and England alike. Great attention was given to polished manners and dress and to the patronage of the arts. Far from these aristocrats were the violence, vulgarity, and simplicity of the lesser nobles. Their education was extensive; Baltic aristocrats, for example, had tutors for their primary schooling and then went on to private secondary schools and often to a university. In general, education was designed to provide grace and polish. Training in the classics and attention to sports were designed to produce general ability and distinction. Well rounded and cosmopolitan, the upper aristocrat could recognize his peers in any country, which was one reason their group long resisted nationalistic loyalties. And in almost every country the group remained in control of the major institutions of society well into the nineteenth century.

Aristocratic Power

Both gentry and magnates constituted the leading political class of premodern Europe. They ran many cities as well as rural areas, serving as judges, representatives in the regional parliaments, and chief executives. They dominated the top positions in the larger political units. Rarely could a nonaristocrat rise to high office level in the military. Dukes and princes ran the armies of the eighteenth century; their leadership ultimately prevailed over the upstart forces of the French Revolution and Napoleon. Beneath the magnates a host of younger gentry, particularly those excluded from the main inheritance, served in the next echelon. Here were important sources of jobs and income and also the fulfillment of the aristocratic code of honor and bravery. No one else could serve as well.

Aristocrats also claimed a particular responsibility for the church. Here the obligation to care for the lower orders of society could be expressed. Here younger sons, trained already in at least the rudiments of the classics, could find a suitable income and social position. It was relatively easy for aristocratic churchmen to arrange for their peers to fill the leading posts in the established churches. Furthermore, religion was an important part of aristocratic life. Some aristocrats, especially in the west, dabbled with irreligion in the eighteenth century, but this was a short-lived trend. Thus in the later eighteenth century the upper echelons of the Catholic, Lutheran, and Anglican churches were dominated by the aristocracy. In 1789 all French bishops were aristocrats. And everywhere the aristocratic dominance of the established churches was a major factor in promoting social and political conservatism within the churches. For as the aristocracy served the church, so it expected service in return.

The most important institution in which the aristocracy took a leading and traditional role was, of course, the state. There was some ambiguity here. There were traditions of state service for both old landed families and more recent bureaucratic nobles, but there was also hostility to the growing central power of most monarchies, which cut into local privileges.

The basic political tradition of the aristocracy was one of weak central government supplemented by the local political power of the aristocrats themselves. Since 1600 particularly, the central state had developed greatly, from France to Russia, and had deprived nobles of full power over law courts, taxation, and the like. It was always tempting to defy the central state and seek a return to localism. Through the *parlements* many French nobles fought the state during the eighteenth century; their resistance, expressed in the Assembly of Notables of 1787, set the stage for the Revolution. Even later the localist tradition was maintained by men like Alexis de Tocqueville.

However, it was in eastern Europe that the localist impulse remained strongest. Most regions still had diets, the regional parliaments, controlled by the aristocracy, with substantial powers over taxation and regional administration. In Russia, by the 1760s, the government had greatly increased local aristocratic power, particularly legal power, over serfs. But this only whetted the appetites of many gentry to cut down the central autocracy still further. In Poland and Hungary the size of the nobility and the fact that central government was foreign led to even more active resistance well into the nineteenth century.

But the aristocracy rarely indulged its penchant for antimonarchism, for it needed government jobs. Frederick the Great, while strengthening the Prussian state, confirmed the Junkers' local power and continued to rely on bureaucrats drawn from the class. Some posts were outright sinecures, paying good money for no real service. In other cases, where nobles served as diplomats or finance ministers, important work was done, but almost always the aristocratic cachet was essential. Only with the French Revolution was there a real effort to drive aristocrats from the government, and ironically this only confirmed the links between monarchs and nobles elsewhere: for when both were attacked, what was more logical than to combine in defense? Thus well into the nineteenth century, even in western Europe, including France after 1815, the aristocrats filled the main administrative posts. And where national parliaments existed they won control as well. In Britain the House of Peers was by definition aristocratic; more important, until about 1850 over half the members of the House of Commons came from the same class, which was adept at wielding influence and even buying votes in a system where suffrage was extremely limited.

Aristocracy as Ruling Class

Individual aristocrats brought great talent to their leadership functions. Some were economic innovators, playing a role, during the eighteenth century, in introducing new agricultural methods and even opening up new coal mines and factories. It was a British earl who first put rails in a mine, to haul coal. Many statesmen served well. The cosmopolitanism of the class was particularly important. It played a major role in keeping wars within some bounds of reason. Leading magnates might seek to aggrandize their state, but not at the cost of totally disrupting the European diplomatic system. The 1815 Treaty of Vienna, which balanced the interests of the states so neatly (while ignoring newer forces, such as nationalism), was a classic aristocratic peace.

But as a ruling class the aristocracy was losing any special claim to dominance, well before the French Revolution. Its military prowess was no longer distinctive. During the eighteenth century the newest, most potent branch of the military was the artillery corps; but leadership here required technical training, and few aristocrats, except very minor ones like Napoleon Bonaparte from Corsica, were willing to take the trouble. So artillery was badly used, until the French Revolution brought new blood into the system. Despite individual exceptions, particularly in Britain, the aristocracy could not find new general goals. In particular, it could not spearhead economic change, because this would conflict with its sense of honor. All ruling classes are parasites, in the sense that they depend on winning disproportionate rewards from the hard work of the bulk of a population. The aristocracy not only sucked up huge wealth, but it depended on maintaining values that no longer had a vital role to play. The class was on the defensive by the eighteenth century. Its death pains were prolonged, and in some cases distorted a whole society, for the power of the class was great.

The ambiguous position of the class, great power combined with functionlessness, was revealed by the aristocratic resurgence of the eighteenth century, which in one form or another touched most of Europe. There were several causes of the resurgence. Population growth hit the aristocracy hard; there were more younger sons to provide for than ever before, and posts in schools, the church, and the military did not expand accordingly. Prices rose, and to maintain an expensive style of life nobles had to increase their resources. There was a growing sense of middle-class competition for economic and social status. This was particularly true in the west, but even in Russia the rise of a small entrepreneurial class in the eighteenth century spurred the aristocracy to protests and some competitive activity. Finally the weakness of the central state in France, and the growing sympathy of governments in Prussia and Russia, led aristocrats to believe that they could regain some political powers that had been taken away by powerful monarchs during the late seventeenth century.

Here, then, was both need and opportunity. And the aristocracy did make gains. But with few exceptions—these mainly in England, where the class helped revolutionize the agricultural system toward increasing production for the market—the aristocratic resurgence was defensive and backward-looking. In politics and religion this meant a growing effort to exclude all outsiders, even the rare talented newcomer, from positions; never had such an outright monopoly been attempted. In economics the resurgence consisted primarily of an effort to tighten the manorial screws. Traditional burdens on peasants were increased in an effort to counterbalance the price rises. Hence French nobles tried to raise feudal dues, and in Russia the *obruk,* or feudal tax, was increased after 1760. Finally, in the social sphere the aristocracy tried to mark itself off from commoners with growing rigor. In France accessions to noble rank from below, previously a normal means of recognizing business success, were virtually eliminated after 1750. Even British nobles tried to draw away from the middle class, forming their own exclusive clubs and cultural groups. By the end of the century musical activities in London, for example, were largely an aristocratic preserve, whereas they had previously been open to the middle class as well.

The aristocracy thus displayed great activity but little power to innovate. Unfortunately, there was a hugh gap between the end of essential aristocratic functions and the surrender of the class to new forces. Everywhere a battle had to be fought, with the aristocracy showing great resilience. In eastern Europe the power of the class retarded the modernization process well into the twentieth century.

East and West

The bitter battle of the aristocracy to retain its class supremacy involved the whole of Europe until the mid-nineteenth century, but it is vital to remember how varied the odds were from eastern to western Europe. Manorial controls were at their apogee in the east, whereas western aristocrats depended on remnants of their dues plus outright money rents. Except in England, the western aristocrats controlled a smaller percentage of the land than was the case in the east and south. Hence they had to be more flexible in their defensive action. They were inevitably more open to new economic methods, on the land but also in industrial investments. In England, where the class was most open to commercial opportunity, they played a major role in economic change. Ultimately, aristocrats in western Europe would also have to come to terms with a strong middle class, interacting with their representatives in parliaments and government bureaucracies.

In the east and south a manorial economy and legal privileges remained the basis for the class. Even when legal adjustments were required, aristocrats sought to maintain a traditional stranglehold on their labor force. In 1807 a reform law allowed peasants in East Prussia to leave the land, and soon thereafter they were permitted to redeem their land from feudal dues. But the Junkers held sway even so. They managed to have the new local administrative districts coincide with the boundaries of their own estates, so they lost no local political power; now instead of holding courts as manor lords they were judges paid by the state. They expanded their landholdings by buying out the poorer peasants. Indeed a peasant could escape his feudal dues only by turning over at least a third of his land to the lord, so either way the Junker won. In fact, few peasants could afford freedom at this price and serfdom remained pretty well intact until after 1848. In other parts of eastern and southern Europe changes in the manorial structure were insignificant before the mid-nineteenth century, except where obligations were actually increased. Four years before the French Revolution destroyed the legal privileges of the aristocracy in much of western Europe, Russian nobles gained the power to buy and sell serfs and to inflict any punishment on them short of the death penalty.

So the gap between the two regions was obvious. Aristocratic adaptation in the West, though often subtle and successful, contrasted with intransigence in the East. At the top of society, the differences between the two main zones of Europe were actually increasing at the outset of modernization.

The Peasantry

Interpretation of the peasantry is the most important item in any survey of preindustrial society, simply because they were so predominant in numbers. Although not all rural residents relied mainly on farming, agricultural peasants constituted at least 60 per cent of any preindustrial population. We have seen that they were poor and that they worked hard, though not intensely in the modern manner. Did they have values and structures that compensated for poverty? Many historians have argued that they did and that modernization, overturning peasant values and communities, involved some tragic losses. The argument has merit, and many peasants, fearful of city life, would probably have agreed. But we must be careful to distinguish fact from fancy. We have already seen that although peasant economic tradition carried over some sense of offering protection to all members of the community, it did not prevent intense suffering and inequality. Peasants did have institutions of great importance and these worked well for many of them. But their success was varied. The reality of peasant life can only be captured with this sense of differentials.

For the peasantry had an internal class structure. The big farmer, the middling landowner, and the near landless laborer were the three main units, and they could cordially detest each other. Their careers were not static. Even under Russian manoralism there was a range of inequality in income and land ownership of 150 per cent among peasants in 1858, with the poor paying a disproportionate amount of manorial dues and taxes. But to be a rich peasant was apparently chancy; on one estate only one fifteenth of the rich peasantry retained their status between 1813 and 1856. In France, peasant mobility seems less extensive, and a rich farmer's family could probably hold out fairly well. But mobility as well as intra-village tension pointed up the profound divisions within even the agricultural group. There were also, in the average village, a handful of nonagricultural people. The ordinary village had a teacher or a scribe (to help illiterate peasants take care of legal business) and/or a priest or pastor; it also had an innkeeper or some other businessman. Thus 1 to 2 per cent of the rural population was middle class. A larger number were artisans, and some villages specialized heavily in some branch of manufacturing such as shoes or clothing. Indeed more manufacturing was done in the countryside than in the cities in a preindustrial economy; this meant that at least 5 per cent of the rural population were artisans, and other peasants did part-time manufacturing work. Even in the typical agricultural village the blacksmith and the miller played an important role. They were more likely to be literate than the ordinary peasant; they had more urban contacts, for they had to deal with city people to buy supplies and tools. The village, with usually no more than 250 to 450 residents, thus had a complex occupational structure. Rural people did not constitute a single class; even peasants did not, in economic terms.

Two other divisions among the peasantry must be mentioned. There was a vast difference in status between married and unmarried adults. In preindustrial rural society 30 to 50 per cent of all adults never got married. These were younger sons who could not inherit land, poor daughters, or ugly daughters who could not find a mate. Their status was very low. Unmarried women, save those in Catholic countries who escaped to a convent, probably worked as servants either for one of the richer farmers or for their own brother (and their sister-in-law). Unmarried men were often agricultural laborers, but they had somewhat greater opportunities to go to the cities, at least part of the year, to earn a bit of money as unskilled construction or transportation workers. Unless they left the village permanently they remained, like the unmarried women, part of a family economy, contributing their income to the family fund; but they too were an inferior part. In dealing with the importance of the peasant family it is vital to remember that almost half the adult population did not have full rights in it.

Rural society also had a distinctive age structure. Children began to work at age six or so. They were a vital source of labor, and this is why rural tradition so commonly stressed the importance of having a great many of them. But children did not necessarily grow up or reach effective adulthood until their mid-twenties. Only when they could inherit land and marry were they really adults. Of course they matured late sexually, reaching puberty only in their late teens. But village society was not designed for the young, in terms of independence and power. Age tensions would add to class differences, and the confrontation between a man in his mid-twenties, wanting to see himself established in village society, and his father could be bitter indeed, for the old man had to die or retire before the young could achieve independence. The adult peasant had twenty or twenty-five good years to enjoy his status. It was not that he would die young necessarily. The shockingly high death rates of rural life were among infants. If a man or woman reached twenty, the chances of living until sixty were pretty good, only about 20 per cent less good than they are today in modern France or the United States. So there were old people in the village. We are accustomed to assume they commanded great affection and respect, but the fact is that we do not know much about them. In times of crisis villagers often turned against their elderly, as in the witch crazes that singled out elderly women particularly. A grandparent could help babysit while his adult children worked in the fields. And usually a man or woman fifty years old would still have a younger child of his own to help out, for child births continued into the mid-thirties for women and a peasant father would usually have his last child when he was about forty. This was undoubtedly one of the chores that set aside the unmarried young adults in the village. The fact remains that the older peasant was an economic liability. Although almost as likely to be alive, he was far less likely to be healthy than an old person today. There was the simple matter of his teeth falling out, for there was no easy replacement, which in turn meant immense difficulties for his own digestive process and for anyone who cooked for him. There were, undoubtedly, vigorous patriarchs who continued to help out in the fields and ruled their families with a stern hand. There were also old peasants who had to plead with their children, or more commonly write out careful contracts to make sure they would still have a garden plot to support them even though they were no longer capable of running the family.

Key village traditions thus operated against a backdrop not only of poverty, but also of class division and generational tension. They worked as well as they did because they were economically essential. We cannot be as sure that they provided emotional satisfactions.

Peasant Tradition

The foundation of peasant society was family and village, both of ancient date. Their traditional basis was vital. Not only did peasants have no independent values by which to challenge either institution, but they also frequently had memories of merits that the institutions might no longer have. Peasants had no historical sense, for they learned from stories (and story telling was one important function older people did have) not from books, and peasant legend, passed orally from one generation to the next, could jumble memories chronologically. Hence the peasant might believe the family was supposed to cherish its elderly even when he cordially disliked his own father. He might see the village as an egalitarian institution, owing equal support to all its members, even when the village had long since failed to live up to these standards (if indeed the standards had ever been more than myth).

The basis of the family, however, was economic, not myth. A peasant goes courting in eighteenth-century Bavaria. He chooses a girl whom he undoubtedly knew from childhood. (In a typically small village there were no more than ten to twenty people in their early twenties, which did force some suitors to go to another village.) But he also, if he wants to woo successfully, picks someone of roughly his own economic level. Hence children of rich farmers married children of rich farmers. Sometimes there was no preliminary courtship at all, for an intermediary "marriage broker" did the job. But finally the couple meets and the suitor is given about half an hour to propose. Then the parents come in to see if they have taken to each other. If so, the real negotiations began. The girl's parents had to make sure the son was going to inherit an appropriate amount of property, the boy's to guarantee a proper dowry (and woe to the peasant who had too many daughters, for he could lose his wealth simply trying to marry them off). As it began in economics, so the family continued. In agricultural work there was a certain division of labor, the man working the fields (with his sons, when they passed infancy), the wife and daughters managing the house, caring for the animals, and raising a vegetable garden (they also went to the fields at planting and harvesting time). A rural French mason noted what he expected of his wife:

> We know there are countries where women marry with the oft-realized hope of having to work only in the house; in France, there is nothing of the sort. Precisely the contrary happens. My wife, like all other women of the country, was raised to work in the fields from morning until night and she worked no less after our marriage.

Where necessity required, a husband might go off to earn some money, as in doing seasonal construction work, or his children to serve in a richer farmer's house. Any cash was turned over to the head of the household. Teen-aged children were in fact often sent out to work as servants and laborers for other families. This helped a village economy correct excessive imbalances in wealth; a poor man with many children could survive only by sending some of his progeny to a richer neighbor who had few. This may have had the added advantage of getting rid of older children at a time when they were beginning to resent their parents' authority. They would be kept under strict discipline as employees in another house.

With its economic base the family was a tightly knit unit, normally broken only by death. It was normally an extended family, in the sense that uncles, aunts, and grandparents normally interacted with a given parent–child unit. Contrary to some impressions the extended family rarely lived under the same roof. As we have seen it was not necessarily ruled by an elder patriarch. In parts of the Balkans and Russia, the extended family nevertheless served as an economic entity, pooling all earnings under the direction of the family's head; in Serbia this unit was known as the *zadruga*. Even in western Europe members of the family stood ready to help each other out. Above all, if only from its role in providing a rudimentary division of labor, the family gave the peasant his primary sense of identity. He worked and lived not for himself, but for the family. This was a concept instilled very early. Infants were a burden to peasant society, for they were an economic drain until old enough to work. Busy mothers had little time to spare. They fed their infants when they wanted to, not when the infant demanded. Typically they wrapped the baby in swaddling clothes, so that he could not move around, often hanging him from a peg on the wall while they worked outside. Lack of attention was not a matter of economics alone. Half of all infants would die; it was risky to invest emotion in them until it was more certain they would survive (though of course this was something of a vicious circle, for more attention might have saved more of them). And they had to be taught deference. In the seventeenth century the dominant image held that the infant was a little animal, whose will had to be broken. Peasant methods of child rearing assured that most children would learn to respect their parents' order and would identify with the group, not the individual.

The family's economic and emotional role was rather general across peasant Europe, despite great diversity in particular customs. In western Europe, however, peasant society since the end of the Middle Ages had developed an additional trait that complicated family life: late marriage. In eastern and southern Europe peasants married around twenty (that is, quite soon after puberty) and had a lot of children, most of whom died. In peasant society everywhere, unwanted children might be killed by exposure or abandonment. But west European peasants, freer from manorial controls, were more concerned about protecting their property and so wanted fewer children; they continued to practice abandonment until the nineteenth century, but they needed other regulation as well. Although some methods of birth control were known to peasants—notably, using animal bladders as condoms—the most general practice was a delay in marriage until the bride was near her mid-twenties and the husband usually a bit older. And village society strictly prevented sexual intercourse before marriage, for illegitimate children would rock the local economy too. The west European peasant family was thus, typically, a property unit as well as an economic unit and accustomed to rather severe sexual restraint to preserve its functions.

Above the family stood the village, a collection of several extended families who were themselves often closely related. Varying in population, but nowhere composed of more than a few hundred people, villages served a large number of functions. They were, of course, residential groupings. Only in a few regions did peasants live on isolated farms. Normally their houses clustered in a village and their fields spread around it. The village was an economic unit producing most of the goods the peasants required. The village itself directly organized much economic activity. Many villages, as in Britain before 1750, appointed shepherds and cowherds, decided what crops to plant, and governed the use of the commons. Villages also often settled land disputes among their members. After 1861 the Russian central government even used villages as units of government responsible for approving sales of land. Although this is an extreme case, clearly the village served in many ways as an important governing unit.

Further, villages usually had a definite governing structure. In some cases villagers actually met to make major decisions; in Britain before 1750 a three-quarters majority was required to determine what crops should be planted. Russian villages in the late nineteenth century had assemblies composed of all heads of families, which in turn elected elders as officers. Elsewhere leadership was sometimes less formal, composed of the wealthier farmers, for generally the village was strictly based on peasant class structure. In any case, the village was capable of exercising definite direction over its members while claiming some basis of some consensus.

The communal tone of village life extended to recreation. Festivals, religious celebrations, and even marriage involved the whole village. Typically, although specific customs varied, village participation in weddings extended to a celebration around the house of a newlywed couple in some form of charivari. Village leaders usually gave the job of organizing more formal festivals to the younger people, which may have alleviated their discontent at lack of independence and of sexual outlets; the young were allowed a certain amount of prankishness on these occasions. But older people had their role to play as well, telling stories in the evening. In village festivals, operated carefully according to long-standing traditions (in southern Italy some villages celebrated the defeat of Moslem invaders, which had occurred nearly a millennium before, as if it had happened the previous year), we see much of the communal charm of rural life, for here was one area where class and age distinctions blurred. We see the corollary as well: one had to go to these festivals, for the village insisted on communal loyalty. If, in France, the head of a family failed to contribute straw for a ceremonial bonfire on the local saint's day, he was subject to severe public ridicule and popular tradition held that, soon after, he would break a leg or see one of his children die. Accustomed to communal loyalty the peasant would not perceive these requirements as a burden, however, for village life provided no real sense of individual privacy.

Few peasants had much experience beyond the village. In the poorer regions a number of males had to wander off to seek work each year. In Spain up to 10 per cent of the peasantry spent part of their time annually serving as carters, hauling goods to the cities by mule or donkey. The isolation of rural villages should not be exaggerated, and it bore far more heavily on women than on men. Furthermore, there were peddlers and even local fairs, which provided entertainment and news as well as goods, but both were infrequent. Characteristically the peasant distrusted towns and wandering traders as much as he enjoyed them. Both represented forces outside the village and so could not be fully understood. Similarly, agents of the central government reached the peasants only infrequently in the form of tax collectors, recruiters, and rural police. They were known and often disliked, but they were not a regular part of peasant horizons. Even the church affected the peasant primarily by reinforcing localism. The church was a village church, the priest usually a peasant from the region and possessed of little education.

In this situation a peasant's first loyalty was inevitably given to his immediate area. Even dialects and costumes were fairly local, although both extended well beyond a single village. Peasants had little interest in national politics. Their political focus was on the village and local aristocracy; in larger terms they were apolitical. Furthermore local peasant politics was personal. Issues revolved around personalities in the village and, when votes were taken, they were by public declaration. The peasant did not deal with principles or abstract issues; here too he was far from a modern political sense. Hence, well into the nineteenth century, peasants had no demonstrable interest in matters such as civil liberties or governmental structure. There was, generally, a traditional loyalty to the king as protector of his people. Even when peasants rose in protest, as in France in 1789 and in Russia as late as 1905, they would commonly express their affection for the king and blame his advisers for any wrongs. Such risings were over economic grievances rather than political ones, and when land reforms were granted, as in France by 1793, the peasants lost interest in further revolution. Political revolts by urban elements were commonly ignored by the peasants, as in the French revolution of 1830 or the Neapolitan rising of 1820. In these and other cases the issues involved were irrelevant to the peasantry. Similarly, peasants had little active concern for other areas and peoples. There might be some traditional hostility to invaders; Balkan peasants, for example, often disciplined their children by threatening to call in a Turk. From Alsace east the Jew was known and disliked as an outsider and a moneylender. But aside from a few highly traditional general views, the peasant found his standards and goals within his immediate surroundings.

Peasant localism strengthened, and was strengthened by, the pervasive traditionalism. The decisions made by village or family about economic or social matters were based primarily on local custom. The peasant's reliance on custom was quite natural. It expressed his isolation from other groups and regions and his need to rely on oral sources of knowledge. Peasants were predominantly illiterate. In 1800 only 11 per cent of the peasants of one Irish county could read at all; in France during the Restoration, less than 30 per cent could read. Again this was an oral culture and people learned by listening, which meant that peasant knowledge was primarily a matter of traditional beliefs and practices orally transmitted. Aspects of the tradition were ancient indeed. Certain pagan rites and superstitions persisted everywhere. Old medical lore was carried on. Invasions, plagues, and revolts from previous centuries might be remembered as yesterday because they were carried on as part of a living tradition.

Ceremonies of marriage and burial involved an elaborate ritual, varying of course from region to region, but always grounded in tradition. In parts of Ireland in 1830 a bride was supposed to flee with the best man on a horse; the groom would ride after and seize his prize. Elaborate precautions were taken against the presence of witches, who might produce a childless marriage by their spells. Ceremonies existed to cure barrenness and disease. Pregnant women sometimes took mud from long ditches called "Priests' Beds" to avoid a painful labor. Various omens were taken to indicate good or bad luck in ventures such as marriage. Many ritualistic precautions were developed to protect newborn infants against bad fortune and evil spirits; often they intermingled Christian and pagan practices. No general statement can cover the huge variety of peasant rituals; but these rituals entered deeply into the life of the class.

Another vital ingredient of traditional peasant culture was an ambiguous view of social hierarchy. Unless impelled by unusual distress, such as a severe famine, peasants accepted social inequalities both within the village and outside. They saw local nobles as natural leaders in the world outside the village, a world that was not of great interest in any event. Many serfs believed that it would be positively inappropriate for their masters to do manual labor. Often they followed their lords into battles that had little to do with their own interests; and when given the vote, during the nineteenth or twentieth centuries, peasants typically responded by electing their landlord or priest. Daily signs of deference abounded. The British laborer tugged at his forelock as a sign of respect when his landlord rode by.

This deference had several sources. Peasants were too busy with their daily work, often too poor and hungry, to think about protest. They were carefully schooled as children to respect authority; it was easy to carry over loyalty to family to loyalty to landlord or king. Sensible landlords, for their part, played by the rules of the hierarchical game. They were courteous, if patronizing; they left the dirty work of tax collecting to subordinates; they provided services of charity and mediation.

Peasants could also harbor anger at injustice. The egalitarian strain of rural tradition could be carried against rich farmers in one's own village, but more often it was turned against the landlord class or the tax collectors of the state. In many times of stress individual peasants behaved with deference during the day, and then went out to burn their landlord's haystack at night. More rarely there were general risings, in times of bad harvest. Peasants had a sense of natural justice. They could claim that their landlords had no rights over them, that they alone owned the land. This was the *jacquerie* tradition that went back to the late Middle Ages. Peasants could attack the property, manorial records, and even the persons of landlords. This was the tradition that sprang up in Russia during the great Pugachev rebellion of 1773–1775 or in the rural revolution in France during the summer of 1789. More common were local grain or tax riots, in which peasants would try, through violence, to insist that the government owed them protection in times of crisis. Often, as in France during the late seventeenth century, the state organized grain convoys to feed the cities during famine years. Peasants, attacking these convoys, were seizing grain and also expressing a sense that the state should protect them too.

The peasants most commonly able to express the belief in natural justice were those with middle-sized plots of land. The farmers were too rich to bother with protest, the near landless too poor to feel fully part of the rural community; and a community sense was vital to premodern protest. Often other village residents played a key role in organizing unrest. Rural artisans, particularly, were potential leaders. Their literacy and urban contacts set them off from the ordinary villager but could be vital in converting vague grievance into positive action. For protest came hard to the ordinary peasant. It could play a significant historic role, for when roused peasant anger was hard to quell. On the whole, however, deference, more than the protest tradition, was the peasants' political legacy to modernization.

Stability and Tension

Peasant social structures and traditions were designed above all to provide stability. From marriage customs through village economic decisions the peasantry sought to perpetuate the world into which they had been born. Individual peasants changed. Not only was there social mobility, there was also a certain amount of geographic movement. Records of English villages show a surprising number of people born in other communities. Again this was not a changeless society. But it had no culture to accommodate change. Given the frequency of disasters, such as famine, it was more important to try to protect what one had than to think about improvement. Protest itself, when it occurred, was based on past standards: we want the rights we had in the past, or the grain we had last year.

Poverty, economic uncertainty, and social conformity were softened by a pervasive local religion. We cannot assume that all peasants were sincerely religious. The poor, particularly those who had to travel to seek work, may have paid little attention to the church. There were signs during the eighteenth century that peasants who lived near cities, where the culture was more secular, were irreligious, and this sentiment may not have been new. Generally, however, religion and peasant life were closely intertwined. An impoverished French village, run by an absentee landlord, beset by frequent migration and family tensions, was held together only by religion, which gave inhabitants a sense of a higher, if mysterious, purpose to life. Religious ritual was an integral part of village festivals and personal celebrations such as weddings and funerals. On occasion peasants displayed an intense religious emotion; this was a common response to famine or plague. More normally religious rituals provided emotional, even aesthetic satisfaction. For married women, church going was one of the only activities that took them out of the home.

The village had other devices to defuse tensions. Drink was one.

Peasants could not afford to drink a great deal (even in France, wine drinking became common only after 1500), but on feast days and special times of tension liquor provided some release. Agricultural laborers were given drink after the harvest was in. Russian peasants in the nineteenth century, involved in the intense bickering over property lines that bedeviled peasant society, often settled cases in the village court by giving both parties an abundant dose of vodka. Nicknames often helped. Balkan communities well into the twentieth century expressed both humor and dislike by derisive name calling. Festivals provided an occasion for socially controlled violence as well as drinking. Rough games pitted men from one village against men from another, or married men against unmarried. Many were little more than brawls.

But not all tensions could be controlled. Some villagers, lacking property or hating their parents or in trouble with the village council for displaying too much independence, had to leave. They might head for a city or sign up for long stints in the military (service contracts ran up to twenty-five years). But some roamed the countryside, and bands of beggars, even outlaws, could strike fear into the hearts of the village. There was violence within the village. Peasant property was normally respected, for village safeguards here combined with the need, in a subsistence economy, to avoid senseless destruction. But rates of personal violence could be high, and up to 74 per cent of all village crimes were acts of violence. Lacking local police, many peasants took revenge into their own hands. Family feuds, as in southern Italy, constituted an extreme of this practice and could lead to frequent bloodshed. Unwanted infants were often killed, usually by exposure, when peasant methods of birth control were inadequate. There was insanity in the village as well, if only because inbreeding could cause congenital madness. The village idiot was not a myth, and he often had company.

Village conformity thus exacted some toll. Certain kinds of peasants, particularly at certain stages of life, might be open to an alternative. But the attractiveness of village structures made it difficult to think in terms of novelty. Most peasants had a sense of identity, so rigidly enforced that it inhibited choice. Modernization, which necessarily challenged key rural values, would find many peasants ill prepared for change. It would drive some to acts of despair.

The Cities

Urban society was more recent in origin than rural, but it too had a long history in Europe. The cities themselves were old. Their systems of government as well as many of their physical facilities had been established centuries before. The two principal urban classes, the bourgeoisie and the artisans, had both originated in the middle ages. Both classes had been renewed and added to since that time, but many of their institutions and values were extremely traditional. However, the cities were not closed to innovation. Social structures could not be totally rigid; the very physical proximity of a large number of people of varying positions caused a certain tension. The cities themselves were expanding even in the seventeenth century, although at a relatively slow rate; and their wealth was increasing. Finally, the leading urban class was usually mobile in the preindustrial period. The bourgeoisie in western Europe was based on wealth, primarily nonlanded wealth. Though by no means totally venturesome, the class as a whole did tend to try to expand its wealth to improve its social position. Despite important traditional features, then, the cities were sources of considerable dynamism in the preindustrial period. From the cities, in fact, issued many of the innovations that created a radically new social and economic climate during the eighteenth century.

The urban map of Europe at the end of the eighteenth century was rather complex. Cities scarcely existed in eastern and southeastern Europe. There were a few centers, sometimes rather new, such as St. Petersburg. Some commercial activity took place in these cities, but the level was low. The few major cities of eastern Europe existed primarily as political and administrative centers. Cities that lacked these functions were of little importance; Athens, for example, had dwindled to a population of only a few thousand under Turkish rule. Correspondingly, the urban classes of eastern Europe were both tiny and weak. Commercial middle classes and artisans scarcely existed; much of the scanty trade that did go on was in the hands of foreigners. There was a bureaucratic middle class in Russia, but it was tiny and lacked independence. In terms of social structure cities were unimportant in these areas. Along with the distinctive features of rural classes, the effective absence of cities was one of the basic elements of eastern European society.

In western Europe important cities did exist. Urban population in Scandinavia and Spain, at the extremities, was less than 10 per cent of the whole, but significant commercial and artisan classes were present. In France, the Low Countries, and Britain about 20 per cent of the population lived in cities. It was in those areas that cities had been expanding in size and wealth. Even in western Europe, however, most individual cities were small. There were a few giant centers; Paris had a population of 700,000 at the end of the eighteenth century, one sixth of the urban population in the country as a whole. The rest was scattered in smaller cities. Only Lyons had more than 100,000 inhabitants. A few other centers approached this figure, but far more had populations of only 5,000 or 10,000. The largest cotton manufacturing city in France, Rouen, had fewer than 80,000 residents in 1815; vital regional commercial and administrative centers such as Toulouse had fewer than 50,000. In France and elsewhere the average city was modest in size, and such cities were widely scattered over the country as a whole.

The physical organization of the city reflected its size. Cities were compact. Traditions of crowding together for defense and ease of building remained. Many cities still tried to live within defensive walls, even as they expanded. Streets were small and narrow. Houses were also narrow, usually attached in rows. Crowding pushed members of different social classes into close proximity. Many houses were divided into apartments, with wealthy burghers occupying the lower floors and poorer artisans the upper. A large city such as London did have residential areas more clearly separated by wealth and profession, but even there important residential mixing occurred.

City governments generally undertook only limited functions before the industrial revolution. Many were still controlled by aristocrats and churchmen. In England regulation of hygiene and trade scarcely existed. Police forces were rudimentary, fire prevention and transportation left entirely to private hands. On the Continent, central governments took a greater role in city life, and this was to increase in the eighteenth century. They undertook some housing regulation and fire prevention. More streets were paved, more sewers covered. Police forces spread even to small towns.

Even on the Continent the dangers and difficulties of urban life were numerous. Crime and violence were common. Disease was widespread and epidemics frequent. In fact, almost every city before 1800 experienced more deaths than births in a given year; population was maintained or increased only by immigration from the outside.

The economies of most cities were as simple as their physical facilities. Local trade and artisan manufacturing were the economic bases of the typical urban center. Small shops sold foods, clothing, tools, and various luxury items to residents of the city and surrounding region. Products were commonly manufactured and sold in the same shop. Even so, few people were employed in a given shop because the operation was on a very small scale. Only a few enterprises reached out for more than local markets. Major cities like Paris produced some luxury goods for sale all over the world. Some other centers had a specialized production destined for wide distribution. Lyons exported much of its silk production; on a more modest basis, Thiers sent cutlery all over France. Even in these cities the units of production involved only a few workers. But above these units, large merchants exercised important control, bringing in raw materials and arranging for the sale of the products.

Many cities were also centers of a rural textile manufacturing system as well. Large merchants again brought in raw materials, but in these cases sent them out to peasant homes all over the surrounding region. Foremen served as middlemen, allocating raw materials and collecting cloth. Only a few finishing operations took place in the city; but the city was the economic center of the industry, and to the city flowed the profits. Only in a minority of cities did merchants engage in extensive putting-out production; only the most dynamic centers manufactured more than could be sold close to home. Most entrepreneurs and workers alike were involved in small operations in which neither complex tools nor complex business organizations were needed. For every far-flung export concern there were hundreds of tiny shops relying on the manual skills of one or two workers and the simplest of business and accounting procedures. Again it must be remembered that the typical urban resident lived not in a major production center but in a city with less than 10,000 inhabitants, content to serve a local economy.

The Bourgeoisie

At the top of the urban social structure were the bigger merchants and some related professional people, particularly lawyers. They did not necessarily run the city. Many units were controlled, like agricultural estates, by nobles or churchmen. The society and culture, though not the government, of bigger units like London were dominated by aristocrats. The wealthier businessmen might share in this culture, but at some distance. Concerts were advertised as being open to nobles, gentry, and "others," and seating was often segregated. In smaller centers the business community usually had a greater role, and merchant guilds ran the government of places like Mulhouse, Frankfurt, and Elbeuf. But at best wealthy urbanites had only local power and prestige.

In many cities the leading businessmen constituted the *bourgeoisie,* a term which initially meant only a city resident. This had in fact become a legal status group, not unlike the aristocracy. It had special voting rights and tax privileges. Often it was quite small, reflecting the fact that old merchant families were prone to set themselves up rather like an aristocracy and fought the admission of outsiders. The term *bourgeoisie* has come to mean much more, of course, denoting a capitalist middle class. In premodern cities, though individual capitalists flourished, the bourgeoisie as a whole cannot be described in this way. We can see the seeds of a middle class, but not the class itself. Even the term *bourgeoisie* is too narrow, for not all businessmen and professional people had the legal status of this group. It is nevertheless useful to employ this term for the premodern group as a means of distinguishing it from its modern successor.

The bourgeoisie in this broader sense was an economic grouping in part. It was richer than the artisans and lower classes of the cities and less wealthy than the aristocratic magnates. But a successful businessman might rival the earnings of the gentry, which is where the law came in: at the top, a bourgeois was bourgeois because he lacked noble title and noble rights. The class was a large one in the cities, representing up to 20 per cent of the urban population, or about 4 or 5 per cent of the total population of western Europe. Its members ran the larger businesses and manufacturing establishments. It sent some people into the government bureaucracy, at the middle if not the top levels. It was literate, and a few of its members went to secondary school and even the university; some lawyers, for example, were university trained.

However, although its outlines can be roughly defined, in many ways this was not a class at all. Its professional segment lacked many of the modern attributes of professions, though it loomed large as a percentage of the bourgeois, contributing over half the class in Prussia and other areas of central Europe. There were in fact only three premodern professions: law, medicine, and the clergy. In Catholic countries the clergy had its own legal privileges, and as we have seen its upper ranks were dominated by the aristocracy, its lower by bright peasants who had some special calling and/or the sponsorship of a local notable. In Protestant countries the clergy had more ties with the bourgeoisie. Service as an Anglican minister, for example, was a highly respected career for the son of an English merchant. But to obtain the necessary university training and placement it was common to seek aristocratic sponsorship; many ministers initially served as tutors for noble families. Hence, though they received training that can be called professional, clerics formed something of their own group even when not a legal Estate, closer to the aristocracy than to the bourgeoisie. The leading lawyers also served the aristocracy, for the most complicated transactions involved the landed estates. And although some were highly trained, others entered through an apprenticeship system that won them scant prestige. Doctors were trained entirely through apprenticeships and had a rather low status. Neither doctors nor lawyers had any means of assuring the quality of their colleagues (there were no examinations, no licensing) save through individual sponsorship, and no ways of limiting their numbers. Nor did they have much sense of professional cohesion.

Some were in fact quite talented. But those who did well generally profited mainly from aristocratic patronage or from service to the state. Particularly in central and eastern Europe bourgeois elements filled important bureaucratic posts because they had training and expertise that many aristocrats were unwilling to acquire. But as bureaucrats they were directed by aristocratic ministers and were sometimes themselves ennobled.

For their part the larger merchants were unable to provide a distinctive definition to the bourgeoisie. In big cities like Paris they typically aspired to become nobles themselves, for until the mid-eighteenth century if one amassed enough money one could hope to buy a title. In the meantime the wealthy merchants tried to imitate an aristocratic life style, rather than develop a separate sense of values. This was why so many bought land, where it was legal for them to do so. If they acquired an estate they liked nothing better than to rule as lord of the manor. Some won local govern-

ment functions, as was the case with notaries in France and Italy who had
great local prestige. Well into the nineteenth century a number of businessmen essentially agreed with the aristocracy that commerce was degrading,
and sought a more respectable way of life. The same impulse could even
impede their money-making efforts in the city. In Paris, for example,
aristocrats were more daring in their investments than bourgeois businessmen, who typically put their money into real estate at a very low (2½ per
cent) return. The concern for investment security and respectability must
have kept many businessmen from reaching their real goal, amassing enough
to buy a title.

All of this means that the preindustrial bourgeoisie was not capitalistic
in the modern sense or resentful of aristocratic dominance. But most businessmen, particularly in the typical smaller centers, had no chance to
aspire to the aristocracy. There was a bourgeois culture, although not a
modern one. In the first place, the bourgeoisie had a clear sense of distinction from the lower classes. Here businessmen probably shared aristocratic
values, but because they lived in the city, where the poor were more
menacing and not a part of a clear hierarchy, their views could take a fearful
turn. The poor were inferior and there was no remedy for their condition.
As the Bible helpfully commented, "the poor will always be with us." At
most they deserved charity when times were particularly bad, and the
bourgeoisie had a traditional, paternalistic attitude that would lead them
to donate clothing to the poor, give occasional tips to their servants, and
grant alms to the many beggars of the city. For their part the poor were
supposed to be respectful and grateful. But the bourgeoisie was conscious
of another urban group as well, the criminal class, for there were sections
of the cities like London and Paris that were too dangerous to enter.
Criminals were permanently degenerate; here too there was no remedy to
propose. But the perception of two groups within the lower orders was
confusing. Charity was fine, for example, but it should be carefully moni-
tored lest it go to the undeserving, barbaric element. By the same token the
bourgeoisie lived close to some elements of the poor and even shared in
their culture. London merchants, for example, gambled and went to cock
fights along with journeymen. But other elements of the poor were positively terrifying. This ambiguous class outlook was not a modern attitude
toward the lower classes, but it would long influence middle-class percep-
tions.

In business the bourgeoisie valued security and organized to protect
themselves against risk. Many merchants were grouped in guilds that limited
competition. In Frankfurt merchant guilds ran the City Council, which
alone had the power to grant citizenship in the city; and only citizens were
allowed to conduct business. What was sought was a safe income and a
legacy for the children. Wives often helped with accounts or tended shop.
Children were brought into the business early. Most clerical work was done

by sons who could plan to rise to ownership when their fathers died or retired; there was no real clerical class as a result. The bourgeoisie was comfortable, immensely impressed with the importance of owning property but not, for the most part, eager to amass great wealth. It valued a certain simplicity in manners, differing thus from the imitators of the aristocracy. Clothing was somber, quite different from the flamboyance of the aristocracy, though more elaborate than the dress of the lower classes; French burghers wore knickered breeches, whereas the lower classes had only trousers, a distinction that would be given political meaning by the French Revolution, which designated the urban mobs *sans-culottes*—"without breeches." Bourgeois food was abundant but simply prepared.

This middling bourgeoisie had something of its own ethic. It stressed the importance of family life and sober behavior. It wanted disciplined respect from children, modesty from women, who were supposed to be subservient to their husbands. Family and economy were intertwined in this group too, and marriages were carefully arranged to provide economic security for the new family; dowries and inheritance thus loomed large. The bourgeoisie valued hard work and condemned idleness. It frowned on spendthrift behavior and praised savings. But it also disliked excessive ambition. This was a group quite satisfied with its position in the middle of society; in Germany it was in fact called the *Mittelstand,* or middle order. He who tried to rise too far was taking too great a chance; modest achievement was preferable. Regular religious practice was part of bourgeois respectability, and the class gave important financial support to urban churches and religious charities.

In sum, the bourgeoisie had certain values that could carry over into a modern middle class. The "early to bed, early to rise" ethic could form the basis for a dynamic capitalism or a challenge to the idleness of the aristocracy. But the attachment to modest property had a role for the future as well, which would keep many bourgeois from ever accepting the implications of modernization.

The Artisanry

Right beneath the bourgeoisie was the artisan class. Indeed there was some overlap, and a successful artisan master (a wealthy goldsmith, for example) bore much resemblance to the bourgeois. But the classes were largely separate. Artisan guilds, for example, rarely had much voice in urban government, although economically they served many of the same functions.

The artisanry was the largest urban class, usually about 40 per cent of the city population. Wealthier than the urban poor it lived close to the subsistence level in most cases; it was highly vulnerable to economic crises, for when harvests failed food prices rose and demand for manufactured goods fell off as well, hitting the artisan hard. So it was not so much a distinctive average income that defined the class as the possession of a definite, traditional economic skill. Artisans made lace and embroidered fabric. They wove and finished cloth, particularly expensive cloth like silk with luxurious patterns. They worked as tailors, printers, bakers, and butchers. They were the leading construction workers in the city, carpenters, painters, roofers, and masons. They made furniture; they made tools and other metal objects. In other words, they comprised the basic labor force of the urban economy, manufacturing most of the products required locally and some important items for more distant markets as well. Their methods of work were largely traditional. They worked with simple tools, lacking elaborate mechanical contrivances. They worked at home or in small shops, usually with no more than five other craftsmen. There was little division of labor in the artisan's work. A few young workers, particularly apprentices, often served relatively menial functions. They carried raw materials and finished products, swept the shop, and assisted in some of the more difficult procedures of the artisan himself. Aside from this, the artisan typically carried his operation through by himself, from preparing the materials for production to taking care of the tools. The complexity of the operation and the simplicity of the equipment meant that real skill was required. Artisans invariably underwent an important period of training, usually in a formal apprenticeship program. Even relatively simple jobs, such as lace making, required at least a year of apprenticeship, and more complex trades involved up to seven years of training.

Artisans built their lives around their work, spending long hours on the job. Their family life and work intertwined. Wives helped with some manufacturing processes, but more commonly kept accounts and sold goods. In some cases their functions required them to be more literate than their husbands. The family lived in the shop. Artisan masters normally housed and fed journeymen as well as apprentices, extending the familial atmosphere. Not uncommonly the journeyman married the master's daughter, a good way to assure the boss's favor. Artisanal organizations favored the sons and brothers of existing craftsmen anyway, which enhanced the association of family and work. As with peasants there was little life outside the job, save for occasional festivals. Again, artisans did not work intensely, except for short periods; these bursts would be followed by slower work that allowed talking and singing with fellow workers. Many artisans, particularly those who worked in heat, causing them to perspire heavily (bakers and blacksmiths, for example), drank regularly on the job. Thus the artisan did not have a modern work culture, for he mixed what we would call recreation with labor.

Urban artisans resembled village craftsmen in many respects. Their skill and training, their relatively common literacy, and their work patterns could draw them together, and many a rural blacksmith or mason could move into urban crafts without much difficulty. But urban artisans had an organizational experience that was much different from rural patterns. They were less individualistic in a way, and certainly more accustomed to grouping in the interests of economic protection and sociability. The key artisan organization was the guild, which served many of the same functions as the village did for the peasant in attempting to provide security but also closely regulating social life.

Most guilds had the legal power to deny a worker the right to practice his trade unless he was admitted as a member. Through this device guilds typically tried to limit the number of workers in a given trade in a city; the guild existed not to maximize production, but to protect the standard of living and the economic opportunity of its members. By limiting the number of workers it tried to assure employment for all. It also tried to restrict production so that artisans would receive suitable pay and prices for their work and products. Guilds therefore maintained strict controls over the methods used in work and generally prevented any major innovation in technique. This not only stabilized earnings but also upheld the value of traditional skills. Opportunities for the ambitious and clever might be limited as a result, but such opportunities were irrelevant to the guild's primary goal of protecting the welfare of all its members.

Moreover, important mobility was provided within the structure of many guilds. Artisans were divided into three major categories: apprentices, journeymen, and masters. Artisan tradition, and to some extent continuing practice, held that each artisan should have an opportunity to pass through all three stages during his productive life. The period of apprenticeship was, of course, vital to the artisan's position. Beginning usually in the early teens, the apprenticeship provided training for the job. A fee commonly had to be paid for the privilege of entering apprenticeship, and a stiff contract bound the apprentice to his tasks. On the other hand, tradition and guild supervision attempted to insure fair treatment of the apprentice. The master was required to feed and house the apprentice and train him to the level necessary for full participation in craft production.

After apprenticeship the artisan typically became a journeyman, working for wages, often supplemented by food and housing provided by the master. Following some years as a journeyman, in which hopefully some savings could be accumulated, opportunity might arise to buy or inherit a shop and equipment, so that he became a master in his own right, often employing other journeymen. This did not mean that the master became separated from his work, for masters worked beside their employees in most cases. Under guild rules and protection the artisan was provided with a social and economic ladder he could climb as he gained skill and capital.

Guilds offered, then, some economic security and protection of skills. They helped limit the gap between master and journeyman. In addition, they provided some political experience, as guild appointments were made by vote of all the masters. In some cases artisan guilds had some voice in city governments. Certainly the general recognition of guilds by city and even national governments gave the artisan significant contact with politics more generally. Guilds often provided travel experience for the young artisan. Journeymen in many trades often traveled throughout a country for a few years. They obtained social contacts and employment information in each city from the guild in their craft.

Guilds were social groups as well, sponsoring a variety of functions and supervising a number of rituals. Many guild statutes set forth detailed funeral regulations, stating who should attend, who should bear the body, how many candles were to be lit, and so forth. Although artisans had more chance for independence than peasants, particularly when they traveled, guild membership restricted not only economic initiatives but also personal privacy.

Guilds expressed and provided many of the values maintained by artisans well into the industrial period. However, the picture should not be overdrawn. In the first place, not all urban artisans were involved in guilds. Certain populous trades, such as lace making, were never organized in guilds; this was particularly true of work in which women were primarily involved. Even in the masculine crafts certain cities never developed a full range of guilds. On the whole, however, the major artisan professions still had a guild tradition and important guild structures.

More important was the fact that the guild tradition periodically broke down even in the key professions. Usually two related conditions were involved. First, newcomers to the city, in period of urban growth, could overwhelm guild limitations and create competition for jobs and wages among journeymen. In England by the eighteenth century most guilds had totally lost the power to restrict the number of workers in a craft or even to control techniques of work. When journeymen were overabundant it was tempting for masters to convert the guilds to their own ends alone. This had often happened in French and Italian cities and was to occur more massively with modernization. Guild ideals held that masters should be roughly equal, and to this end guild regulations often limited the number of journeymen that any one man could employ, as well as holding open the promise of mobility. But when journeymen were cheap, individual masters often sought to advance their fortunes, at the same time using guild organization to block all but their own sons from rising to mastership. A class wedge could thus be driven within the artisanry. Even here, however, guild traditions were not irrelevant, for the typical response of journeymen was to form their own associations to bargain with the masters and achieve some of the goals guilds were supposed to provide. In seeking to protect wages and limit the number of apprentices, journeymen's associations were a midway point between guilds and craft trade unions. But in 1700 guilds themselves had rarely broken down entirely; they were particularly strong in central Europe. Artisan shops remained small and most craftsmen had personal contacts with the masters that prevented a complete class rift.

Journeymen and masters alike had a definite sense of status. They expected to be treated with respect, even by their social betters. Just as the bourgeois marked themselves off from artisans by distinctive clothing, so artisans wore emblems of their trade to distinguish themselves from the poor. Family organization resembled that of the propertied classes, peasant and bourgeois alike. Artisans married late, for it was improper to found a family without a suitable economic position, preferably a mastership. Marriages typically involved the same kind of economic calculation we have seen among other groups. Brides were supposed to have a dowry, grooms of course their skill and good prospects for the future. From this base stemmed the association of family and work, which was typically passed on to the next generation when the son was sent into his father's trade. It was in fact the father's responsibility to provide the funds to pay for the son's apprenticeship as well as set up dowries for the daughters. Here was another reason for late marriage, which would limit the number of children born to the family.

Finally artisans had political expectations. Not, typically, of the modern sort, the expectations were nevertheless more precise than those of peasants. Artisans were not accustomed to asking for direct voice in government, although occasionally they might attempt this on the urban level. They did expect the state to help them out during economic slumps. In the typical preindustrial economic crisis, the artisan needed cheaper bread, for prices rose precisely as income went down. The response was often a bread riot, in which bakers were attacked for price gouging. But the artisanal protest tradition could spill beyond this. Sometimes rich businessmen were attacked, for artisans had an egalitarian resentment of wealth that could burst out when times were bad. And indirectly artisan rioting called for state action: the government was supposed to bring in enough grain to drive prices back down again. Where possible the state did exactly this, for artisanal rioting was feared. As with the peasantry the basic artisanal protest tradition was backward-looking. It asked for restoration of conditions that had prevailed before, not for new gains. This is why it could occur only in economic crises, for there was no expectation of progress to motivate agitation in good times. But the protest tradition was important nevertheless, and artisans would carry it vigorously into the modern period.

It is tempting to idealize the artisan's life, in comparison with later conditions of manufacturing work. Skilled, respected, able to rise to independence, this might be an enviable lot. Certainly the values involved were important, and many artisans would long try to preserve them. But the system did not work well for everyone. Journeymen had personal contact with their masters but they were by the same token intensely dependent on them, directed about from day to day and supervised not only at work but at meals and guild festivals. As was the case with the peasantry, a large number of journeymen could never marry, because they never acquired sufficient independent means. Many artisans, even masters, were desperately poor, though of course there was great variation from one individual to the next. Many ate little but starchy foods, and the quality of food was often spoiled. Housing was characteristically crowded, especially because the home was also shop and journeymen's dormitory. Health suffered. Many painters and printers died early from lead poisoning. Weavers were particularly subject to chest diseases because they pushed their looms with their chests. Indeed many artisans were deformed by their trade, and were more identifiable by their bent walk or gnarled hands than by the costumes they wore on festival days. Crowded housing, poor diets, and the miserable sanitary conditions of most cities caused a high infant mortality rate. Most urban artisans could expect more than half their children to die before age two; they were even worse off in this respect than the peasants. When a craft was destroyed by industrialization—and many were not, as we will see—important losses occurred that many craftsmen would try to protest. There were also reasons in the traditional conditions of the crafts to interest some in an alternative style of life.

The Urban Poor

Artisans were definitely not the worst off in a premodern city. Approximately 20 per cent of the urban population were domestic servants, mainly though not exclusively males. In Elbeuf, for example, approximately 250 members of the bourgeoisie employed 194 servants in 1785, and of course aristocratic households in larger cities would add to this number. Servants had some economic security, for they were normally assured of board and room. Though their money wages were low, some were able to save. They could also imitate some of their masters' habits; many learned to read. Given hand-me-downs by their employers or dressed in livery, servants might be proud of their dress. A successful servant might indeed rise in society, using his savings to buy an inn or some other business. But the typically modest bourgeois household was not the basis for material comfort. Housing was miserably crowded, and only poor food was provided. Servants as a whole were a highly dependent group. They could not risk protest; they had at least to pretend subservience. They had virtually no free time from their job, for they were expected to help set up the household in the morning and put things to rights at night.

But at least the servants had some compensations for a hard existence. A vast number of floating urban poor had nothing. In the larger cities, the final 20 per cent of the population was composed of unskilled, transient labor, and even smaller centers had a substantial group. These were people who did the cruder kinds of dock work, who hauled carts and wagons or

carried bricks or stones on construction sites, who dug ditches. Their functions were in fact vital to the city, but their rewards were minimal, for
they offered only their muscles, with no special skills or training.

The unskilled were paid low wages and also subject to irregular, degrading employment. Normally they were hired on a day-to-day basis,
flocking to a city square (for example, the Place de Grève in Paris, from
which the French word for *strike* ultimately came), where they would
compete for attention from a hiring boss. Some had to offer bribes to get
any work and all had to be carefully docile to any employer. Many drifted
from one city to the next, or back and forth from the countryside. Unskilled construction workers traditionally came into Paris from several poor
rural areas every summer, hoping to earn enough to tide their families
through a hard winter. Southern Italian laborers wandered even farther in
search of urban work.

The poverty of the unskilled could almost surpass description. Ragged
clothing and the meanest housing, often in cellars or attics, combined with
meager food. Unless they had a rural base the unskilled could rarely afford
a family, and many did not earn enough to form a marriage even in the
countryside. Many had to beg. Some had to turn to crime. This was a
desperate existence.

Yet the urban poor could not protest. They lacked the resources to
take time off from their quest for work. Their diets afforded them no energy
for an unusual effort. And they lacked community structures, which were
essential to protest in premodern society. They moved about too frequently
even to know many of their neighbors. They had no standing or traditions
in the city and no organizational experience. This deprived them of leadership of their own. More than this, the urban poor were rarely able to join
a riot started by others. Rioting required a sense of purpose in society;
struggle for survival was not enough. So except for individual acts of
defiance, such as theft, the urban poor could not protest their plight. The
group remained isolated and disorganized in the city, vital to the city's
economic life, vaguely feared by the propertied classes, but otherwise
ignored.

Popular Culture

Preindustrial cities had their own rituals and entertainments, beyond
those organized by individual classes, that even the very poor could share
to some extent. Urban popular culture expressed many of the hardships and
uncertainties of material existence; it might also provide some distraction
from them.

The culture was violent. As in the countryside urban groups not
infrequently engaged in brutal brawls. Rival journeymen's organizations,

with no apparent differences save separate names and symbols, often came
to blows. Apart from direct fighting, popular entertainment frequently
had a violent element. Animal fights were prized, as in bear baiting or cock
fighting, with bets placed on the winners. Public executions could gather
thousands of people, as the state intended, so that the example would be
clear. Whether they sympathized with the criminal or simply enjoyed the
macabre show, the public rarely stayed away. There were popular songs,
often with a romantic theme, and other casual entertainments as well, but
the theme of violence was noteworthy.

Death played an important role as well. Few people, urban or rural,
were unused to death; virtually every family saw several children die. Hence
the rituals associated with death were essential. The ultimate degradation
was burial in a common ditch, and a family had failed when one of its
members had to end in this way. A proper funeral soothed the tragedy of
death; it could even add a bit of interest to the routine of the living, for
death was too common to be the subject of prolonged lament. Sickness, too,
was seen as largely inevitable. The urban poor shunned hospitals, because
these were just places where one died among strangers, a judgment that
had considerable basis in reality. At most some magic potions were sought,
by a quack drawn from the ranks of the poor themselves. Beyond this it
was up to God's will whether one lived or not.

This was in an important sense a conservative culture, designed to
palliate tragedy but not to seek improvement. Where change was suggested
it was often feared; vaccination against smallpox, for example, introduced
during the eighteenth century met widespread resistance in the cities. Fear
of the unknown was enhanced by suspicion of outsiders, for the urban poor
had little experience of help from the upper classes or established institutions of society. In the cities even the church was often resented as the
creature of the rich, and the poorest elements of the city proved readier to
riot against the priests than against any other target. For the charity given
by the rich and the church was known to be patronizing, and even when it
had to be accepted the necessity was disliked. Worthless in the eyes of the
larger society, the poor would have liked to close themselves off from it to
defend their self-respect.

The changes associated with modernization inevitably shocked the
common people of the cities, and some, because of their traditionalism,
were slower to take advantage of new opportunities than any other element
of society. New urban leaders directly attacked the most common recreational outlets of the city's poor. But other values had to be preserved, at
least until the physical quality of life in the cities underwent enough improvement to warrant a culture based on some hope. Elements of the
preindustrial popular culture survive among the very poor even in cities
today.

A Status Society: For or Against

The complexity of preindustrial society is obvious. Even the poverty, which has to be emphasized, was not absolute except for a minority in both city and countryside. Economic uncertainty was more widespread, rooted in the impossibility of controlling the conditions of agricultural production —hence the protective quality of most economic organizations, from peasant family to merchant guild. For all but the aristocracy and the bourgeoisie, life was full of hard physical toil. For men this was qualified by a work culture that intermingled elements of sociability and a slow or mixed pace. This was true of women in field and shop as well. But married women owed not only their productive labor but also frequent childbearing. To produce three or four children living to adulthood the peasant or artisan wife had to have seven or eight births, which were normally spaced two years apart. Thus the average wife spent fourteen to sixteen years of her life carrying, bearing, or recovering from having babies. Apart from the physical strain, which resulted in frequent death in childbirth, there was the emotional anguish of infant death, which no amount of fatalism or ritual could entirely overcome.

To some extent the economic limitations of preindustrial existence restricted the affectionate quality of life. Economic arrangements came first in the family, and romantic love, though sung in popular ballads and hailed in aristocratic culture, was an accidental result. Infants were seen in terms of labor potential, and not given much attention until this potential could be realized; this was particularly true in southern and eastern Europe. Quarrels over property could poison family relations at a later stage; here western Europe, with its more property-conscious peasantry and bourgeoisie, faced greater tensions. Even death could not be given too much attention. When one marriage partner died he or she was typically replaced, for where there was property it was not hard for a widow or widower to pick up another mate. Given late marriage age and a slightly shorter adult lifespan, the average marriage may have lasted only fourteen years, which is considerably less than in the modern day, for mortality is more inexorable than divorce. We cannot know how much affection a husband lavished on his wife or parents on their children; undoubtedly there were great individual variations, as today. But we cannot assume that the family existed primarily as an affectionate unit.

Preindustrial society did provide other compensations for physical hardship. Religion gave hope for the afterlife. The multitude of small organizations, beginning with family and ranging through village and guild, protected from loneliness and gave an automatic sense of identity, though it is important to remember that a large minority of individuals were not fully embraced by these organizations. Protection entailed intensive personal supervision of life. How one could work, whom one could marry, when one could have sexual intercourse, what one could do on holidays, all were precisely regulated, except for the minority of people who led a precarious existence roaming from one place to another. But except for the wanderers there is little sense that supervision was resented, for no alternative model of existence was available.

Relatedly, the majority of the population had some stake in the existing order. Deference from below, paternalism from above cushioned the basic framework of a hierarchical society. Protest was extremely important but it occurred usually within the social framework, not against its foundations. Rarely did a preindustrial group toss up egalitarian arguments, though this had occurred among small radical sects in the Reformation and the English Civil War. More important, the bulk of the populace had some property or expectations of property. It might be highly qualified, particularly in eastern and southern Europe, with the overlay of manorialism. But most peasants had at least a partial sense of land ownership; most journeymen owned their tools and could aspire to mastership; the bourgeoisie was propertied by definition. Those in the family who did not own were either women, who largely accepted their legal subservience if only because they might wield important informal power in family government, or younger people, who were kept in line by the expectation of inheritance. More than legal status, which defined the outlines of social groupings, property ownership, despite its various objects and gradations, served as the key to societal organization, and this principle would be brought forward in the first stages of modernization even as legal privilege was attacked.

Hence few groups professed active interest in changing the social boundary lines. The people who endured the most intense physical suffering were too remote from the prevailing organizations to have a voice. Individual discontent could be alleviated by mobility—moving to another village or to the town, moving up in society by purchasing an aristocratic title. Because some movement was possible at various levels, most commonly from one age group to the next as skills or property were acquired, the basic social order seemed acceptable and there was no need for an ethic of mobility. The aspiring bourgeois wanted to imitate the aristocracy, not displace it. The itchy journeyman hoped to become a master, not destroy mastership. There was change in life, or expectation of change, without an ethic of individual striving.

Much of this was now to be challenged. And there were a number of groups who might be ready to take advantage of a new social structure, even if they were not overtly discontent in the preindustrial system. Women, youth, the poor, aggressive personality types at any social level, all might find reason to try something new. Others would resist. Cherished institutions, the property stake, and very means of childrearing that stressed loyalty to authority and custom, all promised stern opposition to change. Above all, preindustrial society provided no obvious source of fundamental change. Even when we recognize that, for all its virtues, preindustrial life had a host of drawbacks, in terms of human relationships as well as material hardship, it is not easy to predict how its fundamental character could be challenged. Literally none of the major social groupings believed in change. Even the bourgeoisie, as a class, sought to defend, not challenge. The small organizational units that defined institutional life were all predicated on maintenance of custom, not innovation, and their close supervision of their constituents made deviation difficult. What possible set of forces could unravel this tight social fabric?

3

THE FORCES OF
CHANGE

A number of related developments reshaped the economy and, to some extent, the character of society in western Europe from about 1750 to 1820. Economic relationships became increasingly commercialized, based on selling labor and goods for money and maximizing profits where possible. Commercialization also means impersonal economic dealings, with strangers in unfamiliar market settings. Although cities did not grow with unusual rapidity, urban influences spread along with the market economy. Entertainers from the cities fanned out into the countryside. By the end of the eighteenth century, for example, professional jugglers and other urban-based side shows were a regular part of traditional village festivals in France. Urban influence also showed in new patterns of sexual behavior and, in certain areas, a decline of religious practice. A new sense of time gained usage, as work, at least in urban manufacturing, was measured by the clock. Timing by sunset and sunrise was giving way to hour-by-hour punctuality; the growing sale of clocks and watches showed that more and more people were adopting this time sense, even if against their will. This first phase of modernization brought a newly sharp division between propertied and propertyless people, which came as a particular shock in the countryside. It saw the birth of a more modern political sense, as elements of the bourgeoisie and the urban artisanry learned to demand rights of political participation.

Most fundamentally, modern personality types were clearly emerging at a number of social levels. Some peasants as well as merchants learned to think in terms of rationality and innovation, casting aside a traditional outlook. A new sense of individualism was even more widespread. People began to express and indulge their egos as individuals, reducing their identification with customary groups.

These vast changes occurred in a setting that was, until the end of the period, superficially rather placid. The industrial and political revolutions of the late eighteenth century followed from the modernization that had already occurred. But even when we add their impact to the initial changes we must recognize that European society in 1820 was still highly traditional. This is an ambiguity that will recur in every stage of modernization, for even revolutionary change did not quickly destroy older values and institutions. This was one of the ways change could be accepted. Young people were constantly more open to it than old, and this generational process helped cushion the impact of change. When young people in the villages adopted new styles of dress or began to drink coffee and tea, the old might grumble but, so long as they could maintain their consumption habits, they did not feel too threatened. But young people, too, mixed tradition and innovation, preserving many preindustrial structures, notably the family, in a new setting. Change and continuity may constitute a trite theme but it is a constant one in the modernization process.

The first phase of modernization was confined to western Europe: Britain, France, Scandinavia, Germany, the Low Countries. Its major features were also present in North America. This Atlantic region was already accustomed to market dealings, with a bourgeoisie that, if not highly dynamic, was at least attuned to trade and finance. Peasants already engaged in some trade. The commercialization process simply altered the balance of their economy; from marginal, sales to the market became increasingly central. Comparable commercialization was impossible in eastern Europe. In the Balkans peasants had almost no market experience. They viewed nature with superstitious awe. Tools, to them, were objects of worship as much as implements of production, and elaborate ceremonies were built around the ax or the stove. Only a few objects, in terms of tools and furnishings, were owned by the peasant household, probably less than a fifth as many as in the peasant cottage in western Europe. A new attitude toward things and toward nature was essential before further change could occur, and this came about only gradually in the nineteenth century. This was an extreme case. Commercialization in the Russian countryside was suggested in the eighteenth century, as manufacturing spread and some peasants began to serve as commercial agents, hinting at a rural middle class. But the aristocracy, fearing this kind of innovation, assumed control of rural manufacturing by the end of the century, so neither the position nor the values of the peasantry could change greatly. Earlier changes in western Europe: the growth of cities, the reduction of aristocratic power, the partial independence of both peasants and artisans created the only setting in which modernization could initially occur. The aristocracy could not block the process. Peasant superstition, though real, did not prevent new efforts to subjugate nature. In both city and country-side tools, although respected, could be changed.

But what caused change? It is possible to see it imposed on the bulk of the populace, against their will: a group of greedy capitalists forced the common people into new ways. This leaves the question of where the new greed came from, but presumably this could be tracked down. The approach has some merit, as we will see, but it is too simple. Change came from decisions made by a whole variety of groups in the population. The decisions had unexpected consequences and their impact was severe in many ways. But they were not simply forced down the popular throat. And their results were correspondingly ambiguous. If the common people were merely forced to change, we would expect massive problems of adaptation. If, as we will contend, some change resulted from voluntary and widespread popular action, some adaptation was prepared in advance. Early modernization, particularly early industrialization, has often been seen as a massive attack on a happy, traditionalist society, even an over-turning of the natural human way of doing things. This view, particularly common in England, is nonsense. Traditionalist society was not so uni-formly happy. Its ways were not "natural," for after all only hunting and berry picking were natural to original man. The transformation of pre-modern society did involve great strain, but it brought some rapid benefits as well. Otherwise the masses of people would not have been so stupid as to participate in the process.

Sources of Change

Before the modernization process began at any general level, there was a massive revolution in the realm of formal ideas. The scientific revolution of the seventeenth century produced a belief in progress, reason, and the possibility of grasping the simple laws of nature. In the eighteenth century this mentality was carried forward in the Enlightenment, and philosophers held that human affairs could be ordered as rationally as they believed physical nature already was. The Enlightenment asked for political reform and material progress. Its image of man was very much like the model of modern man as developed by social scientists in the twentieth century: secular, scientific, progressive, and so on. These formal ideas must have had some bearing on popular modernization in its early stages.

The connections are in fact tenuous. New science, for example, did not produce new inventions. Only in the nineteenth century was the linkage made. Eighteenth-century industrial techniques were worked out by artisan tinkerers, who had no contact with scientific thought. James Watt, the inventor of the steam engine, came closest to such contact, for he made precision instruments for scientists at the University of Glasgow. But his steam engine did not embody existing scientific ideas; at most he imbibed a belief that progres was possible and that step-by-step thinking produced new knowledge. Early industrial capitalists seized on Enlightenment ideas. Matthew Boulton, who first produced the new steam engines, joined a scientific society and talked about industry as the basis of world progress. But these interests occurred after his success as an enterpreneur; it is hard to argue that they caused it. The Enlightenment had a more direct role in the first signs of modern political consciousness. Belief in political reform spread to many sectors of the bourgeoisie in France during the second half of the eighteenth century via Enlightenment tracts. Lawyers and other professional people were particularly receptive. By the 1790s a more radical reform interest, also Enlightenment-derived, reached artisans, whose leaders began talking in terms of social contracts and popular sovereignty. But even here the Enlightenment channeled political interests more than it caused them.

The state, particularly on the Continent, played a more direct role in modernization, though without intending to contribute to any fundamental transformation of society. From the late seventeenth century most European governments had been extending the scope of their operations. They tried to increase their contact with distant sections of their country, curtailing the regional power of aristocrats. Bureaucracies were expanded, and bourgeois elements were brought into some of them. Most important, the government began to deal with activities that had previously been left to the control of local and private groups. Many states codified laws on a national basis, establishing clear and presumably rational standards to replace local traditional rules. Governments felt active concern for the economic health of the nation. At the end of the seventeenth century, governments from France to Russia tried to introduce new industries and techniques. Several governments, such as the Prussian, encouraged better agricultural methods; they sponsored drainage projects and supported new products such as the potato. To promote commerce, several states provided clearer standards in currency and in weights and measures; Britain even established a semiofficial national bank. Efforts were made to cut down local tolls and other barriers to a national market. Roads and canals were extended. There were even direct attempts to encourage population growth.

In none of this, however, was there any intention of altering basic class structure. There was some talk of governmental responsibility for the well-being of all subjects. Some rulers increasingly saw their interests as separate from those of the aristocracy and other traditional bodies, such as the national churches; hence nonaristocratic bureaucracies and religious tolerance grew. But above all, Continental governments wished to develop their economic and military power. This required reforms in military techniques and recruitment. It required an improved economy, particularly in the manufacturing sector. It required greater governmental efficiency in many respects. But this was not a revolutionary purpose. Governments avoided challenging major privileges, especially those of the aristocracy, because such challenges would distract from the cohesion of the state. In eastern Europe, as we have seen, nobles were able to increase their power. Governmental action did spur some economic and administrative change, but for an attack on class structure some new impulse was necessary. Even in the economy, governments often prevented innovation by formulating elaborate rules on production methods that supported the craft and merchant guilds. So we must look elsewhere for the basic motor of change.

Population Growth

The massive expansion of Europe's population was the most important disruptive force in the eighteenth century. Elements of every social class were forced to innovate in order to survive. There were, to be sure, areas of substantial population growth that did not modernize; indeed the eighteenth century saw a population explosion outside of Europe as well. Within Europe demographic upheaval in Spain and Italy did not produce new social structures. Again only western Europe had the essential preconditions for modernization; but even here it required the shock of a true demographic revolution to begin a fundamental transformation of traditional society.

In virtually every area of Europe the population increased by 50 to 100 per cent in the eighteenth century, with the greatest growth coming after 1750. The Hapsburg Empire grew from 20 to 27 million; Spain rose from 5 to 10 million and Prussia from 3 to 6 million. France increased from 20 to 29 million, Britain from 9 to 16 million. Growth continued throughout the nineteenth century. Some areas such as Italy and the Balkans, even increased their rate of growth after 1870. In Europe as a whole population rose from 188 million in 1800 to 401 million in 1900. This was an upheaval of truly impressive proportions. Its significance may be measured by comparing the rate of expansion with the 3 per cent increase in Europe's population during the entire century between 1650 and 1750. Clearly, a demographic revolution occurred after 1750.

The expansion of population was European in scope. Certain regions, even whole countries, experienced an unusually rapid rise. Britain and Germany approximately tripled their populations during the nineteenth century after a notable increase in the eighteenth. France barely doubled her population between 1700 and 1900. Obviously, differences in degree must be noted. Distinctions in date are equally important. The demographic boom in western and central Europe was most intense between 1750 and 1850; French population began to rise as early as 1680. The factors promoting this boom touched eastern and southern Europe in a more limited way, and it was the period after 1850 that saw the most significant increase, with the spread of western techniques of midwifery and vaccination playing a leading role. By 1900 virtually every area of Europe had contributed to the tremendous surge of population, but each major region was at a different stage of demographic change.

The unprecedented increase in population was the most important feature of demographic change, but it was not the only one. In the century and a half after 1780, Europe sent 40 million people to the two Americas, Asiatic Russia, and other areas. Emigration was one of the clearest expressions of the upheaval that increasing population brought to European society. In the first generations of demographic rise economic opportunities failed to keep pace with the population. Emigration was most intense when population grew most rapidly and tended to decline once industrialization developed sufficiently to absorb most of the increase. Britain and Ireland supplied most of the emigrants at first, reflecting the intensity of population pressure in the two islands. The agricultural crisis of the 1840s convinced many German peasants that the land could no longer support them, and a wave of German emigration ensued. Eastern and southern Europe provided most emigrants at the end of the century. By 1914, 17 million people had emigrated from Britain and Ireland, 4 million from Austria-Hungary, 2.5 million from Russia, and 10 million from Italy. Only a few countries, such as France, largely escaped the movement.

Though only a minority of Europeans actually emigrated, the movement affected a far larger number. The wave of emigration greatly increased Europe's influence in the world. It brought new economic opportunities and new knowledge to many Europeans. Equally important, it disrupted many families, many villages, and exposed countless people to contact with new ideas about the possibility of mobility and change. Information and myth about the possibility of emigrating and the nature of life in new lands had significant effects on many villages and towns. They represented one aspect of the change in outlook that population growth brought to European society.

The populations of Europe not only grew in the nineteenth century, but also changed in physical character. Health improved. In 1800 the life expectancy of a Frenchman at birth was twenty-eight years; by 1900 it was almost fifty. Physical size increased. In western Europe the average man was about five feet tall in 1800. A century later average height had increased by six inches, and weight was accordingly greater. Physical deformity became less common as diet improved and many forms of manual labor were lightened by the introduction of machines.

The demographic revolution thus serves as a backdrop for social change well into the later nineteenth century. But its consequences were most dramatic during its initial decades. And it is here that we must seek the basic causes of the process.

Causes of Population Growth

The population explosion resulted from a break in the traditional, if approximate, balance between births and deaths in European society. In England between 1700 and 1750 approximately 32.8 people were born annually for each 1,000 inhabitants, and 31.5 people died. Similarly, in Lombardy in the late eighteenth century, 39 people were born and 37 people died for each 1,000 inhabitants. Clearly, major alteration had to occur either in birth or mortality rate before the expansion of population could begin. In fact, both rates changed: families began to have more children and a lower percentage of the population died each year. Much is still unknown about the precise developments in population rates in the eighteenth and nineteenth centuries, but certain general features seem clear. During the period 1750–1800, for example, the population of England grew at a rate of over 1 per cent a year. Approximately 80 per cent of this can be accounted for by a decline in mortality; by 1800 only 27.1 per 1,000 died per year. But there was also a startling rise in the number of children born annually.

Several basic factors contributed to a decline in mortality rates in the eighteenth century. In central Europe and in France deaths in wars declined. Epidemic diseases became less common. Plagues still occurred; in the 1830s cholera killed a large number of people in western Europe. But the historic pattern of periodic decimation by epidemics, like the fatal wave of influenza in western Europe in the 1720s, was really broken. Better methods of hygiene, particularly in the cities, accounted for some of this decline. English cities kept streets cleaner in the late eighteenth century and paid more attention to sewage disposal. In parts of England vaccination reduced the incidence of smallpox, a major traditional killer. There was also an improvement of border controls against entry of diseased persons and animals. The growing efficiency of the Hapsburg government was particularly important in blocking the traditional route of plagues from the Middle East into Europe. But we should not exaggerate the importance of human agencies in this process. Certainly no major medical advance was involved. The decline of epidemic disease occurred outside Europe as well, for the eighteenth century saw a break in the traditional plague cycle, as had occurred before in human history. The germs would regroup and attack again in the nineteenth century, but by this time European society had greatly changed. It was even learning how to deal with disease.

More important than reduction in disease was reduction of famine in the eighteenth century. Better diets improved health, which helped increase sexual activity (hence the birth rate rise) and reduced mortality. A number of factors improved the food supply. The eighteenth century was unusually warm, the warmest century in 800 years, which improved crop yields. New agricultural methods were developed, particularly in England and the Low Countries. Better methods of drainage opened up new lands. Increasingly, cultivation of nitrogen-fixing plants replaced traditional systems of fallow on some of the large estates. By growing plants like turnips every few years, all cultivable land could be kept in use, which implied as much as a 33 per cent increase in agricultural production. New equipment, such as seed drills, also improved yields. In eastern Europe the governments of Prussia, Russia, and the Hapsburg lands fostered colonization of wilderness regions. The Russians expanded cultivation in the rich lands to the south and west, and new areas of Hungary were opened up to agriculture.

But the new lands do not account for most of the increased food supply. Nor, certainly, do new agricultural methods, for although these were known and discussed they were not widely adopted until the nineteenth century. The most important new development was a simple one: the introduction of the potato and, in southern Europe, maize from the New World. The potato's advantages over traditional grains were legion. It could be grown in three or four months, instead of ten, and in poor soil. Its yield was more than two times that of grain per acre, and so it was particularly ideal for small holdings; an acre in potatoes would support a family of five or six people, plus one animal, for the better part of a year. It could be cultivated by hand. It had high caloric and nutritional value. The qualities of maize were somewhat similar, though it could not be grown in northern Europe. Italian peasants grew maize on their garden plots while they raised wheat for their landlords, subsisting on a corn meal, polenta, which is still widely used in southern Italy even though it may cause pellagra. Maize also supported population growth in Spain, southern France, Hungary, and possibly the Balkans during the eighteenth century.

But for the area in which population growth triggered modernization it was the potato that was the chief agent. Population growth indeed varied somewhat with the rate of adoption of the tuber; France, for example, was slow, whereas the impoverished peasantry of Scotland and Ireland expanded massively as they converted to the new crop. England, in the middle position, nevertheless had at least a third of its population subsisting on the potato by 1844. Ironically, peasants had long resisted the potato, which had been brought from the New World, as an oddity, well before the eighteenth century. Traditional fear of novelty was at the root of their resistance. The Bible did not mention the crop, therefore it could not be good. It was held to cause typhoid fever. Russian peasants, in a slight variant, believed it produced cholera, which is one reason the potato did not catch on there until after 1850. But eighteenth-century governments and enterprising landlords promoted the crop, for increased population was a source of military and economic strength. And peasants gradually converted on their own. For the potato initially answered two traditional needs. It helped assure against periodic famines, and grain failures in the eighteenth century played a major role in spreading reliance on the new crop; and it protected the peasant with only a garden plot, particularly in areas where landlord dominance or repeated division of plots through inheritance left a family with insufficient land to survive. A sensible decision, to adopt the potato, but one that had immense consequences.

The initial causes of population growth in western Europe really lasted little more than half a century. By the early nineteenth century the rate of growth was slowing. But expansion would long continue, even increasing in terms of absolute numbers. Basically this momentum resulted simply from earlier growth. More people reaching childbearing age in 1800 guaranteed still more children reaching childbearing age by 1820 even if the birth rate slowed up a bit. By the nineteenth century the undeniable spread of agricultural improvements supported the new population. Ireland suffered demographic disaster in 1846–1848, when the potato crop failed, and never regained her peak levels of total population as death and emigration turned the country backward. But the rest of Europe, despite periodic famines, could now produce even more traditional crops than before. Industrialization also provided new jobs and wealth. Finally, by the later nineteenth century genuine medical improvements, particularly in the care of children, entered the scene. By 1900 death at infancy had been reduced to about 10 per cent in western Europe. The discoveries of Pasteur and others from 1860 onward heralded additional improvements in medicine and hygiene. So populations still grew. But in fact most families in western Europe, by the second half of the nineteenth century at least, were trying to reduce their birth rates. Although demography still had a dynamic impact, the real revolution, resulting from a few simple decisions and an odd combination of circumstances, had already taken place.

Effects of Population Growth: Commercialization

The population increase of the late eighteenth century shook established behavior. Jean Koechlin was a rather ordinary master weaver in Mulhouse in precisely this period. Not particularly dynamic, not an obvious industrial pioneer. But he had twelve children, all of whom survived to maturity. He needed jobs for his sons, dowries for his daughters. So he began to spread his textile operations to the countryside, ultimately directing a large putting-out operation. His sons, in turn, more genuinely possessed of a risk-taking entrepreneurial spirit, set up large cotton factories and were industrial magnates by the mid-nineteenth century. Here is an unusual success story, but something like it occurred many times, which is why population growth is so vital to the understanding of economic modernization. New numbers provided a new labor force and new markets, quite obviously; they also provided new motivations.

It is impossible to say why some families, undoubtedly a minority, responded to population growth through innovation. Previous social position had little to do with the pattern. Large farmers probably had an advantage over other peasants as they converted to more market production in order to support their brood. But established merchants often clung to traditional business practices; only a minority of the bourgeoisie expanded trade and manufacturing. By the same token traditional centers of production often declined in relative importance. Their leaders, satisfied with preindustrial standards, simply did not take the trouble to innovate. Cities outside the traditional merchant and guild orbit, some of them, like Mulhouse, with no special physical advantages, could rise quite quickly. Here was the beginning of the remaking of Europe's urban map. Most artisans tried to cling to old ways. A few did not, and it was from French and particularly British artisans that most of the early industrial inventions came. One could even rise from a rather low position in society. A landless English peasant in the early eighteenth century sets up as a domestic weaver, possibly making a fairly good wage. His son becomes a foreman in the system, distributing raw materials to the workers and picking up the finished product. His son, in turn, sets up as a small manufacturer, for by now the family has a modest capital. And either he or his son, for by now we are near 1800, starts a factory. There was much intergenerational mobility of this sort, for population growth created an extremely fluid society.

Ultimately the economic innovators would coalesce into a modern middle class, but this was not yet. For the eighteenth century what must be emphasized is a division in virtually every traditional class, between those who sought change and those who resented the new pressures upon them.

The aristocracy was sorely pressed by population growth. Although the class had traditionally had much larger families than the poorer masses, it was not accustomed to seeing so many sons and daughters survive. Established positions did not increase apace. The army officer corps, for example, did not grow as rapidly as the aristocratic population. Here was a major source of the aristocratic resurgence, and the main contribution of the aristocracy to modernization was negative. By trying to monopolize both church and state the class helped convert aspiring bourgeois into a middle class, with a consciousness of its own rights and values. By responding defensively, the aristocracy set up a new class struggle. The French Revolution and related political battles elsewhere became middle-class movements for this reason. But individual aristocrats innovated more positively. They could be found introducing new mining techniques or new agricultural methods.

In England the aristocracy found new wealth through the enclosure movement, which was at its height in the sixty years after 1760. The movement involved the withdrawal of massive tracts of land from village tenure. Landlords, predominantly aristocratic, not only withdrew their own lands from peasant farming, but also bought up much of the land of poorer peasants. Government acts, burdening many peasants with obligations to fence in their own land, literally forced many small owners to sell. By the early nineteenth century over 67 per cent of British farm-land was included in large estates. And the British landlords, unlike their Continental brethren, were not content with merely expanding their holdings; they fenced in their land, thus separating it from any remnants of village agriculture. They installed tenant overseers, often drawn from the more ambitious ranks of the local farming population, and paid them well to organize the estates on a basis of rational exploitation. Fallow fields were replaced by fields planted in nitrogen-rich turnips or clover. Drainage was installed. Cattle raising was extended and the stock much improved. Agriculture was geared to produce effectively for the market and to earn the highest cash return possible. Workers were ill paid, to be sure, but the system did not depend on serf-type labor; in fact, with improved methods the productivity of labor was greatly increased.

The peasantry produced agricultural innovators as well. It was a desire to get ahead that produced the rationalizing managers of estates in Britain or Normandy. Other peasants wanted to take advantage of the market on their own, for the class was obviously pressed by population growth and had to find new ways to support its children. Rising prices for marketable grain (up to 100 per cent in some areas during the eighteenth century) provided their own lure for the ambitious. The large farmers in France began in many areas to attack village agriculture. They tried to buy out smallholders to provide a better base for market production. They sometimes moved part of their operations onto common lands. This was the beginning of a very long process of change in village agriculture, for there was no revolution in peasant mentality. Even by 1789, however, the traditional middling peasant was demonstrably upset at the incursions of the big farmers. And a large class of propertyless peasants had been produced. Some families sold out, particularly of course in England, through the pressure of enclosures. Others simply had no land to distribute to a growing family. Here was a newly sharp division, really unprecedented in terms of village traditions, between owners and nonowners.

Something of the same division widened among urban artisans, though with equal gradualness. Faced with population pressure the artisan master was tempted to try to expand his operation a bit, breaking with the guild system. In France and England artisan shops became larger, the master more of a small businessman and less a fellow craftsman. In some of these shops the new sense of time was promoted, for punctuality would increase production. Tasks might be divided a bit more than before, for specialization of labor raised productivity as well. A few shops were indeed on their way to becoming small factories, even without new equipment, and their owners to entering a new middle class.

The bourgeoisie produced its own set of innovators, always with the constant need to compete for new resources for a growing population. Professional people suffered from population pressure. Plum jobs in bureaucracy and church were not growing fast enough, and the aristocratic resurgence offended this group particularly. From lawyers, minor provincial bureaucrats, and even some nonnoble priests would come the articulation of the political aims of the middle class, as Enlightenment principles were translated into demands for new political power. For a reform of the state, with bureaucracy open to talent instead of aristocratic privilege, was one of the most obvious ways for alert professionals to meet the demographic crisis. The impulse was to spread well beyond the borders of France, though it was in the French Revolution that this particular strand of modernization had its first historic impact. But this was not the only professional response. At the end of the eighteenth century professionals in several areas began to form associations and talk about improvements in training. In Prussia the training of Lutheran ministers was tightened up, which was to contribute to a growth of professional consciousness generally; for the new ministers, proud of the training, would commonly use their position to send their sons into better-paying professions such as the law or university teaching. Professionals generally pressed for expansion of secondary schools and universities; by 1800, partly because of the obvious need for better-trained bureaucrats, partly because of the impulse of the French Revolution, this expansion occurred. Finally, even before 1789, new professions were being suggested. Improvements in artillery as well as new economic development created the need for trained engineers, and on the Continent several training centers were established. This was a very early stage in the modernization of the professions, far less visible than the political response, but it laid out lines that would be followed later.

Innovative business elements of the bourgeoisie busily established or expanded banks and trading operations. In France and England colonial trade increased dramatically. But the most important eighteenth-century response to new pressures and opportunities was the dramatic expansion of the system of domestic manufacturing in the countryside. Urban merchants invested in raw materials, particularly in textiles, but also in production of metal tools, nails, and cutlery. They sent these materials to rural producers, who spun thread or wove cloth or forged knives in their own homes. Some of the producers marketed their own product, but increasingly, as the eighteenth century wore on, they served as paid labor and simply returned the finished items to the merchant, who arranged for sale. There were opportunities for great profit in this system, for the rural producers bore much of the risk. They invested in the spinning wheel or loom. It was easy to lay them off when there was a slump, for the skills involved were not great and were easy to replace. New centers of domestic manufacturing, like Mulhouse or Zurich or Elbeuf, along with port cities involved in the colonial trade, supported a booming business community, the embryo of a modern, capitalist middle class.

The Propertyless

Near the bottom of the social scale there was innovation as well. Population pressure, vastly increasing the propertyless class, created great hardships. The structure of a Bavarian village in 1817 reveals a common pattern. Of the family units only five were large farmers who employed labor on their own; forty-three had about 25 acres, enough to live on easily; forty-eight averaged 12.3 acres, which was not enough to support children over twelve, who would therefore have to find something else to do with their labor at a very tender age; seventy-four were even worse off, with 8.2 acres; seventeen had mere shacks; and some day laborers owned nothing at all. The landless or near landless lived in great material misery, and nutritional standards declined in some cases, for ironically the potato kept some people alive who before would have perished with so little land. Rising numbers of people who had to seek paying jobs often drove down the wages of agricultural workers. The big cities were filled with growing numbers of unskilled workers too. Begging and crime increased everywhere. London, particularly, was never more thief-ridden than around 1800, when bands of impoverished children were organized to pick pockets.

But some of the propertyless found compensations. They lived under great compulsion, and some must have resented not only material hardship but the lack of traditional status quite keenly. But elements of this group could modernize in their own fashion. Bavarian farmers found their laborers increasingly uppity, immoral, and money-grubbing. They criticized them for wearing flashy, city-style clothes. There are several important aspects to this judgment. In the first place, the growing gap between owners and nonowners made the owners nervous, for they distrusted people without property. This became a durable element of class tensions in countryside and city alike. Second, the propertyless, although never rich, were not always impoverished. The agriculture of the late eighteenth century was labor intensive. New equipment, when used at all, required more work than before; this was true, for example, of the seed drill. In addition, the most modern estates employed more labor than traditional agricultural units involving the same amount of land could have done. The enclosed estates of England thus displaced small landowners and really destroyed any English peasantry, but they did not displace labor. Women as well as men found paying jobs planting, harvesting, and tending stock. This is why, sometimes at least, agricultural laborers were able to buy new clothing. The propertyless were opening up a new style of life, which is what most obviously offended the propertied.

This theme can be more obviously pursued among the rural domestic manufacturing workers, who usually earned better money wages than agricultural labor. This was a vast group, embracing hundreds of thousands of workers, women and men alike, around each major center. Some worked only part time, but certain families and even whole villages virtually abandoned agriculture, except for garden plots, in favor of this newly expanded system. It took some venturesomeness to set up as a manufacturing worker, which is one way to approach a changing outlook amid the rural lower class. Many had little alternative, of course, for domestic manufacturing was an essential resource to an expanding rural population, now that there was not enough land to go around. But once involved in the system the typical domestic manufacturing worker changed his or her habits rather dramatically. These workers began to buy city-processed food products such as coffee, tea, and sugar. They adopted a more urban, and more revealing, style of dress, with more brightly colored clothing. The concern for dress was important for it provided a new kind of status, a new interest in life, and would be taken further by the industrial working class. Domestic manufacturers reflected urban influences on their lives in other ways. They might resent their status as almost propertyless workers, but some began to learn how to use the market system to maintain a good wage. Scattered strikes and riots occurred among both rural and urban producers during the eighteenth century in an effort to bargain with employers; here was at least the suggestion of a new protest theme. Indeed many of the propertyless were changing their conception of society more rapidly than their employers, which is why the owners found them disrespectful.

Finally, the domestic workers got married at an earlier age, because with no property to defend, the traditional waiting period made no sense.

Able to earn money even in their late teens they were less subservient to their parents' authority. They began to seek more sexual pleasure.

A Sexual Revolution

There were several signs of a major change in sexual behavior that began in the late eighteenth century and continued into the nineteenth. Marriage rates increased in a number of areas. With new sources of income people who previously had to remain single were able to form families, which increased their status and gave them emotional support. The age of puberty began to fall. Boys' choirs were harder to maintain because voices were changing earlier. Though unremarked in the world of music, the age of menstruation also began to drop. Earlier puberty reflected better average nutrition. It also stemmed from the wider contacts, the greater sexual stimuli, possible in an expanding society. The traditional village horizons, in which there were just a handful of possible sexual partners in a given age group, were broadening as population grew and there was more economic interaction with cities. Illegitimacy rates increased. From about 2 per cent of all births in traditional society, illegitimacy rose, throughout the modernizing area on both sides of the Atlantic, from about 1780 onward, reaching a peak of as much as 11 per cent in some cases by 1870.

Increased sexual activity occurred within marriage too. This contributed to the rising birth rate. It also caused a major change in the traditional cycle of births and conceptions. Traditional peasant society produced a peak of conceptions in May and June, which meant that far more babies were born in February and March than at any other time of the year. Why this pattern prevailed is hard to determine. Traditional spring fever, the advent of better weather, the greater privacy possible when children could be playing outdoors, all may have contributed. Probably the most important factor was the desirability of minimal interference with a mother's labor service. Giving birth in mid-winter, when there was no agricultural work to be done, made good sense in a subsistence economy. It was not a good choice so far as infants were concerned, for the early spring and summer constituted the period when food was in shortest supply and parental attention most distracted by jobs in the fields. So March-born babies were smaller and less intelligent than the average. With the spread of urban influence, for the conception cycle had never been so seasonal in the cities, and manufacturing work that could be done even in the winter, sexual intercourse could occur more regularly through the year. The traditional conception and birth cycle began to even out, though there are still traces of it even in the twentieth century. Here, too, was a sign that many Europeans were becoming sexier.

In this case, by producing births at more favorable times of the year, the change may also have improved the size and intelligence of the population.

Peasant society had been sexually prudish. It had successfully prevented sexual intercourse outside of marriage. It had severely limited sex within marriage, because of the need to regulate the timing of children. When intercourse occurred it had usually been hasty and unimaginative— no foreplay, the man on top, quick ejaculation. Probably sex was becoming more diversified as well as more frequent in the first stage of modernization. As part of political reform, laws against fornication were repealed. More important, parental controls over sexual behavior were reduced. Something of a new youth culture was springing up, particularly among the propertyless, who, with nothing to inherit, had every reason to seek new satisfactions in romantic love. Women as well as men found pleasure in these changes. A Bavarian girl suggested her new sense of freedom when asked why she kept having illegitimate children: "It's okay to have babies, the king has okayed it."

The clearest signs of change in sexual behavior occurred among the propertyless. This was the group, certainly, that produced the new rates of illegitimate births. But the decline in the age of puberty and the suggestions of more sexual activity within marriage may have affected the respectable property owners as well. New sexual pleasure denoted a greater sense of individualism, a desire for personal satisfactions, that could be the first step in the formation of a modern outlook.

The sexual revolution had its drawbacks too. Older people, particularly among the traditional propertied classes, began to lament the immorality of the young and the poor (another modern theme that has proved quite durable). More directly, greater sexual activity, in virtually every segment of society, produced more children to take care of. It obviously contributed to the tensions of an expanding population. It seriously conditioned the later life of women. The girl delighted in new sexual freedom at age twenty became a mother worn out by the necessity of caring for six children, of perhaps eight who had been born to her, at age thirty. The late eighteenth century saw a number of efforts to counter the effects of the new birth rate and the greater survival chances of infants. There was an increase in child abandonment and exposure of children. In a number of countries baby farms were patronized by various social classes; ostensibly designed to nurse infants, the "farm" saw most of their charges die from ill care, which is presumably what their overburdened parents wanted. Only in the second half of the nineteenth century did the baby farms disappear. Some abortion occurred. In 1839 over 10 per cent of all women arrested in Paris (156 individuals) were charged with infanticide, and about 1 per cent more with abortion. Yet still the average size of the family increased.

A Balance Sheet

The first stage of modernization had immensely ambiguous results. Rising crime suggested immense personal hardships and dislocation. Violence often increased faster than crimes against property, suggesting that many poor people used traditional crime methods more frequently in response to change; it was hard to innovate even in expressing anger. And it was not only the poorest who were bewildered. Within each segment of society that produced a modernizing element there was a majority that found change unacceptable. The small peasant landowner who wanted nothing more than to perpetutate his family plot now found himself burdened with more children than he could provide for, pressed by his farmer neighbor who wanted to alter village agriculture in order to produce for the market or by a business-minded miller who increased his charges for processing grain. The urban influences that could liberate some peasants infuriated others, who found unwanted city people, strangers, trying to do business with them. In some cases two rural regions side by side had quite different reactions to new commercial pressures. In western France a wine-growing area, accustomed to selling to the cities, adapted to domestic manufacturing and other urban contacts quite well. Right next to it was a region, the Vendée, of large estates run by absentee landlords. Here, new trade, involving contact with urban outsiders, was profoundly resented, and the peasants of the Vendée were to rise up against the French Revolution essentially as a protest against the whole modern order. But within a given village, different personality types, even different ages, produced similar distinctions. And of course many individuals had ambivalent reactions, appreciating, say, the new urban entertainers who embellished their festivals but disliking other trappings of modernity, and above all the relentless pressure of rising population against a limited land supply. Desperation caused a rising tide of rural riots. There were several hundred small riots in Russia in the 1790s. A new current of agitation took shape in southern Italy after 1810. French peasants rose more massively in 1789. Their direct object was to end the remnants of manorial obligations, but they were also concerned about the activities of the big farmers and the urban businessmen. In this case they won and lost; manorialism was abolished but this only increased the pace of economic modernization. Further rural agitation was inevitable.

Artisans could also be ambivalent about modernization, but here protest took even clearer shape. In Britain, Holland, and of course in the larger French cities during the Revolution, artisans began to request political rights in order to defend their traditional values. Guilds were abolished in France in 1791, a middle-class revolutionary achievement. Journeymen did not object to this, for the guilds had been taken over by the masters anyway, but they did want new associations to defend their rights. This being denied, by another 1791 law that forbad all economic associations, French journeymen launched an intense, if sporadic, effort to win control of the state in order to defend traditional goals of protected wages and prices and a traditional economic system. British craftsmen, particularly in London, who sought the vote had similar goals in mind. For the most articulate artisans, political modernization—that is, the demand for a voice in the state—followed from a desire to attack economic change. Here, too, the battle was just beginning.

Within all the lower-class groups—artisans, peasants, and landless laborers—some elements sought to profit by modernization, some to protest it, and some doubtless did a bit of each, depending on the economic conditions of any particular year. And amid all the disruption important continuities with the past remained. The domestic manufacturing system preserved the family economy. It gave new opportunities to women, who normally contributed their earnings to the family fund; women did all the domestic spinning and some ancillary weaving operations as well, almost always within the family context. Many young people did not receive traditional parental support; they avoided some controls as well. But more of them formed their own families than ever before, for the economic functions were not lost. Villages and guilds were not working as well as they had in traditional society, but they had long performed imperfectly and they remained viable throughout most of Europe. The Bavarians who had illegitimate children still went to church, believing themselves good Christians, and attended village festivals. They upset their priests— for the church was quick to attack new behavior, leading the charge against immorality—but they did not believe they had changed greatly.

In other words the sense of upheaval was not yet overwhelming. Even protest was based on an idea that past values could be restored. Immense dislocation and hardship were important realities. But some people found traditional problems alleviated by the new economic trends. Domestic manufacturing cut underemployment in some rural areas. Rising marriage rates and reduced sexual restraints answered longstanding weaknesses in the rural culture of western Europe. Many people, whether aggrieved or not, could believe that traditional values were still functioning or were within reach of recapture. Without these ambiguities, modernization could not have proceeded, for in some areas of Europe, despite population pressure, it was stillborn. New kinds of unrest arose. Traditions were adapted. Some people, the rising urban capitalists but also the rural spinners who bought fancier clothing, began to think in terms of new pleasures.

Two Revolutions

From this volatile mixture two further challenges erupted at the end of the eighteenth century. From France political revolution extended many of the new governmental functions that had been initiated earlier; it also gave reality to the demands for political participation that had been simmering among urban bourgeois and artisans. In England the first industrial revolution had even more sweeping implications.

An aristocratic attempt to wrest more power from the monarchy, part of the class's resurgence in France, triggered political revolution in 1789. Artisans and peasants acted on grievances new and old. The artisans focused on material insecurity and sought government protection against economic change; the peasants attacked their landlords. But the revolution's direction was assumed by the middle class. In terms of personal aspirations many of the leaders were rather conservative bourgeois. They used the revolution to take over landed estates and high posts in the bureaucracy, creating a ruling elite whose interests were not totally different from the aristocracy. But the political measures this group introduced truly revolutionized the legal structure of society. By the autumn of 1789 the legal and economic basis of the aristocracy had been attacked. Feudal rights and privileges were destroyed; government service was theoretically open to anyone with the necessary ability. The church was stripped of lands and privileges; religious tolerance was extended. Peasants were relieved of manorial dues. In matters of law and taxation they dealt with government agents instead of local notables. Guilds were abolished and all combinations of workingmen forbidden. It was now legal for anyone to set up economic operations and to use any methods he desired. In sum, the Revolution altered the structure and personnel of government and drew new groups into political consciousness. It attacked the legal basis of the old regime by replacing hereditary and group privilege with equality under the law. It promoted a capitalistic market economy not only in manufacturing but also to a degree in the countryside. In all these ways the Revolution provided the political basis for the social development of the nineteenth century.

The Revolution was not confined to France. Its principles had wide appeal to various groups, and the appeal was to increase in the next generation. In 1793–1794 merchants and artisans agitated in Holland for a revolutionary change, and there was stirring elsewhere in western Europe. In the east, where there was no significant urban element, the Revolution had repercussions among other groups. Some peasants in Bohemia, Hungary, and even Russia learned vaguely of the Revolution. Some aristocrats in Russia and Poland, chafing under autocracy, were attracted by ideas of the rights of man. Quite generally and for very diverse groups the Revolution promoted an idea of change and showed the path that change should take. Invocation of revolutionary principles was basic to most political agitation in the next century. Furthermore, French armies directly carried the gains of the Revolution to many areas adjacent to France. Guilds and feudal privileges were abolished in the Low Countries, western Germany, and northern Italy. Equality under the law was proclaimed, law codes rationalized, the church weakened.

Beyond these areas, monarchist statesmen were impressed by the revolutionary ferment and tried to prevent comparable disorder at home by timely reforms. Even after this the memory of revolution lingered, leading conservative statesmen to sprinkle their repressive measures with some reforms. More important, the military and political efficiency of the Revolution appealed to rulers in their own terms. Efforts to rationalize bureaucracy were undertaken in Prussia and Russia; new interest arose in improvements in commerce and agriculture. Not all these changes were effective; some were revoked after the Revolution. But a door had been opened to change in every corner of the Continent.

The Industrial Revolution

At about the same time, during the last decades of the eighteenth century, the industrial revolution was taking shape in Britain. Its basis was the application of mechanical power to manufacturing. At first this power often came from water wheels, but the invention of the steam engine about 1770 allowed far more massive mechanical power to be developed. By providing powerful pumps the steam engine allowed deeper mine shafts to be sunk, greatly increasing the amount of coal available for mining. In metallurgy steam engines were soon applied to power the bellows for blast furnaces and to operate automatic hammers and rollers for metals. Productivity in metallurgy was also greatly expanded by the substitution of coal and coke for charcoal in smelting and refining. The new fuels were cheaper than charcoal and could fire larger furnaces and ovens. Through a combination of these technical improvements the output of iron could be vastly increased. Furthermore, the spreading use of steam helped create a growing need for coal and iron to build and power the new machines. Rapid growth of production in both industries, based on important new techniques, was a fundamental feature of every industrial revolution.

Steam engines were applied to many other industries as well. Grain mills and sugar refineries used a large number, though more traditional methods survived for a long time. Far more important, and more extensive, was the mechanization of textiles. Unlike mining and metallurgy, textile production was well developed before the industrial revolution; need for cloth was basic to life. Far more workers and entrepreneurs were involved in the industry and a far more valuable total product was created than in the heavy industries. Therefore although technical changes in mining and metallurgy were vital and the output in these industries increased far more rapidly than in textiles, the mechanization of the textile industry was the change that affected the most people and the greatest product in the early industrial revolution.

The initial inventions in the industrial revolution were developed largely within the textile industry. Well before a practicable steam engine was produced, British inventors had devised major changes in both spinning and weaving. At first these improvements were designed to increase productivity in domestic industry with no change in the source of power. The flying shuttle, invented in 1733, raised the productivity of manual weaving about 50 per cent by having the shuttle, which carries threads across the loom, return automatically instead of requiring another weaver to push it. The spinning jenny, developed a few decades later, wound fibers around a spindle automatically, permitting a single spinner for the first time to operate several spindles. In other words, inventions in textiles decreased the need for direct manual operation in certain key stages of production. They were therefore adaptable to mechanical power. First in spinning, then in weaving, water and gradually steam power were introduced to provide the motive force for production. By the 1780s the basic processes existed in England for a technical revolution in the textile industry, although the development of power looms was not yet complete. Along with new methods in mining and metallurgy, they ushered in the first stage of the industrial revolution in Europe.

The early industrial revolution involved not only technical change but also a new organization of industry, which followed from the new machines but had advantages of its own. Basically, the process consisted of concentrating the forces of production in larger, more compact units.

First, the workers themselves were concentrated in a factory. Utilization of water or steam power required that workers be gathered around the wheel or engine. Instead of being scattered in small shops or their own homes manufacturing workers were assembled under direct central control. Greater supervision was possible under this system. Division of labor could be substantially increased, raising productivity by having each worker specialize in one small part of the productive process. The factory system, in other words, had advantages even aside from the utilization of mechanical power. Early factories were generally rather small, often using only about twenty workers; but they steadily grew as the size of engines and machines increased, and as better methods of supervision were developed.

The factory system concentrated capital as well as workers into units of unprecedented size. The new machines were expensive. Factory buildings themselves cost money. Never before had manufacturing required the assembly of capital on such a large scale. In domestic production workers themselves had usually bought the equipment and the housing;

the manufacturer needed only operating capital to buy raw materials and pay initial wages. With new machines and plants far greater investment was necessary. In metallurgy and mining, where machines were particularly expensive, most new firms were launched only through the participation of a number of wealthy men in some form of expanded partnership. In the textile industry an individual family could often set up a small unit with its own funds, supplemented by some borrowing and perhaps a temporary partnership. Subsequent expansion was usually financed by the profits of the firm itself, and the textile industry has retained traces of family ownership to the present day.

Causes of Industrialization

A number of general factors entered into the industrial revolution in every area. Certain factors were necessary to stimulate the movement; others were needed for the stimulus to be successfully answered. Britain, obviously, possessed the needed combination at the earliest date. Involved were features of government, population, class structure, past wealth, and physical geography. The combination was complex; only such complexity could account for the fundamental economic change.

The key factor in causing the industrial revolution in any area was the creation of a new level of need for manufactured goods, for everywhere industrialization was a response to other changes. Even the major inventions resulted from a pre-established need for new techniques. Hence an expansion of domestic production usually preceded the adoption of mechanical methods and encouraged the development of new productive devices.

New need, or market, for manufactured goods arose from a number of sources. Population growth was essential. In every major case population growth antedated industrialization by several decades, providing a major new market stimulus. Countries where population growth was relatively small, such as France, saw their industrial possibilities correspondingly limited. Rising export opportunities also added to available markets. In western Europe and particularly Britain the expanding colonial trade of the eighteenth century was an important stimulus to manufacturing.

Improving transportation, finally, encouraged the growth of national and international markets. Britain, with a large fleet and an exceptionally extensive network of navigable rivers, had far better transportation facilities than the Continental countries in the eighteenth century. Improvements in roads and canals in western Europe in the same period provided general, though more limited, transportation possibilities. Outside western Europe the industrial revolution could not occur until after a railroad network was established. In France and particularly in England transportation and market possibilities were sufficient to allow initial industrialization before the railroad.

With new markets as stimulus, a region's response depended on several factors. Basic raw materials were needed. Britain had an exceptionally favorable supply of cotton from colonial sources, but it was access to coal and iron that was crucial to industrialization. Britain had substantial deposits of each and they were close together or linked by rivers and sea.

Available labor was provided by population growth and the new food supplies. Already increasing numbers of workers had been freed or forced from agriculture, depending on domestic manufacturing. Now some of them were lured or compelled into factories. The lure was, initially, higher wages than other work provided. The compulsion, broadly speaking, was the havoc factories created in the domestic manufacturing system. Vastly more efficient than rural work (a laborer in a spinning factory was up to one hundred times as productive as a cottage spinner, because of the power-driven machinery), early factories quickly displaced rural production in spinning. The same process in weaving was more gradual, but again displacement occurred. Amid continuing population growth, this forced many workers into the factories. Labor force formation was not always easy even so, for workers rarely moved long distances as yet. A domestic manufacturing group might be displaced but cling to the countryside amid growing poverty. Britain again had advantages here. The enclosure movement, although it did not reduce available agricultural jobs, did limit the flexibility of the countryside to absorb increasing numbers of poor people. In areas of small holding, outmoded domestic workers could hang on, thanks to garden plots and the potato. Britain, in essence, was able to urbanize her poverty with unusual speed. Immigration from Ireland also fed the early factory labor force.

The industrial revolution required capital. Britain and western Europe possessed substantial holdings of commercial capital resulting from internal and colonial trade. Britain also benefited from a banking system.

And one final, less tangible ingredient was necessary. An area could industrialize only if it possessed individuals willing to take the risks of engaging their work and funds in unfamiliar and risky ventures. Competition was rugged in early industry, and failures were frequent. Only relatively hardy souls were willing to engage in this process.

The new entrepreneurs in one sense constituted the culmination of the modernization of business mentality that had been occurring during the eighteenth century, prodded by population growth, amid a minority of the bourgeoisie in western Europe. The pioneers of industry came almost entirely from the ranks of innovative artisans, domestic manufacturers, and wealthy farmers. Only a few aristocrats or lower-class elements entered the picture. Formation of an early factory required more spunk, however, than operation of an expanding farm or domestic production system, because the techniques were far more novel and the capital investment greater. Other factors contributed to this special entrepreneurial spirit. In England Dissenting Protestants, blocked from access to government posts and social prestige, tried to compensate by building industrial empires. Calvinists in Alsace similarly took a disproportionate role in French industrialization. But Catholics, in Belgium and northern France, could manifest a similar spirit, talking of glorifying God by hard work and good profits.

The Spread of Industrialization

The industrial revolution was barely underway by 1820. Even in Britain it involved only a minority of businessmen and manufacturing workers, and most of the population was still in agriculture. On the Continent only a few, essentially experimental, factories had been set up. In most of Europe the legal changes introduced by the French Revolution had to be assimilated before industrialization was possible. Even with expanding population, a factory labor force could not be formed until manorialism was destroyed, for otherwise workers were not free to leave the land. Guild restrictions had to be abolished for new techniques to be widely introduced. Some areas were too poor in capital to industrialize, even when the legal reforms had been enacted. Others lacked the needed resources or transportation. Italy, for example, was extremely poor in coal. Germany and Russia had abundant supplies of iron and coal but lacked natural means of transportation to combine them; this was why the railroad was an essential precondition.

But many of the causes of industrialization were widespread. Population pressure, in particular, provided an almost irresistible stimulus in terms of new markets and the need to innovate. Furthermore the dramatic example of Britain's industrial success served as a cause by itself. Businessmen and governments found it hard to avoid imitation. Britain itself, and then other early industrializing areas, provided ingredients initially lacking. Even by 1820 Britain had new capital to invest, entrepreneurs eager to set up factories abroad, skilled workers ready to earn good wages elsewhere. Impelled by the basic forces of modernization but also by the spur of Britain's lead, the industrial revolution fanned out on the European continent after 1820, spreading steadily farther east and south.

Thus the first phase of modernization, which involved relatively modest economic change, produced far more fundamental agents of transformation. The new values it had created, most obviously among dynamic businessmen but also in other segments of society, including the potential factory labor force, provided the spur for further change and also the possibility of assimilating it.

4

EARLY INDUSTRIAL
SOCIETY

The spread of industrialization and the working out of the legal changes of the French Revolution set the framework for the next stage of modernization. This was the period when cities began to grow rapidly, so that what had previously involved a partial urbanization of outlook now involved literal movement to urban centers. This enhanced the pressure for agricultural change, and new methods spread widely to meet the opportunity provided by a growing urban market and the disruptions caused by population growth and legal reform.

Yet this was not a finished industrial society. Class structure still hovered uncertainly between preindustrial and modern criteria. We are talking about a fifty- to seventy-year period of transition, which opened in western Europe early in the nineteenth century. But by now the forces of change were spreading more widely across the Continent, and we must add diversity to the discussion of modernization. This in turn requires a sense of the differential patterns and pace of early industrialization.

The Spread of the Industrial Revolution

Within any country the development of industrial production was extremely uneven. Established industries changed at very different rates, for many workers and entrepreneurs resisted innovation. Cotton spinning was quickly transformed whenever industrialization began, for cotton was an easy fiber to handle on machines, and cotton production, being relatively new, had few entrenched interests to resist change. Within a decade after industrialization reached a given area, all cotton spinning was done by mechanical means. Wool spinning followed, but linen lagged because of difficulty with the fiber, and a sense of routine in the industry prevented rapid modernization. Weaving always took longer to change, although it too followed the pattern of cotton first, then wool, then linen, then silk. Power looms were less productive than mechanical spindles, so manual workers could compete for a longer time. It took fifty years or more for hand weavers to admit defeat in an industrial country.

The new methods of mining and metallurgy spread rapidly, but traditional firms, employing only a few workers and using simple tools, persisted for several decades. In France, where technical change began around 1820, half the iron produced still came from charcoal ovens in 1848. Many industries were not initially affected by new methods at all. Food processing, the building trades, tailoring, and the like were nowhere significantly altered until after 1850. These were the industries most solidly organized in a preindustrial craft structure.

Furthermore, in any country there were diverse regional patterns. Areas near coal supplies—northern England, northern France, the Ruhr—changed quickly, but other regions long continued to use traditional procedures. They suffered competitively, of course, so that industrialization everywhere heightened the regional concentration of industry. But stagnant backwaters, such as southern England, still contained large numbers of people.

Particularly during the first stage of industrialization this meant that several manufacturing economies coexisted in a single country. Crafts and even domestic production could expand, though never as rapidly as the factory sector. A more rapid death for the traditional forms might have been a kindness, but lack of knowledge, shortage of capital, and positive resistance to change combined to give industrialization an uneven pace.

In terms of the national roster Britain was of course the leader. The initial inventions had been widely introduced by 1780, and by 1850 the major manufacturing industries had been transformed. The pioneering period was over, for Britain possessed enough trained workers, managers, and investment capital to insure the continuation of industrial advance. Belgium and France effectively began their industrialization about 1820. France was held back by relatively slow population growth and a shortage of coal, but her major industries were transformed by 1870. The French growth in manufacturing production was slightly slower, per capita, than that of Britain or Germany; a more dramatic spurt began in the 1890s. But the transformation even before then was comparable to early industrialization elsewhere. Germany began to industrialize in the 1840s and reached substantial industrial maturity about 1900. Sweden entered the industrial revolution about 1850; Italy, Austria, and northern Spain about 1870; and Russia clearly in the 1890s. All were to reach industrial maturity in the twentieth century, with the Italian process taking the longest time. By 1900, then, most of Europe was caught up in some phase of the industrial revolution, with only the Balkans relatively untouched. But the chronology of the first industrial stage must vary with the region. The dates 1800–1870 fit Britain and western Europe. Central Europe underwent much the same process about twenty years later, the east and south almost fifty years after that.

Furthermore the nature of industrialization differed from one major region of Europe to the next. The later the industrialization, the more important the heavy industrial sector. All industrializations from the German onward were preceded by railroad development; in Russia's case railroads began to be widely built a full two decades before industrialization. Railroads provided an obvious market for coal and iron, and this fact, if no other, assured the predominance of these industries. In France, Britain, and Belgium lighter industries, particularly textiles, played a greater role. These industries were inherently less concentrated than mines or metallurgical firms, for their equipment was less complex. Early industrializers thus had a less bureaucratic industrial structure, more opportunity for relatively small businessmen.

The later the industrialization the greater the role of government. In Germany, and even more in Russia, the lack of a large preindustrial bourgeoisie and of massive commercial capital required the government to play some of the role private entrepreneurs did elsewhere, and these were areas of a strong state tradition anyway. Foreign capitalists also took a greater hand in late industrial revolutions; almost half of Russia's industrial capital came from abroad before 1914. Industrialization had to be induced, for modernization had not gone far enough for it to be spontaneous. This not only meant the absence of vigorous native entrepreneurial spirit, it also meant that potential workers were less attuned to a market economy. On the whole, induced industrialization caused greater shock than was the case in western Europe, where its roots went deeper in terms of preindustrial social change. It might be rapid and successful, as in both Russia and Germany, but it offended more traditional sensibilities. It was also true that later industrializers imported relatively sophisticated equipment from the west, so that technological change was less gradual. Here, too, was a source of disturbance. Economic modernization in a country like Germany could outstrip more general social modernization, a disparity with serious implications.

We will return to this kind of differentiation in subsequent discussion. For now, the early industrial period is taken as something of a unity, applying of course to a given country in its appropriate time slot. Just as the main causes of the process were similar, so certain effects flowed from industrialization in every case. Even major differences are partly a matter of degree. Industrialization was a shock even in England, undoubtedly viewed with disfavor by the majority of the population, even in the middle class, in 1820; it would take time for society to catch up here too.

Immediate Effects of Industrialization

The first three generations of the industrial revolution witnessed continuing economic change. New machines, once introduced, were quickly improved, becoming larger and more productive. The number of spindles on spinning machines steadily rose during the early nineteenth century. Weavers were given one, then two mechanical looms to operate. The average size of the factory steadily increased, in part because of this growing sophistication of equipment. It was early discovered that large engines were more efficient than small. More important, the large firm had other advantages over a small enterprise. It had greater control over its supplies and might in fact produce its own raw materials. There was an increasing tendency for cloth producers to add a spinning plant or for metallurgists to acquire a mine. Large size permitted greater control of markets. A big firm could afford a better marketing organization, sometimes dictating terms to its buyers; in France the seven big producers of rails were fixing prices by mutual agreement as early as the 1840s. So the theme of concentration of organization, with its implications for economic power and the development of managerial bureaucracies, was suggested quite early, even though the average firm remained small.

The introduction of machines and factories had a number of more obvious economic consequences. Where new techniques often increased the productivity of an individual worker ten or fifteen times, or where many new workers were added to the manufacturing force, as in coal and iron, production rose greatly from the first. In 1800 Britain produced twenty-six pounds of iron per person; in 1880 she produced 260. Her gross production rose twenty-seven times between 1800 and 1860. Germany's per capita output of iron rose from 41 pounds in the 1860s to 170 in 1890. Coal production rose even more strikingly. Even France increased her output from 1 million to 13 million tons between 1840 and 1870. Prussia's coal production rose from 1.5 million tons in 1825 to 20.5 million in 1865. Output in certain other industries rose comparably. The machine-building industry grew from almost nothing to a position of major importance in the early stages of industrialization. Sugar refining in France increased 900 per cent during the July Monarchy alone. Even textiles, which had been widely manufactured by older methods, expanded greatly. During the July Monarchy French production of cotton and wool cloth doubled. In every branch of industry touched by the new methods a sharp rise in production was one of the major results of the industrial revolution.

The rise in production was accompanied by a change in the balance among industries. Industry as a whole, of course, became the major producer of wealth in society by the third or fourth decade of the industrial revolution; agricultural production also expanded in value, but it could not keep pace. Within manufacturing certain traditional products declined because they failed to adapt. The linen industry, hit by the competition of cheaper machine-made cotton cloth, faded in importance. Lace making and a few other artisan artivities lagged for similar reasons. The importance of the textile industry as a whole steadily declined in the face of rising heavy industry, but textiles remained dominant until after 1850. A steel industry arose almost from nothing. The chemical industry, at first confined to the production of dyes, expanded and later in the century developed into an industrial leader.

Increasing production drove prices down fairly steadily. On the whole, rising productivity allowed industrialists to meet the need to lower their prices without diminishing their own profits. In individual cases, however, falling prices put real pressure on companies. Particularly before 1850, when business activity was not accompanied by a sufficient increase in the supply of money, the downward trend of prices was severe indeed. Between 1830 and 1848 prices of cotton goods in France fell 66 per cent, of woollen goods 31 per cent. After 1850 prices of manufactured goods still declined, but at a much slower rate, because of the increased availability of precious metals. Nevertheless, the general tendency was clear, and price drops in turn opened new markets for a variety of goods previously too expensive for ordinary use. Significant changes in consumption patterns resulted. One observer in France hailed 1830 as a revolutionary year not because of the political upheaval, but because at about that time ordinary urban workers found they could afford stylish cotton clothing. In France and elsewhere in the west around the same period forks became a common utensil in the average home. Increasing availability of goods, through falling prices, was a necessary result of the industrial revolution.

Cheapness alone, however, did not insure sales. New marketing techniques were also necessary. National and even international trade rose greatly, displacing earlier local patterns. The international trade of every industrial country expanded rapidly. In 1820, 2 million tons of goods entered British ports; by 1870 British ports handled 15 million tons. Every industrial country quickly became involved in literally a worldwide network of imports and exports. Major companies set up factories in leading cities all over the world. Within an individual country the effects of expanded production on market structure were even more revolutionary. New facilities for mass marketing everywhere followed industrialization. Firms sent out trading agents, and contacts were set up in centers all over the country. In rural areas small shops gradually replaced itinerant peddlers; there was too much to sell to rely on occasional opportunities. Similarly, local fairs declined in favor of permanent wholesale and retail outlets. In larger cities the department store developed as one symptom of the greater need to sell. Beginning in Paris in the 1830s, the store specializing in masses of products spread all over urban Europe during the nineteenth century.

New transportation facilities, essential for the expanding markets, everywhere accompanied industrialization. At first the main emphasis was on increasing numbers of ships, improving paved roads, and building canals. Then in the early nineteenth century in Britain the omnipresent power of steam was applied to transportation as well as to manufacturing itself. The steam locomotive, invented in the 1820s, was first economically applied in a line between Liverpool and Manchester in 1830. In the 1830s local lines were built in Britain, Belgium, Austria, and between Paris and Versailles. During the next decade Britain and various German states began to build a more general system. France planned such a system, but completed it only in the 1850s and 1860s. By the 1870s the major countries of western Europe had a substantial network of trunk lines. Local lines had been established in Austria and Italy, and plans existed even in more distant regions. Along with the telegraph, which spread during the 1830s, the railroad provided more rapid communication of news as well as transportation of goods and people. It cut into local isolation and allowed more effective contact between central governments and outlying regions. Most important of all, it represented a major development in the quest of industry for more widespread and substantial markets.

Improvements in shipping increased trade and communication among nations and continents during the nineteenth century. Before 1850 both iron and steam had been applied to shipping. This improved the speed of shipping and increased the capacity of each vessel. After 1870 ships were sufficiently large and rapid to allow intercontinental competition even in agricultural goods.

But the economic interest of this first industrial period lay in production, not marketing or distribution. Leading economists stressed the virtue of increasing production; an extreme liberal, J. B. Say, even asserted that sales would take care of themselves. Industrialists themselves devoted most of their attention to problems of investment and technology. The industrial revolution was first and foremost a change in the technique and organization of manufacturing goods. It was stimulated by new market opportunities. But, once started, the process could outstrip the growth of the markets.

It was natural that the disposal of products caused the greatest economic difficulties of the early industrial revolution. European society was still poor. The resources of the masses were barely if at all above subsistence level. Their numbers were increasing, and their ability to consume rose gradually as prices fell. However, no change in consumption power occurred in the nineteenth century to correspond to the real revolution in ability to produce. Many of the economic difficulties of the century, and even beyond, were based on this disparity.

The disparity between what society could produce and what it could consume gave rise to fierce competition for the available markets. Many innovations in technique resulted from the competition for lower costs and greater production. Many bitter individual failures resulted also, particularly during the early decades, when many new firms were established. An atmosphere of conflict permeated the early industrial revolution. Even successful entrepreneurs felt hemmed in by the forces of competition. As transportation improved, the sense of competition from distant areas grew. Particularly on the Continent, where British rivalry was keenly felt, a desire for tariff protection resulted. Everywhere competition encouraged pressure on working conditions because of the need to reduce prices and seek sales that would keep pace with production.

The most agonizing symptom of disparity between production and consumption was the frequency of economic crises in the nineteenth century. In the first half of the century such crises generally occurred as a result of bad harvests, which decreased the income of peasants and raised food prices generally, leaving everyone less able to buy manufactured goods. Crises such as this were not new, but their effects were felt keenly when a larger percentage of the population moved into the cities. Production declined, prices of industrial products fell, and employment, profits, and wages dropped.

Most people managed to survive, and some even profited. Difficulties in sales induced many entrepreneurs to undertake major technical improvements in the hope of cutting costs; such improvements set the stage for the next expansion of production and of consumption. During a crisis itself, however, there was real misery. And crisis years were frequent. Major slumps occurred in the late 1820s, in 1837, in 1846–1847, in 1857, and other declines occurred in certain localities and industries even more frequently. Crisis seemed to be a part of industrial life. It created a sense of insecurity among manufacturers and workers alike.

On the whole, however, industrialization steadily created new wealth through its expansion of production. This new wealth was by no means uniformly spread, but it came to benefit most elements of the population. Within a few generations it reduced the numbers living on the borderline of subsistence from a majority to a minority in the industrial areas. At the same time the industrial revolution changed the residence of the average person in Europe. It changed the type of work he did; it changed his pace of work. Along with population expansion and a new legal structure, it freed or forced the population of Europe from traditional ways of action. None of this was accomplished without difficulty and hardship; none of it occurred overnight. The novelty of industrial development dominated many aspects of society during the nineteenth century. Established social classes had to contend with this, as of course did the new groups that the industrial revolution created. In combination with the changes in law and the continuing population growth, industrialization caused a real social upheaval in Europe.

Ironically, during the early industrial period most people remained outside the factory system, even outside the burgeoning cities. Only after 1850 in England and after 1870 in Belgium and Germany did factory production predominate. What industrialization did for most people was to heighten the commercialization process already spreading in the eighteenth century. New wealth, new markets, new transportation system brought change to every sector of society. They deepened the sense of disturbance that had been growing in the previous period. We return again to the theme of transition. In this period premodern social classes and institutions remained supreme. They could only feel challenged by the new intrusion. Even apparent advantages of industrialization, such as rising wealth, could be resented. Only when resistance to the basic principles of industrialization was abandoned, and the idea of recurrent change in technology and wealth accepted, could a truly industrial society be created. Important adaptation occurred even in this first period, but it was hard to perceive amid the loud, anguished clamor for a return to the old order.

The Agricultural Classes

Market Agriculture

During the nineteenth century the system of market agriculture almost entirely displaced the previous system of local subsistence production, already challenged in the previous period. Peasants and landlords alike depended increasingly on sales to distant markets. Production expanded to take advantage of new opportunities for sales. The growing trend toward market agriculture was spurred by the population expansion and particularly by the rise of cities as part of industrialization, both of which extended the potential market. The changes in transportation also furthered the process. Railroads and rapid and capacious shipping both allowed more substantial shipments of food to population centers. New manufactured goods were brought to rural areas, attracting many landlords and peasants to the sort of production that would allow them to buy outside goods. Changes in law also encouraged market agriculture. Abolition of feudal dues meant that landlords increasingly depended on commercial profits from their land rather than on traditional revenues. Peasants were released from the protection of their former lord. No longer were the charity and other services of the lord readily available. Again, the only major recourse was to produce increasingly for the market. In many countries, peasants were also subject to new taxes by governments once they were considered free agents; their needs for cash rose. German and Russian peasants also required some cash, for a certain period, to pay the redemption fees demanded for the abolition of manorial obligations. Both opportunity and necessity existed for the development of market agriculture.

Substantial profits could be made on the market. Demand for agricultural goods rose steadily and prices remained favorable until the 1870s; producers in a country like England, where methods were relatively advanced, knew a golden period of earnings. However, market agriculture involved certain pressures and even risks that were new to most peasants and landlords. Production for the market meant subjection to the whims of demands. The railroad brought the products of one region into competition with those of another. Despite rising consumption, this competition increased steadily during the nineteenth century, to the detriment of less efficient producers. For now the market required adoption of new agricultural methods.

Ironically, and sometimes tragically, the economic traditionalism of of the agricultural classes was peculiarly ill suited to such radical novelty. Changes did occur; European agriculture vastly increased its production and efficiency. By 1830 England, for example, produced two to three times as much grain as it had in the eighteenth century. Huge cities could therefore grow, and famine became a thing of the past after 1850 in all but a few eastern regions of the Continent. Such immense development put real pressure on the customs and structures of agricultural existence and even on the economic well-being of many producers. Much of the life of the agricultural classes during the nineteenth century was determined by the clash between new economic forces and a highly traditional way of life.

The increasing pace of economic change, added to population pressure, heightened the division of all the agricultural classes between adapters and nonadapters. At all levels many people sold out. In the most tragic case, small peasants were tempted or bullied, as soon as they acquired legal freedom, to sell their plots, for the abrupt abolition of manorialism plus new needs for cash to pay taxes left many confused. In Prussia 100,000 small holdings disappeared between 1815 and 1848. The same collapse occurred in southern Europe after 1850. But aristocratic land changed hands as well. Here was the source of new class relationships, confirming the trend toward separation of owners and nonowners. Finally the countryside was increasingly conditioned by the exodus to the cities. This reduced further population pressure, which was a blessing. It removed some people who could not make out in the new economic setting, and their problems of adaptation now became part of urban development. Temporarily it gave the village new contacts, as many emigrants returned to tell of their experiences in the cities even abroad. In the key period of rural unrest this was a factor in articulating discontent. In the longer run, however, too many departures were permanent, driving out of the villages a dynamic, younger element. This weakened the ability of rural society to respond to innovation, for gradually the villages became the haven for older people whose hostility to change only increased with age.

Methods and Products

Market agriculture required major changes in agricultural methods, equipment, and products to meet the need for greater efficiency. Existing land had to be used more fully. Better drainage methods spread, allowing use of marshy land. The planting of nitrogen-fixing clover or turnips increasingly permitted the suppression of fallow land on the Continent, as it had in Britain in the previous century. Common lands were gradually divided and cultivated at great cost to peasant traditions and to the livelihood of many poor peasants. Finally, animal and chemical fertilizers were developed early in the nineteenth century, and their use slowly spread, increasing the yield of the land.

Changes in agricultural equipment also heightened productivity and decreased labor costs. Such a simple improvement as the use of the scythe instead of the sickle raised the productivity of harvest workers by up to 50 per cent. More massive equipment became available also, but it spread slowly. Heavier, larger plows were manufactured. Threshing and reaping machines were invented. In agriculture, as in industry, it became increasingly possible to substitute machines for human power and labor.

Finally, market agriculture required specialization in a cash crop; general production of many crops could not be efficient. Europe became increasingly divided into grain-growing, wine-growing, and stock-raising areas. Such areas were dependent on the market for the purchase of foods that they did not raise. Although this specialization greatly improved productivity, it had certain dangers. Failure of one crop could wipe out one's whole livelihood; for example, great misery resulted from the destruction of French vines by phylloxera in the 1860s. Constant attention was necessary to keep a specialty crop up to rising standards of quality. Particularly in stock breeding, improvements in the product were fairly steady in the nineteenth century. Changes in consumption patterns could threaten the profitability of a specialty crop. Sheep-growing areas were hit by the rise of cotton fiber and the declining popularity of mutton. Growing wealth in western Europe caused a general movement away from the cheaper grains, such as rye, and toward wheat by the mid-nineteenth century. Again, substantial adjustment had to be made by producers.

More productive methods, better equipment, and new crops created great possibilities for agricultural development during the century. They were encouraged by government information programs and by many agricultural societies, which tried to introduce and expand a variety of new techniques. Nevertheless, in many cases development was very slow. By 1870 only one third of even the large farms in northern France had threshing machines, and only after 1890 did such equipment become really common. Not until about 1880 did use of mineral fertilizer expand significantly in France. In all these cases it had required decades of spreading information plus a new rise in competition to produce major change in equipment. Similarly, many of the necessary changes in crop specialization occurred only slowly if at all.

Ignorance and traditionalism accounted for much of the lag between what was possible and what was done. The illiteracy of many peasants and the aristocratic hostility to commercial activity favored the status quo in most areas. Furthermore, major improvements in equipment or the quality of the crop required capital. Peasants and small landlords alike had little monetary capital; what they owned was the land itself. Credit facilities were not extensive in rural areas. In the early part of the nineteenth century loans still could only be obtained at rates of interest up to 60 per cent. Later, government and cooperative funds were established to ease the situation, but credit remained tight. Finally, many peasants' plots were too small to apply machines successfully. Even simple improvements, such as the suppression of fallow, proved impossible for many farmers. They did spread, causing the great increase in production, but they ruined many peasants and aristocrats in the process.

Despite the transformation of agriculture, the agrarian classes were unable to maintain their traditional importance in society as a whole. Their production sank steadily as a percentage of total national output, and agriculture employed a declining share of the total labor force. Most of the population increase in western and central Europe went into the cities. The agricultural classes grew only slightly in the century as a whole, and in a few areas, such as France and Britain, they began to decline in absolute numbers after 1870 as improved methods and increased competition curtailed the need for labor. In the extreme case, only 10 per cent of the population of Britain depended on agricultural work by 1900. It was easy for those who remained in the countryside to feel that modern life was passing them by.

The Aristocracy

Economic Base

The decline in the relative importance of agriculture hurt aristocrats severely, particularly in the West. Control of much of the land no longer assured them economic supremacy. Their average earnings were rapidly challenged by the owners of industry. In 1800 the British aristocracy controlled almost 20 per cent of the annual production of the nation; by 1850 it commanded less than 10 per cent. It became increasingly difficult to maintain a style of life distinguished by luxury. Some aristocrats attached themselves to the rising fortunes of industry despite the general prejudice against commercial activity. Few of them actually managed enterprises, but a number invested and served on boards of directors. However, aristocrats never rivaled the middle class for control of industry, and by mid-century in western Europe their wealth could be matched by the top businessmen.

This meant also that the class had to abandon its pretense of serving as principal patrons for the arts. They had to admit middle-class rivalry in sponsoring musical events. Authors now made money by writing for the middle-class public, not a noble patron. Throughout western Europe the first half of the nineteenth century saw something of a battle between the two classes for cultural leadership, with the aristocrats typically defending classical styles and the middle class forming groups to support the newer Romantic trends. But war could be only temporary, for the aristocracy, no longer the dominant economic class, could not prevail.

Concomitantly, the changes within agriculture challenged aristocrats directly. The demands of market agriculture for commercial ability and technical innovation touched even eastern Europe during the early nineteenth century. There were definite attempts to adapt to market opportunities. Junkers and Hungarian nobles increased their landed holdings at the expense of the peasants. Production for export did rise. Some eastern landlords introduced crop rotation and even machinery quite early. By the 1840s Baltic aristocrats began converting to stock raising in the interests of improving their markets. And generally the use of wage laborers spread. However, only a few individuals modernized their agriculture substantially. There was relatively little general change in method; in Hungary, many nobles depended primarily on extending servile work obligations for their commercial product. Nowhere was there so fundamental a conversion to market agriculture as was occurring in Britain.

Yet a conversion was increasingly necessary, even aside from market pressures. In western Europe by 1800, in central Europe by 1850, and in Russia after 1861 manorial dues were abolished. Aristocrats who had depended on dues rather than domain, as had the majority in the west, lost much of their traditional income by this change. Even where there was a domain, adaptation was essential.

Many landlords retained considerable power over peasant labor. Russian nobles received redemption payments in return for the abolition of feudal dues. Elsewhere some peasants continued to pay rents. In southern Italy and southern Spain many peasants were so poor in land and capital that they became sharecroppers for the lords. Here and in Prussia many landlords successfully pressed peasants to sell out; in southern Spain three quarters of the peasantry was landless by 1890, earning about 9 cents a day as agricultural laborers. In none of the large domain areas except Russia did the abolition of feudalism break up the big estates, and even in Russia the lords kept much of the best land. The Rumanian abolition of serfdom in 1864 actually destroyed peasant small holding and divided almost all the land into large estates for the first time. There and elsewhere freed but landless peasants were available for cheap labor.

However, the traditional sources of income were irrevocably lost. Peasant labor had to be paid in cash, even if wages were low. In the south sharecropping meant little if the sharecropper's product was not profitable. In other words, the abolition of manorialism inevitably forced the landed aristocracy to participate in market agriculture. Even where the class exploited peasants shamelessly it could decline.

Most landed aristocrats were unable to respond to the new conditions of agriculture. They failed to introduce new equipment and new crops. Many went heavily into debt to compensate for the inadequacy of their income from the land. Many became impoverished or eked out only a meager living on the basis of sharecropping or tenant returns. Many lost their land. Even in the early nineteenth century, when market conditions were excellent, many aristocrats had to sell out to more dynamic landlords from the middle class or from their own class. They lacked the capital and technical knowledge to keep going. In Prussia a third of the Junker estates were sold out between 1815 and 1848 alone. By 1885 about 87 per cent of the east Prussian estates had changed hands. In 1855 only 55 per cent of the land was in aristocratic hands, by 1889 the figure had declined to 32 per cent. Except to a limited extent in Russia, estates were seldom broken up; the peasantry did not gain in the large estate regions. But increasingly many estates were administered by the middle class or a few rich aristocrats on a commercial basis. Only in scattered regions, such as England, where aristocrats converted to radically new methods, or the Baltic provinces of Russia, where new methods were combined with semifeudal control over peasant labor, did the aristocrats avoid major competition from new landlords.

Social Status

Aristocrats faced a crisis of legal and social status. Their sense of superior status had depended on high incomes and consumption power, both of which were now under attack; it had also depended on real legal privilege. The abolition of manorialism and the establishment of equality under the law destroyed such diverse privileges as exclusive hunting rights, the right to try certain crimes in manorial courts, and the right to have one's word accepted in other courts without challenge. Some privileges remained. Suffrage systems based on ownership of property, particularly landed property, gave aristocrats disproportionate voting power in many countries. France retained such a system until 1848, Prussia until 1918. On the whole, however, the legal status of aristocrats was little different from that of other citizens by 1815 in western Europe and by mid-century elsewhere. This fact, along with growing economic pressure, made it increasingly difficult for aristocrats to maintain their traditional feeling of hereditary superiority.

Two general lines of action could preserve some sense of special status. The social exclusivism of the class could be asserted against the rise of the middle class, and special political powers could be maintained, which could provide income as well as status.

Everywhere in the early and mid-nineteenth century aristocrats tried to protect their distinctiveness in new ways. They made more formal use of their titles than before, when an appropriate social order could be taken for granted. They formed exclusive social clubs, in which they could conduct distinctive activities such as gambling. Intermarriage with the middle class may have declined, as in Germany; it was certainly disapproved. Rigid social barriers were maintained against contact with nonaristocrats in hunting groups and at dances. Until 1918 Prussian nobles used a rope to separate themselves from the middle class at any dance. After 1815 Parisian nobles began to build a purely aristocratic suburb, the Saint Germain quarter. Aristocratic schools often sought to exclude the nonaristocrats, and continued to stress subjects such as classics that were suitable for refinement and leisure rather than for economic utility. German universities maintained an aristocratic code of honor in their dueling societies. Wealthy urban nobles perpetuated and even increased when possible their association with cultural activities. In a variety of ways, then, large and small aristocrats continued to seek a distinctive pattern of life and society.

In addition to its stress on style of life, the aristocracy tried to maintain its special political importance. The class continued to believe in its peculiar fitness to rule. Political activities allowed aristocrats to exercise their traditional concern for the well-being of society. They brought jobs that were dignified and provided income. Political power could be used to defend traditional aristocratic values such as religion and military prowess. Hence in countries like Germany poor aristocrats crowded into universities and the bureaucracy after 1815, competing with middle-class professionals and often worsening standards of training. Political jobs also allowed defense of the agricultural interests. Junkers could push for free trade to help their exports and subsidies to large estates; French nobles sought and obtained agricultural tariff protection.

Finally, through politics some of the more objectionable features of the middle class could be attacked. In the early nineteenth century many aristocratic politicians in Britain and France encouraged the passage of legislation limiting the rights of employers over workers by defining conditions of child labor and hours of work. In Britain the Earl of Shaftesbury promoted the Ten-Hour Law of 1847; in Germany aristocratic parties supported restoration of guilds after 1848 and later backed the first social insurance laws in the 1880s. Only a minority of aristocrats took an interest in these efforts, and a fear of the unruliness of the masses increased in the class as time passed. However, aristocratic paternalism and hostility to the middle class, expressed through the use of political power, provided one of the foundations for more vigorous state regulation of industry in the nineteenth century. Here, as in many other ways, the aristocracy tried to use its political voice to support traditional position and values.

The aristocracy retained a number of types of political power in the nineteenth century. It continued to dominate the military and generally tried to limit the opportunities for nonaristocrats to enter the ranks of officers. Control of some of the leading positions in the state churches gave aristocrats another important form of institutional power. Aristocrats generally defended the established church with great vigor during the nineteenth century as one means of protecting tradition and stability in society. During the French Restoration aristocratic politicians passed a law decreeing the death penalty for sacrilege in the Catholic Church, and the British House of Lords long resisted measures passed by the Commons to allow Jews to become members of Parliament or to permit Nonconformists to enter the universities. It was in government, however, that the main aristocratic power lay; even church and army were increasingly defended by political means. Nobles retained considerable local authority. In Russia and Prussia the local administrators established after the abolition of feudalism were usually aristocrats. In Spain landlords continued into the twentieth century to nominate local officials. Their nominees controlled much of the local police and were therefore able to intimidate the peasantry; they could also defend the aristocrats' interest against the central government. In France and Britain many regional administrators were aristocrats, and many more were subject to aristocratic influence. Despite changes of regime in France, for example, the regional prefects changed little in social type between 1815 and 1850; they were not exclusively aristocratic, but the aristocracy played a considerable role.

The aristocrats had legislative power in government also. Their local popularity and prestige encouraged their election even in countries where universal suffrage was established. In 1905 one twelfth of the British House of Commons was aristocratic; this was a notable decline from the figure of one sixth in 1860, before the establishment of universal suffrage, but it was a significant figure nevertheless. In France aristocrats played major roles in parliaments in such crisis years as 1848 and 1871 because of their local prestige among new peasant voters. Furthermore, many legislative bodies preserved an even greater role for aristocrats until 1914. The British House of Lords retained a full legislative veto until 1911. Suffrage limitations in Italy and systems of class voting in Prussia and Austria, by which every class (as defined by property) got the same number of votes regardless of its size, returned large numbers of nobles to legislatures in these countries until the late nineteenth century and even after.

It was in central administration, however, that the real political power of aristocrats lay. Even after democratic parliamentary regimes were established in Britain and France, administrators tended to be appointed by cooption rather than by determination of the populace or legislature, which reserved many of the principal roles for aristocrats. In eastern Europe, where the power of parliaments and democratic bodies was small, aristocrats played a fuller role in administration. There the principal ministers as well as the leading diplomats and civil servants were aristocrats. In France the aristocracy saw its hold on the ministries weakened after 1830 and largely destroyed with the establishment of the Third Republic in 1875. In England nobles shared the ministries with commoners throughout the century. Even in France and England, however, many of the chief administrative bodies beneath ministerial rank, such as the diplomatic corps, remained largely in the hands of the aristocracy.

Aristocratic dependence on administrative positions made the class an increasingly conservative force. There were three notable exceptions to this. In Poland and Hungary resentment against foreign rule and the deteriorating economic position of the gentry caused a rise of rebellious nationalism after 1815. There the lesser aristocrats had little political power to defend, so it was understandable that Polish risings in 1830 and 1863 would be led by nobles. The liberal, nationalist Hungarian revolution of 1848 was primarily a rebellion of the gentry. Only after 1867, when the Hungarian aristocracy won great national and local political power, did the switch to conservatism come. In Russia some members of the gentry, particularly educated bureaucrats and military men, had grievances against the autocracy; a few of them led the abortive December rising of 1825. By the 1830s liberal gentry were forming the first elements of the discontented intelligentsia, but this radicalism was not characteristic of aristocrats generally, even in Russia. And by the 1860s in Russia, even the minority was being weaned away from opposition to the tsar. The factors in this process were familiar ones. Economic difficulties increased with the abolition of serfdom; the gentry depended on state help. Local political power grew; the gentry filled most of the positions on the *zemstvos,* the new regional assemblies.

Generally, aristocrats provided the principal support for formal conservative groups during most of the nineteenth century. In France many nobles defended the Bourbon, or legitimist, tradition of monarchy into the 1870s and later despite three intervening regimes. In Prussia the aristocrats also gathered increasingly around the king. Politically as well as religiously, the class defended traditional institutions and through them their own customary leadership.

By 1870 the position of the aristocracy had been altered substantially. Land remained a source of power but an increasingly shaky one. Social distinction remained also, but it had to be defended with new and formal devices. Titles were generally recognized, usually supported by the government. Only in Norway had aristocracy been fully abolished. In politics the nobility retained great power and used it consciously to defend the whole range of aristocratic interests.

If one notes the important legal and economic decline of the class, one must also note aristocratic resiliency. Even in the economic sphere all was not lost. Certainly in politics and administration the nobility remained the dominant element except in some parts of western Europe. The class felt increasingly beleaguered. Its actions were often belligerently defensive. Because it was dying but not dead, the class remained a surprisingly important social force.

The Peasantry

Changes in the situation of the peasantry during the nineteenth century in some ways mirrored those within the aristocracy. Both classes were traditional and tradition-minded. Both were faced with major economic and legal change. Both defended many of their customs against change and with some success. Aristocrats and peasants both remained more religious and more politically conservative than did urban classes during the same period. Both were opposed to certain values of the triumphant middle classes and to the rise of the urban masses. Unlike the aristocracy, however, the peasants were not a traditionally privileged class. Less conscious of social status, many were able to adapt more fully, if gradually, to the needs of market agriculture. Poor, even destitute, they were capable on occasion of turning violently against existing society, against the aristocracy itself, in a way aristocrats could not because of their continuing stake in the existing order. Peasant life altered fully as much as did that of the aristocracy, but the alterations inevitably took vastly different forms.

Despite many changes, certain aspects of peasant traditionalism persisted. Local festivals continued to constitute one of the major forms of peasant recreation. Even in England peasant songs and folklore were continued into the 1840s. Distrust of distant regions, including the city, was still common. A great attachment to the land remained. Many peasants gave up or left their land reluctantly, usually under the pressure of considerable misery. If they could, they commonly tried to counter economic novelty by confirming their hold on the land and even acquiring more.

Traditions of village and family unity loosened during the century, but both remained a vital focus for peasant life. Many villages maintained some supervision over local agriculture and law. Village courts in Russia continued even at the end of the nineteenth century to rule on land and inheritance disputes on the basis of quite local customs. Peasant families maintained tighter traditional links than did families in other classes, and peasants typically had more children per family than other classes did. Religious practice remained important for most peasants, although there were de-Christianized rural areas in several western countries. In southern and eastern Europe peasants might respond to new pressures by a wave of religious fervor. Old Believers in Russia, though not new, continued to insist on a return to a purer church, and in Italy small sects, notably the Lazzaretti, gained peasant converts with the hope of an imminent millennium that would restore equality and dignity to the land. Even in western Europe material acquisition remained a less important goal for the peasant than for the urban classes. An interest in material gains developed, but most peasants seemed content with a lower standard of living than that prevailing in the cities. Traditional recreation, the land, the family, and the church provided satisfactions that supplemented the material standard of living.

Economic Pressure

Major alterations in peasant existence were brought about by massive pressures that the peasant could neither resist nor fully understand. Population growth was the most general and fundamental problem. Decline of domestic manufacturing increased the economic pressure. New legal and market systems encouraged the growth of a landless element. Finally, market agriculture brought great difficulties even to landowners.

Throughout Europe the land available per person continued to contract, with the worst problems spreading to the east and south. The number of peasants in European Russia doubled by the end of the nineteenth century with no notable expansion of the land under cultivation. Real land hunger developed in such circumstances, violating village and family traditions of a stable relationship to the land. Common lands were no longer capable of supporting the growing number of landless people. The opening up of new lands, through drainage and suppression of fallow, did provide new jobs for both men and women, but in every country there was a decade or more when demand did not keep pace with population given the simultaneous decline in domestic manufacturing. By 1780 many British laborers were dependent on charity for survival. In 1830 the introduction of harvesting machinery provoked a major riot from laborers in parts of England, trying to defend the jobs and wages they had. This was an unusual expression of collective consciousness, which followed from the high level of agricultural commercialization in Britain. But a less articulate crisis mentality prevailed elsewhere. The 1840s and 1850s were the crucial decades in Bavaria, as crimes against both persons and property rose even in prosperous years. Here and elsewhere in western and central Europe the agricultural laborers were not capable of formal protest. In the 1848 revolution, for example, landless peasants in Bohemia, lacking leadership, talked of their own sinfulness and the need for a purer religion; reflecting changes in the village structure they also asked for a hereditary right to cultivate some common lands. But they did not raise basic demands. In these same areas emigration to cities and abroad, along with the related rise of successful industrialization, soon reduced the worst pressures. An important landless element remained but they were not to be heard from for some time. Even in Prussia, where there were 2 million landless by 1849, only vague grumblings could be discerned. Continued deference to landlords or village notables, fear of going to the city and satisfaction at clinging to rural existence, the enervating impact of poverty, all must help explain the relative quiescence of this group after a decade or two of disorganized crime and unrest.

In eastern and southern Europe the landless loomed larger numerically, for far more were dispossessed after manorialism was abolished. Rural crime rose rather persistently in Ireland and southern Europe. In central and southern Italy this fed into more organized brigandage against government agents and the wealthy landlords or their minions. In Italy, where 3.275 million peasants had less than 2.5 acres of land by 1894, the landlords' officials could enter some estates only under armed guard. Even in Russia, where peasants received most of the land after emancipation, the pressure remained intense. Population growth was not matched by migration outlets and the law still tied many peasants to their village. Aristocratic landlords, though controlling only a minority of the arable land, had the best soils. Furthermore some of them were bought out by a commercially minded middle class, and by 1900 one seventh of the large holdings were in nonnoble hands. Finally, throughout eastern and southern Europe these changes, occurring late in the nineteenth century, took place in a framework of declining agricultural prices. Small wonder that their impact was more severe and durable than previously in the West. Apart from formal protest, increased drinking, growing hostility to the church as a tool of the upper classes, as well as crime marked the dilemma of the rural poor.

The peasantry that did have land, though impeded by traditionalism and lack of capital, might adapt more positively. Many did produce for the market; many did enjoy the more diversified goods available as the commercial economy spread. Peasants did not become like city folk; they maintained contact with distinctive traditions. But they were not all averse to a gradual adaptation to new ways. Their key activity was the attempt to purchase new land to take advantage of market opportunities, for this made sense in terms of traditional status as well. Hence in western Europe they nibbled at the holdings of their poorer brethren and at the common lands. Even in the large estate areas of Prussia a minority of peasant farmers did well, which helped reduce tension. And in Russia the emancipation of

1861 provided the average peasant with over twenty acres, albeit not always fertile ones. The continuing restrictions were galling. Russian peasants could not leave their village without village permission. In some villages land was to be redistributed every ten years; these repartitional villages allowed no permanent ownership. The obligation to pay redemption to the state, at rates sometimes higher than the rental value of the land, was terribly burdensome to all. But here, too, adaptation occurred, and a minority of peasants was able to buy new land during the last three decades of the nineteenth century. Only in southern Europe was the division among the peasantry, between owners and nonowners, almost nonexistent because of the pervasive large estates; there was a difference between a sharecropper and an outright laborer, but it was not great. Elsewhere a minority, varying in size according to the previous land tenure systems, could make do.

Peasant Rebellion

In the early stages of this transition a third group of peasants, with some village allies, played a crucial role. If we project a very simplified trend, whereby peasants converted sufficiently to the market to survive or entered an agricultural proletariat (or, of course, left the land altogether), we must recognize an intermediate phase in which the middling peasant was being squeezed but still tried to make do. His neighbors might want to buy him out but land was his life. Taxes and other money obligations were rising rapidly. Real conversion to the market was impossible because of lack of enough land and capital. A future of landlessness seemed ominously close, the final degradation. Add to this middling group domestic manufacturing workers, not yet displaced, who also saw the handwriting on the wall as they were increasingly hardpressed by their employers, suffering declining wages and growing periods of unemployment. Add, finally, village artisans, like blacksmiths, who faced competition from factory products and who could play a particularly good leadership role. This was the formula for massive peasant rebellion in most parts of Europe during the early industrial revolution. The richer peasants did not join in, though they might sympathize; English farmers, for example, supported their laborers' demands for better treatment in 1830, claiming that they had adopted new machines only because competition forced them to. Except in England and, later, southern Europe, the landless laborers were generally too disorganized to be effective rebels. But middling peasants and their manufacturing allies were quite strong enough to make a last attempt to restore a better society. They won some victories, particularly when they attacked the manorial system; here they had major historical impact. But they lost the war, because they could not stop the advance of industrialization and, when they gained the downfall of manorialism, they actually opened the way to further change.

A rising tide of riots focused on the apparent causes of misery. Merchants were often attacked during periods of high prices as a result of the increasing dependence of peasants on outside purchases. Here traditional protest focus was simply heightened by modernization. In 1795 British peasant women rioted in a number of market towns. In the years of poor harvests in France, such as 1828 and 1847, peasants often attacked shops and grain convoys. Grain dealers were attacked in Italy in 1898, again a symbol of resentment against the condition of market agriculture.

In periods of agitation peasants often refused to pay taxes or redemption payments, as in Russia in the late nineteenth century. Rioters sometimes attacked tax offices; more than resentment was involved in such attacks, for peasants often burned records in the hope of eliminating the hated assessments. Domestic workers frequently attacked factories and machines. This Luddism, though not confined to peasant manufacturers, was often an important concomitant of more general peasant discontent.

The most bitter and extensive riots, sometimes a part of major revolution, were directed against the landlords. This was often the focus of crime. Poaching and thefts were the responses of many English peasants to the hardships of the late eighteenth century. In Russia 144 landlords and twenty-nine stewards were killed between 1835 and 1854. Generally much rural crime expressed the idea that the land belonged to the peasant and that the lords' property could be legitimately attacked in these new times of hardship. When it was most purposeful, peasant agitation tried to destroy manorial obligations and to acquire more land. Such agitation was usually precipitated by a year or two of bad harvests and resulting misery, but it sought more than temporary material relief. In response to population pressure the peasants sought more land and outright control of the land they already had.

Peasant risings against landlords employed many methods. Refusal to pay rents was a common preliminary to an actual rising. Angry and violent attacks on the house and more rarely, the person of the landlord were part of many riots. Rioters usually stole from the lord's property. Peasants on large estates often went on strike. Two features of the major risings were most indicative of the basic purpose. The records of the landlord were pillaged and burned to destroy manorial and sharecropping obligations where these still applied; or government offices collecting redemption payments were similarly treated. Peasants wanted to remove the burdens placed upon them by the lords and felt that no compensation for this removal was justified. Furthermore, peasants often took over part of the lord's land and cultivated it. Here was a naked expression of the land hunger of the peasantry during its time of crisis.

Peasant risings were largely apolitical. They might coincide with political revolution, as in France in 1789, Germany and Austria in 1848, and Russia in 1905, but the peasants had little concern for political goals. Most commonly, they expressed their loyalty to their traditional monarchy, blaming bad advisers for any mistakes the government had made. If they obtained their demands concerning manorial payments, they were content; hence after 1793 the French peasantry largely lost interest in the revolution. In the Russian Revolution of 1905 there was a Peasant Congress, which formulated political demands, but it was in no way representative of the bulk of the peasants who had risen.

Most of the peasant risings lacked any clear doctrine. Russian peasants actually resisted the efforts of university students to spread agrarian socialism during the later nineteenth century. There are, however, two cases in which an ideological element was present. Sicilian peasants accepted the leadership of urban socialists during the Fasci revolt of the 1890s, and they expressed demands for equality of bread and work and even the realization of a new fraternal order in the countryside. Peasants saw in socialist concepts a way to express their old ideals of sharing and equality. In Andalusia in the same period peasants found a doctrine, brought in by foreign and urban agitators, that expressed many of their own hopes. Andalusian peasants were massively converted to at least some of the slogans of anarchism. They tried to free themselves from the encroachments of the central government by eliminating government in favor of purely village rule. They wished to divide all the land equally. By these means misery would be destroyed and a perfect social order established. Both southern Spain and Sicily were areas in which peasant poverty and lack of land were particularly acute; there was really no way for even a minority of peasants to adapt to change. Both were areas of traditional resentment of the state; southern Italians in particular resented controls and high taxation from the new northern-dominated government of united Italy. Both were areas of religious fervor that could carry over into the new ideologies. Even in these cases, although doctrine was brought in by outside agitators, the basic purposes of the peasants continued to be expressed. More commonly, doctrine was neither needed nor available, and peasants sought their own goals in their own way.

The organization of peasant risings was vague and informal. They usually spread from one locality to another by contagion rather than by advance planning. Leadership even among Spanish anarchists was local, because the movement was hostile to organization. There were no special funds to support peasant agitation, and it was difficult to sustain the agitation for more than a few months. Rebellions might recur, as they did in Spain about once every ten years after 1870, but they usually burned themselves out fairly quickly. In its organization as well as its main purposes peasant agitation drew from the traditional importance of the land and local structures, which is why landed peasants and artisans played the key role. Peasant rioters in Russia in 1905 came clearly from the middling landed group; anarchist leaders in the Spanish villages were most often craftsmen.

Regional patterns and dates of protest varied greatly. British peasants rioted frequently up to about 1850. They used some distinctive methods, notably burning of buildings. They might attack merchants, as in 1795, or new taxes and tolls, as in the 1843 Rebecca riots in western Wales. As we have seen, the 1830 riots in Kent and elsewhere were directed against threshing equipment in the name of just wages. Some rural domestic workers attacked the source of their competition, the new machines and factories. In this Luddite agitation, beginning in 1811 and cropping up occasionally later, small groups of weavers and others destroyed many machines in northern England by well-coordinated night attacks. The Luddites developed a doctrine based on the presumed virtues of manual methods.

In France the major rising occurred of course in 1789. Although manorial dues were abolished in the autumn of 1789, agitation continued until redemption payments were eliminated in 1793. Even after this there were brief local riots in famine years until the middle of the nineteenth century. Domestic workers, pressed by increasing factory competition, occasionally struck and rioted locally. In many of the poorer regions, such as the mountainous Auvergne, peasants rioted during the ferment of 1848. But most peasant regions were now immune to major agitation and some actively opposed the urban risings of 1848.

German peasants rioted occasionally in the early nineteenth century; banditry also increased. In 1848 peasants in many sections of Germany and Austria followed the lead of revolution in the cities and attacked their manorial lords. After two years of bad harvests peasants in several areas, especially in the southwestern part of Germany, pillaged and burned many castles and record repositories. In eastern Germany there was less revolutionary activity, but peasants were restless and some urged a redistribution of property.

Southern and eastern Europe witnessed some major peasant riots in the early part of the nineteenth century, but there agitation increased after 1870. Because of the deteriorating conditions in agriculture generally as well as the unusual poverty and pressure on the land in these areas of big estates, the period of agitation was often more extended than it had been in western Europe. In Andalusia anarchism spread after 1870. There were a number of major strikes by workers on the latifundias; anarchists even seized land and tried to set up an idealized village government and economy. The Sicilian revolt of the Fasci in 1893 followed three years of declining wheat production and wine prices and a concomitant rise in unemployment. Peasants tried to seize the land, claiming it was theirs by a tradition of possession akin to the possession of common land. Rioting broke out again in 1898 in Sicily and central Italy against grain dealers and bakers; many town halls containing tax records were attacked.

Riots were frequent in the Balkans in this same period. Rumanian peasants rose several times in their hunger for land; a major outburst in 1907 resulted in thousands of deaths. Bosnian peasants rebelled against their Moslem landlords in 1875; they were spurred by a crop failure and by their resentment at having to surrender up to half their crop to the lords. There was one distinctive element in some of the Balkan agitation. Nationalist doctrines attracted increasing numbers of peasants as a means of expressing the common grievances. Nationalist agitators found considerable support among the peasantry on Bosnia, Serbia, and Macedonia. Peasant nationalism was directed particularly against the Moslems because they were landlords and unbelievers; but it could be turned against other outsiders, such as the Austrians. The assassin of Franz Ferdinand in 1914 showed how peasant hardship could take a nationalist form: "I have seen our people going steadily downhill. I am a peasant's son and know what is happening in the villages. . . . All this had its influence on me and also the fact of knowing that he [the archduke] was a German, an enemy of the Slavs."

Russian peasants engaged in some riots in every year of the century; between 1826 and 1849 there were about sixty local outbreaks a year. After 1856 petitions to the government or to landowners for freedom from servile obligations increased, spurred by the discontent of soldiers returning to the villages from the Crimean wars. News that the government was going to emancipate the peasantry and then dissatisfaction with redemption payments and lack of land caused a rise in the numbers of riots. In the first months of 1861 alone there were 1,340 outbreaks. This number was unusual, but in succeeding decades a great deal of agitation occurred, particularly in years of bad harvests and famine, such as the 1870s. In Russia as elsewhere, a combination of population pressure and dissatisfaction with legal changes created a high pitch of discontent. The culmination came in 1905, when peasants rose in many areas, spurred by bad harvests and the failures of the war with Japan. They pillaged landlords' forests and estates, refused to pay rents, and burned records in the familiar pattern. Peasants in the repartitional communes, who lacked firm individual ownership of land, were most active in the rising, which extended over a two-year period. After 1906 the pace of rioting declined quite notably until war and revolution brought renewed agitation to the countryside.

At some point in the nineteenth century, peasants in most areas tried to protest their changing situation. They tried to defend and increase their traditional attachment to the land by attacking outside ownership and obligations. Their level of discontent was high, just as the pressures upon them were considerable. Large numbers were roused from customary resignation into an active defense of their dearest traditions. The period of protest, whenever it occurred, marked a major turning point in the lives of the peasants.

Adaptation to the Market

The period of protest in almost all cases reached an end during the nineteenth century. Only in a few areas, notably in southern Europe, did conditions remain so stagnant that the protest period extended well into the twentieth century. In France and Britain risings were over by 1851. German and Austrian peasants were largely quiescent after 1848, and Russian peasants were relatively calm between 1907 and the March revolution. Peasants who still had land were largely able to adapt the new conditions of agriculture. The landless had to knuckle under or leave.

A number of factors combined to relieve the pressures on the peasants. The full abolition of manorial dues and redemption payments was crucial in satisfying much of the peasantry in France after 1793; in parts of western Germany, northern Italy, and the Low Countries soon thereafter; in Austria and Germany by the 1850s; and in Russia after 1906. This abolition often resulted directly from peasant risings. It helped placate peasants particularly where individual holdings predominated, as in Western Europe and in Russia. But even in east Prussia a minority of peasants had satisfactory holdings. Peasants who owned land now owned it free and clear, although in Germany some rental fees were still paid.

At the same time the rise of new factories provided an outlet for most of the excess rural population. Certain areas, such as Brittany, remained poor and overcrowded because they were too far from industrial centers; it was still difficult to travel very far. On the whole, however, industrial growth absorbed those who could not find a place on the land, sometimes with the help of emigration. In Germany, for example, the expansion of cities accounted for almost the entire increase of the total population after 1840. This alleviated discontent even in the eastern areas of large estates. In addition, domestic production was viable now only as a supplement, for older workers and women; and though this continued to involve many thousands of people, the full-time workers had given up. Here, even more than with middling peasants, modernization finally shunted aside leading protest groups, after a bitter period of transformation.

Alleviation of population pressure and the traditional obligations to landlords created a new environment for peasant agriculture in much of Europe. The landed peasants not only continued their quest for more land, gradually dividing common lands into private ownership and partially consolidating scattered strips, but they also increased their specialization for the market, some going into truck or dairy farming. Their effort was aided, after 1850, by the development of better agricultural credit through government and cooperative banks. Consolidation of the land was also encouraged by the state, and though peasant traditionalism retarded the process, some units were big enough to allow individual economic decisions about land use and to permit grazing of animals or use of machines in cultivation. All this naturally heightened the divisions between owners and nonowners, but even the landless might benefit as the cessation of population pressure stabilized their wages.

Nowhere was the readiness for adaptation of a large minority of peasants more dramatically apparent than in Russia after the 1905 revolution. Between emancipation and the revolution peasants had been held to a rather traditional village agricultural system; villages made economic decisions and protected common lands and the division of holdings into strips. After 1906 the government, under the leadership of Stolypin, tried to alleviate peasant discontent by releasing peasants from the hold of the village. Peasants could, on petition, abolish common land and repartitional communes and could consolidate strips. Taking advantage of these possibilities, most peasants withdrew their land from repartitional communes; almost half applied for some consolidation of strips. In a very short time the new economic interests of the peasant leaders became clear.

The final ingredient of peasant adaptation was the cessation of periodic famines. Their own improved production plus better transportation through railroads eliminated famines even when there was a poor harvest. In western Europe, 1846–1847 represented the last case of real starvation in the countryside. In normal years also the extension of the market system gave many peasants increasing access to urban goods, ranging from coffee and sugar to more stylish clothing.

For all these reasons the great age of peasant protest ceased toward the end of the early industrial period. It revived in Russia during World War I; its bases remained active in southern Europe and the Balkans, though these areas had not really industrialized significantly yet. The countryside was not forever to be quiet. A massive rural uprising in southeastern France in 1851 suggested new elements, for these peasants, including many agricultural laborers, were protesting the end of republican government; the revolt followed the authoritarian coup d'état of Louis Napoleon. Peasants could gain new political interests. But on the whole they had forged a unique blend of the old and the new in Western Europe, and there were hints of the same combination in Russia after 1906. Their villages retained recreational functions. Their family structure had been jolted when they realized they could not provide land or jobs for all their children. In Russia after 1906, for example, children were free to leave home without parental consent after the age of twenty-one; previously they had been pledged to their father's authority and turned over their earnings to the family fund. But an individualistic strain did not destroy the peasant family. Some peasants, as in France, rather quickly reduced their birth rate to maintain the relationship between children and land. But this was in part because French law required equal inheritance. In other areas large peasant families long prevailed and the belief in the economic importance of big broods remained. Large numbers of peasants in southern Germany, for example, carefully got their bride pregnant before marriage, saying they wanted to make sure of their deal. This was not age-old tradition. But greater economic opportunity, including the chance to leave the countryside, let peasants indulge their customary desire for children and child labor more fully than before.

And peasants still protected themselves somewhat from the outside world. Government directives, aside from taxation and military recruitment at least, could be avoided; hence what the state wanted for agriculture, in terms of new methods and more commercialized tenure arrangements, differed considerably from what it got. There were increasing urban contacts, through market agriculture and the return of now urban relatives, but these did not totally break through the combined envy and distrust that peasants felt for the city.

None of this should suggest perfection. Peasants were in many ways lulled by their own image, which conservative politicians carefully enhanced, of the superior virtues of rural life. They took land over standard of living. And even this conservative adaptation escaped the rural laborers who worked for landlords or rich farmers. Agricultural life need not be idealized. What is clear is that, despite some hints of new political interests in a few areas, a time of quiet descended. Whenever the old spurs to protect—manorialism, famines—were gone, peasants made do with an adapted tradition. Some of the least protected or most aggrieved elements simply left.

Urban Society

Growth of Cities

Urbanization was a natural result of population growth and industrialization. Expanding population and rising agricultural productivity released hundreds of thousands of people who were not needed and could not be supported in the countryside. Improved food production, along with better transportation, made it easier to supply urban populations.

The most rapid rates of urban growth occurred in the new factory centers, for mechanized industry required a large pool of labor. Many of these cities were essentially new, for factory location was increasingly determined by access to coal, and many of the coal-rich areas had been only sparsely urbanized before. And the peak rate of urban expansion corresponded to the rise of the factories, usually two or three decades after the industrial revolution began—1820–1840 in England, 1850–1870 in France, 1870–1890 in Austria, and so on.

Other types of cities grew in the nineteenth century, without necessarily developing an elaborate factory system. Cities with port facilities were encouraged by the industrial revolution, because the expansion of trading and exports increased the need for commercial outlets. Even in agricultural areas market opportunities spurred the growth of some big centers, such as Budapest. Trade, banking, and government encouraged the growth of traditional political centers such as London, Paris, and Amsterdam, and newer ones such as Berlin, more than industry itself. So urbanization and factory industry should not be too closely linked, and some cities grew faster than their functions warranted. In this there was real tragedy, for traditional migration patterns brought many peasants to the capitols, flooding them with unskilled workers, at a time when the most dynamic cities were trying to recruit labor. This was an obvious source of the unusual crime and unrest in the political centers as well.

One of the reasons for the growth of big cities, whether new or old, was the stagnation of many regional towns, which resulted in a major change in Europe's urban map. Improved transportation and marketing reduced the need for purely local trading and manufacturing cities. Even artisan production tended to move from local towns to a small number of cities, such as Paris. The railroad itself operated most efficiently between large centers. Even when lines were built it was uneconomical for trains to stop and start too often and the systems of trunk lines left many cities without service and usually doomed to decay. Similarly, the need for a pool of labor and massive capital and commercial facilities dictated the expansion of cities best located with regard to resources and transportation. Urbanization involved, then, the concentrated growth of some new industrial cities and of major centers generally. Many older towns, such as Norwich in Britain and Vézelay in France, actually declined as part of the urban movement. Even when a regional center merely stagnated, urbanization could again cause tragedy, as established groups could no longer rely on their local position to feel important.

Overall, however, the main fact of urbanization was the sheer rate of growth involved. Favored cities expanded rapidly. In Britain, many northern manufacturing cities, such as Leeds, Birmingham, and Sheffield, grew by 40 per cent between 1821 and 1831. Between 1801 and 1851 Birmingham grew from 73,000 to 250,000, and Liverpool expanded from 77,000 to 400,000. Manchester rose from 25,000 to 367,232 between 1772 and 1851. London also continued to grow but at a slower rate. French industry and population expanded less rapidly. Between 1830 and 1851 four fifths of France's population rise went into the cities; between 1851 and 1871, eleven twelfths did so. Some industrial centers grew with great rapidity but never to the size of the British giants. Saint-Étienne rose from 16,000 to 56,000 between 1820 and 1850 and Roubaix from 8,000 to 34,000. The great growth of Paris overshadowed the provincial centers during most of the century, making French urban development far less balanced than was the case in other countries.

In Germany urbanization had clearly begun by the 1860s, for it was that decade that city growth first absorbed the whole German population gain. Berlin and the industrial centers in Saxony and the Ruhr grew most rapidly. In 1870 there were eight cities in Germany with populations of more than 100,000; in 1900 there were forty-one, and five were over the half million mark. Scandinavia and the Low Countries entered their period of urban growth around mid-century also, and eastern Europe soon followed. Austria's city population rose from 18 per cent to 32 per cent of the total between 1850 and 1890. During the last three decades of the century Warsaw grew by half a million, and the industrial city of Lodz rose from 31,000 to 310,000. Russian cities grew rapidly, with Moscow rising by 400,000.

In 1800 Europe had twenty-two cities with a population over 100,000; in 1895 she had 120, and their inhabitants represented 10 per cent of the European population as a whole. Several areas, in fact, were over half urban. Britain passed this point in 1850, and by 1900 over four fifths of her people lived in cities. Germany was over half urban by 1900, France by 1930; and the trend spread widely.

City growth slowed down in most countries after the first decades of industrialization, though there was still substantial increase. By that time the nature of the cities and their place in society had been radically altered. New urban areas had risen, more massive agglomerations than had ever before been known. For a large amount of Europe's population the most distinguishing feature of the early industrial period was the move to the city and adjustment to its life.

City Population

The initial decades of urban expansion depended largely on immigration from the countryside. The cities themselves had only scant margins of births over deaths in this period; they were not capable of significant natural increase. In some of the fastest-growing centers two thirds of the residents had been there less than fifteen years. Many rural residents were attracted to the cities by the opportunities and excitement of urban life, but more were forced to come. Population pressure, loss of land, and more productive agriculture made many peasants unnecessary in the countryside, and factory competition displaced domestic manufacturers. After a period of declining wages and lengthening periods of unemployment, huge numbers of rural people sought refuge in the cities. Often they went first as transients, hoping to return to their village after a period of factory work. Gradually, their contacts with the countryside declined and they became fully urban.

Some of the cities' new residents had traveled long distances from their homes in towns and villages. Large cities such as Berlin and Paris drew from all over the country. Barcelona attracted thousands of southern Spanish peasants. A substantial number of foreigners came into many cities. Irish peasants sought work in the new British centers, and Belgians and Germans helped build up towns like Roubaix and Mulhouse; Poles later came into the Ruhr.

But one of the themes of rapid urbanization was an effort to cushion shock. Some long-distance migrants were simply unusually venturesome. Others expected to return home after earning a bit of money, planning to support the family economy or even buy land. Particularly before the railroad most migration was short-hop. That is, a displaced young peasant son moved twenty or thirty miles nearer a city, where the economy was more commercialized and jobs more plentiful. His children, in turn, moved into the city. Correspondingly many cities (the capitals are the leading exceptions) drew primarily on their own regions even as they expanded rapidly. Finally, some long-distance migration followed traditional patterns. Servant girls coming to Paris, for example, originated disproportionately in poor agricultural areas that had always sent servants to Paris; only their numbers had greatly increased. None of this should minimize the jolt of urbanization. Cities provided a distinctive way of life. But not all people moved blindly into a strange environment. They took it one step at a time and/or hoped to pull out as soon as possible. This is one reason they could survive the shock.

For cities were strange, bustling, hurried. They had been different from the countryside before, and the new urbanization increased some of the differences. The city population was young. The bulk of the immigrants from the countryside were between twenty and forty years old, the age at which one had the vigor and courage to tear up ties with the village or town. The youth of the urban population in turn contributed to the dynamism of the cities. The immigrants were at the most economically productive age, and this helped build the prosperity of the new cities. The energy of the young newcomers might also contribute to rising urban agitation.

In the cities illegitimacy and crimes against property had long been higher than in the countryside. Urbanization extended these trends to a larger population. At the same time urban residents were physically larger, on the average. They were less afflicted with congenital idiocy, because there was greater cross breeding in the cities. The percentage of women was higher in the city because of a higher male death rate and the fact that the ratio of males to females at birth was lower than in rural communities. In vigor, in composition, and in many basic habits the people of the new cities were different from the people of the villages. There were many vital distinctions in class and behavior within the city, but urban life imparted some common features to city residents as a whole. Above all, cities were messier and more exciting places.

Material Conditions

The most obvious general influence in the rising cities was the material setting. The great influx of immigrants put real strain on urban physical facilities, which had often been poorly developed even before. A positive deterioration of conditions occurred in many cities during the first period of urban growth. British cities, which had been paying growing attention to street paving and to covering sewers in the late eighteenth century, could not build rapidly enough to keep pace with their rising population. An increase in urban mortality rates was the inevitable result. Rapidly growing French cities such as Mulhouse had similar problems, but centers that expanded more slowly, such as Lille, managed to improve their facilities throughout the period. Later in the century similar material pressures occurred in the cities of southern and eastern Europe.

New numbers created a great need for housing. Old buildings were divided and redivided; the poorest families had only one room or even had to share a room with another family. New buildings were hastily thrown up, providing cramped, flimsy accommodation. Rents soared, doubling or even tripling in a decade or two. Intense crowding, inadequate conditions, high prices—these were the inevitable consequences of the influx to the cities.

The expansion of cities created needs for transportation as well. New streets had to be built. Many older streets were still unpaved, and the new ones were often little more than rutted paths. Vehicular transport was in private hands and expanded only slowly; the carriages and horse-drawn omnibusses were too expensive for most of the new residents. The crowding of the cities was partly due to the need to be within walking distance of the place of work, and even so some new workers had to walk many miles each day.

New population meant increasing need for wells and for sewage disposal; these too were provided only slowly and inadequately. Many sewers remained open, and many rivers were increasingly polluted by the disposal of wastes. This was in fact the peak period of urban water pollution, unmatched even in the twentieth century. The poorer areas of most cities were unbelievably filthy and smelly. They were naturally subject to diseases and even epidemics, such as the cholera epidemic that raged through western Europe in 1832.

Danger from fire and from criminals was also high. Cities had few police facilities. In 1848 Berlin had two hundred policemen for a population of 400,000, and this was one of the best-policed cities of Europe. With unlighted streets, hugh numbers of new and poor inhabitants, and few regular police patrols, it was small wonder that crime rates rose rapidly. The pressure of population on already limited facilities created a vast array of material problems in the cities.

City Government

Gradually, private groups and particularly urban governments themselves developed new concepts of what a city should be like. They tried not only to catch up with the needs created by a rising population, but also to go beyond what older cities had offered. New systems of fire prevention and of mass transport were developed; new ideas of police action and government inspection arose. By the mid-nineteenth century in western Europe, and soon after elsewhere, new institutions were transforming urban life.

In many cases the development of new urban activities was promoted by changes in city government. New elements in the middle class, such as factory owners, sought urban political power. In Britain this change was slow. Manchester was governed as a noble manor until 1844, when the administration was opened to election by middle-class property owners. Even before then, however, industrialist groups had supplemented the manorial officials with activities of their own, especially in matters of police and hygiene. Cities elsewhere in western Europe were more abruptly freed from the control of aristocratic or church officials. The French Revolution established election procedures for mayors, with the franchise usually limited to property owners. Most cities in France and the Low Countries were governed by middle-class administration. The mayors of most factory centers were usually industrialists, but older elements of the merchant class controlled other cities. In eastern and southern Europe urban administration was opened to new personnel later in the nineteenth century.

National governments, too, played an increasingly active role in the cities; in central Europe this continued the earlier trend. By 1850 the British government began to suggest and then require the establishment of local boards of health and education. The French government, more active in local affairs, played a major role in such projects as slum clearance.

Municipal governments took a hand in the matter of housing. By the 1830s French cities established some inspection of houses and even closed some of the worst slums. During the Second Empire the national government sponsored housing projects in Marseilles and elsewhere. In Paris the prefect Haussmann tore down huge slum areas in order to build a network of boulevards. The object was to eliminate the twisted, crowded streets that were so easy to barricade in revolution and to replace them with avenues down which troops could march and fire. The result was a major change in the housing and transportation of Paris, and also a considerable reduction in the possibility of riot. In Britain cities were empowered to inspect houses in 1851 and to clear slums in 1865; by the 1890s minimum standards of space and sanitary facilities were established in all houses. Elsewhere in Europe, in many German cities for example, stronger traditions of government action promoted regulations even earlier.

Cities also began to build parks. Paris removed many old cemeteries, health hazards in themselves, and replaced them with parks. At the end of the century Vienna tore down her peripheral walls and substituted a ring of boulvards and parks.

Problems of transportation were attacked by private companies and cities. Increasing controls were placed on bus companies. Streets were broadened and paved. Most important, commuter trains and later subways offered rapid transport at a low price. By the later part of the century rapid transportation and municipal housing regulations had greatly reduced urban congestion; the boundaries of cities spread and suburbs proliferated beyond them.

Urban governments also attempted to deal with crime and public hygiene. Gas lighting was installed on many city streets by the 1830s. Police functions were greatly expanded. New forces, such as London's bobbies, set up in 1829, provided far more numerous personnel. Cities also established fire departments, long supplemented by private brigades such as those provided by many insurance companies. Cities built new covered sewers quite rapidly and worked to improve the water supply. They began to clean the streets. Municipal officials checked water supplies, market conditions, and slaughterhouses. Schools, factories, and hospitals were also subjected to city inspection. Many cities required vaccinations of all residents.

The result of these various efforts in housing and hygiene was a major improvement in urban health. By the 1830s French cities had a large annual surplus of births over deaths. German cities such as Frankfurt achieved a similar surplus in the 1840s. Everywhere urban mortality rates fell much more rapidly than rural after the first shock of urban growth passed, and in a few countries, such as Austria by the end of the century, they had actually dipped below the levels of the countryside.

So the cities were not helpless even as they received their great onslaught of new people. Some government patterns were suggested that were later taken over by national states in their own response to industrialization, for cities forecast a host of welfare and regulatory measures. But for urban residents, old as well as new, the early industrial period was dominated by confusion and material horror as traditional facilities were overwhelmed by new numbers of people. Adaptation might occur, even among some of the poorer elements, but it was hacked out in an exceedingly harsh environment. The material problems of the city affected all classes. The rich began to separate themselves from the poor far more rigorously than before. Some feared crime, though their imagination often exceeded reality. Still more tried to flee dirt and pollution; it was no accident that most of the wealthy quarters shifted to the west of the center city, for prevailing winds came from the west and conveniently blew most of the filth on the older sections. This kind of reaction left each urban class somewhat isolated in its efforts to come to grips with city life. The poorer classes obviously, but also the new middle class had to deal with an environment that was unexpected and to a significant degree out of control. Finally, the speed of urbanization not only created new social classes but overwhelmed older groups with new numbers; there was no chance for any large element to maintain the contact with tradition still possible for rural landowners.

The Rise of the Middle Classes

The rise of the middle classes is a familiar theme, expressing the most important change in social values in the early industrial period. The middle class was not the most rapidly growing segment of society, but it outstripped all the purely traditional elements. The growth of business and of governmental activities increased the need for professional people, and relevant educational opportunities expanded sometimes faster still. Between 1809 and 1842 attendance at French *lycées,* which had been set up primarily to train bureaucrats, doubled. Russian university enrollments rose from 1,700 in 1825 to 4,600 in 1848. Some of the students involved were aristocrats, but there was a growing middle-class element. In Britain the professional ranks grew by 185 per cent from 1803 to 1867. A distinct lower middle class arose as retail shopkeeping expanded everywhere. This was a vital economic function, now that there were more goods to distribute, and shops replaced fairs, peddlers, and some craftsmen as the purveyors of goods. From almost nothing, this group grew to about half of the mid-century middle class in cities such as Paris. The upper middle class profited from new economic opportunities too. In Paris the wealthiest segments of the middle class rose from 2.4 per cent of the population to 3.6 per cent in 1847, and the city's population itself had risen during the same years. Middle-level businessmen, new factory owners and wholesalers, proliferated as well. This was no tiny elite. Although it did not quite keep pace with urban growth, it rapidly increased as a percentage of the overall population. In Britain, for example, the middle class grew by 223 per cent, compared to the 206 per cent rate for the population generally.

New numbers meant new wealth, and although the lower income levels of the class grew more rapidly than the top segment there could be no doubt that the class commanded a rising share of the national income. The very rich in the class also increased their wealth per capita; an upper-middle-class family in Paris was richer in 1848 than its counterpart thirty years before. Many industrialists and bankers gained great fortunes. Even a more modest manufacturer could steadily increase his living standards. The Alsatian Thierry-Mieg began with a small textile operation and within twenty years was earning three hundred times as much as the average textile worker he employed; at which time he proudly noted, "My fortune is made."

New numbers, new wealth were capped by a reshuffling of positions. Between 1820 and 1848 most of the richest middle-class families in Paris were replaced by new men, drawn from lower in the class. The same process occurred in Vienna. Industrialists in smaller cities gradually shunted aside traditional merchants, who were unwilling to innovate. The majority came from among well-to-do farmers, former artisan masters, or foremen in the putting-out system; they had not been born to their station. This was a period of maximum mobility. Toward its end opportunities decreased somewhat. The new upper middle class closed its ranks, and manufacturing families often monopolized even the new techniques. But for several decades talent and luck could really pay off.

The rise of the middle class was thus very tangible. And the class could be easily measured off from other groups. There was a bit of fuzziness at the bottom. Perhaps 15 per cent of all shopkeepers were close to the artisan level, intermarrying with this class and sharing its living standards. By the same token some master artisans claimed middle-class status, if they owned their own ships and directed a few employees. Factory foremen and business clerks were another ambiguous group. But on the whole distinctions were clear. The middle class owned property. The average big-city shopkeeper possessed at least twenty times as much capital as the average artisan. Most married within their own group; in Paris approximately 80 per cent of the daughters of shopkeepers married shopkeepers during the period 1820–1848. At the top, only a few wealthy businessmen could rival the aristocratic magnates until late in the early industrial period, and of course they were untitled as well, and frowned upon by aristocrats who were trying to defend their own position. A growing group, definable in fairly clear economic terms—it should be easy to go on to talk about the class's clear triumph and the new values it stood for. In fact, there were at least two middle classes, an old and a new, and traditional motives could intrude upon apparently new economic functions. The middle class, so often praised as the engine of progress or damned for its exploitation of workers, has rarely been studied in detail. Not only were there discrete segments within the class, but there was almost total conflict in goals.

The Conundrum of the Middle Class

The middle class did not grow uniformly with industrialization. Where the state took a prominent role in industry, as in Russia, the business segments remained small and dependent; professional elements were long more important. The new middle class varied in size and strength as a function of the previous size of the non-aristocratic property-owning groups.

Luddite acts, though undertaken by only a small number of craftsmen, met with tacit approval from many middle-class elements. Shopkeepers sometimes cheered the machine breakers on, and magistrates were often inclined to be lenient. Most middle-class elements, even in England, did not like the raw new factories and would have voted against industrialization.

In 1848 the Bavarian government sponsored an essay contest on the state of society. Contributors were mainly middle class: teachers, pastors, master artisans, even some local businessmen. Almost uniformly they damned the changes they saw around them. The lower classes were immoral, witness their fancy clothes. The rich were getting too rich. "Destruction of these machines . . . would be the most beautiful way to get the disastrous things off the face of the earth."

A sentiment that many manufacturers would echo, or almost. In 1840 a young French industrialist, Motte-Bossut, impressed with what he had learned in England, set up one of the first big spinning factories in Roubaix. His parents, owners of a putting-out system with modest wealth, invested in his plant (he was their son, after all) but refused ever to set foot in it; such a gigantic operation was immoral. Another manufacturer in the same city urged that mechanization be limited and that England's horrible example be avoided, for above all the middling property owner should be protected from voracious capitalism. But other French industrialists wanted nothing better than to beat the English at their own game; to Motte-Bossut, England was "the center of the universe."

The middle class constantly criticized itself, or so it seems on the surface. Middle-class publicists, including many women, berated the average middle-class housewife for idleness, living beyond her means, and frivolity. They were wrong, as we shall see; but the housewives read the criticisms, for they hungered for guidance. Happily they did not follow the moralistic advice, but they may have been troubled by it.

"Middle-class" political regimes were rarely so. "The" middle class was not liberal. Many were hostile to liberalism, and most distrusted pure liberal theory. The middle class was not yet eager to seize political power directly. When the whole class got the vote, as occurred for all intents and purposes in England in 1832, they elected about the same types of people as before, including many aristocrats. More commonly suffrage reforms divided the middle class, with only the top property owners gaining the vote. In the July Monarchy in France only about 250,000 males could vote, with landowners predominating. In Italy only 2 per cent of the population could vote from unification to the 1870s. To go from "middle class" to a defined political interest is usually misleading.

The Middling Class

One can begin to get at some of these anomalies by looking at the origins of the nonaristocratic, urban, property-owning group that is normally called the middle class. The old bourgeoisie, in the first place, did not simply roll over and die. Small-town bigshots—the local judge, the miller—carried on even as their towns declined in relative importance. Even in large older cities (Rheims is an example) big merchants, although adamantly refusing to adopt factory equipment, long dominated the town's social life and kept the new industrialists at a distance; some industrialists, because of the stigma of novelty, long preferred to call themselves merchants. Even a small manufacturer might see no point in innovating beyond a certain level, because his goals were not really new.

In the second place the cities were filled with former rural property owners, the middling peasant who had sold out, the former village teacher or grain merchant. For the countryside had concealed a large number of business and professional people, along with landed peasants. Some of these, upon reaching the city, hoped to attain new heights; some joined the innovators. Far more hoped to preserve old values in new ways, now that the rural economy was so confused.

A case in point is the shopkeeping group. As noted, their economic functions were new. Many brought their capital in from the countryside; in Paris 60 per cent of the shopkeepers were of rural origin. This much they would venture, but no more. They saw their business strictly in family terms. Wives and children worked the same long hours as the men, preserving even the traditional pace of work by building their whole lives around the sporadic activity of the shop. There was no desire to expand, and the shopkeeping group improved its economic position not at all during the nineteenth century. The group asked nothing more than to remain in the middle of the social scale.

The ministry was another channel for traditionalists. Many small-town bourgeois and artisans became Catholic priests or Lutheran pastors. This was mobility; it was certainly a respectable alternative to remaining in a stagnant job. Hence the peasantry was increasingly displaced in this profession by more urban elements, who often scorned the countryside and hoped for positions in the city. This was a particular source of tension in the German Lutheran church, for peasants did not like the new type of pastor. But the ministry remained a conservative force; its members were eager to preserve the old social order, not to adapt to the new.

Hence it is useful to conceive of a middling class, representative of older values. In the long run this group would be economically different from the real middle class, becoming notably poorer though still defined by its property ownership. In the early decades of industrialization some of the modernizing elements of the middle class would be little better off. Values, more than economics, marked the split.

Finally the middling class provided some of the moralizing tone that has often been attributed to the middle class as a whole. Churchmen particularly led the charge against greed and a more luxurious style of life. Religious writers attacked the real or imagined frivolities of middle-class women. Many members of the middling class early tried to restrict their birth rate, for they wanted to be able to pass their property on intact, not divide it among too many children. This promoted an ethic of sexual restraint, as well as a relatively late marriage age, for abstinence was one of the only sure ways this group knew to limit births. This group, though profoundly uneasy about modernization, lacked direct outlets for protest; they were too respectable, too conscious of defending their property, to take to the streets. Even in petitions they rarely attacked the middle class directly. For in the early industrial period they could make do; they were losing ground but not displaced. Their agony would come later, when society was more fully out of hand according to traditional norms.

The Middle Class

This was a class that accepted change. It had its own anxieties. Big businessmen could talk of the evils of cities and the unbearable tensions of risking a new investment. Housewives might read the religious magazines even as they tried to work out a new style of life. The uncertainties surrounding innovation created some links between the middle class and the middling class, particularly in the first generation of industrialization. Later, businessmen shook off some of the fears and spoke more consistently of expansion. The principal women's magazines in Britain deliberately avoided a religious tone after 1850.

For the middle class thought in terms of science and material progress. It was sure a better world was being built through industrialization. It could accept the idea of social mobility. Members of the middle class hoped themselves to rise in society. They were eager to acquire a new standard of living. They were conscious of the need to save money, for this was the source of investment funds and dowries for daughters, but they were quickly open to new pleasures as consumers. They wanted better furnishings for their homes. They wanted new recreational outlets, like the fancy bars that sprang up in Paris around 1850 or the music gardens in London that drew a fashionable crowd of young clerks and professional people for drinking and dancing. At the top, the upper middle class indeed began to separate itself from the rest of the group by a really luxurious standard of living. Successful businessmen bought large mansions and had at least three servants. They increasingly took over patronage of concert groups. This kind of wealth came only to 5 or 10 per cent of the class, though the numbers were sufficient to make a real change in the cultural tone of society. The bulk of the middle class had to be content with more modest improvements, but the desire for new pleasure was there even so. Ultimately this would be the source of a new leisure ethic. In this first industrial period the middle class spent long hours at work, twelve or more a day, and its work ethic overshadowed all else. But there was room for experimentation with a new style of life. Although set apart most obviously by property ownership, the bulk of the middle class pulled in three or four times the annual income of the working class —£200 in England, for example, compared to £60 for a skilled worker. This margin, though not as great as might be imagined and inadequate for elaborate recreational expenses, served as a source of innovation in the household. Finally, the middle class was open to the idea of mobility for others. Its myth was not that the poor were uppity and immoral when it saw them wearing fancier clothes, but rather the fiction of the self-made man. Few people actually did rise into the middle class in this period from below. As we have seen, recruitment was almost entirely from the ranks of existing property owners. Only 10 per cent of entrepreneurs in Berlin had other than solid middle-class backgrounds. But a handful of examples were genuine: Cail, ultimately owner of a machine works in Paris, who started as an apprentice metal worker, or Joseph Brotherton, a successful manufacturer who was the only member of the House of Commons of working-class origin. And the idea that people could and should rise by their merits was central to the middle-class ethic, in contrast to the middling class impulse to want everyone to remain in his place.

Increasingly the middle class won out. Its modernizing values converted part of the middling class and even part of the aristocracy. It had a number of important weapons even though, at the start of the industrial revolution, it was a decided minority among urban property-owners generally. Success bred imitation. The middling class might rail against large fortunes but the fact is the new fortunes were there. A minority of younger people might be tempted to pursue the same goal. Hence although most shopkeepers remained stagnant, they sent perhaps 30 per cent of their sons into the higher ranks of the middle class, and many sons of Lutheran ministers used the scholarships to which they were entitled to enter more modernized, better-paying positions like law or teaching. Generational changes thus muted some of the conflict that existed between the two groups.

Moreover, there was overlap between the values of the two groups, for both appealed to a fund of bourgeois wisdom. They could agree on the importance not only of property but of hard work, savings, and respectable moral behavior. They agreed that the family was the proper basis for society and the goal of economic effort. They agreed that sons should be given a good start in life, through some education and a solid inheritance, and that daughters deserved a dowry to start a proper marriage. They agreed in marrying relatively late, the men often in their late twenties, so that the family would start out on a proper footing. Important differences existed, for the middling class thought in terms of passing on the same station in life whereas the middle class strove upward. But there were similarities in what children were taught, which gave some basis for a son or daughter in the middling class to decide to move beyond their parents' station.

Furthermore the middle class issued its own propaganda. Although religious literature was widely read in the first industrial decades, so were works such as those of Samuel Smiles in England, which preached a slightly different ethic of success. Hard work, respectability to be sure, but crowned by steady advance up the social ladder. This was a classic self-help approach produced in every industrializing country. The worker who saved his money and restrained his animal appetites could go from rags to riches. The literature was widely read by shopkeepers and artisans; Samuel Smiles, for example, won his main audience in these groups. Here was another way that the idea of social mobility and technological advance spread widely. Furthermore, modernizing values crept into the educational system. In the eighteenth century Prussian schoolbooks stressed the importance of social hierarchy and respect. By the 1840s they had switched emphasis to discussions of hard work, material progress, and self-disciplined control of impulse; they criticized selfishness and irreligion too, but clearly the balance had changed.

By the mid-nineteenth century the most advanced industrial areas were ready for industrial festivals. Beginning with London's Crystal Palace Exhibition of 1851 millions of people could be drawn to displays of the most modern machinery and the new arrays of material goods these machines spewed forth. By no means was the whole society converted to an ethic of material progress; even the middling class still held out to some extent. But given the combination of example and propaganda, it was hard to resist the middle class entirely.

The Professions

A crucial element in the development of the modern middle class was the conversion of the professions to a modernized outlook. There are real ambiguities here. Many people entered professions to achieve respectability in older social terms. Aristocrats, as we have seen, might take this path, and professionals retained more contacts with the aristocracy than most segments of the middle class. Even some businessmen admitted the greater prestige of the professions by sending a son to the university so that he could become a lawyer or government bureaucrat. This pattern was developing as early as the 1840s in France and Germany. By the same token respectable professions like law were often overcrowded while new ones, such as engineering, had many unfilled jobs. The prestige of the professions rested on job security, at least when a government job was in the offing, and on the older place of the professions in the bourgeoisie. Professionals did not make as much money as successful businessmen, so their high status had to have these partially anachronistic roots.

For their part professionals were constantly tempted to distrust the world of business. This was the only highly educated group in the middle class, for most businessmen sent their children to work after at most a few years of secondary school. It was not hard to see the business world as filled by money-grubbing, ignorant men. In turn, businessmen often distrusted professionals as theorists, for they had a pragmatic streak that called any elaborate intellectual life into question. Professionals saw their role in local government threatened, as businessmen used their greater funds to capture the mayor's office and the city council. Factory owners partially displaced professional people as leaders of local social groups. Professionals in a city artistic or philanthropic society had to pay increasing deference to the power and wealth of businessmen. In Mulhouse a young chemistry teacher named Achille Penot began a career of public service by attacking the industrialists who dominated the city. He investigated the conditions of the poor and found them horrible; and he said so. The local industrial society, which was proud of its devotion to spreading knowledge of new scientific and technical developments, responded with horror: they had been attacked by one of their own. So Penot tactfully withdrew his first book, was readmitted to the society, and thereafter made more modest suggestions for reform, such as better treatment of child labor, while writing panegyrics to the local industrialists.

So there was tension between professionals and businessmen and they had somewhat separate worlds. The professionals' concern for their prestige showed vividly in their tendency to live beyond their means. At best they saved a bit of money for their children's education (and this was another group that early reduced its family size, so that it could afford the proper education); as much as 25 per cent of capital could go to this purpose. But the professionals also wanted a fancy house and servants. Even Karl Marx, eking out a living as a journalist, had his two maidservants. The professionals' impulse to spend for show, which endures to the present day, derived from their reaction to the world businessmen were creating, in which money was the key to social position. Lacking elaborate property, for their capital was in their training, they tried to put a good face on it even at the risk of constant money worries.

But the main point is that they did accept and even propagate the middle-class set of values, at least in this first industrial period. Penot did swallow his pride and work within the businessmen's framework, where he could in fact tactfully push for change. Professionals might lament their inability to match businessmen's earnings, but they tried for a similar style of life.

Above all, professionals began their own kind of occupational modernization in this period. Three key elements were involved: formation of professional associations to defend standards, insistence on regular formal training capped by an examination, and, usually a bit later, a state licensing procedure. In 1832 the British Medical Society was formed, against an older, looser group of London physicians; its impulse immediately was to push for better training and a clear association of medicine with scientific advance. In 1858 the Medical Act provided state licenses and examinations. In addition, universities in London and Edinburgh began to provide more careful medical training, in contrast to the older tradition of a gentlemanly liberal education followed by a bit of apprenticeship. Somewhat more slowly, lawyers followed this same pattern. And other groups joined in. Surgeons, formerly associated with barbers, advanced their status and income by professionalizing. They formed their own societies, improved their training, developed new specializations such as gynecology. Pharmacists professionalized; in 1815 British apothecaries won a law that established examinations and licensing. As the century wore on, architects, engineers, and upper-level teachers joined the professional ranks, while accountants moved toward the same goal (achieving it only in the twentieth century). A few groups, admittedly, tried but failed. Primary school teachers talked about better training and licensing but were never able to enforce these on the majority.

The modernization of the professions, both old and new, had a distinctive flavor. Licensing and examinations were designed among other things to restrict entry; here was a guildlike approach that actually restricted mobility into the professions, for the requisite training was expensive. But the process meshed with modernization in other respects by increasing the training levels and associating the professions with scientific advance. Here, obviously, was the way professionals maintained themselves in an industrial society.

There were several more specific reasons that professionals chose the modernization route in the early industrial period. In their schools, particularly on the Continent, they encountered consistent barriers to the free flow of ideas. Conservative governments restricted reading matter and fired liberal teachers. Suppressions of freedom of the press obviously mattered to an educated group. The frequent student riots of the early nineteenth century in Western Europe and later in Russia and Italy set the stage for more persistent reform agitation. In their jobs the professionals encountered other barriers. Young lawyers in Germany who sought to enter the bureaucracy were forced to spend years in junior positions, or even on waiting lists, while their clothing and morals were carefully supervised. Relatedly, there was a constant tendency toward overproduction of professionals. It was easier to get through the universities than to find jobs afterward; this was one reason for the intense competition for bureaucratic posts in Germany. All this tempted middle-class professionals to think in terms of capturing the state and turning it to new purposes. If the aristocracy was reduced, if the state took over manorial functions, there would be new jobs for lawyers and judges. If the state encouraged economic growth then the well-trained bureaucrat would be in the driver's seat, for with his knowledge he would easily outperform the aristocratic dilettante.

The modernization of professionals, which allied them, even if somewhat uneasily, with businessmen, had immense consequences. It was the professionals, with their interest in formal ideas, who served as the main propaganda agents for the middle class. (Samuel Smiles, for example, was a doctor.) It was they who helped revise the schoolbooks. And above all it was they who, if only for their own interests, served as the political arm of the middle class in the final period of class struggle against the aristocracy.

The majority of the members of political societies such as the *Carbonari* were from the professional element, and middle-class revolutions were led by professional people. Journalists directed the French revolution of 1830. Professors led the delegation to urge reforms on the king of Prussia in 1848, and lawyers took the major role in the activities of the Frankfurt assembly. As parliamentary regimes spread, professional people again took a leading part as middle-class representatives. In all these activities the professional group worked for interests that the business elements also supported; but it continued to be the most politically conscious segment of the middle class.

In eastern and to an extent southern Europe, professional people served as an embryonic middle class by themselves by the beginning of industrialization, in the absence of a large, independent business group. By the mid-nineteenth century nonaristocrats were entering the professions in Russia in substantial numbers. Many were sons of Orthodox priests, another instance of the transfer from older to newer forms of professional mobility. By the end of the century there were over a half-million doctors, lawyers, and related professionals, many employed by local government agencies. In the typical pattern they too began to form professional associations and also raise political demands, playing a major role in the 1905 revolution.

Middle-Class Politics

Generalization about middle-class politics is difficult. Many businessmen had no particular political interest. They did not necessarily clamor for political rights. And they certainly did not insist on direct monopoly of political power. When they acquired the vote, as in Britain in 1832, they were content to let aristocrats continue to hold key ministries. But they did insist that government, no matter who ran it, fulfill certain key goals, and in this way they contributed to the continued modernization of the state. Very generally, most politically articulate members of the middle class were liberal. They wanted freedom of the press and of religion. They certainly wanted the state to get out of some traditional activities, such as support of guild restrictions and manorialism. Middle-class reformers worked further for the abolition of the slave trade and for state-sponsored education.

But the middle class also valued order. Riots ruined shops and factories, strikes and crime impeded the conduct of business. So the class supported restrictions on workers' rights to associate and the provision of new city police forces. It saw education as a means not only of training workers in new skills, which would make them better workers and possibly capable of rising in society, but also as an acculturation device that would make them docile. So the schools should teach religious and moral values, discouraging drink and disorder. Prison reform, similarly, was meant to be humanitarian; the middle class could grow appalled at the brutality of traditional punishments and pushed for reductions in torture and the use of the death penalty. But prisons should also teach criminals proper values and should keep them hard at work, for work was a panacea. Middle-class liberalism was thus a double-edged sword. It advocated new freedoms and was based on a genuine belief that men could be good. But it wanted the state to educate and rehabilitate, and in this way sought new political controls over the lives of the lower classes. Even lower-class entertainments had to be supervised. New middle-class city governments quickly abolished bear baiting and cock fighting as brutal and sometimes moved against gambling as well.

The middle class wanted an efficient state that would not waste money. There was a profound suspicion of government, a holdover from the age when aristocratic elements had used the state to restrict economic growth. Even after obvious anomalies such as guilds had been destroyed many middle-class politicians had to fight the aristocratic effort to win special support for agriculture. British businessmen, particularly, were driven to a high level of political interest by their opposition to the Corn Law of 1815, which set high tariffs on grain and therefore, by making food more expensive, increased their wage costs. Their political agitation helped lead to the suffrage reform of 1832 and twelve years later the Corn Laws were abolished. There was a general impulse to believe that, if the state would leave people alone and keep its activities to a minimum, the public interest would be best served.

But the middle class also saw new, more positive roles for the government. This view was stronger in Germany, where the government was traditionally active and relatively efficient, than in France or England, but the impulse was fairly widespread. Reformers who wanted to moralize and control the lower classes usually turned to government support. It was the state that could outlaw gambling. It was the state that could undo some of the worst effects of industrialization, by regulating child labor, for example. Most elements of the middle class, including many industrialists, came to accept the notion of some minimal state regulation in the general interest, and child labor laws were passed throughout western Europe during the 1830s and 1840s. Though not fully enforced, they did limit the age of entry to work and the hours children could be employed. Still more obviously the state could promote the economic interests of the middle class by providing tariff protection for industry, transportation facilities, and the like. Urban administrations were urged to build streets, drainage systems, parks, libraries, and schools. The growing vigor of city governments was due primarily to middle-class demands and interests.

The middle class came to recognize that the kind of state it wanted could only come from middle-class participation. Typically, politically active elements of the class pushed for municipal reforms that would give them control of city governments; and they advocated national suffrage systems based on property qualifications that would associate the vote with success in business. Correspondingly, they pushed for a parliamentary system that would give their representatives a voice. Parliaments were installed in all middle-class revolutions, from France in 1789 to Russia in 1905 and 1917, and the power of parliament was jealously protected and promoted by all major middle-class parties, such as the Prussian Progressives in the 1860s. Only with a constitutional, parliamentary regime did the middle class feel that its political interests could be realized.

Middle-class political interest was increasingly attached to the concept of the nation as well as to the ideal of parliamentary rule. This was the class to which nationalist doctrines particularly appealed. The middle class saw the nation as a vital economic unit. It needed a national market for its goods and national protection of its economic interests. Nationalism also gave the class a focus distinct from attachment to traditional dynasties and aristocratic political principles. After the revolution of 1830 the new king, Louis Philippe, ruled not by hereditary right but as king of the French. In Britain,

France, and Belgium, where national existence was established by the 1830s and where the middle class participated in government, nationalism was expressed in pride in existing national institutions and the belief that one's own nation was morally superior to others. Elsewhere, as in Germany and Italy, the middle-class interest in nationalism obviously worked for political change. Middle-class political groups sought national unity along with constitutional, parliamentary regimes. In parts of eastern Europe a small middle class was often instrumental in introducing nationalism. Greek and Serbian merchants were exposed to nationalism in trade with the west during the French revolutionary period. Bulgarian merchants, a new group after 1850, inspired much nationalist activity. Middle-class intellectuals spread nationalist ideas in many areas. Here again a passion had been aroused in the middle class that was to have profound political consequences.

During the first half of the nineteenth century, and later in parts of eastern Europe, the middle class was dissatisfied with existing regimes, although few members of the class agitated actively. Where there was sufficient liberty of the press, middle-class newspapers attacked governmental conservatism and aristocratic rule. In Restoration France and before 1832 in England, meetings were held and groups formed to agitate for reform of the suffrage, greater protection of liberty, and real limitation of the role of the aristocracy in government. In Spain, Italy, and Germany middle-class activity could not be so open, but there were some publications and discussion groups that condemned the established order. A minority of the middle class, drawn particularly from young professionals and students, went beyond discussion and actually joined groups for agitation. Masonic groups in Spain, the *Carbonari* in Italy, and the *Burschenschaften* in Germany drew significant numbers into vigorous political discussion and sometimes protest.

In certain circumstances the middle class countenanced direct action, even revolution, in pursuit of its political goals. It is incorrect to say that the class itself revolted. Businessmen were seldom on the streets in revolutions, although they might shut their shops and encourage their employees to riot. The interest in personal security was too great for participation in actual violence; and after revolution broke out, the class was quick to form and join national guard units to preserve order. There was, nevertheless, a series of middle-class revolutions in the first half of the century in most western and central European countries. Middle-class intellectuals prepared the doctrines for these revolutions, doctrines that were accepted quite widely in the class. Middle-class groups typically provoked the revolutions and controlled the revolutionary governments, which sought liberal parliamentary and nationalist goals.

Most of the revolutions failed to establish a government wholly conforming to the middle-class ideals, but even where revolutions were directly defeated, as they were in Germany and Italy in 1848, the succeeding years brought some of the reforms the middle class desired. Parliaments were established, although their powers were limited. Middle-class economic interests were promoted, and national unities were achieved. The middle class did not rule in its own right; it shared power with the aristocracy and compromised its principles with those of the old regime. Nevertheless, a major political role was now assured.

After 1848, in fact, the era of middle-class revolutionary activity was over in western and central Europe. The class had made sufficient economic and political gains that it could be relatively content and the revolutions themselves had heightened its interest in order. Particularly in 1848, the agitation by the urban lower classes, culminating in such bloody riots as the June Days in Paris, attached the middle class to existing governments even when such governments were not fully satisfactory. The class did not lose an interest in parliamentary rule and other reforms, but efforts for change worked within the legal structure. In most countries the class had won some freedom of the press, through which opinions could be expressed. It had won a parliament, albeit often a weak one, in which further changes could be proposed. It had gained new bureaucratic jobs. After the 1848 revolution thousands of new judgeships were created in Prussia, and the Austrian bureaucracy expanded mightily to fill the void left by the abolition of manorialism. The middle class had dislodged the aristocracy from total control. It would now defend its interests in a calm and orderly way.

Middle-Class Economics

What the middle class did economically was more important than what it thought about the economy, but a general outlook was significant as well. The middling class most typically wanted an economic structure based on small, family-owned units. They valued a wide distribution of property. This could lead them to a laissez-faire view, in which the virtues of free competition were praised. Certainly liberal economists in the early industrial period urged the good effects of individual effort, which through competition would produce more and more goods at lower and lower prices. But the middling class feared freedom too, and might turn to the government for assistance.

The leaders of the middle class rarely thought in laissez-faire terms. They used the theories on occasion, particularly to defend against government interference or criticism of industry from the outside. Liberal theories were popularized in many middle-class journals, which spread the ideas and slogans. But the middle class was interested in promoting security as well as individualism and it differed from the middling class in being open to new forms of organization. It steadily modified the family firm approach by developing larger, more bureaucratized business units. And, even in this early industrial period, it went beyond the individual firm.

Cooperation was one means of reducing competitive pressure. Industrialists' associations developed early to share technical information or even to allocate markets and supplies. The middle class also sought government encouragement for the economy. Except in Britain almost all entrepreneurs insisted on tariff protection. They might feel that internal competition was valuable, but they certainly had no desire to face foreign goods. Most businessmen also sought government encouragement of experts, provision of better transport systems, and the like. A smaller number of manufacturers sought government controls on quality and on conditions of work in the interest of modifying excessive competition. There were even proposals, fairly common during the July Monarchy, for example, for a system of government licensing aimed at restricting overproduction and crises. The middle class remained fundamentally optimistic about the course of the economy, for usually its purposes were being realized; but it was not wedded to a concept of complete individualism. Its openness to new forms of organizational control would become progressively more important.

Middle Class and Lower Class

The middle class did not innovate as fully in its view of the lower classes as it did in politics or economics. There was a great deal of ignorance of working-class life, particularly as businessmen and professionals moved to separate areas of the city in order to avoid the worst urban problems. Many never penetrated the poorest quarters of the city. They saw some workers and beggars, but knew nothing of their life, so it was easy to accept general stereotypes. Their own servant girl was often dirty and ill mannered, in their view, which might enhance the barriers to understanding. There were many gaps between the middle class and the urban lower classes. Speech was different. Many artisans and workers had distinctive accents or dialects; some were even foreign. The middle class usually prided itself, after the first generation at least, on pure pronunciation. The class stressed cleanliness and respectable clothing. Workers, in contrast, were often dirty, ragged, even diseased, and to middle-class eyes they were unpleasant to look at. The middle class urged hard work, whereas many workers valued leisure and took time off when they could. The middle class valued saving; the lower classes had little to save and often preferred to spend any margin for enjoyment. The drinking and sexual immorality of many workers were widely criticized. The lower classes seemed often disorderly because of their penchant for rioting and the roughhousing in which many workers engaged.

All this led the middle class to a firm belief that workers were inferior. It brought some to a fear that the poor were becoming increasingly degenerate and brutal. The middle class was prone to exaggerate crime waves and, at an extreme, to see the urban poor as virtual animals, who had to be controlled.

This was not the most common view, however. Exaggerated optimism was at least as widespread. The middle class was uncomfortable with poverty; this was one of its innovations in outlook, even though it produced few quick results. The class was thus open to arguments that poverty was not really there. Publicists often exaggerated improvements in clothing or diet. Great stress was laid on political reforms that freed the workers from the restrictions of guild and feudal lord. Technical developments such as gas lighting were assumed to be of benefit to all. Many observers claimed that workers could always earn enough in good times to cover their needs in bad. Others noted the beneficence of the factory system in giving work to women and children, who would otherwise be left without resource and without proper discipline. Mine owners might claim that their employees gloried in the possibility of working in a soothing pit, sheltered from the glare of sun and the beating of rain. The tendency to see a silver lining in every lower-class cloud relieved the consciences of the middle class and dulled any willingness to take positive action for reform.

However, optimism was not the only reaction of the middle class to the problems of the poor. The class could not be blinded to some of the horrible features of working-class life. Employers, after all, did see their own workers in the plant at least. Crime, riots, and begging indicated that all was not well. Government investigations of the conditions of child labor, carried on in Britain and France in the 1830s and 1840s, were covered by the press, and private reports by doctors like James Kay in Britain and René Villermé in France received considerable publicity. Local middle-class groups also sponsored surveys of labor conditions. Only the most fatuous members of the middle class persisted in asserting that all was well.

Confronted with the evidences of lower-class poverty, the middle class sought a scapegoat. Some said the fault was with the cities; others blamed foreign countries or distant regions for unfair competition that forced conditions down. Some still maintained that poverty was inevitable; did the Bible not say so? Many employers were honestly if occasionally saddened by their workers' lot but felt powerless to do anything about it. Many blamed the conditions of the poor on the poor themselves. There was a deep-seated belief that poverty must somehow be the result of moral inadequacy. Anyone with merit could rise in middle-class society. If workers would save, they would be protected from misery and could even rise; middle-class pamphlets pointed out how easy saving was. If workers would stop drinking, they would have both more money and more energy. Some manufacturers in France claimed that workers spent a quarter of their income on drink and that if they gave up drink they might be rich. If the poor had a decent family life, they would work harder, train their children better, and avoid the exhaustion of sexual debauchery.

The view that the poor were immoral justified a great deal of neglect of social problems. Why help those who would not help themselves? In 1834 the British parliament passed a new Poor Law designed to make poor houses as unattractive as possible. As the poor were to blame for poverty, they should not be encouraged to take charity. Middle-class city government quickly outlawed begging, a major departure from traditional urban life. The same belief in the immorality of the poor justified such political measures as restricting the vote to the well-to-do. Society was fundamentally a hierarchy with the meritorious rising to the top. The same view of the immoral poor conditioned many of the reform efforts that were made. This approach, harsh and unfeeling as it was, came closest to being innovative. For it had some optimistic roots: if workers could reform morally, they might become civilized, that is, just like the middle class. British manufacturers, who began their conduct of factories with a traditional belief that workers were inferior but deserved help from charity, moved increasingly to a view that workers could or should take care of themselves, like any human being. This excused neglect: workers were responsible for industrial accidents, even when no safety devices were provided. But it left workers considerable personal freedom. Some, by showing ambition, could win the respect, even friendship of the employer. Finally, on a more general level, the moralistic approach could lead to reform efforts. It obviously supported the effort to spread education. As one English observer noted, "Virtue is the child of knowledge, vice of ignorance: therefore education, periodical literature, railroad traveling, ventilators, and the art of life, when fully carried out, serve to make a population moral and happy." Industrialists actively promoted technical training, if only out of self-interest, and although there were a few that felt education was dangerous, in giving workers new ideas, the expansion of schools, by private associations and by the state when in middle-class hands, was extremely rapid. Reformers also worked for limitations on child labor, for it was hard to argue that workers could improve themselves when they were committed to hard labor at six or eight years of age. Efforts to encourage saving were in the same vein. So was the periodic belief that workers could be political allies. The middle class, responsible for much harshness toward the poor, was also responsible for many efforts at amelioration. The real reformer was rare. Most middle-class people spent little money or effort on moralization programs. But the ameliorative streak did produce some results and it did leave the middle class open to later change.

Neither harshness nor reform efforts characterized the most typical approach toward the poor. The middle class did not, in this period, really abandon the traditional attitudes. Although not liking poverty they did not believe that much could be done about it. Although disliking charity, not only because it cost money but also because it provided no basic remedy, they saw no other solution, and continued to rely heavily on it. Hand-me-downs and tips to the servant, a bit of money for the worker who was sick, an annual contribution to a charity fund—these were all that could be done. The poor were not seen as unusually degraded, but rather as naturally inferior people. Of course they drank too much, of course they were sexually immoral, but these were really the simple pleasures necessary for a life of hardship. Workers were often compared to children, who could be allowed a bit of frivolity but who should also be controlled by their natural superiors. As long as they were grateful and did not trouble the social order, they deserved charity when they fell on hard times.

In the bigger factories this approach, combined with the need to tie skilled workers to the firm, produced a paternalistic program that was often quite ambitious, particularly on the Continent. Companies built houses for their workers, set up aid programs for illnesses, constructed clinics, and so on. The result could be of real benefit to the worker, but it could severely limit his freedom as well. For the worker who offended his employer could be evicted from his home; if fired, he would have no right to claim the funds he had contributed to the company insurance funds. All of this followed from the interests of the firm in having a stable, docile labor force, but also from the broader view of the worker as an inferior incapable of helping himself.

During the first industrial period the failure to modernize social outlook, even if modified by hints of a new approach, did not have serious repercussions for the middle class. Servants stole a bit or made fun of their masters behind their backs; workers sometimes robbed materials from the factory. Both groups changed jobs often, to maintain a sense of freedom. But there was no general attack on the middle class, and these individual efforts simply heightened the belief that the lower orders were irresponsible. The general unrest of the period was not directed at the middle class specifically. Only in the next stage of modernization would the class's social outlook be explicitly tested.

Middle-Class Culture

The middle class had sufficient funds and education to develop cultural interests, and middle-class values accordingly had great influence on the general development of the arts in the nineteenth century. At the beginning of the industrial revolution the cultural interests of the middle class were relatively simple. The tastes and habits of many members of the class reflected those of their parents in lower levels of the middle class or in rural society. Few businessmen had substantial resources for cultural activity, and fewer still had time. In London, for example, even substantial businessmen could not afford to attend concerts regularly until after 1840.

On the Continent, particularly in the larger cities, there was a tradition of theater-going even for the lower middle class. But in industrial cities, and in Britain generally, simple amusements were the rule.

Cultural activity centered around the home and was largely confined to furnishings and decorations, items useful in daily life that provided some status among friends. The middle class sought comfort, neatness, and some sentimentality in its decorations. Typical of this taste was the Biedermeier style, which dominated German bourgeois furnishings and paintings during the mid-nineteenth century. The Biedermeier style stressed simple, manageable furnishings that would not take up too much space, decorated without great imagination or luxury. Wallpaper was crowded with picturesque designs; it was cheaper than it had been in the eighteenth century and became common in middle-class homes for the first time. Paintings in middle-class homes were generally either portraits or sentimental country scenes. Again, the interest was in a setting that would be at once comfortable and respectable. The class had neither the time nor the background for ostentatious designs.

The reading interests of the middle class also centered in the home. Men kept up with political and economic news in their newspapers and journals. Both newspapers and magazines increasingly stressed accounts of technical and scientific developments. Many middle-class views on progress were reflected in and furthered by this reading. Beyond this there was a general interest in stories suitable for family reading. Families often read aloud in the home. Newspapers and magazines provided serialized stories for such reading; authors such as Charles Dickens derived most of their income from these stories, sentimental narratives that were particularly pleasant for the women, whose formal education was slight. Such a magazine was *Die Gartenlaube* in Germany, which jumped from 5,000 subscribers in 1853 to 225,000 in 1867, as the middle class rose to greater prominence. *Die Gartenlaube* offered articles on science and education, the paths to progress; it editorialized against traditional superstition and for humanitarian causes. Its stories stressed the moral value of family and property. It condemned the aristocracy and often in stories portrayed the idleness and immorality of nobles as a shocking, but somewhat exciting, contrast to bourgeois virtue. Novels for the lower middle class in Germany went even farther in sensationalism, as well as sentimentality, although they too were always careful to let morality triumph.

Apart from home decoration and reading, the principal cultural interest of the middle class in the early nineteenth century was religion. In cosmopolitan centers such as Paris, where educational levels were unusually high, the middle class inclined to skepticism in matters of religion. Generally, however, the class maintained a firm tradition of church attendance and religious interest. Some industrialists came from intensely religious backgrounds. The Nonconformists in England entered industry in large numbers and long preserved their religious fervor. Protestant leaders of industry in Alsace and Switzerland tried to combine work and prayer. Some began each workday in the factory with collective prayer and Bible reading; many attributed their economic success to the will of God. Catholic manufacturers in northern France displayed similar religious intensity. Later, fervent Old Believers played a major role in early Russian industrialization, again combining religious zeal and economic activity. Church attendance was important to the middle classes during the early industrial period; for women particularly, religious practices provided an important outlet. Children were trained in the principles of religion and often were sent to church schools.

The middle class had little interest in theology and ceremony. Doctrines of sin and the afterlife were accepted, but were not the focal points of middle-class religion. In fact, the middle-class values of material success and the ability of the individual to improve himself tended increasingly to contradict the traditional stress on otherworldly goals and original sin. Beyond this the middle class was generally opposed to the political powers of established churches. In countries where there was a tradition of a dominant state church, as there was in France and the Scandinavian states, the middle class proved particularly hostile to religion generally. In Britain and Germany the multiplicity of religions reduced the political issues surrounding the churches, although even there important conflict arose. The middle class resented religious intolerance and its enforcement by a state. It resented the power of aristocrats in the established churches. Neither traditional theology nor church politics attracted the middle class to religion.

Religion did fulfill three vital functions for the middle class. It provided a social focus; for most women church attendance was one of the only regular contacts outside the home. Religion was regarded as useful for the masses; it promoted morality and the acceptance of hardship on earth in the expectation of reward in heaven. Most important, religion served as a source and sanction for morality for middle-class families themselves. The class sought sermons and religious reading that would explain the beauty and utility of moral behavior. This did not add up to intense religious interest necessarily, though it gave churches a new source of funds. With each new generation middle-class religious interest in fact declined.

Outside of home and church, the cultural activities of the middle class were few. Some women did a bit of painting and took music lessons, but this was rare. Music was not widely known except as part of church services or family entertainment; by 1800 most homes in the English upper middle class had pianos. Theater attendance was generally uncommon; in England many businessmen felt that it was a waste of time, and some regarded it as immoral. Not until 1850 did the British middle class begin to show an interest in drama. When it did, it applied to the theater the tastes it had developed in reading. It wanted sentimental and instructive plays, and it insisted on more comfortable theater seats.

These early trends in middle-class culture were not permanent. They did, however, contain certain durable principles. The class demanded that literature and art be moral. Erotic references were unacceptable, and governments during the period often tried to ban works such as *Madame Bovary,* which seemed too daring. Literature was to portray the value of hard work and thrift and show how these qualities allowed men to rise in society. It was to avoid subjects such as crime and was not to dwell on life among the poor, for such topics could not offer proper lessons for family reading.

Cultural products were also to be useful. They should provide information. The class did not care for flights of fancy; it preferred moderately realistic portrayals. Purely aesthetic experiences were not sought; art should decorate and represent, or it was a waste. Sentiment was entertaining and informing, but great emotions were dangerous. Scientists were particularly esteemed among intellectuals because their functions were so obviously useful; in fact, the middle class tended to confuse science with technology and praise both as motors of progress. Other intellectuals and artists were regarded with some suspicion, for they seemed preoccupied with abstract theories and were not motivated by a proper respect for wealth. Middle-class reading often contained portrayals of the wild life and subversive quality of some artists. The legend of the Bohemian artist was being born and would increase middle-class doubts about the morals and motives of writers and painters.

The middle-class cultural canons of utility and respectability both reflected and caused its educational interests in the early industrial period, for most members of the class had only primary schooling, plus some technical training. By the second or third generation of the industrial revolution, however, the cultural interests of the middle class broadened notably. By mid-century in Britain and France and a bit later in Germany the intense efforts of the middle class to found businesses had paid off in secure and rising incomes. The class had more leisure, for many businesses now had large staffs, which reduced the time required at work. The class developed the inclination to enjoy itself, although the stress on hard work and saving did not disappear.

The religious interests of the class tended to decline as material success became greater and as other opportunities for recreation arose. The class did not abandon the churches. It still regarded them as morally and socially useful, but its religious zeal abated. By the second generation it was noted that manufacturers in Zurich had become somewhat apathetic in religious practice; the same trend appeared later in Russia among middle-class Old Believers. By 1850 religious interest had declined notably in Britain, even among middle-class women, without turning to explicit hostility. In the second half of the nineteenth century some churches tried to accommodate the new interests of the middle class. Modernist movements in Protestantism and the rise of Reform Judaism were attempts to harmonize religion and science and de-emphasize unappealing doctrines such as original sin and the possibility of damnation. These trends reflected not only the continued attachment of the middle class to aspects of religion but also their lack of traditional piety.

After the first generation or two of industrialization, the wealthier elements of the middle class began to patronize music, art, and literature extensively. New levels of education played a great role in this process. Sons of successful business families were given more education and were sent to more traditional schools. In the early nineteenth century the middle class derided the classical stress of traditional secondary schools. Middle-class magazines urged the importance of science, modern languages, history, and other useful subjects, and the class sent its sons to schools that provided such subjects. About mid-century, however, the focus changed. Business families in France began to abandon the cheaper colleges in favor of the more prestigious and more classical lycées. The great British public schools were investigated in the 1860s and did introduce some modern subjects; but although they changed only slightly, the upper middle class supported the schools eagerly now that its sons could enter them. The educational interests of the upper business group, the leading professional families, and the aristocracy increasingly merged. The bulk of the middle class could not follow this pattern; its education remained more limited and utilitarian. In fact, it was cut off from the upper-middle-class families by the new educational gap.

To demonstrate their social prestige middle-class families sought clear, almost official canons of taste. They shunned cultural innovations that might prove socially unacceptable in favor of firm, respectable standards. As vacations and travel became fashionable, travel guides were printed, and travel agencies formed to arrange safe and respectable itineraries for the increasing numbers of eager but inexperienced middle-class tourists. In the 1840s Thomas Cook opened in London the first major travel agency. Spas such as Brighton and Folkestone were patronized in imitation of aristocratic resorts. They might be dull, but they became symbols of status.

The middle-class interest in creating socially acceptable institutions led to growing support for opera companies and symphony orchestras, institutions that enjoyed aristocratic patronage as well. Permanent symphony orchestras were established in many cities for the first time. Concert prices were reduced, which allowed many middle-class families to attend, and the new numbers and wealth of middle-class patrons increased the professionalization of concert music. German symphony performances even in Beethoven's time had usually involved a temporary collection of semiprofessional musicians, and the quality of playing was often very poor. The change in middle-class culture promoted a real improvement in musical performances.

The new patrons of art preferred works that met the conservative standards set by established academies, such as the British Royal Academy. Aside from portraiture, middle-class purchases of art were concentrated on the old masters, whose paintings had clear prestige and would be trophies as well as decorations. The new interest in the old masters was so intense that the forgery of masterpieces became a substantial business.

Middle-class libraries, similarly, were heavy with the older, safer works. The upper middle class in Paris in the 1840s bought more eighteenth- and seventeenth-century classics than contemporary works.

Magazines and books like J. C. Louden's *Encyclopedia* in Britain gave guidance for taste in furniture. The interiors of wealthy homes were elaborate and often showy. They scorned unity of design for an interest in accumulating decorative objects. Heavy furniture and fringed curtains were combined with Chinese figurines. An impression of wealth and profusion, with a continued interest in comfort, dominated many middle-class homes.

In many ways the architectural standards of the nineteenth century best exemplified the taste of the rising middle class. Expensive, ornate mansions became badges of middle-class wealth. Standards were again sought in the past. Imitations of classical and even byzantine style rivaled re-creations of the Gothic. These imitations, however, were usually modified to reflect a new interest in massive form and luxuriant detail. The French architect Viollet-le-Duc restored many Gothic buildings in France and England, often adding battlements and ornamentation unknown to the middle ages but appropriate to the new age of luxury. If the nineteenth century cannot be viewed as a triumph of taste, it can be seen as a vast development of a self-conscious interest in culture. The middle class, massive in numbers, rose from simple, traditional taste to an eager search for cultural prestige.

Finally, growing interest in dancing, choral concerts, and cafés gave new impetus to what might be called a professional recreational industry. Though not rich enough to contribute to formal architectural styles, sometimes too poor to furnish more than a single room with any luxury, the bulk of the middle class had a bit of money to spend on entertainment and it was beginning to move this interest outside of home. Here was the beginning of what would, in the next stage of modernization, constitute a new definition of what leisure is for.

Middle-Class Families and Middle-Class Women

It was within the context of the family that the middle class made its final contribution to modernization in the early industrial period. Indeed its action here was more significant that its impact on formal culture, for this was an area of vital importance to the class as a whole.

The tight official structure of the middle-class family is well known. Children were expected to be respectful and discipline was strict. Careful economic arrangements were made for them. On the Continent legal marriage contracts stipulated levels of dowry, and many weddings were carefully arranged with an eye to economic advantage. Many a textile fortune was made when a spinning plant married a weaving mill, in the persons of their respective male and female heirs. In England dowries and contracts were less general, but economic interest was seldom absent. Many businessmen everywhere liked to marry their daughters to professional men; this gave the professional some needed capital, and the businessman gained a sense of prestige. In western Germany, about half of the women married to government bureaucrats in the early nineteenth century were from business families. Concern for the future of sons was obvious, in the effort to build up a firm for him to train in and finally take over and/or the interest in a solid education. The desire to assure the family's future gave much of the sense of purpose to the hard work and economic innovativeness that characterized the class.

With wives relationships often seemed formal as well, but a middle-class woman had to hope for marriage (and the vast majority did marry) because there were few respectable jobs open for women in the period. Yet wives were typically inferior to their husbands in law. In England the wife had no independent legal standing and could neither testify in court nor divorce her husband. Any earnings or property belonged to the husband. Much public culture, including that promulgated in many novels, suggested that women should cultivate their beauty, wear stylish clothes, learn social graces such as the piano, and in general serve as rather useless ornaments in the home. There undoubtedly was a sense in which businessmen, edgy after a long day spent in a rather novel and competitive economic effort, liked to return home to an attractive, submissive wife. Hamburg businessmen, for example, wanted wives who would know their place, embellish the home with embroidery, and rely on the dominant male; one wife, taken to London on a trip, dutifully burst into tears whenever she lost sight of her husband.

Women were also supposed to be guardians of morality. Here too might be an important refuge from the cutthroat business world. Certainly the morality publicists urged on the middle class was often severe. Particular attention was given to sexual restraint. There was a widespread belief that undue sexual activity was damaging to one's health, that sex involved expenditure of vital energy that could not be replaced. Certainly most doctors claimed this to be true. Women were held responsible for restraining their husbands, for their own sexual drives were believed much slighter. They should also train their children to be sexually pure, for not only premarital intercourse but above all masturbation were dangerous as well as disreputable. Elderly adults were also supposed to refrain from sexual activity. Much of this sexual ethic was quite traditional, from classic authors onward, simply receiving greater publicity in the nineteenth century with an expanding readership.

It is not hard to embellish this picture of a middle-class family caught in a network of inhibitions, ruled by the husband-father in authoritarian fashion. Unquestionably legal structure and the opinions of doctors and publicists played a role in actual family life. However, the real developments in the middle-class family went in quite different directions and would begin to change both culture and law. Many were spearheaded by the wife.

Toward children, middle-class families became increasingly attentive and affectionate. Concern began with infancy. Mothers were no longer willing to let the infant cry, as had been previous practice; a crying child needed loving attention. The practice of leaving infants in the care of others declined. Parisian mothers, long in the habit of sending babies out to the countryside to be wetnursed, began by the mid-nineteenth century to keep the wetnurse in the home, where she could be supervised, or to nurse themselves. British mothers almost entirely abandoned wetnursing and either nursed themselves or adopted bottle feeding. New attitudes toward the infant led into a revision of disciplinary ideas. Physical punishment was increasingly replaced by discussion. Children were indeed to be respectful, but they received more love (and took more of their mother's time) than before.

Older children were something of a problem, though this is an area just beginning to be explored by historians. The middle class did marry rather late, for economic reasons. Females, and males even more, married several years after puberty. Males might find some sexual outlets through prostitutes or even abuse of the family's servant girl; but such practices were frowned upon and certainly not universal, though many a French school boy spent part of his holidays in a local brothel. Middle-class girls, needless to say, were supposed to remain chaste until marriage. So the middle class did have to promote a rigorous sexual ethic for one stage of life, and the particular concern over masturbation, whose evil effects were held to range from sterility through brain damage, reflected this dilemma.

Between husbands and wives there was a growing division of labor. Except in the small shops, wives stopped participating in their husband's business after the first generation of industrialization. But this did not deprive them of functions, for their household was increasingly complex and they made the major decisions about family consumption patterns. The middle class, by definition, embraced growing numbers of people who had a disposable income, well above subsistence, for the first time. Wives administered much of this. Their desire for respectability meant a great deal of hard work, for the typical middle-class family could afford at best a single servant (indeed, despite the rapid growth of the servant class there were fewer servants than middle-class families even in the mid-nineteenth century). And not only child care but also notions of cleanliness were changing, perhaps in response to the filth of the cities. Wives put more and more effort into cleaning clothes, dusting furniture, scrubbing floors. They also sponsored gradual improvements in the household. By the mid-nineteenth century middle-class homes were acquiring indoor plumbing and a separate bathroom; flush toilets would soon follow. Other new equipment was added, notably the sewing machine. Middle-class wives were thus open to new technology, and their efforts spurred an important segment of the economy. Indeed it was to women, as the main agents of consumption, that advertising was principally directed. Finally, successful operation of the household required planning. Women learned to keep accounts and budget books. They bought major items on time, for a sewing machine was too expensive otherwise. In all this they asked for a great deal of advice from women's manuals and magazines.

For, although confined to home and family, middle-class women were developing a new outlook. They were becoming consumer-oriented. They were learning, if imperfectly, to think in terms of rational organization, just as their businessmen husbands were increasingly doing on the job. They were beginning, again hesitantly, to strive for material progress and technical improvements. They were, in sum, beginning to modernize.

New attitudes were also developing in the field of health. Women were becoming less fatalistic about pain and disease that had previously seemed inevitable. Increasingly they switched from midwives to obstetricians for childbirth. They consulted health manuals. They bought quack medicines because they were advertised as being scientific. They made some mistakes in all this. Sometimes indeed they caused their children's death by overfeeding, the first reaction to prosperity, or by dosing them with harsh drugs. But their interest was in improving the health of their children, and gradually they had some success. Fewer developments benefited their own health. Women did welcome the reduction of pain in childbirth that came with the use of chloroform, although ironically many doctors opposed this.

But the most important development in the middle-class family came with the reduction of the birth rate. By the 1820s in France, if not before, and at least by mid-century in England and Germany the number of children born to the average middle-class family began to drop steadily There were obvious economic reasons for this. Given the need to provide education and dowries, too many children were an obvious burden. The new concern for the individual child was possible only when there were fewer children to command attention. And the women wanted more time for their other functions and, quite possibly, less exposure to the pains and risks of childbearing. Probably wives and husbands in most cases jointly decided to limit their families to three or four children, but occasionally women may have decided on their own. For from about 1820 onward devices were introduced that allowed artificial birth control. Sponges and diaphragms were widely used by women, and their quality steadily improved. With the vulcanization of rubber in the 1840s condoms, which had long been known, also became more reliable and cheaper. Some middle-class women may have suffered a certain role confusion as their families became smaller, for motherhood had long been their proudest function. More commonly, concern for the quality of the child replaced concern for quantity. All of this represented an important step in the modernization of family life, and it would later spread more widely in society.

The new orientation of the family did cause strain. It was hard to keep pace with a consumer economy with a limited budget. Rents rose rapidly, which hit the middle class hard just as it was trying to improve living standards in other respects. Many had to flee to the suburbs, which were cheaper but involved commuting expenses; by the 1860s suburban populations were growing more rapidly than urban from London to Vienna. The desire for better family health outstripped the quality of medical practice, and many women suffered from health problems. A few, overburdened by their functions, turned to drink or, more commonly, the use of opiates, for opium-based drugs were widely sold. More commonly, women were able to adapt, particularly when birth control began to relieve their lot.

But what of husbands and wives? They did not see each other as often as in a traditional bourgeois family, for the husband's work increasingly took him away. But division of family labor was modified by a certain mutuality in decision making. At the same time marriage, though still based in part on economics, became somewhat freer; a couple made its choice with less parental guidance and with more chance for mutual affection. Within marriage sexual pleasure probably increased. The traditionalist advice was often ignored. Birth control devices certainly eliminated one customary inhibition on the wife's part. And they were advertised as doing so. For actual middle-class culture was by no means entirely strait-laced, and man and wife were urged to enjoy sex. Even a prosaic English doctor suggested: "During connection both husband and wife should endeavor to be in a happy state of mind. The wife especially should have happy thoughts when having connection." A more radical writer, widely read in the English middle class around 1820, was more explicit:

"The hypocrisy, the cruelty that would stifle or disguise a passion, whether in the male or in the female, is wicked, and should be exposed, reprobated, and detested. Young Women! Assume an equality, plead your passion when you feel it, plead it to those to whom it applies."

We are far from knowing the state of sex life in the early industrial middle class. Obviously there were criticisms of this and other changes in the class's life style, particularly from religious observers, and this may have caused some confusion. The need to avoid sex before marriage (at least for women) could hamper response once marriage occurred. But it is safe to assume that a new, more affectionate, and actually sexier relationship was developing in some middle-class households. And this new relationship began to inspire changes in law. The legal rights of married women were improved in several measures in Britain from 1857 onward, culminating in the Married Women's Property Act of 1870, which gave a wife the right to own her own property.

Middle Class and Modernization

Thus the middle class was caught up in a host of changes, of which economic innovation was only the most obvious. It sponsored an important new stage of political modernization. It took over the principal patronage of cultural activities, though with directions that were as yet less clear. There were lapses in the pattern of change, particularly in the outlook toward the lower classes. And the middle class, though now dominant in terms of values, had not wrested full power from the aristocracy. Finally, the rift between middle and middling class slowed the pace of change, and again not only in economics. The revolutions of 1848 revealed, particularly in Germany, that the middling class could be used to support a conservative regime, against the political goals of the middle class. But increasingly the framework of society was being set by the middle class, and its pioneering efforts, whether good or bad, were being extended to family functions and the position of women.

The Urban Lower Classes

The early industrial revolution compelled two quite different reactions from those who now found themselves in the urban labor force. The most obvious was the need to adapt to, or protest, strangeness. Factory workers new to both city and power machinery were the most rapidly growing social group. Right behind them were servants, almost entirely female. In both cases population had outstripped economic opportunities in the countryside, so like it or not something radically new had to be undertaken. But a large group of workers, still growing if more slowly, were not new to their jobs and many not new to urban life. Artisans remained a distinct force in urban society. They faced change too, but from a more established position. There is no possibility of discussing a single working class at this point. It is not even entirely clear which of the two main situations—total novelty or the temptation to defend established ways—was more troubling.

Finally, there remained the urban unskilled, whose ranks were swollen by immigration into traditional centers such as Paris. Their lot, bad before, was shared by more people. Some were young, both male and female, and cut off from parental direction as they moved to the city. Some were unable to get factory work, for cities like Paris had few factories as yet. Others worked as servants but were raped by an employer and then fired for having an illegitimate child, and so tumbled into the urban dregs. With new numbers, the slum section of all the older cities became increasingly foul. That crime went up among this group is hardly surprising. Urbanization seems to have brought a fairly steady rise in thefts, fraud, and suicides, though little or no increase in murders (the murder rate dropped in cities like Paris) and a decline in arson (the traditional rural crime). On the other hand lesser interpersonal violence (assault and battery) rose, and especially rapidly during the fastest period of urban growth. Here was a sign of tension that went well beyond the very poor, though it must be remembered that cities were not the only center of personal violence; many rural areas had higher rates. In some cases (this has been argued for England) crime of all sorts went down again once the worst urban confusion had passed, for more of the "criminal element" could find regular jobs. More commonly the increase in crime rates simply slowed. But we know little else about the condition of the urban poor in this period, and it obviously should not be assumed that most of them turned to crime. Their existence and extreme poverty could affect the attitudes of the middle class, as we have seen, though again they were concentrated mainly in a few centers, not in cities generally. They could affect the consciousness of other lower-class elements as well, for one might protest out of a fear of falling into this group or remain self-satisfied because it had been avoided.

The Artisans

Artisans remained the largest urban group for several decades and were widely distributed in cities generally. They were particularly prominent in major centers such as London and Vienna. As late as 1850 there were as many artisans as factory workers in Great Britain. In the 1860s artisans represented 60 per cent of the Prussian manufacturing force. In France artisans maintained a greater importance than in other European countries. At mid-century there were only 1.306 million workers in firms with over ten employees, and many of these were, of course, domestic manufacturers. The remainder of the industrial population, including 1.548 million employers and self-employed, worked in firms averaging two employees. Twenty years later, at the time of the Commune, the bulk of the Parisian workers were artisans. Of approximately 500,000 workers in a population of 1.8 million, 100,000 were construction workers; 110,000 worked in jewelry, furniture, and other luxury industries; 34,000 were printers; 41,000 worked in food processing; 115,000 worked in clothing and textiles, mainly in small tailoring and dressmaking shops. This was an unusual concentration; Paris served really as a center for craft production, exporting artisans' wares all over the world. But even factory centers in 1870 depended on artisan labor for most food processing, clothing, and construction work.

Until about 1850 in Britain and until at least 1870 elsewhere the number of artisans increased in proportion to overall population growth; for as population expanded and wealth increased with both agricultural and industrial improvements, the need for artisans rose. Industrialization itself fostered the development of some new small-shop crafts, notably in machine building. Flourishing cities required more carpenters and masons, more butchers and bakers, more tailors and shoemakers. With a very few exceptions early mechanical processes were not applicable to the kind of work done by urban artisans; in some cases they have not been widely applied to this day. A few urban branches of textile manufacturing, such as the finishing of wool cloth, were quickly affected. The printing industry underwent increased mechanization, although in this case artisan skills were not entirely displaced. Some female artisans, such as lace makers, were affected by the rise of competitive factory products. For the most part, however, it was rural home workers, not urban artisans, who were displaced by the new industrial processes. The decline of a few urban groups was more than balanced by the heightened demand for other major crafts. Most of the history of what has often been loosely termed "the working class" in the early industrial revolution is in fact a history of artisans. Workers in the crafts were increasing far less rapidly than workers in the factories, but they long continued to dominate in numbers, wealth, social cohesion, and purpose.

Stability of Habits

Before 1870 artisans were fairly distinct from factory labor. They usually worked in different places; artisans still relied on traditional skills and techniques and worked on their own or in very small units. Even residentially, there was only limited contact between the two classes. There were relatively few factory workers in major artisan centers such as London and Paris and in large numbers of traditional towns. Furthermore, artisans had traditional quarters of residence, usually in the center of a city, which factory workers did not fully penetrate. Sections such as the Faubourg Saint-Antoine in Paris remained artisan preserves. However, particularly in factory cities, there were opportunities for contact. Artisans saw factory workers as important potential allies in such movements as unionization and Chartism. To some extent they served as mentors to the new class, and workers often imitated artisan movements. But most artisans viewed the workers with some suspicion. They abhorred the factory system and its products, and they distrusted the coarseness and the violence of the working class. Ultimately, they found some kindred interests with the skilled elements of factory labor, but almost never did they identify with the working class as a whole.

Artisans remained a relatively stable class in personal habits and family structures. They had traditions in their work and in their city life to which they constantly referred. Even new artisans coming in from the countryside were assimilated to artisan values. Many had a craft background in the village that gave them a sense of status and dignity that few other workers had.

Many observers noted that even poor artisans were often better off than factory labor because they avoided showy spending on drink and on clothing. Thread twisters in Lille, for example, who earned about half the wage of factory spinners, frequently had better diets and cleaner housing and depended less on charity during crises. They were thriftier in good times, worked more steadily, drank less. Artisans generally, though they earned little more than workers, were far more inclined to save money. Similarly, their family structure was tighter. Artisans retained an interest in establishing their children in their own trade and educated them accordingly. Wives worked in the home, not in the factory. Most artisans carefully limited their family size by delaying marriage until their late twenties, in the interest of maintaining their material well-being and caring properly for the children they had.

The material standards of artisans still varied greatly. Single women had to work long hours to earn enough to survive. Craftsmen facing mechanical competition received low wages for increasing hours of work. Many Lyons silk workers labored sixteen or eighteen hours a day for pay that was barely sufficient to sustain life, though artisan masters usually had some comforts. Among the leading crafts, pay levels usually rose slightly. Carpenters or butchers could afford more stylish clothing and furnishings and could often save. They seldom needed to put their children to work until they were in their teens.

There were still many hardships. Construction workers and some others suffered from long periods of seasonal unemployment. Personal disasters, such as illness or age, could reduce a family to dire poverty.

Artisans suffered severely in economic crisis. Their wages fell, and they often experienced higher levels of unemployment than did factory workers. The need for artisan products, often in a semiluxury category, fell far more rapidly than did the need for factory staples such as clothing. And this crisis of falling wages and rising unemployment was, of course, usually accompanied by rising food prices. Only bare subsistence expenditures, appeals for charity, and sale or pawning of furniture and even vital tools could permit survival in these conditions. But the leading groups of artisans were not ordinarily impoverished; they had a small though insecure margin above subsistence.

Forces of Change

Other aspects of the artisan's life were changing far more steadily than purely material conditions. In times of prosperity as well as times of crisis some of the foundations of artisan economic and social values were being undermined, and far more radically than in the previous period.

Most basically, the principles of the rising new industry clashed with the principles of artisan economy. Artisans relied on stable skills; industry involved rapidly changing methods and the use of large numbers of unskilled workers. Skill and training were not eliminated in industry, but they were new and on the whole more easily learned; in few cases, for example, was prolonged apprenticeship required to enable a worker to perform his job adequately. The artisan's pace of work, involving frequent breaks and holidays, was threatened by the new machines. Artisans traditionally tried to protect themselves against competitive pressure by restricting both techniques and the size of the labor force. In industry limitations were removed; workers were hired as they were needed, machines introduced at will. The artisan interest in restraining the degree of inequality within manufacturing was also ignored in the new factories. Factory owners often acquired great wealth and tried to expand this wealth without clear limit. The gap between them and their workers was great, and it was rare for a worker to rise to the ranks of the manufacturer. The novelty of the factory system was a real shock to the artisan stress on stability.

Few urban artisans, of course, were forced into the factories. The threat of the factory system was more subtle. The rise of mechanized industry displaced artisans from a fundamental control of the urban economy. Their numbers rose, and their earnings grew slightly, but their relative position steadily declined. The working class expanded far more rapidly than did the ranks of the artisans, four times as rapidly in Germany by midcentury. The wealth of the new elements of the middle class eclipsed any increase in artisan pay; even some factory workers earned more than craft labor. Furthermore, factory industry was obviously dynamic and expansive. It had displaced many workers and might displace more. There was real concern among artisans, even those remote from branches of industry touched by machines, that the new principles of production might spread to their own trade.

A fear of displacement, more than actual displacement, dominated artisan activity in this period. The realization of the new challenge to artisan economic values caused many attacks on the factory system. Some artisans, directly threatened by mechanical processes, tried to destroy the factories themselves. Most areas went through a period of Luddism by urban artisans as well as some domestic workers. Nottingham glove makers destroyed a thousand new stocking frames in 1811–1812, and Yorkshire wool finishers attacked machines also. French wool finishers destroyed several machines after 1820. Craftsmen in Barcelona attacked new spinning machines between 1854 and 1856. Artisan newspapers, pamphlets, and petitions to the government often urged removal of machines. Pamphlets in Germany in the 1860s attacked the stock exchange, department stores, and the principle of division of labor. The Parisian newspaper *L'Atelier* warned constantly of the evils of factory industry.

Artisanal conditions were changing directly at the same time that factories posed their challenge. Not only guilds but also all worker associations were outlawed in Britain and France by the end of the eighteenth century. The French Revolutionary government spread the abolition of guilds wherever its armies conquered, and in most cases the abolition was retained even after the Revolution. By 1815 many west German and northern Italian states, and the Low Countries, had eliminated the guilds. Spain abolished guilds by 1836.

Most of Germany, particularly Prussia, was slower to act. Conservative governments continued to enforce guild exclusions until mid-century. In the 1840s the Prussian government, without abolishing guilds, removed the official support from guild exclusiveness; workers could now enter crafts without guild permission. After the revolution of 1848 aristocrats tried to ally themselves with discontented artisans by restoring the legal position of guilds. Only in 1868 did the Prussian government again allow work in the crafts without guild permission. The German guilds did not die as a result; they continued privately to enforce some exclusions and to serve as centers for defense of professional interests. There fundamental powers were nevertheless radically limited. But the tardiness of the attacks on the guilds allowed German artisans to remain attached to a traditional, even conservative, outlook that set them off significantly from artisans in the west.

In addition to the abolition of the guilds, the relationship between journeymen and masters changed rapidly during the nineteenth century. Although the number of artisans grew steadily, the number of masters did not. Masters increasingly tried to protect their own social and economic position in a changing economy by limiting their ranks. Some became employers rather than masters, for they had enough workers to avoid most manual labor themselves and concentrated instead on arranging for materials and sales. In the construction industry, large crews were formed with the master serving as a contractor. Masters in this situation increased their capital for the purchase of supplies and equipment, and thus made it more difficult for a journeyman to rise. The social relations between artisan and master were changed. It became less common for journeymen to be housed and fed by the master. The gradual development of a purely and permanently wage-earning status for journeymen, though not entirely new, was a profound shock to artisan tradition. All of this also reflected the vast immigration to the cities, for urban journeymen faced massive competition from village-trained craftsmen.

In other instances, masters and journeymen alike were forced into virtual employment by merchant capitalists. This was particularly common in the textile industry, where industrial capitalism was spreading rapidly, but it also occurred in some construction work and in some branches of metal work. Embroiderers, knife makers, and the like were increasingly assigned tasks by a foreman employed by a large merchant. They might work in their homes or in a master's shop, but their conditions were set outside the artisan system.

Finally, many new employers, whether merchants or masters, showed some tendency to neglect traditional methods of apprenticeship. If they hired children, they expected them to work more than to learn. Journeymen themselves, involved increasingly in a wage system, were often reluctant to delay their work by training a child. Apprenticeship continued except in a few decaying trades such as lace making, for the old traditions were not entirely violated. In a limited way, however, aspects of industrial organization were being applied to the crafts without a real introduction of a factory system. There were also efforts to speed the pace of work.

The social as well as the economic position of the artisans was changing. The artisan lost the social contact of the guilds at the same time that his links with his master were declining. His place in the city was also slipping as factory workers became more numerous and as new elements of the middle class rose to prominence and took a growing role in city government. Neither destitute nor uprooted, the artisan was nevertheless faced with major challenge.

The Reactionary Impulse

Artisans reacted to the challenge to tradition in a number of ways. There were some efforts to retain the old customs. The various attacks on machine industry, sometimes physical but more often verbal, were an important sign of traditionalism. A number of groups tried to maintain the guilds. British joiners and shoemakers retained some guild structure into the nineteenth century. This retention was primarily for social purposes, as the organizations raised few economic demands. Similarly, French carpenters joined traditional secret groups called *compagnonnages,* which were related to the guilds. The *compagnonnages* dealt with matters of apprenticeship and working conditions but again were primarily social organizations. They arranged for the traditional tours of France by young journeymen and provided an elaborate ritual for the entertainment of their members. The importance of these various guild remnants gradually declined and never involved more than a minority of the class as a whole.

Only in Germany and Austria was there a persistent effort to preserve the guilds, for only in Germany did conservative classes have sufficient power to allow some hope of success. Hence the major demand of German master artisans in the revolution of 1848 was for full restoration of the guilds, which had after all only recently been threatened in states such as Prussia. The German artisans, spurred by two previous years of intense economic crisis, rioted in many cities, petitioned the revolutionary government, and even assembled a national congress of their own in June 1849, in an effort to win their demands. They wanted guilds to restrict the number of workers, wanted regulations and taxes to limit the output of factories, and wanted the state itself to guarantee work. In Prussia during the 1850s the restoration of the guilds simply encouraged the artisans' attachment to a conservative social order. Having been rebuffed in their revolutionary demands by the middle-class assemblies, which sought economic freedom instead of guild restrictions, they turned against middle-class liberalism. The attacks by artisan pamphleteers on new industrial and commercial methods increased even in the 1860s; and as they acquired the vote, many German artisans attached themselves to conservative parties.

The German case represented an extreme of the general suspicion of modern trends. Even in Germany artisans west of the Rhine, where guilds were abolished during the Napoleonic period and where regimes were relatively liberal, did not concern themselves greatly with restoration of the guilds. Less formally, however, journeymen as well as masters almost everywhere tried to retain some guild benefits through other associations. German journeymen, now at odds with their masters' restrictiveness, did not ask for guilds in 1848, but they did want the right to associate to control their wages and conditions of work. In many towns even journeymen continued to be able to monopolize certain occupations. In Marseilles, several trades were dominated by sons following their fathers into work; hence 69 per cent of all masons had been born in Marseilles, as against 50 per cent of the skilled labor force in general. So we need not exaggerate the disruption of artisanal traditions. The adaptation of most artisans consisted of a clever mixture of older habits, based around defense of a rare skill, and newer goals; craft unionism was ultimately one product of this mixture.

The Self-help Impulse

At the opposite pole from the reactionary impulse, many artisans adapted older habits in an effort to seek individual improvement. Traditions of training could convert to a new interest in education; habits of saving might be diverted from purchase of a mastership to the establishment of a more modern small business.

Most commonly artisans attempted to earn more money by working hard and improving themselves within their craft. Many developed a great interest in education, and artisan groups and publications commonly stressed this as a means of self-improvement. In Britain, Mechanics' Institutes were established to provide a variety of technical and commercial training. Courses in accounting, chemistry, practical mathematics, and the like, established in most French cities, were attended particularly by artisans, although often intended by their middle-class founders to benefit factory workers.

The vast majority of urban artisans were now literate, and some purchased and read books and newspapers fairly regularly. By the 1840s a number of artisan newspapers were appearing in Britain and France, often with great stress on political and social problems. Artisans sought entertainment above all from their reading, however, and cheap novels and periodicals were more popular. They stressed sentiment and sensation, and they purveyed tales of supposed aristocratic immorality.

Artisans also tried to improve themselves by saving. Savings banks spread fairly widely during the period, and artisans and servants were their principal patrons among the lower classes. Many artisans undoubtedly banked the funds that in an earlier period they would have devoted to buying a master's position. Elements of the artisan class were patterning themselves upon the values of the rising middle classes. The interest in self-improvement, education, and saving was frequently urged by the middle class, in speeches and in pamphlets, as the path to happiness and success. These recommendations undoubtedly caught the attention of a class that had a sense of pride and that sought a respected place in a society increasingly dominated by the middle class.

Some artisans rose out of their class altogether. It was not unrealistic, once guild restrictions were lifted, to start a small business on one's own. In an artisanal city such as Vienna small firms proliferated in the first stage of industrialization, ironically reducing the average size of the firm (to only 1.3 workers per company). Many little shops failed; a few started their owners on the ladder toward middle-class status; still more swelled the ranks of the middling class, for a tailor or shoemaker was proud of the small family business. And artisans interested in mobility were found entering the noncommissioned army officer corps in France, the priesthood, and some of the lower professions. Far more artisans sought mobility than found it, without doubt, but this was a questing group and even hope for advancement might long sustain a journeyman. Finally many artisans left the shop for the factory. Early industrialization required masses of skilled workers, and the artisanry was a vital source of recruitment. Particularly in machine and metal factories, artisans with training as blacksmiths or locksmiths were in high demand. They could earn more money than their journeymen brethren, and although they were subjected to more rigorous supervision, their values of skill and pride in their work were not lost.

Many artisans thus had some range of choice in reacting to industrialization. Although pressed increasingly into the status of paid labor, journeymen were not yet proletarianized; even when they entered the factories their earnings and mutual interactions made them an aristocracy among labor.

Political Interest

Artisans also tried to raise their political and social status. They increasingly wanted the vote, particularly in western countries where the middle classes possessed or actively sought suffrage. In Germany, where political interest even in the middle class was relatively low, artisans were also less active. During the revolution of 1848 they made some demands on the government, including free state education, provision of credit for artisan shops, and support for the ill and maimed; but they showed little interest in political rights or in changing political forms. Even so, there was political consciousness: in the city of Halle in 1848, 81 per cent of the artisan masters and 71 per cent of the journeymen voted, compared to 46 per cent of factory labor.

In France, where the Revolution had provided a brief experience of universal suffrage and political action, especially in Paris, and in Britain, where the middle class sought and gained the vote in 1832, political activity made even more sense to many artisans. French artisans who filled the streets in 1830 were acting specifically against the existing monarch and for a change in the political system. During the July Monarchy some artisans joined republican groups and pressed for universal suffrage. British artisans were even more persistent before 1848 in seeking the vote. Before the Reform Bill of 1832 many joined with middle-class elements in associations and meetings to promote an extension of the suffrage. After 1832 artisans, particularly in London, took the lead in forming the Chartist movement to seek universal male suffrage and other political reforms. They held meetings, passed resolutions, sometimes threatened violence, and circulated gigantic petitions to further their cause. On three occasions, in years of economic crisis, the movement drew a great following, including factory workers as well as artisans. In 1839 a Chartist petition was signed by 1,280,000 people, and in 1842, 3,317,702 signed a new appeal. After a final abortive effort in 1848 the movement collapsed, and many artisan organizations turned away from politics.

The artisans sought political change for many reasons. They wanted the state to aid their self-improvement efforts by providing educational facilities. They hoped that their votes would induce the state to take economic action in their behalf. The Chartists, for example, had a vague belief that political reforms would result in the ending of poverty. Parisian artisans in 1848 felt that their control of the government would bring a new organization of work that would restore artisan forms of production and eliminate unemployment. Finally, artisans sought political participation as one means of obtaining respect from other elements of society. The German artisans in 1848 who insisted that they be addressed with the formal *Sie* instead of the familiar *du* were expressing a general desire to be treated as equals by employers and other members of the upper classes. The search for political equality was an important effort along the same lines. In an age when established social positions were eroding, the artisans attempted to assert their place in new ways.

Mutual Aid

In addition to efforts at self-improvement and at political reform, artisans utilized a variety of methods to better their economic position and provide greater social cohesion. These efforts continued some of the artisan economic traditions but in a new framework. They involved co-operation in the interest of collective economic security. They were organized along craft lines and were usually local.

The simplest and earliest form of artisan cooperation was the mutual aid group or friendly society. Most major cities had a variety of such groups for the leading crafts, which grew up quickly after guilds were abolished. The groups were far more extensive among the artisans than among factory workers. They provided aid in sickness and in death and often established technical courses, libraries, and recreational programs. Occasionally, aid groups conducted strikes as well.

Many crafts also formed unions to protect their economic interests, usually a few decades after aid groups began to form. Artisan union movements waxed and waned in most countries according to economic conditions. However, some individual locals persisted from the 1820s or 1830s in Britain and France. Groups such as printers' and carpenters' unions began in Paris in the 1830s and in London even earlier. Lyons silk workers had several large unions in the early 1830s, but government repression eventually reduced the movement. Printers and hatters formed short-lived associations in Italy in 1848, and in the 1860s more permanent unions grew out of aid groups.

In Britain artisan union efforts were unusually elaborate, aided by the easing of legal restrictions in 1824. In the early 1830s about half a million workers, led by members of the building trades, joined the Grand National Consolidated Trades Union under the leadership of Robert Owen. This group went well beyond the purposes of ordinary artisan unions and tried to reconstitute the economy on cooperative lines. After the failure of Chartism in 1848 and with the rising economic prosperity of the 1850s, the union movement among artisans and skilled workers increased substantially. Carpenters, iron founders, engineers, and the like dominated this movement, known as New Model Unionism; and they intentionally ignored the mass of factory workers. These unions attempted to be respectable and solid. They had large funds and professional officials. They urged temperance, saving, and hard work on their members and provided the benefits of a friendly society. They preferred to negotiate with their employers for improvement of wages and hours and conducted strikes only with reluctance. This was a quiet, exclusive movement operating on principles of collective benefit for members, very much in the artisan tradition.

The New Model Union movement was the most extensive and elaborate union effort developed among artisans before 1870 and the only one that went beyond purely local associations. But the methods of New Model Unionism were quite common. Parisian groups and the shorter-lived Lyons unions tried to established solid gains for their members in terms of wages and hours. They attempted to bargain collectively with their employers and a few cases did succeed in winning contracts that set the conditions for the whole profession in the city. Whether unionized or not, many artisans attempted strike movements that had a similar modern ring. Although not yet typical of artisanal protest, many small strikes in France as early as the 1830s were designed to take advantage of prosperous years to win better wages and shorter hours. In Italy, similarly, the first modern strike movement developed with printers in the 1860s. And always, in this first industrial period, the artisanal strike rate was higher than that of other workers. Some artisans were thus learning to use organization and moderate protest to win gains within the new economic order and to regain the voice in job conditions that they had lost with the collapse of the guilds. The more enduring artisan unions, then, worked carefully for major general gains within the existing system. They tried, with some success, to win a voice in craft conditions to compensate for the loss of guild controls.

One other form of organization elicited considerable artisan interest, though again only a minority of the class was involved. By mid-century a cooperative movement of some importance had developed in western Europe. There were two hundred cooperative associations in Paris in 1851, principally among artisans. A number of similar groups existed in Britain, particularly in London, and involved tailors, hatters, and the like. These groups tried to establish a new system of production based on artisan principles. They stressed the need for a period of apprenticeship and limited entrance to their group. They hoped to eliminate competition and mechanization at the same time. Some of the groups collapsed, and even the successful ones failed to gain control of the economy as their founders had often hoped. Many groups did provide economic assistance and social contacts to their members, and a cooperative consumer movement, involving competition with private retail stores, had more enduring significance.

Protest

The first stage of industrialization everywhere saw massive artisanal protest. Many artisans, content either with maintaining sufficient traditions at work or with their individual adaptations, had no part in this. The Marseilles craftsmen who monopolized their jobs, for example, were slow to develop political protest, although artisans born elsewhere, precisely because they were excluded from the most prestigious jobs, began to react. Many artisans undoubtedly alternated attempts at adaptation with protest, depending on the state of the economy; for massive unrest occurred only after a slump. But there is no question that many artisans were concerned about the basic direction of society. The cooperative movement expressed such concern and frankly hoped to restore a more artisanal system of production. The Chartist movement vaguely sought a new organization of the economy. Movements such as the Grand National Consolidated Trades Union intended to take over the whole of industry and organize it on a cooperative basis; government itself would be put into the hands of the unions. These various movements enlisted only a minority of the artisans, for challenges to established order are always difficult to follow. They represented, nevertheless, a significant impulse within the whole class. And there were many occasions when artisans defied the legal order by action as well as by doctrine.

Although most artisan strikes were relatively well organized and nonviolent, on occasion strike action took a more menacing tone. Huge strikes in the Lyons silk industry in 1831 and 1833 sought a minimum wage for the whole area, harking back to the craft tradition of mutual protection through joint action. Repressed by government troops and attracted by republican propaganda, artisans actually took over the town for a period. Violent protest riots by Parisian artisans followed the repression in Lyons as well. In England, defeat of strikes in 1818 in Birmingham led many artisans toward political agitation. Luddite action, conducted by urban craftsmen such as cloth shearers, directly displaced by machines, had some strikelike aspects, for machine breaking had often been used to force employers to bargain over wages. But there was hatred of the machines as well, and English Luddites developed a vision of a utopian, egalitarian society run by artisanal units. Everywhere artisans sparked the bulk of the urban unrest that occurred during the first stage of industrialization. In western and central Europe their strikes and riots crested in the 1840s and flowed into the great revolutionary movement of 1848.

Artisans provided the street fighters in the three French revolutions of the nineteenth century, all of which were centered in Paris. Parisian artisans were distinguished from others in France and elsewhere by their number, their revolutionary tradition, and their exposure to the doctrinal and political ferment of the capital. In 1830, 1848, and after the siege of Paris in 1871 they rose in revolt. The 1830 revolution, though sparked by middle-class protest against the Restoration government, was manned by artisans. Members of the leading crafts composed the bulk of the street fighters, with carpenters and masons playing a particularly large role. During the 1848 revolt artisans rioted not only in February, but also in the succeeding four months; and they manned the barricades during the bloody June days. Finally, in 1871, artisans and some small shopkeepers provided both the troops and the government personnel during the Commune.

Artisans played a major role in the rioting in Vienna and in Berlin during the 1848 revolutions there. Fighting in Berlin during March was concentrated in the artisans' quarters. Only a minority of artisans were ever revolutionary; of about 350,000 artisans in Paris in 1848, only 15,000 were on the barricades in June. Only a few other French cities stirred significantly during the same year. Nevertheless, the artisans provided a greater number of actual revolutionaries than did any other urban class.

Artisan revolutions occurred shortly after a major economic crisis, though usually after the worst point was past. In Paris before the Commune, 90 per cent of the workers in some major crafts were unemployed. The 1848 revolution followed two years of intense hardship. The goals of artisan revolutions were quite broad, in the economy and usually in politics as well. In 1848 French artisans clearly pressed for the establishment of a democratic republic and in the Commune sought a new political regime for the city of Paris. In the economic sphere artisans sought protection from unemployment and government sponsorship for small artisan shops. In Paris in 1848 a significant number of artisans were acquainted with utopian socialist doctrines, particularly those of Louis Blanc and his book *The Organization of Work*. Blanc, like most other socialists of the day, offered doctrines with distinct appeal to artisan traditions. The stress of utopian socialism was on small, cooperative units of production working without elaborate equipment and distributing wealth equally among members of the unit. This was not the old guild system restored, but it urged some similar principles. Hence when Parisian artisans clamored for the organization of work in 1848, they were shouting for more than a system of relief from unemployment through public works. Public works were all they received, however, in the form of National Workshops; and even these were abolished in June, touching off the June Days. The leaders of the Commune, finally, were largely in the tradition of Proudhon, himself an artisan and a socialist. There again the stress was on small, cooperative, egalitarian units of production and in this case also the abolition of the state in favor of self-government by these units.

Generally, the revolutionary movement tended to die after midcentury as artisans found new ways of dealing with their economic situation. In France, and later in Barcelona and parts of Italy, a utopian feeling lived on and was to reappear even after 1870. These were countries where industrialization had begun but proceeded slowly and where artisans were caught in the pressures of the industrial revolution for many decades without losing their sense of strength and tradition. A minority of them could continue to hope for radical change. Before 1848 this utopian hope influenced artisans more generally in western Europe. It represented one aspect of the complex process of artisan adjustment to industrial society.

At the end of the first stage of industrialization the artisans remained a distinct and growing class. They had fairly firm personal goals and had developed important collective institutions in their effort to adapt to change. A minority was periodically interested in more than this, in remaking the whole of society in the artisan image.

The Working Class

As a group, factory workers were distinct from artisans by their rapid rate of growth, their work on new, faster-paced machinery, their lack of collective tradition. Fewer were highly skilled; more entered the class from a peasant or agricultural laborer background. The units of employment were larger, averaging twenty workers and sometimes rising to the hundreds; inevitably this meant less personal contact with employers. Unlike the journeyman, the worker did not own his own tools; he was more completely propertyless. There were, as we have seen, former artisans in the factories but they generally skimmed off the top positions. In Mulhouse during the 1840s, for example, almost the only factory workers who had been born in the city were skilled machinists and cloth printers. Often this top group deliberately avoided social contacts with the mass of workers, many of whom served under their direction. So workers were deprived of a possible leadership element that could help them adjust to the newness of urban and factory life.

The industrial working class was at first rather small and very unevenly distributed in any country. In new factory cities such as Manchester, Mulhouse, or Essen, workers formed the majority of the population. But more traditional centers, such as Paris and London, long harbored very few factories. Other older cities did develop an industrial working class but only as one element of a diverse population. By 1902 approximately one tenth of the inhabitants of Moscow and St. Petersburg worked in factories, and they tended to concentrate in a few sections of each city. By no means, then, did the working class dominate urban society in the early industrial revolution. Precisely because the new machines were so productive, they required relatively few workers; in the French wool industry of the 1840s there were 31,000 workers in the mechanized spinning factories, but weaving, with half a million workers, had been scarcely touched by new processes. Small wonder that by 1850 factory workers, numbering 400,000, constituted only a tenth of the French manufacturing labor force; even in Britain they had risen only to half the manufacturing force, with 2 million in the class.

Factory workers thus had special conditions setting them apart from all other workers. They were growing more rapidly than any other social group but their numerical importance must not be exaggerated.

The main source of factory workers was, of course, displaced rural labor, people who lacked land and could no longer continue as domestic manufacturers. Frequently it was only their misery that could have induced the new workers to abandon the countryside. Peasants often resisted factories even when the conditions of labor were exceptionally favorable. Manufacturers in Décazeville, a new industrial city in central France situated in an area of poor agriculture but extensive peasant smallholding, found it very difficult to recruit workers locally. The methods and discipline of the factory were simply unappealing even though the wages were much higher than in agriculture. In France more generally, the lack of severe population pressure on peasant tenure made it difficult to recruit a large labor force. There were, of course, individual cases of attraction to life in the factory and in the city. Some peasants were delighted at the opportunity of leaving the economic and social limitations of village existence. More commonly, however, the labor in the early factories was recruited by no positive attraction. Often there was little conscious choice at all. The hundreds of thousands of Irishmen who crossed to English industrial cities, the Flemings who flocked to the mines of southern Belgium, and the Russian peasants who reluctantly left their villages in the 1890s were impelled by the increasing hardships of rural life. Often miserable and even more often confused, their origins were to exercise a profound influence over the early conditions of their class.

With little positive choice in entering the factories, faced with novelty on every hand, factory workers encountered anguishing problems of adaptation. The simple but basic question is: how did they make it through their lives? The first step toward the answer flows from their own origins. Their rural lives had already been disrupted; factory employment, for all its burdens, might provide welcome stability. Some had already begun a process of adaptation, by changing their sexual and consumption habits as domestic manufacturing workers. On the whole factory workers could continue these adaptation patterns. Without minimizing the shock of entering factory labor, it is vital to realize that few workers stepped directly from a purely traditional village into the city. Traditionalist areas, like Décazeville, simply did not provide much factory labor. Potential workers moved toward the city in stages. All this helps explain why, as in Germany, factory labor was hard to recruit even amid rapid population growth. It suggests that some of those workers who did take factory jobs saw some possibility of adaptation.

Material Conditions: Progress or Decline?

The second stage of an answer involves a subject long discussed by historians. Despite their many difficulties, most workers were better off in some respects than they or their parents had been in the countryside. The question of whether conditions deteriorated or were improved by early factory employment has been hotly debated, particularly in the case of the British industrial revolution. There is evidence on both sides. Many have tried to prove that early industry was evil; others have asserted its beneficence. Even during the industrial revolution itself the question was argued with much partisan feeling. The issue is not merely an academic one. In order to understand the workers themselves, it is vital to know whether they experienced a deterioration in conditions as they entered industry. That the workers were in misery from a modern point of view cannot be denied; that they were severely limited in their conditions is obvious; but whether they felt themselves to be miserable, judging by the standards they knew, is far from clear.

Several points must be considered as a preliminary to this major issue. In the first place, there are obvious national and chronological differences to be noted. The possibility of deterioration of conditions was greatest in Britain, for several reasons. The standard of living among the British peasantry was relatively high until the early eighteenth century at least; in rates of meat consumption and quality of housing particularly the peasants were better off than their counterparts on the Continent.

Furthermore, British industrial growth and the corresponding urban crowding were very rapid, and this put pressure on the working class in the early decades that was less severe in France or Italy, where the process was slower. Also, British cities were far less regulated than those of the Continent; this affected housing and hygiene significantly.

Early British industrialization stressed the textile industry. This was a highly competitive industry, with small firms battling vigorously to stay alive and grow. It involved relatively little skill and employed large numbers of women and children. In contrast, later industrialization, as in Germany and Russia, involved more employment in large firms and in heavy industry. Competition was reduced because of the size of the firms, and the greater skill and strength required of workers encouraged better treatment. Finally, countries industrializing after 1850, when the supply of money was increasing rapidly, were less pressed by falling prices than industrializing areas had been in the earlier part of the century. Working conditions in Germany in the 1850s and in Russia in the 1890s were far from good. But there and even in France there can be little question of deterioration in material standards for workers entering factory industry.

Furthermore, in England and elsewhere, rural conditions had usually been declining before the industrial revolution began. This was, after all, the main impulse for peasants to accept factory jobs. Peasant standards of living were low anyway; preindustrial society was simply poor. And the people entering industry were often drawn from the lowest categories of the peasantry. These were the people who suffered most from expanding population and declining domestic industry. There was deterioration of material conditions in the early industrial period, but it occurred primarily in the countryside among the landless and the domestic producers and among the unskilled in the slums of cities like London. When they found factory employment, workers seldom could note a significant worsening of their situation and often benefited from some improvements.

The worst problem for factory workers, as for the poorer classes even in premodern times, was the instability of conditions. The sick worker was rarely paid and sometimes lost his job. With age a worker's skill and strength declined, and so his earnings. Machine breakdowns caused days and even weeks of unemployment. Most important, recurrent industrial slumps plunged many workers into profound misery. Wages fell, sometimes by as much as 50 per cent; up to a quarter of the labor force lost their jobs. Some returned to the countryside to seek work or to roam in bands to find food. Some survived on charity, and the charity rolls of manufacturing cities often embraced over half the working class, though only meager support was offered. Some sold or pawned their possessions. All reduced expenses by eating potatoes instead of bread and ignoring rent payments. Working-class life was thus punctuated by a number of personal and general disasters, creating a sense of insecurity that haunted workers even in better times.

More generally, the worst feature of the average worker's material standard of living was housing. Rural cottages had often been flimsy and small, befouled by animals, but city housing was sometimes worse. Many workers had less than a room for their families in a filthy slum. More commonly factory workers could afford two rooms and sometimes even a garden if they lived on the outskirts of a city, where factories were most commonly located, or in a smaller factory town. Most factory workers thus were not the worst housed in the whole urban population. But their space was limited and related services, such as toilets and sewerage, were typically foul. Furnishings were also meager.

With poor housing and urban crowding, along with the pressures of factory work itself, many workers were in poor health. Rates of infant mortality were high, and many workers had a life expectancy at birth only half as high as that of their employers. Even as adults they suffered frequently from illness and often aged rapidly, becoming decrepit by forty. But was their health worse than they would expect, according to their own previous experience? It is clear that urban health deteriorated in Britain between 1820 and 1840, improving thereafter, but this comment does not bear on factory workers specifically. In Lille, a fairly large industrial center in France, workers' life expectancy at birth rose from twenty eight to thirty two during the early industrial decades. In this same area the rate of rejects from the army on grounds of health was higher in some of the poorer adjacent agricultural regions than in the factory centers. Health conditions were dreadful but it is not clear that workers could sense a deterioration.

For there were significant improvements in some aspects of life. Diets were limited, with food commanding three quarters of the average budget; starches predominated, and much of the food purchased was of poor quality, for workers had little power to resist frauds or shoddy goods. Workers in metallurgy and mining earned enough to eat some meat regularly, which they needed to endure their strenuous jobs, but for other workers meat was a once or twice a week treat and half of all earnings went to buy starches. But meat consumption was higher than rural levels even so. Similarly, the working class increasingly ate wheat bread instead of black bread or potatoes alone. Here, admittedly, was an anomaly. White wheat bread was a symbol of better living and so was eagerly adopted, but it was less nutritional than other bread. Workers also consumed more coffee, sugar, and alcoholic drink. Clothing became more stylish and varied. There were workers in rags, coming to work barefoot, but far more had at least one change of clothing, including a pair of leather shoes. They liked to dress up on Sunday and no longer looked like the traditional urban poor. Machine-made cloth made clothes cheaper and more colorful. The same impulse toward fashion that distressed traditionalists in the middling class, who found the workers uppity, gave some pride and status to workers themselves. Workers were also able to afford new items such as forks and umbrellas.

Unquestionably factory wages were better than those of the countryside. Highly skilled male workers, many of them former artisans, were paid three to six times as much as ordinary laborers. For early mechanization did not eliminate the need for skill, merely the changing the type required; hence the men who built and installed machines, or who puddled iron, or who ran the more complex spinning machines required years to learn their trade fully. But even lesser skilled workers could command a money wage that was higher than what was available in the countryside or to the transient workers of the cities. There was little left over for purchases beyond food, housing, and clothing. A bit of tobacco or a small contribution to a mutual aid group were all that the ordinary worker could afford. On the other hand, wages tended to go up with time. They definitely rose in England after 1840. The main factory centers in France saw an increase in real wages in the 1830s and 1840s, and there was improvement in Germany in the 1840s and 1850s, in Russia in the 1890s.

So it is safe to conclude that material conditions, though bad, provided some solace for workers during the early industrial period as a whole. On the average, conditions were better than the new worker's traditions had led them to expect. Hence strikes for better wages were relatively rare. Factory workers did rise occasionally in slumps, often attacking bakers and other merchants in the traditional manner of the bread riot but sometimes asking for a restoration of previous wage levels. But material conditions were not, in normal times, the subject of articulate concern. Indeed many new workers were demonstrably uninterested in maximizing their wage gains. They enjoyed a few new amenities: better clothing, some changes in diet, and tobacco. But rural expectations were long preserved. This in fact allowed some workers a certain margin to adjust to other aspects of factory life. It was common, for example, for better-paid workers to stop work periodically to enjoy a period of leisure, instead of earning well beyond subsistence. Many French spinners and machine builders regularly worked only four or five days a week. Employers tried to put a stop to this by fines and other penalties, but they were not entirely successful.

Workers were beginning to establish a culture of living for the present that would long endure. Savings had little meaning for them, and their use of savings banks was far lower than that of artisans. Immediate enjoyment was more to the point: buy a new suit or a cut of meat for Sunday dinner. The need to compensate for hard work, the uncertainty of an existence that was basically out of their control and dependent on the whims of

employers, economic cycles, and disease, but also the delight in unex-
pectedly high wages at times, all help to explain a distinctive reaction. But
it was to work and family patterns, rather than consumer behavior, that
the new working class devoted most of its attention during the early
industrial decades.

Work

Factory life juxtaposed the traditional work rhythm that the labor
force brought in from shops and countryside with the new pace of the
machinery and the dynamic work ethic of the entrepreneurs. Steady pressure was put on workers to discipline them to a new pace, and there was
some change from one generation to the next. But workers were not
just passive victims, and they preserved important elements of the work
tradition.

The physical environment of the factory was extremely harsh. Machinery was unscreened and it was not uncommon to catch fingers in it.
Children had to crawl under textile machines to clean them while they were
still in operation. Textile work involved heat, dust, and dampness; mining
and chemical production involved exposure to gases. Few precautions
were taken by manufacturers that would add to the expense or difficulty
of production, and a host of accidents and occupational diseases resulted.
There was some improvement with time. Bigger machines and rising
profits encouraged manufacturers to build bigger, airier factories and reduce the level of dust. Some factory workers were accustomed to job
hazards anyway. The craft tradition involved a variety of occupational
diseases, and domestic spinning and weaving had been less salubrious
than factory work. Workers were acutely conscious of job dangers, but
they did not yet find new targets of blame.

Hours of work were long. In textile factories the average was about
thirteen and a half hours, though with rest periods some workers spent
fifteen hours at the plant and a few factories required that many hours
of outright work. Metallurgical firms usually limited work to twelve hours
so that two shifts could be set up for the whole day. Mining work varied
but was usually under ten hours a day. There were few days off. Sundays
were usually honored, although some employers required workers to show
up briefly to clean their machines. A few traditional saints' days were
celebrated in Catholic countries, such as the festival of Sainte-Barbe, the
patron of miners. In Russia during the 1890s factories closed for more
than forty such holidays. Generally, however, work and walking to work
consumed virtually all the waking hours of the labor force, at least six
days a week. The new sense of work time was dramatized by the factory
whistle, which piped workers to the job each morning; fifteen minutes late
and the factory gates were locked, leaving tardy workers without pay and

liable to a fine. Hours did decline a bit within twenty to thirty years after the beginning of industrialization. Manufacturers realized that long hours were not necessarily productive, and child labor laws, regulating the work day for children, prompted some to rethink their whole schedule. By the mid-nineteenth century textile hours were down to twelve in Britain and France.

But even with such slight changes the long work day remains one of the most vivid impressions of the early industrial revolution. How did workers stand this? Countless workers undoubtedly hated the regimen but felt powerless to fight it. But others did not find long hours unusual. They were accustomed to work from sunrise to sundown in the fields, and as domestic workers they had sometimes labored up to eighteen hours a day. A slightly better diet could make the hours endurable, and some of the machines lightened the purely physical burdens of labor.

What was novel was not hours but pace. The machine operated at considerable speed. Foremen were set to supervise workers and shop rules insisted that workers be diligent. For machines did not allow the worker to take a break when he wished; if one stopped, the whole machine might have to shut down. Through fines, supervision, and the use of inducements such as the piece rate, which would reward workers who produced more, employers sought to enforce this new assiduity. Unquestionably workers were troubled by this, but they found some means to counteract it. New workers wandered around the factory, even at risk of fines. They were still given long lunch breaks and other rest periods. When their wages permitted they took days off. And, at least while they were single and in their earning prime, they often quit their jobs. Job changing was one of the most important defenses workers could mount against the new work pressures. It gave a chance to look for better conditions but above all it provided a precious interval between jobs. Many new factories faced up to 100 per cent turnover a year except during slumps; an important minority of workers were stable, but many young men and women, not yet burdened with families, switched jobs often.

So the vaunted new factory discipline was incomplete. Workers were pressed, but not yet forced to adopt a totally new work ethic. They took individual measures to keep some of their traditional sense of control and of relief from steady labor. Obviously the poorer workers could not afford the luxury of quitting. Obviously new conditions, such as the sheer din of machines, sorely troubled workers who were accustomed to sing and talk on their jobs. But for many there were means of keeping the job within some bounds of traditional expectations.

Other aspects of factory life might facilitate adaptation. The paternalistic employer who had a kind word for the workers he knew and who helped them out in sickness or sent a gift for the child's communion corresponded to some traditional standards of upper-class behavior. Small wonder that many former German peasants transferred their sense of deference from landlord to industralist or that some French workers, given the vote in 1848, went to their employers for guidance.

Family Life

But the most important element in working-class adaptation involved the ability to preserve or reform a rather traditional family structure. There were of course immense problems in the first generation of industry. Many workers came into factory towns alone, unmarried or leaving their families behind. Many in fact confidently planned to return to the countryside after earning a bit of extra money, and during the early years an important minority did go back at least to do harvest work. This retarded the development of new expectations. But single young people in the cities obviously faced many problems of adjustment even if they thought their lot temporary. Factory girls, paid a low wage, were frequently forced to add prostitution to their working day in order to survive. Where men and women worked in a steamy room, often in partial undress, sexual temptation ran high.

But the most lurid stories of worker immorality were exaggerated, and as workers themselves often noted, sexual behavior had become at least as loose among the rural poor. It was true that many working girls had one or two illegitimate children before marriage, with no great stigma attached. But these were often fathered by the same man; Wendel Holek, a German worker, described how he lived "on trial" with his woman for seven years, siring two children, before they married. Workers thus continued the sexual revolution; they did not begin it.

It was at least as significant that workers developed high marriage rates, often at a rather early age. Because of better money wages, marriage rates in the factory towns could be higher than those of the countryside. In a strange city the family developed an emotional importance that it had not assumed in the preindustrial countryside. There were no property considerations to block a marriage that, at least at first, was based on love or sexual attraction. But the working-class family also had economic functions. Particularly in the early factories the family was able to work as a unit. Children served as aides and apprentices to their father or mother. Use of child labor was high, particularly in textiles, for children's wages were low and they were held to be adept at operations like tying thread on machines. There was immense exploitation here, for long hours hurt children's health. And children were often beaten to keep them alert. But much of this system was regarded by workers, as well as employers, as perfectly natural. Children were supposed to work. What upset workers came a bit later, when more advanced machinery either cut off children's jobs or forced them into separate units of the factory, away from parental supervision.

At this point, as in the 1820s in Britain, many workers decided that child labor was inappropriate and pressed for legislation limiting it. But long past this point the family and work were closely associated.

The same applied to some working-class wives. In textiles, a large percentage of the labor force was female, and when child labor was reduced by legislation and technical developments female employment went up. Unmarried girls and wives alike were thus able to contribute to the family economy. Their wages were lower than those of men, but this did not matter to most because they were working not as individuals but as part of the family unit. Even grandparents might have their role to play, taking care of young children while the intermediate generation worked. The desire to form a producing family, and the ability to do so even in the strange environment of the early factories, explains workers' acceptance of many conditions that we find repellent today, from long hours to unequal wages for women.

Outside of the textile industry the employment of married women was relatively low. Some girls were employed in the British mine pits, and women often could do some surface work at the mines, but this was not a female preserve. The same was true of metal and machine work. And workers, outside of textiles, showed an early desire to pull their wives out of the factories. Because wives could not normally work alongside their husbands, the unity of the family economy would be disrupted by their work. It early became an important sign of failure for a family to send the wife to work: a sick husband or one unusually low-paid, an unskilled worker, a drunkard, these were the only men that put their wives to work. Instead, some women continued to do work in the home, making lace or clothing. Many took in boarders. Wives were expected, even if they did not earn money themselves, to keep their husbands fit. Some had to cut down on their own consumption in order to give their husbands enough to keep going. This made sense when the family was seen still as an economic entity. By the same token the male worker, along with the children, normally turned over most or all of his earnings to the wife, who was responsible for buying food, paying the rent, indeed serving as a consumer agent in the working-class version of division of family labor.

The working-class family quickly developed ties to other relatives, re-creating many aspects of the extended family. Usually it was the wife's relatives who were most important, in contrast to the village situation where the husband as inheritor of property set up the family network. The workers' extended family met for social gatherings and served, again, key economic purposes. One family member could help another get a job or lend money in times of trouble.

Aside from specific adaptations necessary to preserve a rather traditional family structure, the working-class family faced one key problem: how many children to have. Most married early, unlike both middle class and artisanry. Some long viewed children as a pure economic asset, when factory jobs for children were plentiful. But the factories changed, as we have seen; increasingly the family had to bear the expense of raising children until they were twelve. It took time to adjust to this situation. Some workers kept their family size low through abortions; hence in Nottingham in 1851 the average working-class family was only a bit bigger, with 3.6 members, than the middle-class family. But a general working-class conversion to reduction of family size, by any means, was still in the future. Here was another responsibility for the working-class wife, and not always a pleasant one. Wendel Holek's wife, soon the mother of six, was not surprised by having to endure so many births; this, after all, was traditional. But she was surprised that none died, for death had traditionally reduced the burden of child care. Small wonder that she berated her husband when he came home from work.

Disorientation

At the family level and on the job, working-class adaptation was painful and incomplete. The impulse to use traditional values to counter novelty, although surprisingly successful, produced strain. And to a substantial extent the working class was alone in its effort to hack out a response to factory and urban life. Village festivals were gone, except for those workers who made it back to the countryside. Although an important minority of workers continued religious observance (the Welsh miners who were devoutly Methodist or the Alsatian textile workers who remained Catholic), the relevance of religion declined for the working class as a whole. Urban churches were too fancy, their rituals strange for people accustomed to peasant religion. Workers did not necessarily lose their faith—if they went back to their village they would often resume church going—but they lost their habit of regular church attendance. Small wonder that the English religious census of 1851 revealed that only half the population attended church. And certainly the government was no help. With rare exceptions workers encountered agents of the state only as policemen, in cases of riot; or during slumps, when on the Continent many city governments revoked work licenses to send potentially disorderly unemployed workers out of the city; or, on a more limited basis, as a do-gooder trying to limit child labor or require education or insist on vaccinations. For a long time the state was either a hostile or an irrelevant force for the working class.

In a confusing environment, with few recreational outlets and little money to spend, many workers turned to drink. The bars that spread quickly in working-class neighborhoods were mean and crowded, but they did provide some social life and escape from an ugly room. Many workers spent Sunday drinking, and Monday too when they could afford it; women often joined in. Consumption of alcohol rose 40 per cent among Russian workers between 1904 and 1913. In Lille during the 1830s some parents doped their children with laudanum so that they would be free to spend long hours in the bar. Here at least they might find temporary solace.

Servants

The largest employment category for urban women was servanthood, throughout the early industrial period. The number of servants rose massively in all the urban centers. Most servants were girls born in the countryside but no longer supportable there. They would typically have worked as servants for a peasant or farmer before marriage in preindustrial rural life, so it was logical to seek the same kind of job in the cities. Servanthood was thus the counterpart of factory work for redundant rural males, and because it kept the girl in a home environment it was in many ways less of a jolt.

Servant girls faced long hours and sometimes abusive employers. Rarely did they have time off. With scrubbing, marketing, and cooking they had a hard job. Their rooms were cramped and ugly, if indeed they did not have to sleep in a hallway or kitchen, and their diets were meager. But there were compensations, and servanthood can be seen as an important means by which girls made the transition to city life. In the first place though money wages were low they were higher, in combination with board and room, than what factory girls could earn. So many servants saved money. Some sent it back to their family, in the traditional pattern. But others saved it toward a dowry, and a significant minority of servants were able to marry shopkeepers or established artisans, in what constituted upward mobility in society. Many learned household skills, new habits of cleanliness, and other middle-class values. Not a few were taught to read. Even those who married workers, which was the most common pattern (for only a minority of servants remained single and found servanthood a lifelong career), could bring some new values to the family. They might think about caring for their children in new ways, as the middle class was beginning to do, about educating their children and trying to help them move up in society, even about limiting their birth rate. Some of these impulses would have a clearer effect on the working class in the next stage of industrialization.

Servanthood also taught docility, for the servant was told to be respectful to her master and mistress. This could confirm traditional deference within the working class; it helps explain why many working-class wives took orders from their husbands without complaint. To be sure, servant girls might compensate for harsh discipline by stealing from their employers or changing jobs, again a close analogue to factory behavior.

As in the factories, a minority of servants could not stand the pressures of the new life. Some took to drink. More committed suicide than in the overall lower-class population. Some turned to prostitution, often after having been made pregnant by an employer but sometimes because prostitution provided a way to earn more money with less nagging supervision.

Discontent and Protest

Working-class life thus presented a host of ambiguities in this first stage of its development. The class was driven by need. Its ability to adapt traditions was surprising, and more than any clear modernization of values this allowed factory life to be endured. Some outlines of a durable working-class culture were forged quite quickly. But adaptation could not meet all the problems encountered, and some individuals were clearly disoriented. Ironically, both adaptation and disorientation inhibited protest. Workers proud of supporting their families, with their children grouped around them at the machine, might be loath to risk a strike. Workers who sought solace in liquor might storm off the job in anger, but go to the bar to discuss their problems, down a few drinks, and return to work in a day or two, somewhat the worse for wear but incapable of articulating their discontent.

There were genuinely angry workers. A British cotton spinner in 1818 wrote of his employers: "They are literally petty monarchs, absolute and despotic, in their own particular districts; and to support all this, their whole time is occupied in contriving how to get the greatest quantity of work turned off with the least expense." Comparable expressions of class-consciousness could be found in many factories. But the same cotton spinner admitted that most of his fellows were "docile and tractable," though he explained this by the fact that all their energies were consumed by their work. How many workers harbored articulate grievances about their condition cannot be determined. A variety of evidence indicates that most, if asked about their jobs, would have said they found no pleasure in them. British workers interviewed by parliamentary commissions during the 1830s reported many complaints. Many Germans polled around 1900, some still new to the factories and mines, said they had no enjoyment in work. But they did not necessarily expect pleasure, for traditional work had often been boring. And although they missed the opportunity to talk and sing freely, the ability to preserve the family might compensate in part. Finally, even if aggrieved, it was hard to translate discontent into active protest.

Of course there were formal barriers to unrest. Strikes and unions were illegal. The French Le Chapelier Law of 1791 and the British Combination Acts of 1799 and 1800 were typical of the measures that prohibited any association of workers. Strikes were treated as rebellions in most of Italy until 1859. Though England removed the harshest restrictions on unions in 1824, as Russia did briefly in 1906, most governments repressed worker agitation firmly in the early industrial period. Leaders of strikes were often arrested, and troops were used to break up any major demonstration. Employers also resisted expressions of discontent. They fired potential leaders and sometimes blacklisted them locally. They called in government troops, when agitation was merely threatened. And if a strike did occur, they typically tried to outlast it or to retract any gains they might be temporarily forced to grant.

But these barriers affected artisans about equally. It was true that workers had more sense of being among strangers, with fewer familiar faces to appeal to in times of anger. They were also less literate. Although reading ability spread rapidly in industrial centers—if only because employers had reason to encourage literacy, which would improve the ability of their workers to read directions and shop rules—many workers had no schooling and others who went to school were taught briefly and badly. So workers were less open than artisans to political propagandists; utopian socialists, for example, made little headway among them by 1848. Most important, workers lacked the organizational tradition that even inadequate guilds had provided. Hence workers were slow to organize mutual aid societies, although a few developed among the highly skilled soon after industrialization began. Beyond this, partial adaptation, traditional resignation and deference, and sheer confusion differentiated workers from artisans in protest action. Far more workers expressed their discontents individually, through stealing materials from the plant or changing jobs, than could combine for action.

Worker agitation was infrequent and poorly organized during the early years of the industrial revolution, usually for at least the first four decades. There was little worker unrest in Belgium until the 1860s. The whole of French factory labor produced only eight strikes a year during the 1830s and 1840s, and these were usually small and brief. The most common action was more a riot than a strike, occurring during a slump that brought violent attacks on merchants or employers. Only a few groups broke through this pattern. Miners conducted several large strikes in France and Germany, fairly early on. They had more leisure and funds to plan an effort; their dangerous work easily stirred them to anger; and they had a nucleus of traditional mine workers who helped shape goals, for most mine areas had conducted small operations for decades before the industrial revolution. Many of the early strikes concerned work conditions and relations with employers. Silesian miners, for example, first stirred over changes in traditional work patterns and a reduction of customary benefits from their companies, such as free heating coal. Only later would large numbers of industrial workers turn to issues such as hours and wages, except in cases of massive deterioration. But strikes to preserve tradition were hard to win, for employers were insistent on their right to command greater efficiency; so this discouraged strikes even further. Gradually, of course, more workers acquired the ability to protest. The revolutions of 1848 spread new consciousness to some; in Paris, some workers in the new railroad yards even joined the artisans during the June Days. Factory strikes during the French Second Empire involved increasing numbers of metallurgical and textile workers. But the rate was still low, and few permanent organizations arose within factory labor to give leadership and coherence to worker discontent.

Britain offered a slightly different pattern. Again, there was little agitation for the first forty years. Factory workers showed no interest in machine breaking, for example, because this was their livelihood and they could build family work around the new equipment. But in the decades when urban material conditions deteriorated they did stir, often following the lead of artisans. Strikes by bricklayers and carpenters in Birmingham, for instance, were imitated by cotton workers in 1818. Britain was just pulling out of a slump, and workers struck against unemployment and reductions in pay. As in France, then, the first efforts were defensive, to protest deterioration. But here some workers had gained enough experience to go on to form unions, and important organizations developed among cotton spinners and miners, lasting into the 1830s. Workers also participated in the Chartist movement. The political reforms may have meant little to them, but Chartism gave them a way to protest economic slumps; as a result Chartist agitation in the industrial areas was more violent than where urban artisans were in firm command. But with the failure of Chartism and the advent of more prosperous times in the 1850s, worker agitation fell off once more. Only the highly skilled workers pulled away, in the sedate New Model Union movement, but this simply reduced the chances for general unrest. Major, persistent agitation among factory workers throughout western and central Europe was not to develop until the 1870s or 1880s.

The same pattern did not hold true for industrial workers in Italy, northern Spain, and Russia. Large strike waves occurred, along with surreptitious unions, as early as the first or second decade of industrialization. Workers raised not only economic but political demands, asking for parliamentary reform and voting rights. A massive general strike was the backbone of the 1905 revolution in Russia, yet industrialization was only fifteen years old. Milanese workers conducted a major rising in 1898, Barcelona textile workers surged forward a decade later. This agitation had immense political implications, when joined to rural unrest and middle-class demands; in Russia it was to overturn the government and ruling class in 1917. Several factors explain the different working-class potential, including of course the fact that the political regimes in these countries were unusually backward and repressive:

1. Workers in all these areas were recruited from a peasantry that was extremely aggrieved. This obviously played a major role in Barcelona, where workers were recruited from the south and brought their peasant anarchism along with them; this was the only case in which large numbers of factory workers were anarchist. But peasant unrest formed a vital back-drop for workers in Italy and Russia too.

2. There were far more revolutionary doctrines and propagandists at work than was the case earlier in the west. Socialists, communists, anarchists—this was a rich menu to choose from. In Russia, at least, workers were probably more widely literate than their western counter-parts seventy years before. Over 60 per cent of the whole population could read by the 1900s, thanks not only to schools but to training in military service. Comparable levels were reached in France only by 1870, at a much later stage of industrialization. Again this opened factory workers more easily to radical literature.

3. Factories and equipment in these early industrial revolutions were almost as sophisticated as those in the west at the same time. In Russia the average factory was larger than anywhere else in Europe by the 1900s, employing a thousand workers. Workers here lacked the ability to defend traditional work patterns that had been possible in smaller shops with slower machinery.

But if, in Russia particularly, unrest is the overwhelming theme of the early industrial working class, the more general point still must be the limitations on working-class protest potential in its formative years. Protest required a sense of community and tradition, and workers lacked this. Hence, whether satisfied or not, whether benefiting by perceptible improvements in living standards or not, workers had to try to adapt to their new situation. They could not successfully oppose the industrial revolution and, unlike the artisanry, few even tried. So the effort to find new sources of status and pleasure, in clothing, or to re-establish tra-ditional values in altered form, as in the family life, set an enduring tone for working-class culture.

Conclusion

The early industrial period stands out, in the history of social protest, for the frequency and vigor of agitation. This was not a rising of the whole society. The very poor, both in city and countryside, were largely left out. Factory workers participated only haltingly, with a few major exceptions. But large numbers of artisans and peasants were attempting to call a stop to change. They might hark back to an idealized village or guild or they might use anarchism or utopian socialism to paint a new society based on the same principles of egalitarianism and small-group organization.

Neither the forms nor basic goals of the protest were new. The form was a riot, the goals were backward-looking, pointing to old rights that had been challenged rather than new ones deserved. Hence the timing was usually associated with an economic crisis, when conditions deteriorated; when times were good it was hard to form goals, for the present had to be seen as worse than the past for this protest to be possible. Much of the protest involved elaborate rituals, religiouslike symbols, and mythical leaders such as Ned Ludd or Captain Swing. Yet the depth of feeling involved should not be minimized. Though triggered by economic problems, the major protests involved fundamental hostility toward those held responsible for change.

Yet the protests failed to halt change. Often unpolitical, they rarely attacked the state directly. Peasants and artisans worked separately. Even when they rose in the same year, they did not join hands. Furthermore peasants, focusing particularly on the manor lords, were attacking an old enemy, not the source of modernization. They were spurred by newer developments such as population pressure and the growing commercialization of agriculture, but they did not attack these directly. This was why they often won their leading demands, for the modernizing forces, and particularly the middle class, could readily agree that manorialism was evil. But this simply opened the way for further change, as the aristocracy was weakened and the traditional legal structure of the rural world overturned. Artisans hit at the modern economy more directly, by attacking the principles of the capitalist order. Alone, they could not prevail. They were hampered not only by the separate action of the peasants, but by the positive hostility of the rising middle class, which seized control of the leading revolutions. The middle class might not win its revolutions either, preferring defeat rather than the artisan victory that would mean a return to the old order, but it could certainly block the craftsmen. Artisans were also hampered by the ability of many of their number either to defend tradition without revolution or to find individual ways to profit from the new economy.

Partly as a result of repeated failure, this last great wave of traditional protest ended during the early industrial period. Already in England the Chartist movement suggested an adaptation of protest to less violent, more political goals. Some Chartists might dream of a return to a craft economy, but others, asking for votes and education, were ready to try to improve the new economy. The revolutions of 1848 marked the end of preindustrial protest in France and Germany. The peasants in central Europe won the abolition of manorialism, as those in France had done earlier. The artisans were defeated. New elements were beginning to enter the protest scene, like the railroad workers who participated in the June Days. Protest was becoming more political; when artisans and agricultural workers rose in several parts of France in 1851, to oppose the abolition of the republic, they were trying to defend their new political rights, not return to the past. All of this was tentative still, and many elements would still hanker for the past. But in terms of overt collective action, a major turning point had occurred.

Furthermore the 1850–1870 period brought a strange return to calm. These were prosperous years for most elements in society. Famine had ended in western Europe, thanks to improved agriculture and transportation; this classic trigger of protest was gone. Some traditional protest groups were now vanishing—the middling peasant, the domestic manufacturing worker. Artisans were still vigorous, but were turning to new forms of action and adaptation. Governments, frightened by the 1848 risings, became more adept at handling crowds; police forces were bolstered, their weaponry improved. And the middle class turned against protest. It was winning partial political gains, as parliaments and constitutions spread through central Europe. Even leading conservatives conceded that the state should further, not oppose, industrial growth. The Prussian government thus turned from a policy of discouraging industrial investment, in the 1840s, to support of giant investment banks. The peasantry was quiet, with population pressure reduced and manorialism gone. When protest resumed, it would be on quite another basis.

The fate of early industrial protest in eastern and southern Europe was rather different. Sharecropping in southern Italy and Spain, the continued limitations on the peasantry in Russia until the Stolypin reforms prevented the calming of the countryside that occurred in western Europe. Rural agitation remained endemic in Spain into the 1930s, in Italy into the 1920s. In Russia the peasantry might have followed the western pattern after 1906; certainly rioting decreased. But the hardships of World War I, in a situation where adaptation had just begun, roused the peasants once more. The early contributions of the working class to protest also marked this area. And the middle class was weak. Lacking a large, independent business group, liberal professionals tried to master the revolutionary current, as their counterparts had done in the west in 1830 and 1848, but they could not. Finally, with the western experience behind them, revolutionaries like Lenin were far more adept than the smaller band of avowed revolutionaries in 1848 had been. So revolution triumphed in Russia in 1917. Agitation rocked Spain and Italy for decades.

In western and central Europe, the established institutions of society emerged from the early industrial period in apparently good shape. The leading churches had the firm support of the aristocracy, and with a prosperous agriculture some landlords were able to contribute large sums to religion. Middle-class elements, sincerely pious or eager for respectability, also gave money. This was a major period of church building and restoration of ancient edifices. Money went into missionary activity as well, and on the intellectual level there was a revived interest in theology. In England the nineteenth century has, with reason, been called a great age for religion, and the phrase could with some justice be applied elsewhere.

In fact, religion was crumbling as a social cement. The churches retained most of their hold on the peasantry, though in key areas peasants attacked the clergy along with the rest of the established order. But the peasantry was a shrinking majority of society. Middle-class interest in religion was ambiguous at best. The class ethic ran counter to traditional belief. Its optimism and belief in individual ability implicitly undermined the tenets of original sin and damnation. The middle class did not really believe in hell. Its faith in science overshadowed its interest in theology. With the popularization of the theory of evolution after 1859, even greater doubts spread about the validity of religion. The middle class, particularly in Catholic countries, also distrusted the church as an institution, allied as it was with the aristocracy and suppression of freedom of speech and expression. Middle-class leaders, as in the French revolution of 1830, readily countenanced a reduction in the political powers of the church. Religious freedom was declared in every major revolution and church property was often seized, following the example of the French Revolution of 1789. Even in England the political rights of the Anglican church were steadily diminished.

All of this tended to turn the established churches against modernity. In 1864 Pope Pius IX issued a Syllabus of Errors that summed up the position of official Catholicism: he condemned liberalism, socialism, freedom of worship, nationalism, modern science, and the belief that change is good. Effectively he declared war on the modern world. Many Catholics disagreed with his position, but increasingly modernity and religion moved in opposite directions. Obviously, conservatism heightened the difficulties urban churches faced in dealing with the working class. When even Methodist leaders, in England, opposed social reform, workers had to begin to wonder whether it was worth waiting for the afterlife.

The states of western and central Europe were in better shape. With few exceptions they had weathered the amazing wave of revolutions that hit almost every country between 1820 and 1848. They had not been required to give over full power to the middle class. But they had introduced an important series of changes to retain what they could of stability and the old order. They had established parliaments and broadened the vote to include some of the middle class or, as in Britain in 1867, the working class or even, as in France and Germany by 1870, the whole adult male population. They had developed a host of new functions. The abolition of manorialism put the state in direct touch with every citizen, for tax collection, military recruitment, and preservation of order—all rather traditional functions now expanded; but the state was also in touch with citizens for technical training, extension of credit, and, increasingly, primary education. At least in the cities the state inspected housing and factories. It licensed doctors. It kept census records and took over the functions of registering births, deaths, and marriages. This was a state on its way to becoming modern even when, ironically, not fully controlled by a modern social class. Even when in conservative hands it now promoted change. It no longer relied on repression alone, even against the lower classes, as it abortively attempted, even in Britain, for a few years or decades after 1815.

If the state was expanding, other traditional institutions had loosened their hold. Guilds, by 1870, had either disappeared or were voluntary. When peasants could freely leave for the city, villages had lost their traditional control. Despite new state functions, despite even the powers of new institutions such as the paternalistic factory, individuals were freer than before. Some, in desperate misery or confused by the new order, saw freedom as confusion. Not only the very poor but the middling class had reason to question the process of modernity, and even with the decline of traditional protest society was not lacking new voices urging a halt to change. Other groups adapted more successfully to a situation in which individual choice was heightened. For choice meant not only middle-class decisions about what kind of professional education was best or what new machine was most reliable, it meant housewives' decisions about what to buy amid a growing array of consumer goods, or workers' decisions about what job to take or what city to go to, or a girl's decision about whether servanthood, factory work, or perhaps prostitution would best serve her interests. The lower one went on the social scale the more choice was hemmed in restrictions, of course, but behavior patterns were far less closely guided than before.

To adjust to this situation, the family proved of key importance to most of the major social classes. It, too, was freer in important ways. Children or young adults, able to earn on their own, could leave home at an early age, and some did, defying their parents. Choice of mate was more open, even in the middle class. But despite some signs of disorganization, such as the still-rising illegitimacy rates among the rural and urban propertyless classes, most people chose the family. The nineteenth century was a marrying century. By 1850 in England 859 per 1,000 girls reaching the age of fifteen would marry by the time they were fifty, and this figure long held steady. It was much higher than in premodern society. The family remained an economic necessity. Its producing role had changed, though not entirely disappeared; wives were less commonly producing agents than before. But, with the middle class leading the way, it was increasingly becoming a consumer unit, with wives here taking the leading role. It was not yet clear how these changes would balance out for women, but for the moment there was neither time nor interest for questioning the importance of new functions and it was significant that a higher percentage achieved the status of marriage than ever before. Here is one key to the first adaptation to modernization; marriage, an old goal, now was achievable by almost every adult. Finally, to an incalculable degree, the family became a unit of affection. Greater choice of marriage partners, the beginnings of greater choice of how many children to have, created new possibilities here, and the strangeness of industrial society encouraged a search for love as a replacement for stable traditions.

It was not clear whether the family could live up to these new demands upon it, although for the moment its economic functions sustained it in any event. For adaptation had just begun. In all the major urban social classes, men and women alike were trying various combinations of tradition and modernity. A host of traditional values still seemed preservable: the importance of property for the middle and middling classes, the customary work ethic for many workers and artisans. It was on this basis that some change had been successfully assimilated and the effort to halt the tide of industrialization abandoned. But this first stage of adaptation left the door wide open for further change. The next stage of modernization would challenge many groups that thought they had found a safe niche in the new world of the cities.

5

MATURE INDUSTRIAL SOCIETY

Within sixty to eighty years after the beginning of the industrial revolution in any country, most people had become accustomed to some of its effects. It is useful to think of an industrial society as mature when about half a population lives in cities, a situation reached in England as early as 1850, in western Europe around 1900, in Russia around 1950. For this substantial urbanization means that most people remaining in the countryside have converted to market agriculture and are exposed to other urban influences. It means that most urban workers are no longer brand new to industry; increasing numbers have lived in cities and worked in factories for several generations. Even the middle class, though most alert to the possibilities of modernization, has had a chance to adapt more fully. By the later nineteenth century the west European middle class was relaxing a bit, able to enjoy the fruits of earlier labor; from this class in fact would emanate a new ethic of leisure. At various levels of society people, now accustomed to their new work and setting, began to become more articulate about their goals. They no longer had to apply purely traditional standards to their life, but were able to formulate new demands. This effect of the maturation of industrial society helps explain why rates of protest were much higher, but protest itself more moderate, than in the first industrial stage. More people could express grievances, but largely within, not against, the industrial framework.

The idea of a society settling down, becoming more accustomed to industrial conditions, helps explain a number of other developments toward the end of the nineteenth century. Crime rates stopped increasing rapidly. The "modernization" of crime continued, in that property crimes, particularly thefts, continued to gain over crimes of violence. Rates of assaults and suicides declined in several areas. It was after 1870 also that illegitimacy rates stabilized or even dropped slightly. In some areas, the dislocating effects of World War I reversed some of these trends; crime in England and Wales began to rise from 1920 onward. But it is legitimate to see personal dislocation as declining at least until the war and in some cases beyond.

Mature industrial society involves more, however, than the fact that some of the novelty had worn off the industrialization process. Important new developments were occurring that make the mature industrial period a new break in the course of modernization. From about 1870 to 1940 in western and central Europe, basic structural changes were taking place. This chronology is approximate; industrialization was far newer in Germany than in England by 1900, so that a second wave of change was less clearly distinguishable from the initial impact of industrialization. Many German workers were still coming into factories for the first time; they had to adjust to a second generation of technology and business organization simultaneously with their first reaction to city life. But for purposes of generalization, the idea of a new seventy-year span covering all those areas where industrialization had been well begun before 1870 has considerable validity.

Of course, in the midst of this period, an unprecedented world war occurred. World War I sharpened many of the trends visible already, bringing a near collapse of mature industrial society. The special effects of the war must be discussed, but only after the more fundamental trends of industrial maturation have been established.

Some of the features of industrial maturation spread to eastern and to a lesser extent southern Europe around 1900. Big business could be copied; so could socialism. But real industrial maturation took shape in Russia and Italy only toward the middle of the twentieth century. Again one can see important common elements to the maturation process, but at discrete chronological intervals.

The student of modern society should look at a number of key topics to decide when a new break has occurred in the modernization process. Mature industrial society involved a new kind of social protest. It developed a new class structure, particularly with the rise of white collar labor. More fundamentally a new basis for class structure was suggested, though just in embryo; property declined as a measurement of social stratification. Mature industrial society brought a new stage in the decline of religion and the rise of alternate loyalties and beliefs. It saw a new definition of work and of work's role in life. It represented a distinct new demographic period. In mature industrial society the birth rate fell rapidly. Population kept growing for a time but at a much slower pace, and only because of a drop in the death rate plus the cumulative effect of earlier growth. Quickly, however, population headed toward a zero growth rate. France led the way here, as not only the urban classes but also the peasantry, eager to protect their land holdings from the divided inheritance that French law required, cut their birth rates early. By 1820 the major period of French population growth was over. But this pattern emerged by the mid-nineteenth century in Britain, by the 1870s in Germany, and by the 1920s in Russia and Italy. At a very early stage of industrial maturation, thus, or even slightly ahead of its advent, population growth slowed dramatically. This reflected important changes in family relationships and had significant effects on the economy and politics. By the 1930s under the impact of World War I and the Depression, population in Britain and Scandinavia had totally ceased to grow, and in France the native population was actually shrinking, with birth rates lower than death rates; France expanded only by admitting large numbers of immigrant workers.

All of these developments, particularly the new class structure and the new demography, form a vital part of the definition of mature industrial society; several must be explored further, in their relationship to specific social groups. But there are four more obvious criteria for measuring this period off from the first stage of industrialization. The nature of technology changed. So did the organization of the economy. So did the nature of key economic problems, as Europe clearly moved out of the traditional economy of scarcity. So, finally, did the relation of people to the government.

Technology

Although nothing so dramatic as the application of steam power to manufacturing marks off the maturation of industrial society, technology was changing sufficiently that the late nineteenth century has often been termed the scene of a second industrial revolution. The pace of technological change within existing factory industries speeded up, with a new generation of inventions. And machines now spread to literally every branch of the economy.

Between 1870 and 1890 the application of inventions such as sewing machines transformed many craft industries. By 1900 most shoes and many items of clothing were made in factories or in sweatshops. In the food-processing industries machines prepared, processed, and canned many products. Even the baking of bread was partially mechanized, although factory production was not installed. Printing developed automatic composing machines that greatly speeded production. Cranes and electric saws were introduced in construction work, which, along with the use of metal scaffolding for the larger buildings, altered many traditional skills. Cranes also changed the nature of dock work. Crucial to many of these developments was the utilization of electric and gasoline motors, which gained ground particularly after about 1890. Now even small shops and homes could use powered equipment. And regions distant from a coal supply could industrialize, although the heaviest concentrations of industry were still attached to mining centers. Areas with potential for hydroelectric power, such as the Alpine regions, experienced a real burst of industrial development after 1890.

Technological change was not confined to manufacturing. Agricultural producers increasingly applied mechanical equipment to their work. Cream separators in the dairy industry along with cultivators and harvesting machinery spread even to many peasant producers. In office work, typewriters and telephones reproduced some of the impact of the early machines in factory industry: work became more routinized, faster-paced, and noisier. A host of producers thus had to adapt to new equipment, really for the first time. Some were displaced; artisanal shoemakers and tailors increasingly had to concentrate only on luxury production and repair work. The total size of the artisan class, particularly outside the construction industry, began to stabilize or decline after 1870. Even where artisanal forms still predominated, as in baking, craftsmen might fear later displacement by some new invention, and almost everyone had to accept some changes in the methods of work. The same was true of many factory workers. In textiles machinery became increasingly sophisticated. Multiple looms were developed for weavers, allowing them to man first two or four looms and then, with the Northropp loom invented in the United States, as many as sixteen or thirty-two. The new machines did not spread immediately, for there was much resistance, but productivity did rise in the industry. This meant not only a new pace of work but also, given the limited market for textile goods, a stabilization or even slight shrinkage of textile employment.

Other factory industries were growing more rapidly, but here too technical change loomed large. Heavy industry was massively transformed. In 1856 the Bessemer process allowed the elimination of carbon from iron ore by chemical means. This increased the possible size of blast furnaces and also permitted the reintroduction of carbon to make steel on a widespread basis for the first time. The Gilchrist–Thomas process, developed in the 1870s, allowed the utilization of iron ore rich in phosphorous; this opened the iron ores of Lorraine to industrial exploitation and pushed the metallurgical industries of Germany and France to unprecedented levels. Such technical developments vastly increased the potential output of metallurgy and at the same time raised the capital needed by any metallurgical firm; the new devices were extremely costly. By the 1890s digging machines were gradually applied to mining. More important, the machine tools industry was transformed by the introduction of automatic lathes, riveting machines, and the like. These processes greatly reduced the skills necessary in the manufacture of machines and ships, while encouraging a more rapid pace of work. By about 1910 similar devices were changing automobile production from a small-shop, almost artisanal operation to a major factory industry.

New technology propelled the manufacture of electric equipment and the chemicals industry to new heights. By the 1920s these industries were replacing less dynamic branches such as textiles and even mining as the manufacturing leaders. Not only new methods but also new products such as rayon and radios challenged traditional industries severely. Mining found a vigorous competitor in petroleum products. The vitality of the industry declined even before 1914, and by the 1920s this was a sick branch. New technology thus brought displacement home to factory workers themselves. Where workers and manufacturers tried too hard to cling to traditional methods, as occurred in some branches of textiles, productivity did not increase rapidly enough to match the dynamism of other industries or competition from other regions. Whole areas of traditional industry, such as Lancashire, South Wales, and the mining districts of Belgium and northern France, seemed permanently blighted, as the emphasis switched to new regions such as Lorraine or southern England. By the 1920s unemployment stood at 16 per cent in British mining and textiles. More generally, the new equipment first slowed down the growth of the working class and then brought it to a virtual halt by the 1920s, as demand could now be met by increased productivity per worker.

The key symbol of the new technology became the assembly line. Suggested before World War I, mainly by experts from the United States, assembly-line methods spread increasingly in industries such as automobiles and machine tools. Semiskilled workers, using electric-powered equipment, repeated simple operations such as riveting bolts as a part of an engine or a chassis moved by them on a conveyor belt. Not all factory skills were lost. In 1914 a full 60 per cent of British machine tools workers were skilled, the rest evenly divided between semiskilled and unskilled. But the challenge was there. Factory workers, even more than artisans or office help, had to adjust to new methods and the fear of technological displacement.

Big Business

The assembly-line mentality involved more than technology. The leading branches of industry grew steadily more concentrated after 1870, and the new industrial magnates thought in terms of rationalization in all aspects of their operation. Technological change helped spur big business, for the new machines, particularly in heavy industry, were extremely expensive and required a massive investment. But the big business outlook outstripped technological change. The chemical industry, for example, developed gigantic firms at least a decade before extremely expensive equipment was introduced. There was a new spirit in many branches of industry, a spirit that tried to use size to modify competitive pressure and even to reduce risks of failure during business crises.

A big firm with extensive capital at its disposal could afford a research staff; technical improvements could be produced more regularly, and the dependence on competition for occasional inventions could be reduced. A large professional sales force decreased the hazards of the market. Greater size allowed the integration of more operations to assure supplies and to eliminate dependence on any single product for profits. Finally, a firm sufficiently large could have direct control of much of its market. It could partially dictate terms to its buyers rather than rely on the forces of supply and demand, which were so difficult to predict and control.

By the 1890s well over half the labor force in Germany, Britain, and Belgium was employed in firms with more than twenty workers. By 1910, 88 per cent of Russian manufacturing labor worked in firms with more than fifty employes. Everywhere the number of large companies increased at a far faster rate than did the number of small enterprises. The trend of expansion touched virtually every industry, but the most significant development was the giant firm. In an extreme example of size, the German electrical industry was dominated by just two firms, the *Allgemeine Elektrizitäts Gesellschaft* and the Siemens concern, which controlled over 90 per cent of German production and had important international links as well. Each firm could set the terms for many leading buyers on the strength of its great size; beyond this, the firms made agreements with each other on market allocation, which made price fixing even simpler. In the German chemical industry the I. G. Farben company possessed a tremendous influence over its own sales, because of its size alone. Few firms approached outright monopoly, even in Germany; and the concentration of German industry was greater than that of Britain or France. Nevertheless, the trend was general. The steady growth of firm size allowed the utilization of more massive and efficient equipment. It also allowed a greater possibility for profits, even aside from efficiency, by permitting greater control of research, supplies, sales, and position in the market.

The development of huge firms was significant in itself. The position of labor in such firms inevitably differed from the situation in small factories. New techniques of management had to be devised to administer the giants. Equally important, the large firm required new methods of finance. These methods altered the nature of industrial ownership and increasingly encouraged the formation of still larger economic units.

A few firms grew large and wealthy by judiciously plowing profits back into the business. Old metallurgical companies such as Le Creusot in France expanded and developed a variety of new operations without changing their fundamental structure of family ownership. Even there dependence on bank loans increased, and the prodigious expansion of industrial banking aided capital formation of all sorts. With the rise of railroads and heavy industry, the association of the financial power of banks with industry became absolutely essential. During the 1850s Napoleon III encouraged the *Crédit mobilier* as an investment bank to support the development of ports, railroads, and urban clearance. The bank ultimately failed, but in the next decade similar banking enterprises, such as *Crédit lyonnais,* were formed to channel funds into industry. In the German areas the association of banks and industry was even closer. The Vienna *Kredit Anstalt* was formed in 1856 specifically to lend to industry. The German Darmstadter Bank and *Diskontogesellschaft* arose in the same decade, along with a number of less solid banks that collapsed after contributing to a speculative mania. Other investment banks, such as the Deutsche and the Dresdener, arose in the prosperous period of the early 1870s, when the French war indemnity was filling German coffers. The Dresdener Bank developed close ties with the Krupp industrial complex and served as a major source of Krupp's funds. In Germany particularly, but to some extent everywhere, industrial investment banks greatly increased the amount of capital available and thereby promoted the development of larger firms.

The most important source of funds for large enterprises came, however, from the growing use of the corporate form. Banks might contribute to stock purchases, but funds could be drawn from an even broader base, from hundreds and sometimes thousands of investors, large and small. Corporations spread rapidly in every area toward the end of the century, and the rate of corporate formation increased as well. In France corporations required special authorization from the government until 1867, when a change in law encouraged a first burst of corporate growth; but the slow pace of French industrial advance restricted the number of corporations until the 1890s. By then the expansion of French heavy industry required massive financial support and so required extensive use of the corporate form. During the 1890s up to a thousand corporations were formed every year in France. Rates of corporate formation in Germany and elsewhere were rising in the same period, although Great Britain maintained a lead in the sheer number of corporations.

The use of corporate forms greatly increased the size possible for an individual enterprise, either new or old, by extending the amount of capital available. It also changed the nature of ownership, reducing personal control over a firm and substituting divided and substantially anonymous ownership and responsibility. Along with investment banking, the growth of corporate organization tied industry to essentially novel financial forms. This development was almost as important as the growth of the sheer size of firms.

Capping the growth of big business was a search for organizational forms that could bridge the gap even among giant firms. Lobbying associations were formed, such as the *Comité des forges* in France, to coordinate the relations between a major industry and the government. More important, cartels were developed to restrict or eliminate competition within an industry. The *Stahlwerkverband* in Germany, created in the 1890s as a successor to several smaller steel cartels, allocated set market quotas in some goods for each member of the association and fixed limits on all other types of production. In the 1890s a cartel was established among coal producers in the Rhineland–Westphalia region. Each company had votes in the cartel proportionate to its output, and a central commission was established to set production quotas and to determine prices. By 1900 there were three hundred cartels in Germany, and many more were created before World War I. A similar, if less intense, movement developed in Britain, Russia, and elsewhere.

Many governments favored cartels as a means of providing more rational direction to industry. Big investment banks encouraged them; many cartels and even trusts were formed by banks that owned shares in several concerns in an industry. Most important, however, the cartels developed because manufacturers increasingly realized that they could control market conditions through association as they never could in isolation. The movement began in Germany as a result of the crisis of the 1870s, which provided a clear motive to seek more rational organization in industry. It was taken up almost exclusively in industries dominated by large firms; hence cartels were common in coal, steel, and chemicals but literally unknown in textiles. Large firms could make contacts easily because of the small number of units in the industry. Their owners recognized the value of size and coordination and were not committed to a system of family control and mutual rivalry. Increasingly, the principal branches of factory industry were dominated by a small number of giant firms with various mutual links. Coordination and control rather than competition provided the motive force for much of the economic activity within most industrial countries.

Rationalization and concentration continued steadily during the 1920s and 1930s; World War I heightened the trend, if anything. Giant new combines arose, such as the *Vereinigte Stahlwerke,* which controlled almost half of the German steel industry. The role of industrial investment banks increased. Cartels proliferated, some on an international basis.

Big Business: Some General Social Effects

The rise of big business was obviously important for the working class. Growing firms needed new workers, often in tasks requiring considerable strength and skill. Reduction of competitive pressure gave many large firms greater margin for increasing wages and other benefits to their workers. With the great growth of heavy industry up to 1900, those same firms had to offer better conditions to attract the quality of labor they required. Big firms were normally inclined to extend the paternalistic approach to labor that had been suggested earlier. They liked to tie workers to the company by elaborate housing programs and pension schemes. They hoped thus to reduce protest, for big industrialists were particularly angered by any effort at interference from labor. They also hoped to reduce costs, for benefit programs were often cheaper than the equivalent improvements in living standards through higher wages, given the economies of scale in company housing; paternalism, which maintained a rather traditional view of what workers were and deserved, meshed with the rationalizing mentality.

At the same time the development of large units of employment reduced any opportunity for personal contact between workers and owners. It was easier for workers to see the owners as enemies than it had been in the days when the character and even the hard work of owners had been personally known. The huge profits of big corporations invited attack in the hope of obtaining a larger share for labor. Yet workers became increasingly accustomed to large organization. They learned to abide by certain rules; they learned to operate as part of a mass of fellow workers. Many of the causes of new unions and other groups among factory labor can be directly attributed to experiences in huge enterprises that encouraged both the ability and the motivation of workers to take action to improve their lot. But the power of the giant firms was such that successful action would be difficult if the firms chose to resist. The resultant conflict contributed to the rising tide of social tension before World War I.

Big business created new groups of employees during this period. Huge firms, directed by professional managers, required large bureaucracies and growing numbers of clerks. In commerce, large enterprises required clerks and salespeople. A new lower middle class was being formed that neither owned property nor worked as manual labor and whose members were salaried, but did not work with their hands. This new class was one of the most important social results of the development of large economic units dependent on masses of paperwork for their successful administration.

For the industrialists and bankers, the most obvious result of the new business structure was a great increase in profits. Larger enterprises and larger investments permitted an unprecedented concentration of profits. With the reduction of competitive pressure, the bulk of the vast new wealth industry was creating went to the owners of big business. Wages rose, to be sure, but not nearly so rapidly as production increased. During the period 1870–1900 the workers' share in the gross national product declined by 26 per cent in Britain and by 55 per cent in Germany. But the owners of industry had larger incomes than ever before. Their investments rose; giant firms became ever more gigantic. And their standard of living became more luxurious. The upper middle class attained the highest level of material prosperity it had ever known.

Other members of the middle class, and virtually the whole of the middling class, were disturbed by the trends toward concentration and impersonal ownership. They harked back to the pioneering days of industry, when a man could be personally associated with every phase of his enterprise, when his economic effort had a direct relation to his family. Ironically, small businesses steadily increased in number. Between 1882 and 1895 shops employing one to five people grew 24 per cent in Germany, and companies with six to ten workers increased 66.6 per cent. And this was the famous center of big business. After 1900 the rate of small business formation slowed; in England the number of firms actually began to decline in manufacturing by 1906. But still the small owner held on. In Germany there were still as many master artisans in 1926 (about a million and a half) as in 1895, and many were organized in voluntary guilds. Small electric motors and the rise of new goods that could be serviced by small units—the bicycle repair shop, the automobile parts manufacturer—kept the form alive even in new fields. Some small owners hoped to expand and rise into the central or upper reaches of the middle class. But more maintained the old middling class mentality, as the existence of guilds in central Europe suggests. Some were directly threatened by big business, for the growth of small firms conceals many individual failures. Others realized that small firms were no longer proliferating rapidly enough to provide for more than one son; a large family would have to find something else for many of its children to do. The sense of insecurity was heightened beyond any actual displacement, for the relative decline in importance of small ownership followed from a growing cleavage in the values businessmen professed. Modest ambition and direct family control now clashed with a rationalizing mentality in a battle that was unequal from the first. It might have been kinder had small business been killed outright, but modernization has never been kind to traditionalists. A clash was suggested that might be more important than the obvious conflict between business and labor.

Economic Trends

The economic emphasis of the first phase of industrialization was on production, for in a poor society increasing the goods available was essential for any further change. Now, as production continued to expand, the emphasis shifted to problems of distribution. In every branch of manufacturing there were more goods to dispose of than ever before. World pig-iron production tripled between 1870 and 1900. French output of iron and steel expanded more than fourfold between 1890 and 1913. Coal output soared in the last three decades of the century, until affected by the growing use of oil. Britain doubled her already massive production, France tripled hers, and Germany raised hers fifteen times. New needs for acids, dyes, fertilizers, and explosives caused a rapid boom in chemical production. Germany's output of sulphuric acid increased three hundred times by the end of the century. Expansion of older areas of production and the addition of new branches created an unprecedented, though not uninterrupted, industrial boom during the latter part of the nineteenth century.

Many new products were designed for individual consumers. The chemical industry began to discover new kinds of cloth. Novel products such as bicycles, telephones, and automobiles began to flood the market. Here was an extremely significant development, for the early industrial revolution had concentrated primarily on goods already in use. The nature and amount of these goods had changed with their mechanical production, as in the growing use of cotton cloth. The growth of general wealth and of technical knowledge now allowed the development of totally new consumer items. Some, such as automobiles, were reserved for the wealthier classes. Others, such as telephones and electrical lighting, were seldom purchased by the lower classes but affected their way of life as public telephones and lighting systems developed. Finally, some items, such as bicycles, spread to many workers directly.

The dislocations of World War I partially interrupted the surge in production. The French economy continued a substantial boom. Growth in Britain and Germany was slower, but even here new goods received wide currency. The ownership of radios, for example, spread well into the middle class. There were new fibers for clothing, new cosmetics; the list of consumer items grew increasingly long.

The expansion of industrial and also agricultural production spurred new developments in marketing and transportation. In these areas the industrial trends of spreading mechanization and creation of more complex forms of business organization were also apparent. Railroads were extended. Western and central Europe, having completed the development of trunk lines, began to concentrate on local lines. The speed and capacity of railroad transport were brought to increasing numbers of small towns and even villages, expanding both market opportunities and social contacts for rural residents. In eastern and southern Europe trunk lines were now built; the completion of the trans-Siberian railroad in the 1890s was the most notable example of the spread of railroad transport to the European hinterland and beyond. Oceanic shipping expanded greatly in the same period. Metal steam-driven ships dominated ocean transportation for the first time, raising the capacity and speed of shipping. The development of refrigeration allowed perishable items to be sent long distances. Oceanic cables and, late in the century, the radio combined with new shipping to allow increasing international trade. Exports and imports rose massively. European business sought, and often found, new markets in all parts of the world. Even within cities, transportation facilities increased greatly. Electric subways and trams speeded the movement of people. Larger trucking companies and the growing use of gasoline-powered trucks and cabs transformed urban transportation.

New marketing methods followed naturally from the increase of production and the expansion of transportation and communication facilities. Large wholesaling firms arose to supply major cities with consumer products, including foodstuffs. Department stores and even chain stores played a growing role in retailing. Expansion of business structure was a vital part of commerce as well as of industry. Advertising increased, particularly in the mass press, as a means of speeding the circulation of goods. Newspapers and other publications were filled with large, presumably eye-catching notices.

Expanding production obviously produced new wealth. New marketing techniques depended on this wealth, for increasingly industry required a mass market above the subsistence level. Both profits and wages rose significantly during the latter part of the nineteenth century. During much of the period wage increases were accompanied by a drop in prices. Between 1870 and 1914, for example, the wages in French industry rose 14 per cent and prices dropped by the same amount; the result was a major expansion of purchasing power. The cost of housing continued to mount because cities remained crowded, but the declining prices of food and clothing more than compensated for this change.

In Britain real wages rose by a third between 1850 and 1875; between 1870 and 1900 they rose 45 per cent. German real wages increased 30 per cent in the last three decades of the century; French wages rose 33 per cent, and Swedish workers benefited by a 75 per cent gain. The expansion of purchasing power for workers was a general phenomenon even in Russia, where industrialization was just beginning; major differences in standards of living remained, of course, and the older industrial countries offered far higher standards than did newer arrivals such as Germany.

For the first time in human history real poverty, life on the margins of subsistence, was a minority phenomenon in the industrial regions. In

Britain only a third or less of the population lived really near subsistence by 1900; a century before, two thirds had done so. Wealth remained unevenly distributed; in fact, disparities between the middle and lower classes increased as the profits of industry soared. Nevertheless, the masses had gained.

The rise in real wages was translated into a number of improvements in living standards for the lower classes in the countryside and particularly in the cities. Diets became more varied. Consumption of starches tended to stabilize, and the quality of starch improved, especially through the growing use of wheat for bread. Milk and milk products came into greater use. In France the consumption of butter rose 50 per cent between 1870 and 1884. Meat consumption increased notably. In Britain meat consumption per person rose 20 per cent between 1880 and 1900, whereas the rate of bread consumption remained unchanged. Germans bought an average of 59 pounds of meat per person in 1873; by 1912 they were buying 105 pounds per person per year. The consumption of tobacco, tea, coffee, and sugar increased. British consumption of sugar rose 33 per cent between 1880 and 1900, and Germans tripled their average annual consumption (from 12 pounds to 34 pounds per person) between 1870 and 1907. The use of drinks such as beer increased; German consumption of beer rose from 78 liters per person per year in 1872 to 123 liters in 1900. There were still cases of grossly inadequate nutrition, particularly among some agricultural workers and the large group of irregularly employed in the major cities. Class differences were reflected in the fact that, as late as 1930, the average British worker was 2 to 4 inches shorter than his middle-class counterpart. For the majority of the lower classes, however, diets were above the levels of mere subsistence. This was an important precondition for the new vigor that elements of the lower classes showed in many aspects of behavior.

With rising wages and declining food prices, the masses could devote less of their budget to food and still purchase more and better food than ever before. By the 1890s in France only about 60 per cent of the average budget was used for food instead of the previous 75 per cent. The amount and stylishness of clothing reflected the greater resources that the masses could devote to their attire. Furthermore, prices of shoes and clothing fell rapidly. Cotton goods in France cost 50 per cent less in 1896 than they had in 1873. By the late nineteenth century it was virtually impossible to determine a man's exact station by his clothing. The steady democratization of costume, though by no means complete, was an obvious symptom of the rising purchasing power of the masses.

Housing for the masses was still cramped and expensive, after 1870, especially in the larger cities. An increasing portion of the budget had to be devoted to rents, but the teeming tenements of the early industrial period vanished from the most advanced industrial nations. In Prussia over 6 per cent of the families still had only one room, but in Britain this was true for only 1.6 per cent of all families; indeed 94 per cent had three rooms or more. Clearly, housing construction had begun to catch up with the worst needs of the new cities even though rents rose.

Even with all the significant gains in food, clothing, and shelter the lower classes increasingly had money left over for other expenses. Purchases of newspapers and inexpensive novels became common among the masses. Many workers could now pay union dues and contribute a portion of their wage to insurance programs. Popular theaters and music halls arose in the cities to attract the masses; after 1900 moving pictures provided entertainment as well. Sports events, such as soccer football, became commercialized in this period because the urban masses could afford tickets. Railroads offered Sunday excursions for a clientele drawn from the lower classes, and hundreds of thousands of workers and clerks in western Europe bought bicycles, the most expensive consumer good not related to basic needs that had ever been available to the masses. At the same time small savings accounts increased rapidly, and new facilities such as postal savings systems were established to handle them.

The rising average wealth of the masses undoubtedly brightened the lives of most people. The increasing opportunities for diversion were a major new element for the masses in the cities. With more wealth, there was less chance of absolute economic disaster, even during a depression. Savings accounts and sometimes insurance programs provided some protection against illness and old age. There was still great economic insecurity but no longer so many risks of absolute destitution. Better housing and food promoted noticeable improvements in health. This was the period, after all, in which declining mortality rates provided the bulk of the continued expansion of population in western Europe. Increasing numbers of people began to think in terms of improving their health, buying new medicines, and consulting doctors when sick; traditional resignation toward illness declined.

Finally, the fairly steady increase in well-being encouraged a new interest in material enjoyments among the European masses. The masses, particularly in the cities, began to expect further improvements in the standard of living. They developed a concern for new technical devices that would make their lives more pleasant. They were gradually affected by the same attachment to material and technical progress that the middle class had developed earlier. The popular press, even the union movement, both encouraged and reflected this attachment. On the other hand, the rising standard of living, significant though it was, did not take the European masses into an era of abundance. A substantial minority remained desperately poor. Many others had only a small part of their budget free for expenditures beyond the necessities. The conflict between rising expectations and continued limitations on means was to affect both social and economic developments for many decades.

Weaknesses in the Economic Structure

To many observers, particularly in the middle classes, the economy seemed stronger about 1900 than it ever had been before. However, the new economic trends brought with them certain major difficulties. The fundamental problem was that the opportunities for production were not matched by consistent and comparable opportunities for sale. Production was expanding mightily as new countries joined old in industry, and everywhere improved equipment steadily increased possible output. In a real sense the industrial revolution had removed, for the time being at least, any major problem in the production of goods. What remained difficult was the sale of goods produced in growing profusion. Improvements in sales outlets and in transportation were a great help, and trade increased steadily. Nevertheless, there were real weaknesses in the available markets that affected economic conditions and attitudes.

In the first place, the new demographic structure meant that population growth no longer provided the rapid and almost automatic extension of the internal market that had existed during the earlier period of the industrial revolution. Furthermore, important elements of the existing population were severely limited in their ability to buy. Despite rising wages workers could not increase their purchases as rapidly as production was rising. At the same time, the income of agricultural producers was relatively stagnant. Agricultural prices were falling as competition from fertile new regions increasingly pressed farmers. The price drop was partially compensated by major improvements in agricultural equipment and methods during the period, but the incomes of peasants and other landowners did not rise significantly. It was difficult, then, to extend the sales of industrial products among this group. Some new tools and machines were sold because farmers often went into debt to try to improve their production. But again, there was no increase in buying power comparable to the rise in industrial output.

In fact, the only major social group whose income was growing at a huge rate was the business community. Businessmen increased both their consumer and investor purchases during the period. However, they did not spend their money as rapidly as production rose, for they were not pressed by primary needs and were therefore inclined to hold much of their income for a time before deciding to spend. The wealth of Europe as a whole was rising rapidly, but its distribution was such that the principal gains in purchasing power fell to groups that spent rather slowly.

Europe had developed the capacity for massive production but had not yet made the change to a mass-consumption economy.

The disparity between production and market was by no means constant. Utilization of new export opportunities, the high rate of investment in new productive facilities, and the expansion of population and purchasing power allowed a rapid increase in sales. However, there were periods of slump even before 1900. Each of the last three decades in the century saw several years of depression in most areas. The crisis of the 1870s was particularly severe because it came after a period of great confidence induced by the building of basic railroad lines and other outlets for heavy industry.

The slumps of this period were new in some respects, reflecting the novelty of industrial development. They were triggered not by agricultural failures, but by financial crises. The increasing investment of banks and private individuals in stocks could create an artificial speculative mood. The values of stocks soared not because of any corresponding increase in the possibilities of production and sales but because of the rising demand for the stocks themselves. Eventually the speculative bubble burst, sometimes by a failure of a major firm or even of a bank. Investors then became more cautious and funds for further investment harder to obtain. Firms producing capital goods, which depended on investment for their sales, would be forced to reduce their production and employment. This would affect other industries in turn, as the purchasing power of workers and others declined, and the spiral of depression would take its course.

Although levels of unemployment rose during every crisis, suffering among workers was not as intense as it was in earlier depressions. More workers had some savings, and they were not plagued by a concomitant rise in agricultural prices. The inevitable fall in industrial prices made life easier as well. Nevertheless, living standards did decline during the major slumps. And many depressions, such as that of the 1870s, lasted for several years. If crises were not as intense as they had been before, they were more prolonged. Only gradually would the level of investment be built up again as capitalists tried to dispose of their funds; only gradually would sales recover, spurred by lower industrial prices.

The frequency and duration of economic crises was an important symptom of the weakness of the industrial market. It was far easier to invest in industry and produce industrial goods than it was to find corresponding sales opportunities. The growth both of investment and of production continued at a high rate during the period as a whole. Tremendous boom periods, such as much of the 1890s, compensated for periods of difficulty. Nevertheless, a certain structural imbalance in the economy was not removed.

Hence, even the industrialists showed some concern about the tightness of the market for industrial products. Well before 1900 it was clear that many felt that international competition was increasing and that economic activity was becoming more difficult. The feeling of growing pressure was deliberately exaggerated to obtain public support for the demands of the industrialists, but there was real and growing worry. Industrialists and their lobbying associations began to demand new political measures to protect existing markets and promote other sales. They sought tariff protection with greater insistence than ever before. In Germany groups such as the German Industrialists' Union joined hands with protectionist Junkers to press for tariffs on both agricultural and heavy industrial goods. Their greatest success came with the Bülow tariff of 1902, which put a 25 per cent duty on many food and metal products. France passed a high tariff in the 1890s, and Russia, Italy, and most other countries increased or established high levels of protection. Only Great Britain resisted the new wave of economic protectionism until after World War I, despite the growing demands of British industrialists for high tariffs. There was a general desire to mark off national economies and protect the internal market, but in practice tariffs often worsened the situation by making exports more difficult. The pressure for tariffs, however irrational, was symptomatic of the growing anxieties for the future that prevailed among the captains of industry.

The owners of industry urged other panaceas for their marketing problems. Industrialist groups were among the principal promoters of imperial expansion. They argued that colonies would provide both protected sources of raw materials and great markets for finished goods. These arguments were also largely incorrect. Some raw materials were drawn from the new colonies, and certain firms profited hugely from empire. Most of the colonies cost more than they earned, however, and almost none provided useful markets. Trade continued to be most active among industrial countries rather than between an industrial nation and a poor, semipastoral colony. Nevertheless, the intensity of the desire to find secure supplies and markets was another indication of the changing attitudes of industrialists.

Certain industrial groups were also active in promoting increased military expenditures by their governments. This was another, and very realistic, effort to obtain new markets for goods, particularly the products of heavy industry. In Germany owners of metallurgical firms joined with military leaders in the Navy League in a successful effort to stir up public support for the creation of a large navy that would both reflect Germany's national greatness and use an encouraging amount of iron and steel.

Finally, even the investment policies of the businessmen showed a clear realization that economic opportunities at home were less enticing than those elsewhere. More and more, investors poured their funds into foreign enterprises, where interest rates were higher and the chances of major economic advance more abundant. The end of the century saw a significant movement of capital abroad, especially from Britain and France.

The movement was not entirely new, but the pace increased notably. By 1900 over a quarter of British assets were invested abroad. Fifteen per cent of the total French capital and 7 per cent of the German were invested in foreign countries or in the empires. Many of these investments brought handsome returns, helping businessmen to maintain and even improve their economic position during the period. There remained, nevertheless, a certain loss of confidence in the internal economy.

After 1900 the symptoms of economic imbalance became more pronounced. Industrial production faltered, as we have already seen in the case of mining. There were two recessions, in 1901–1902 and 1908–1909; though not particularly severe, they caused high unemployment levels. More novel was a nagging inflation that began with the turn of the century. New sources of gold, in South Africa, helped raise prices, but more than this was involved. High tariffs pushed food costs up. Big business, increasingly able to manipulate markets, could also help keep prices high except in outright recessions. For workers, this meant that real wages stopped rising, for even though money pay increased the price changes ate up the gains. In Britain, real wages actually fell by about 4 per cent before World War I. Profits were not affected, and even rose significantly, because of the growing vigor of big business. But high profits would not help sales as much as mass purchasing power, and this was now challenged.

World War I brought the inflationary spiral to incredible heights. The new pressures were based on governments' printing of new money and extensive borrowing during the war. In essence this increased the demand for goods without any corresponding improvement in the ability to produce goods. Held down by government controls during the war itself, prices nevertheless doubled or tripled in some countries by 1918. Thereafter, except in Britain, which deflated prices by returning to the gold standard, inflation spread like wildfire.

In Austria the cost of living was 2,645 times higher in July 1922 than it had been in 1914. In Germany the inflation of the early 1920s made money virtually valueless as prices rose to astronomical heights. The process was stopped only in 1923 when the government set the mark at a more realistic, but far lower, level than ever before. In France inflation later in the decade was ended only in 1928 by pegging the franc at a quarter of its previous value. Inflationary pressures of this sort affected most groups. Some elements of the working class suffered, for their wages rose less rapidly than prices. Unions were massively damaged as their treasuries were depleted both by the inflation and by the subsequent government devaluation of money. Members of the middle and lower middle classes now suffered even more. A few, to be sure, seized on the inflation as a chance to borrow money cheaply for speculative investment, but the larger element that relied on savings and previous investments saw their holdings virtually wiped out. This encouraged an interest in enjoyment rather than in saving. But the price rises during the war itself, the new taxes imposed by many governments, and the postwar inflation severely reduced opportunities to spend. The loss of savings was also a blow to the confidence, to the very sense of identity, of many in the middle class, which relied on property ownership to provide wealth and status. A new fearfulness arose in the class, which could be translated into active discontent. The class did not lose its esteem for property and its sense of separate status, but it recognized that these values were increasingly threatened by the workings of the economy itself.

Inflation did not necessarily dent production, though it reduced the consumption power of many middle-class elements. Production increased in most countries, though wartime disruption limited gains in some areas. Britain found it hard to recapture export markets that had been lost to the United States or Japan during the war. Germany suffered from the loss of key resource areas. Austria and Czechoslovakia, industrial states, were now cut off from areas like Hungary, their traditional agricultural hinterland. New European boundaries, drawn with no thought to economics, hampered sensible development. Along with inflation itself, this encouraged much unsound investment. Many new business combinations, particularly in Germany, were formed for their speculative possibilities, their potential drawing power for investments, rather than for any improvements they would make in production or distribution. New promoters such as Hugo Stinnes found it easy and profitable to buy firms of extraordinary diversity as vehicles for attracting speculative investments. The rapid price rise of the early 1920s made it easy to borrow with the expectation that the sum would be less valuable when the time for repayment came. Furthermore, massive American capital was available for speculative investment, particularly in Germany, Austria, and the new states of eastern Europe. These funds were not always directed to projects with real productive possibilities (some went into building fancy townhalls), but this simply heightened the speculative spiral. Shaky investments could be bolstered only by further investments, which would raise the value of a stock whether production possibilities were good or not. The result was an economic structure highly vulnerable to shock. When American capital was withdrawn after the 1929 financial crash and when the faith of European investors in their own holdings was correspondingly reduced, collapse of the speculative bubble was inevitable.

For long before this, it had become increasingly difficult to market goods. Wartime interruption of established trade added to the problem. By the mid-1920s areas that produced raw materials entered a severe depression; this was true of agricultural regions in Europe, such as the Balkans, but also the colonial territories. Raw materials were being issued more rapidly than industrial production rose; so their prices fell, which in turn reduced the ability of these areas to buy industrial goods. These new developments were added to the older weaknesses of the mature industrial economy. Agricultural incomes remained low as competition reached new levels. Elements of the working class suffered from unemployment or poor wages, particularly in the older industries. The further reduction of population growth removed yet another possible market. Tariff barriers, which even England now adopted, continued to distort export opportunities.

For a variety of reasons, then, Europe's productive capacities exceeded the possibilities of sales. Production on the Continent as a whole increased only 1 per cent a year after 1923, in contrast to a 3 per cent annual rise before 1913. In a few countries, such as Germany, the speculative boom created a façade of prosperity, but it was highly vulnerable. With the collapse of export possibilities after 1928, and then with the financial crash in the United States and the withdrawal of American capital, Europe entered, inexorably, a period of unprecedented economic depression. The depression was the same type as those before World War I, but much worse than any of its predecessors.

The depression touched every aspect of economic life. It represented a financial crisis. Many banks closed, and credit was restricted; coming on the heels of inflation, faith in money and in financial institutions was severely shaken. Sales fell off sharply even with massive reductions in prices. As a result, production tumbled; German production had fallen 39 per cent by 1932. Profits declined, wages fell, and unemployment increased tremendously. All major social classes suffered. Members of the middle class were hit by declining profits and by loss of stock investments. Their morale was shaken by the mere fact of depression; confidence and optimism about the economic system were reduced. Many managers and recent university graduates suffered from unemployment or were forced to take jobs beneath their station. The lower middle class, similarly, lost many jobs. Peasants were able to sell fewer agricultural goods because of the decline in urban income, so their earnings were reduced still further. But it was the working class that bore the brunt of unemployment and loss of income. In Britain 22 per cent of the workers who had some social insurance were unemployed by 1932. Over 6 million people in Germany and 850,000 in France, not exclusively workers, were out of work. This massive unemployment made recovery from the depression difficult, because it proved hard to stimulate sufficient demand to set the economy in motion once more. And the fact or fear of unemployment greatly weakened public morale. The unemployed survived on some insurance payments and on charity, but they could do no more than survive. Consumption levels fell drastically. Prolonged joblessness reduced many to apathy and stirred others, including those with jobs who feared unemployment for themselves, to new anger.

European economies recovered only slowly and partially from the crisis. The depth of the depression was reached in 1932–1933, although France experienced her trough a bit later. Production after this low point rose; by 1938 the British economy was turning out more goods than ever before. Yet even then more than a million and a half were still unemployed. France did not manage to recover her previous levels of production or employment before World War II. Germany under Hitler did restore full employment and greatly increased production, largely through state programs of investment, military purchasing, and labor service. Wages, however, did not rise to their earlier levels.

Conclusion

The economic trends of mature industrialization thus had diverse implications. It is misleading to look only at weakness, even though the mature industrial period ended in an atmosphere of crisis. Economic change added to the list of innovations that had to be assimilated as part of modernization or exposed new groups to the basic list. Almost everyone had to come to terms with technological change and a new organization of work, as mechanization spread beyond the factories. Everyone had to become accustomed to rising general prosperity. This was not necessarily a simple matter. Traditionalists might take offense at the new spending habits of the lower classes. Many groups might find it difficult to figure out appropriate ways to spend new earnings. Adaptation was obviously complicated by the fluctuations in the economy; too much reliance on material improvements left one open to disappointment.

The possessing classes were faced with a decline in the importance of property ownership. Specialized training and one's position in a bureaucracy were increasingly more important to social success than ownership. Here class attitudes changed more slowly than reality, for the more traditional property-owning groups found it hardest to adjust to the new terms of modernization. Most generally, modernization now depended on ability to deal with large, impersonal organizations. In economic transactions but also in education, even in protest, willingness to interact with strangers and to handle orders from an unseen leadership became increasingly important. Here was a challenge that faced all social classes.

Obviously, some groups that had successfully weathered the first stage of industrialization found the new developments immensely distasteful. Adaptation for everyone was complicated by the periodic economic crises, particularly after 1918 when they bore on the middle as well as the working classes. The gap between the productive potential of the new generation of technology and the overall development of mass purchasing power suggested that society failed to make an important turning. The leaders of the economy, for all their rationalizing genius, were locked into a paternalistic conception of the lower classes. They could not think in terms of a rapid improvement in the general standard of living, which is why they so easily became defensive, turning to tariffs, to empire, to investment abroad, rather than seeking to open up a new kind of market at home. Ultimately not only the working class but also newer elements of the middle class were profoundly affected by the structural imbalance of the economy, which remained beyond their power to control. Important changes in life style were sketched by all these groups, benefiting from new levels of prosperity, but they could not come to full fruition in this period.

Political Change

The Rise of Democracy

Political changes during the mature industrial period were less fundamental than before. Nothing altered the structure of society as had the legal abolition of manorialism and the guilds. Many reforms were rather superficial, in terms of their impact on ordinary life. But political change must be sketched, for three reasons. First, new government functions added to economic rationalization in exposing most people to impersonal organizational structures. Second, the limitations on government activities affected the reaction to the basic economic problems. Third, new political rights increased the interest in the political process. Here was yet another new element of modernization. Popular grievances were now brought into the political arena, and the direction a group's politics took indicated a great deal about its level of adaptation to modern life. In periods of economic collapse, when it became clear that government functions had not changed to match new political rights, politics threatened to become polarized between groups that wanted to use the state to turn back to an earlier society and those that wanted to press forward.

The revolution of 1848 had extended the vote to all males in France and, temporarily, to all males in Germany. French voters had little real choice, however, during most of the Second Empire. Only in the 1860s was there any real opportunity to vote against official candidates; with the establishment of the Third Republic during the 1870s the choice became even more free. The new German Empire, created in 1871, granted universal suffrage for the lower house of the national parliament. Great Britain extended the vote to urban workers in 1867 and to most other males in 1884. Belgium established universal suffrage in 1892. Italy extended the vote in 1882 and made it universal for males in 1912; Austria established universal male suffrage in 1907. Finland and Sweden even allowed women to vote in the 1900s. Britain and Germany did so after World War I. By this time all industrial countries had parliaments with at least one house elected by universal suffrage.

Furthermore, the powers of elected parliaments tended to increase, and parliamentary bodies were established in many nations where no regular instrument of popular representation had existed before. In 1911 the British House of Lords was stripped of the right to veto legislation, fully establishing the House of Commons as the basic authority in British government. The formation of the Third Republic during the 1870s established the supremacy of the French parliament over the executive branch. Elsewhere parliaments were less powerful. In Germany, for example, the functions of the elected Reichstag were severely limited and Prussia, the leading German state, retained a class voting system for its own legislature until 1918. Even in Germany, however, the government paid careful heed to the political composition of parliament, and the masses received increasing attention. They did not rule, but they did not rule in other countries either. It remained generally true, except in Spain and eastern Europe, that the masses gained a regular political voice for the first time during this period; the spread of democratic parliamentary structures was the basis for that voice.

Other reforms promoted effective mass political power. Ballots were made secret in most countries, making it less easy to control votes. Parliamentary representatives began to receive pay, so poor men could serve. By the 1870s most parliaments contained a small number of representatives of working-class origin.

The political reforms, including the extension of suffrage, were largely the work of middle-class and even aristocratic politicians. Few elements of the lower classes had intense political consciousness, although the rising of Parisian artisans in 1848 was the direct cause of the establishment of universal suffrage in France and the Chartist precedent influenced the 1867 voting reform in Britain. Around 1900, after universal suffrage had been established elsewhere, political agitation by the masses, often under socialist leadership, promoted voting reforms in Italy, Belgium, and Austria. Generally, however, the extension of the vote resulted most directly from other considerations.

Conservative–liberal rivalries prompted politicians of both persuasions to broaden the vote in the hope of finding support among the masses. Most important, middle-class political interests continued to stress effective parliaments and even universal suffrage. The class modified a desire for a political hierarchy based on wealth with some sincere interest in equality of political opportunity. And lower elements of the middle class actively supported voting reforms as a means of obtaining political rights for themselves as well as others.

After World War I governments in the new states of eastern Europe, such as Poland, initially granted universal suffrage in imitation of western patterns. Here too, democracy created, rather than followed, political consciousness among workers and peasants.

Hence there was often a conspicuous lag between the extension of suffrage and the development of any clear new political trends. The masses were not accustomed to the vote, and political rights remained meaningless for many. Initial voter participation in German elections was low. Up to a third of all British adult males were excluded from the vote, even after 1884, because of residence requirements; they moved about too often, yet they showed few signs of resenting their deprivation. Those in the lower classes who did vote normally turned first to established political parties and leaders. In France the crisis of the Franco-Prussian War caused many peasants to support local landlords, in the election of 1871; the result was a royalist parliament. In Germany democracy caused little change in the political spectrum for a decade. Only in eastern Europe, where the vote was extended amid early industrial conditions and intense rural population pressure, did new political patterns emerge quickly; during the 1920s a host of peasant parties arose to seek land reform to benefit the rural masses.

Even in western Europe, however, universal suffrage had its impact on established political parties. By the 1880s the professional politician had begun to emerge. Older groups, such as aristocrats or university professors—the "honorable people" of preindustrial society—began to drop out of parliamentary life. Only lawyers retained their place, for democratic politics meant active campaigning, talking to the people, raising campaign funds. So a new group began to enter political life, often as a means of mobility, for parliamentary service paid money, and there were opportunities for profitable contacts beyond this. Ideologically, too, the major political currents had to adapt. Conservative parties by the 1880s had begun to beat the drums of nationalism, even though this was historically a middle-class tradition. Because conservatives wanted no major changes in social structure, they converted to a cause that might rouse the passions of the masses, and with some success.

Middle-class parties were also altered by the need to obtain mass backing. Liberal politicians obtained the support of many elements of the lower-middle class, artisanry, and even the working class by offering support for the extension of free education to the masses and many important measures of industrial legislation and social welfare. The parties were still committed to the protection of middle-class economic and political interests, and on the whole liberal parties found it difficult to win or retain mass support.

The most distinctive result of the new political power and consciousness of the masses was the rise of the socialist parties, an obviously new political force that was at least partially representative of the interests of the working classes. The socialist parties also appealed to some members of the lower middle class and to professional groups such as teachers. The rise of socialism did not follow immediately from the extension of the suffrage, for socialist leaders were not always ready to take advantage of the new opportunities, and the industrial workers were certainly not prepared for such a novel use of their new political rights. In Britain the Labour party developed real strength only after World War I, although it had eighty representatives in Parliament after 1906; the Liberal party continued to win the support of most workers before the war. German socialist activity began in the 1860s but was slow to attract voters until the 1890s, when it regularly polled about a million and a half votes. By 1913 the party received 4 million votes and had 110 deputies in the Reichstag; it was the largest single party in Germany and the strongest socialist party in the world. French socialists, split into several groups, had forty-nine representatives in parliament as early as 1883 and about a hundred by 1913; a socialist had even entered the cabinet in 1899. Socialist parties in Italy and Austria remained smaller because the laboring class was smaller and gained the right to vote only after 1900. Even on the basis of middle-class support, socialists gained importance in parliament, only to become the largest single party once universal suffrage was extended.

Mass Education

The spread of political democracy formed the most notable new link between the masses and government, but it was not the only one. Impressed by the power of Prussia's conscript armies, most Continental governments instituted systems of universal military conscription during this period. By the 1900s most healthy young men of all classes spent two, sometimes three years in military service. This service gave the lower classes experience in discipline and organizaton and provided important training in national loyalty. The Russian army even taught its recruits to read and write. Everywhere military service provided new experiences for many individuals and tended to standardize certain habits regardless of class or region. Particularly for the peasantry, it loosened the force of localism and tradition. Just as military life and tactics changed greatly because of the development of massive conscript armies, so the military experience became an important part of the lives of the masses.

In most countries governments took over functions of record keeping and even marriage from the clergy, usually during a time of church–state conflict. The state registered births, deaths, and weddings for all its citizens.

Most important, the state in all western and central European countries developed free universal public education systems during the period and required school attendance by every child. Education had, of course, been increasing steadily among the masses even before 1870; government expenditures on schools had risen. But many schools remained in the hands of private groups, particularly the churches, and the quality of education before 1870 had been spotty. Many teachers were ill trained, and there were only loose regulations for entry into the teaching profession. Many children who attended school retained little from their experience, often not even the ability to read, and many children could not attend at all because of long hours of work in the city or their distance from schools in the country. Far less attention was paid to the education of girls than to that of boys. Most schools charged small fees, which deterred many parents. Literacy rates rose in industrial countries, but a large minority still could not read.

By about 1870 this situation began to change rapidly. Governments developed a great concern for the education of their citizens, as part of the growing consciousness of the importance of the masses. If the masses were to vote and serve in armies, they would have to be educated. It was vital to attach the loyalties of citizens and soldiers to their governments through education. Middle-class politicians supported educational improvements actively, and the middle class had increasing political influence in this period. The interests of industry also created a greater need for mass education. Industry required growing numbers of people who could read instructions and do simple calculations. It also increasingly needed a population that could read advertisements. Like the state itself, industry required some participation by masses of people who had a basic education. Finally, groups within the urban lower classes, such as artisan unions, pressed for the extension of public education. This was an old demand given greater force by the new political power of the masses.

For a variety of reasons, then, the nations of western and central Europe developed systems of universal primary education during the 1870s and 1880s. Even in Russia primary schools spread rapidly, and in the west schools were available for all. They were quickly made both free, as in Britain in 1891, and compulsory, for girls as well as boys. By 1900 most of western Europe required school attendance until fourteen years of age, and states were providing technical and secondary schools for later years of education. There was even a small movement to broaden university education. New provincial universities were established in France. University extension-course movements and institutions such as Britain's Ruskin College were set up in the hope of drawing talented workers to the universities. These movements had little effect except to extend university training to more members of the middle class. More important was the opening of secondary schools and universities to women. The expansion of higher educational facilities continued after World War I, though again without breaking down basic class barriers.

But mass primary education did have a major impact. It was often of poor quality still. Early schoolmasters frequently thought that disciplining the wild beasts produced by the lower classes was their most important function; not a few school riots broke out among working-class children. Peasants long remained reluctant to send children to school at all, for strangers had no right to interfere in their families and no advantage was seen in book learning. Gradually, however, education became accepted and the quality of schooling improved somewhat. The most important result was the extension of literacy to virtually the whole population of industrial countries. In 1900 two thirds of the people in Spain and Portugal, half of those in Italy and Hungary, and a third of those in Austria still could not read. In all those countries education and literacy were spreading, but the development was too recent to have eliminated extensive illiteracy. Often it required a generation of schooling for a family really to absorb education to the point of being literate, and this generation had not passed in these areas. In the mature industrial societies, however, nearly universal literacy was obtained. Britain rose from 66 per cent literacy in 1870 to 95 per cent in 1900, France rose from 60 per cent to 85 per cent, Belgium from 55 per cent to 86 per cent, and so on. The masses could read, and they did so increasingly. Newspapers preferred by the masses attained circulations sometimes in the millions. Inexpensive books and other publications were widely read also. Mass education, simply by creating the ability to read, was fundamental to the new interests and activities of all the lower classes.

Mass education required significant changes in the organization and curricula of education, which in turn guided the cultural development of the lower classes. In the first place, the educational systems were increasingly standardized under the control of the state. Central bureaus developed uniform course programs, textbooks, and teachers' qualifications for use in all public schools throughout the nation in countries such as France, where the government was highly centralized, or throughout a state in a federal nation such as Germany. The French ministers of education boasted that at any given moment the same lesson was being taught all over France. Local dialects and other parochial interests were specifically fought. One French minister stated that "for the linguistic unity of France, Breton should disappear." Not only Breton, but also Basque, Flemish, Provençal, and, after World War I, Alsatian were attacked by the French school system. Local customs as well as languages were combatted by an educational program consciously designed to provide uniformity. Peasants, obviously, were most affected by these trends, as their localism had been most intense, but all classes were involved. An expectation of uniformity and some cultural guidance from above were among the most important products of the new public education.

The systems of public education also encouraged secularization of the attitudes of the masses and the reduction of religious influences. In most countries the period was marked by major conflict between church and state over the degree of religious influence permissible in the schools.

In Germany education was largely secularized during the *Kulturkampf* of the 1870s. Priests and pastors were removed from the schools, and a number of Catholic teaching orders were suppressed, although Bavaria continued to give public support to church schools. Teaching orders, especially the Jesuits, were suppressed in many other countries during the 1860s and 1870s. Belgian Catholics lost a long and bitter political struggle with middle-class liberals for control of education. In France laws establishing public primary education in the 1880s banned priests from teaching in the public schools and closed all Jesuit schools. The state in most countries sought full control of the education of the masses. It was supported by large elements of the middle class who traditionally combined an interest in education with a dislike of religious influence. The result was an educational experience for the masses that was largely secular in all countries and entirely, even militantly, secular in some.

In place of localism and religion in education, the new systems promoted useful patriotic subjects. Courses in civics and national history were intended to provide the knowledge necessary to a good citizen and particularly to encourage national loyalty. Systems of public education were one of the most important forces in the development of mass nationalism during this period. Training in the national language and literature supplemented the nationalist orientation of the social sciences.

Otherwise, the new education systems pointed toward economic utility. Mathematics, particularly arithmetic, and some technical and scientific training (including discussions of better agricultural methods, in the countryside) completed the typical curriculum.

Education had a number of diverse implications. By spreading literacy and breaking down tradition it opened the lower classes to the new kinds of propaganda. But only a minority—perhaps 5 per cent of the adult working class, according to several surveys—developed intensive new reading interests. Mass politicians, including socialists, long found that speeches were essential to capture their constituency, for the oral tradition remained strong. Reading ability might lead others to seek self-improvement, by obtaining an office job instead of factory work; educational achievement began to be a factor in social stratification among the lower classes. This was not incompatible with radical politics, for an aspiring worker might be an ardent socialist, and indeed leadership ranks of socialist parties and trade unions served as a means of mobility for many bright young workers. But against these dynamic implications of education was the fact that few members of the lower classes had either desire or ability to rise very high on the educational ladder, for schooling was a foreign experience. And the nationalistic tone of the educational systems helped turn many people away from any effort to rock the boat; here was a new form of deference.

Welfare Reforms

The advent of democracy and the rise of socialist parties prodded governments to a series of social reforms. By the 1890s the burning political issue was known as the "social question," which meant, fundamentally, what to do to keep the urban masses quiet. This involved some traditional methods: police forces became ever more adept at riot control, and in most industrial countries major unrest called out the army. But governments expanded their role in other directions to deflate some grievances. The result was an important expansion of state functions, a major element in the growing bureaucraticization of society.

With the growing political consciousness of the masses as a backdrop, there were many sources of support for limited reforms. Conservatives introduced many measures, such as the German insurance laws of the 1880s. A clerical, royalist majority in the French parliament passed in 1874 the first effective factory inspection law. Conservative parties hoped by these measures to win working-class support, and the idea of regulating middle-class business and extending paternal assistance to the poor still had some appeal for conservative aristocrats.

Far more support for welfare functions came from liberal middle-class politicians. There was opposition, of course. The liberal tradition was opposed to expanding the functions of government. Many businessmen feared the expense of welfare programs; German industrialists, for example, opposed the initial social insurance laws of the 1880s. However, there was much middle-class support as well. Many came to see that welfare measures did not harm business interests; in Germany the business community supported some later welfare laws. Many saw welfare measures as a necessary response to the agitation of labor; the middle class was not inflexible in its attitude toward working-class desires. Finally, the humanitarian traditions of the middle class prompted some to see the justice of welfare measures, the need to eliminate some of the worst forms of material insecurity and abuse. Knowledge of the conditions of the poor was promoted by various public and private reports and by the propaganda of socialists and union leaders. There was some realization that reforms were needed not just to assuage labor but also to approach more closely middle-class ideals of general prosperity and opportunity.

Prior to 1870 or 1880 relatively little had been done by national governments to meet the social problems of industrial societies. There had been minor protective legislation, covering particularly the field of child labor. National laws had permitted action, sometimes by localities, to protect certain minimal standards in health, housing, and education. Food and drug inspection began in the 1860s in much of western Europe. Municipal governments had led in developing new functions by providing parks, libraries, effective sewage disposal, and a wide variety of other facilities for their citizens. But the total amount of welfare activity was small and limited in concept. Most of it involved simply an extension of the middle-class idea of the state as policeman, removing abuses but not engaging in positive action to construct new conditions. Vigorous protection was extended only to categories of people, particularly children, who were clearly incapable of defending their interests.

After 1870 many older welfare concepts were extended, and new principles were developed, especially in the field of social insurance. Even relatively new industrial countries participated in the movements toward some welfare legislation, in imitation of the more extensive programs of the mature industrial countries. Germany was the first nation to develop a comprehensive welfare system. In 1883 a compulsory insurance program against illness was established for most industrial workers; up to thirteen weeks of sickness were covered. Both workers and employers contributed to the program, which was administered by local groups, including some old mutual aid societies. In 1884 accident disability insurance was passed, paid for entirely by the employer, novel recognition that the employer, not the worker, was responsible for accidents in the plant. Finally, in 1889, a program was passed to support the aged and invalid, with premiums paid half by employee, half by employer, with government subsidies if necessary. These three laws established the basic welfare program for Germany in the period. They were extended several times to cover more people, including agricultural workers. Between 1885 and 1900, 50 million Germans received from the program benefits worth $750 million, $250 million more than the workers had contributed. Germany also passed various laws regulating hours of work and conditions of pay; even domestic workers were protected. The state promoted industrial courts to arbitrate disputes between employer and worker. With a massive program of social insurance and various other protective measures, the German state offered the most complete welfare program of any nation in Europe.

Britain, somewhat later than Germany, developed a series of measures almost as comprehensive. There was a great deal of regulation of sanitary conditions, of hours for women and children, even of the conditions of children in schools and in homes. In 1909 an eight-hour law was passed for miners, the first law directly regulating the hours of work for adult males. In 1912 a new type of protection was added, again for miners, with the establishment of a minimum wage. A 1905 law, passed by a Conservative administration, admitted new state responsibility for unemployment by establishing state funds for the relief of deserving unemployed, and in 1908 a tax-supported pension plan was established. In 1911 the National Insurance Act was passed, the most extensive scheme developed in Britain before the war. It covered both sickness and unemployment and was compulsory for those categories of workers to whom it applied. A third of the funds for the program came from workers, a third from employers, and a third from the state.

Other European states developed welfare programs, often patterned on the German. Austria passed an accident-insurance plan in 1887 and a sickness-insurance scheme the next year. Denmark created similar programs between 1893 and 1903. Italy passed legislation providing insurance against accidents and old age in 1898, and Norway, Spain, and Holland established accident compensation in the 1890s. Most European states also passed laws limiting the hours of work; regulating the labor of children; setting minimum standards of ventilation, light, and sanitation in factories; and eliminating abuses in fines imposed on workers and in payments of wages in kind. In France insurance against illness and accident was passed, but coverage was voluntary rather than compulsory. A ten-hour day for factories employing both men and women and a six-day week were established by law. In 1910 a voluntary pension plan was set up by the state.

The welfare programs set up during the period all followed several general principles. They extended the concept of the state as policeman on guard against abuse by regulating many new aspects of factory and market activity. Some traditional limits on regulation remained, however, as in the general avoidance of direct regulation of the hours of adult males (with the exception of mineworkers). Another middle-class principle, self-help, guided the insurance programs of the period; participants in most of the programs paid most of the costs. This self-help feature was acceptable to many workers, who could thereby regard the programs as something other than charity, and it helped make the programs more compatible with middle-class ideals, for it seemed to encourage self-reliance and also did not threaten to cost much in tax money.

Many of the insurance programs went beyond the self-help feature by making them compulsory for the categories of workers covered and by adding state or employer contributions. Compulsion was necessary to spread the risks from an insurance standpoint, but it did reduce the liberty of workers to go their own way. Few programs depended on workers' contributions alone. The 1908 pension plan in Britain relied entirely on general tax funds. There was an embryonic concept of the state as a redistributor of income through taxes, and most states established graduated taxes, although mainly to support military expenditures. The Lloyd George budget in 1909 established special taxes on land, raised the taxes on upper incomes and lowered them for the poor, and provided some deductions for children. The British tax schemes, in combination with tax-supported welfare programs, effectively set aside 1 per cent of the national income each year for redistribution. This was only a halting step, but it was the most novel extension of state responsibility during the period.

The early welfare laws did a great deal of good. In Germany and elsewhere insurance programs contributed significantly to the resources of many workers in times of misfortunes. Regulations of conditions eliminated many abuses in factory conditions and were responsible for many of the gains in leisure time and in health by the working classes. However, most of the plans were quite limited. Regulations often applied only to factories and left artisans, shopkeepers, and rural workers unprotected. Insurance schemes, even where compulsory, often covered a minority of workers. The National Insurance Act in Britain was intended to be experimental and applied to only 2.25 million men. None of the plans covered dependents, widows, and orphans. The poorest people, such as rural labor or single women working at home, were left almost untouched by these various schemes; only in Germany did measures go significantly beyond factory workers alone. Even those who did benefit received relatively little. Pensions and insurance payments in Britain were set deliberately low to discourage idling. It was assumed that these plans would merely supplement other savings; but other savings did not necessarily exist. The little redistribution of income that occurred was more than offset by the growing gap between profits and wages that developed everywhere after 1900.

The welfare programs, particularly in their insurance aspects, were important indications of the new political power of the masses and the flexibility of the upper classes in response. They showed that some new ideas about government functions were developing. They were not, however, major contributions to the well-being of the masses. They did not notably stem the discontent that arose among factory labor and even among some segments of the peasantry during the period. The measures taken obviously accorded with the expectations of the masses for direct government aid; but they did not yet go far enough to assure contentment.

The limitations on government action were agonizingly apparent after World War I. In the first flush of enthusiasm following the war, often under the auspices of socialist parties that had grown in strength, new welfare measures were adopted. The French government, for example, proposed a compulsory social insurance program, though this was passed only a decade later. Germany extended its social insurance programs to new groups of workers, and in 1928 passed an unemployment insurance scheme. The hours of adult male workers were limited in several countries. But there was no major breakthrough, and when depression came government policies throughout western and central Europe initially ignored the pressing needs of the working and even the middle classes. Government employees were fired, unemployment compensation funds kept to a minimum. New taxes burdened shopkeepers, who were already angry that they received less attention from the state than the workers did. The general reluctance to use the power of the state to take any new economic initative contributed to the worsening of the depression for several years.

It was only in 1934 that the British government agreed to commit tax revenues to the unemployment insurance program, even though funds had run out long before under the impact of depression, and even then the duration of assistance was severely limited. Only toward the middle of the 1930s were there suggestions, often halting, of a new kind of state to match the novel problems of mature industrial society.

Conclusion

All told, there was more noise than substance to the political changes during the mature industrial period. The character of formal political structure changed, and the contacts of state with ordinary citizen were increased. But the state was bent on maintaining the social system, not overturning it. This accounted for the controls exercised over education and the limited duration and quality of the education offered. There was a commitment now to industrialization, though sometimes qualified by continued protection of a retrograde landlord class. To this extent the state at least did not impede a far more basic force for change. But new state functions failed to keep pace with the altered nature of society. This is why, admittedly after the additional burden of an unprecedented war, most states neared paralysis.

The limited nature of political change obviously encouraged the politicization of grievances, whether new or old. Not only the working class but also middle-class and peasant elements developed new ways to express discontent, because their political rights had outstripped their political power. For the new voting rights, the new parties and campaign methods, did not effect rapid changes in government personnel or outlook. Professional politicians altered the composition of parliaments, drawing in even a minority of ambitious or dedicated workers. But the ministries these parliaments produced were still predominantly middle class and aristocratic. Even top socialist leaders were usually middle class. Still more important, the bureaucracies behind the parliaments, and often substantially beyond their control, were drawn heavily from a conservative amalgam of aristocrats and traditional professional people, open in turn to the pressure-group activities of landlords and big businessmen.

Hence many of the key developments in the further modernization of behavior and values occurred beneath the surface. A changing economy provided much of the framework, as in the rise of new means and new needs for leisure. The state was barely relevant. Even in years of political strife many people were trying to forge a new style of life. Changes in the activities of women or in the treatment of adolescents were rarely reflected in the formal political arena. It remained true that society was modernizing more rapidly than the state and that this ultimately had dangerous political consequences.

The Upper Class

Every major social group was caught in some tension between old and new. Was impersonal economic and political organization acceptable? Were political rights useful, and how should they be employed? How could the class adapt to new economic opportunities and problems? The new tensions explain, among other things, why no social class produced a unified political response. The middle class spawned socialists, liberals, and fascists, all in some abundance. For all the social classes that had been defined by the first stages of modernization were now forced into a redefinition, depending on their relationship to the new forms of production.

Nowhere was this more apparent than at the top of society, yet nowhere was the complexity of redefinition greater. Not a few of the weaknesses of the economic and political structure derived from the curious nature of the European elite.

The aristocracy could no longer serve as the upper class. This, plus the rise of big business, might suggest that a new, rationalizing class of men took over upper-class status in mature industrial society. In part this is correct. What had been, before, the richest segment of the middle class now split off because of its immense wealth and political influence. But it did not take over sole control. It did not directly staff the state bureaucracies, for it preferred to deal with government through pressure groups. Government bureaucrats came mainly from a mixture of professionals (mainly lawyers) and aristocrats, and their outlook and training left them ill prepared to deal with the newer social and economic problems. Big businessmen themselves accepted direct partnership with the aristocracy in education and many political activities. There was increasing intermarriage between the two groups, and in many countries the great industrialists adopted or were granted aristocratic titles. The magnates of the Ruhr regarded their firms as something of a family fief, despite the rise of the corporate form; hence they often named mine pits "The King" or "The Baron." And of course their paternalistic outlook toward the lower classes resembled that of the aristocracy. Big businessmen, in sum, although adept at utilizing new technology and new organizational forms, did not form an entirely modern upper class. They retained admiration for the prestige of noble birth and for the sumptuous life style of the landed magnates. Their great mansions and hunting parties, in which aristocrats increasingly intermingled, maintained other elements of an older tradition.

The aristocracy suffered important new setbacks in mature industrial society that forced it to accept membership in the amalgamated upper class. The key to its dilemma was the unprecedented crisis in agriculture that opened up after 1875. Huge imports of grain, especially wheat, from areas outside Europe reduced grain prices steadily. Aristocrats, dependent on grain sales to the market, suffered along with the peasantry. Not only their earnings but also land values tumbled. At the same time political changes, including parliaments that gave power to middle-class politicians and then new suffrage systems that enfranchised the masses, threatened the class's political hold. But it was through politics that the class salvaged something from its agony, for the state could help preserve the land and give compensatory jobs and power beyond this.

The aristocracy confirmed its grasp on key bureaucratic jobs. They could no longer buy offices. Civil service reforms in all the industrial countries opened the bureaucracy to competitive examination around 1870. This was one reason aristocrats increasingly intermingled with middle-class bureaucrats. But with their wealth, even if dented, and social connections it was still easy to get into the better schools and universities. Moreover, the schools that trained for government service retained a significant amateurish element that the aristocracy found congenial. England offered a classic case in point. Middle-class efforts to reform the great public schools were largely abandoned in the 1860s once these schools admitted the sons of wealthy businessmen along with aristocrats. The schools added a bit more emphasis on science and modern languages, but continued to stress the classics, games, and a nonutilitarian approach. Knowledge of Latin, plus the social graces, were far more important in gaining access to the top civil service job than was specialized training in economics. Small wonder that here, as on the Continent, aristocrats were heavily over-represented in the diplomatic corps and the military and that middle-class elements who served with them took on much of their culture.

Positions in the bureaucracy gave aristocrats pay, and also the means to influence government in their favor in other ways. Militarism and imperialism, so dominant in the policies of the European states during the mature industrial period, owed much to the aristocracy's desire for new bases of power and new ways to express traditional values. Imperialist pressure groups in France, beginning with the "geographical societies" of the 1870s, were led by aristocrats. Big businessmen played their role, supporting imperialism because of presumed market benefits. But the imperialist movement owed at least as much to a new aristocratic reaction as to advanced capitalism.

The aristocracy also entered the political arena, even when they did not run for office directly. They retained a dominant influence in conservative parties. They could still appeal for peasant support on the basis of traditional deference. Groups like the German Union of Agriculturalists advocated high tariffs on grain even though many peasants, converting to stock breeding, bought grain and suffered from any movement toward higher feed prices. Yet they won peasant support on the basis of the unity of agricultural interests and, increasingly, the invocation of nationalism. Traditionally hostile to nationalism, aristocratic interest groups, along with conservative parties, began converting to it in the 1880s because it let them retain political influence. The nation's interest demanded protection for agriculture, a strong military, and an expanding empire. Beneath all these resounding arguments were benefits to the aristocracy.

Small wonder, then, that aristocratic influence won direct support for agriculture. The Prussian Junkers managed to obtain state subsidies for rye; along with the high tariff protection this allowed them to continue fairly traditional agricultural methods, employing a low-paid agricultural labor force, and keep some hold over the large estates. In Russia a Nobles Land Bank was established in 1885; by 1900 aristocrats had borrowed 660 million rubles, much of which they used simply to maintain their standard of living.

Both political and economic efforts brought the aristocracy into growing unity with the upper middle class. Big businessmen and bureaucrats bought land. Some aristocrats moved into corporate directorships. Economic interests became increasingly intertwined. In politics the two groups agreed to scratch each others' backs. Big businessmen, through their political influence, agreed to agricultural tariffs and aristocrats accepted protection for industry; the 1902 Bülow tariff in Germany resulted from this kind of agreement among Junkers and industrialists. Both groups supported military spending. Both increasingly united in opposition to socialism and other lower-class demands. Again in Germany, aristocratic politicians enjoyed tweaking the noses of businessmen by supporting the social insurance laws of the 1880s. But when workers refused to be quietly grateful, when they pressed into the socialist party, the aristocracy took fright. By the 1900s a solid alliance of aristocrats and big businessmen resisted any major labor gains.

The size of the new upper class is hard to determine. Radical politicians talked of 200 families in France controlling French industry and banking, and certainly there were great concentrations of power in a few hands. In the 1930s there were 144 men who served as directors of at least ten companies, and many of their families were intermarried. It was also true that many aristocrats went under in this period, which further limited the size of the upper class. Some lost their land; others huddled on small estates in poverty, damning the modern world but unable to maintain the political flexibility that the upper class now required. But in all probability the upper class was larger than the traditional aristocracy had been. In 1900 in France 2 per cent of all the people who died left 50 per cent of the wealth that was passed on. In Britain between the wars, 5 per cent of the population controlled over 75 per cent of all earnings from private property. The upper class had great political power, dominant wealth, and not inconsiderable numbers. Partly because of their inclusion of the aristocracy it enjoyed wide social prestige. Popular newspapers were filled with reports of the marriages and parties of the wealthy, stirring some readers to envy but more, perhaps, to a bedazzled admiration. For this new upper class benefited from much of the deference many groups had long given to the aristocracy alone.

One final element enhanced the power of the upper class in the mature industrial period. Its emergence coincided with a prolonged crisis in the older professions, which drove many professional people into tacit or direct alliance with upper-class political efforts. As university enrollments soared (they rose from 14,000 in 1870 to 61,000 in 1914, in Germany) the number of jobs for lawyers and doctors did not keep pace. Many were only too eager to ally with aristocrats in the state bureaucracy. Many sought parliamentary careers (not only lawyers but unemployed doctors took this course), and although some served as political radicals, even socialists, others worked easily with the interest groups representing landed and big business interests. Many also filled the ranks of nationalist and imperialist groups like the Pan-German League, under upper-class leadership. Most important, the older professions did not insist on a further modernization of their own education. They were content with the classical orientation of the leading secondary schools and universities, taking their cue from the respectable culture of the upper class that in turn derived so much from the aristocratic tradition of genteel amateurism. The result enhanced the difficulty government bureaucrats and politicians had in coping with new economic problems. The French parliament, filled with lawyers, dealt successfully neither with inflation nor with depression during the 1920s and 1930s. Not the least of the reasons for this was the fact that law schools offered only an optional course in economics.

The new upper class, with its allies from the older professions, was no more malevolent than upper classes in other periods of history. But it was somewhat ill adapted to the needs of modern society. It stressed property ownership—the big business fiefs—and a traditionalist education, with an overtone of a still more traditional esteem for gentle birth. Adept at political manipulation, it avoided outright revolution, and in this sense might be counted rather successful. But it could not manage the economy that it so largely controlled and it could not stem growing political challenge.

The upper class was damaged by World War I. The aristocracy had supplied many army officers, whose death rates were higher than those of ordinary troops; its ranks were seriously depleted. Professional men of good education also generally became officers and suffered greatly. The result was something of a demographic crisis in the leadership ranks, which reduced the quality of bureaucrats and politicians, drawn from a less competitive pool of newcomers, and damaged morale. Aristocrats were also frightened by the example of the Russian Revolution, where the class was expropriated and eliminated by law. The example of refugee nobles serving as doormen or taxi drivers in Paris or Berlin hardly inspired confidence.

Outside of Russia, aristocratic landlords in eastern Europe faced new challenges. New states and old set up democratic regimes. Middle-class politicians talked about liberal land reforms while militant peasant parties pressed hard in the same direction. Actual change was slight. Only in Rumania were the large estates broken up, and even there aristocrats received substantial compensation that allowed them to invest in business. Elsewhere, even in relatively liberal Czechoslovakia, less than 10 per cent of the land was redistributed. Furthermore, in all these areas, including Rumania, aristocrats were able to force much the same alliance with the upper middle class that had occurred in western and central Europe earlier. For both groups grew frightened by peasant and worker radicalism. In combination they were able to replace the democratic, parliamentary regimes with an authoritarian state everywhere except in Czechoslovakia. Much the same pattern developed in Spain. A republic was established in 1931, vaguely talking of land reform though doing little. This frightened aristocrats, and growing socialist and anarchist agitation terrified leading businessmen and professional people. Here a bloody civil war resulted, but the upper classes retained their hold through the ultimate victory of the Franco regime.

The upper class was less beleaguered in the more advanced industrial areas of Europe but it had distinct problems. The continuing agricultural crisis hit the landed estates. Prussian Junkers had to find ways to persuade the new republican government to give them special subsidies, although their success was a testimony to the continued validity of upper-class action. Big businessmen might pile up speculative profits during the 1920s, but investment patterns were disrupted. Big French investors lost heavily from the collapse of tsarist Russia and the Habsburg monarchy, for they had poured funds into both areas. The depression hit individual big businessmen hard. There was no general collapse, but there was growing uncertainty. It was not surprising that the French upper class turned eagerly to a new book, published in 1935, entitled *The Art of Managing and Protecting One's Fortune.* For the upper class, in its capacity as economic and political leader, could not resolve the economic and political crisis of the interwar period, if only for want of appropriate training. Its immediate reaction was defensive. Big businessmen and landowners in Germany, Italy, and France began to support authoritarian political parties that might restore order in their troubled countries. Rarely fascist, for they recognized fascism as an attack on the existing social structure, they often subsidized fascist parties in return for a promise of noninterference in big business. True to their word, Mussolini and Hitler supported big business profits and made no move against the large estates.

So the upper class struggled through the 1930s. Its fortunes were fairly clearly tied to those of the new regimes in central and eastern

Europe and, after 1940, to the reactionary Vichy government in France. Elsewhere its political role was less reactionary but it was no more successful in resolving the basic economic problems of mature industrial society. Called into being by new industrial wealth, the upper class had not really embraced the principles of advanced industrial society.

The Middle Classes

From the middle ranks of society came a new style of life that combined enjoyment and work in a persuasive manner. From the middle ranks of society, during this same mature industrial period, came support for a politics of reaction, ultimately fascism. How can this dual product be explained?

Our ignorance of the middle classes is partly responsible for the superficial conundrum. Very little work has been done on this vital sector of society during the later industrial period, although they constituted the most rapidly growing element as well as, still, the dominant class culture. Variations in time are involved. The middle classes worked on their leisure ethic in good years, turned more to politics in bad. Variations in place play a role. Middle-class political reaction was strongest in Germany, next in France and Italy, while Britain and Scandinavia were not greatly affected; on the other hand the leisure ethic emerged most clearly in England. But the most important single factor was the differentiation of the middle ranks of society into four distinct groups. The true middle class could be defined in terms of income; it was the second wealthiest group in the population, but earning, at its upper limit, less than 25 per cent as much annually as the lower limit of the upper class. It could be defined increasingly in terms of education, for this was a class that now went regularly into secondary school. But the class was now divided between those who could not accept the further development of modernization and those who could. Beneath this divided middle class was the old middling class, now increasingly disgruntled, and a really new, white-collar group, propertyless but with values similar to the modernized middle class. From the modernized middle class and new lower middle class came the new life style. From the disgruntled middle class and middling class came the new politics. This complexity is unfortunate but essential in understanding the period. The products of disgruntlement have thus far received most attention, for they briefly captured the political arena during the 1930s. The new middle-class culture was, in the long run, more significant.

There were of course points of overlap among the four groups. The children of one might feed into another. The son of an embattled shopkeeper could easily become a clerk or a store manager. He might carry over something of his father's sense of grievance against the modern world, but he would also begin to develop other interests. The middle classes had some common problems throughout the period. It became progressively harder to find servants. This caused much complaint but may not in fact have been totally resented, for servants had been a mixed blessing and new household appliances helped replace them. Many middle-class families, increasingly close-knit, may have preferred to live without a stranger in the house. Urban rents rose dramatically, which burdened the middle-class budget and forced increasing numbers into the suburbs. There were new sources of income, too, though we do not know if the average middle-class income increased much even before the inflationary inroads of the 1920s. Educational opportunities were more obviously important. Professional people still went further in their education than businessmen, but both remained more highly educated than the lower classes. In France and Germany about 10 to 15 per cent of the population went to the most prestigious secondary schools, the *lycée* and the *Gymnasium*. Perhaps more important, new secondary schools were developed to offer a more pragmatic training in science and modern languages; the German *Realgymnasium,* in particular, drew many students from lower middle-class ranks. Educational opportunities in England remained more haphazard until the development of a state-supported secondary school system after 1902, but here too the middle classes—their women as well as their men—steadily improved their educational level. In all major cases most of the middle class received primary education under the auspices of the secondary schools and so was separate from the lower classes at all stages.

The Disgruntled Middle Class

A variety of situations could produce middle-class anxiety. The middle-sized industrialist, who believed in the family firm, was increasingly squeezed by larger corporations. Some might decide that it was safest to sell out and become a manager in one of the giant firms. But this involved a crucial loss of property ownership, and with it much of the traditional sense of status; hence in 1899 almost 20 per cent of all British industrial managers felt they had been downwardly mobile in entering their new career, whereas another 40 per cent had not, in their opinion, improved their status over that of their fathers. The middle class was often tempted into new investments, as the stock market expanded, yet these could easily fall through. Financial crisis like that of the 1870s ruined many. Fraudulent investment schemes robbed others of their savings even in prosperous years. The Panama Canal scandal in France affected almost half a million investors.

But it was from the older professions, not the business groups, that the most persistently aggrieved segment of the middle class emerged throughout the mature industrial period. Several factors were involved.

First, the professions did not keep pace with the new upper class in income or status. Some slipped badly, like the French university professors who, miserably paid, spent much of their time discussing their hatred of upstart businessmen. Second, the older professions were producing more people than there were jobs. Many groups continued to measure society in terms of older occupational status rankings and so urged their sons into law or university teaching. Professionals themselves wanted their sons to follow their footsteps, for entry into business would be degrading; hence 65 per cent of German university professors were sons of university-educated fathers. Shopkeepers or even successful businessmen might opt for this older success ladder. The son of a second- or third-generation industrialist who turned against his father's money-grubbing was another common phenomenon. As soon as they were free to enter the professions, Jews in central Europe flocked in; by 1890, only twenty-three years after their legal emancipation, Jews constituted 34 per cent of all university students in Vienna. To the prestige of the older professions was added one new element in this period: those professionals who entered state service, which was itself a traditional goal, now after retirement received pensions. French civil servants, for example, were covered by pensions after 1853. Interest in protecting one's old age became an increasingly distinguishing feature of this segment of the middle class, for this was a group that expected to retire with some security. Consciousness of the importance of old age was in itself an extremely promising development, but for the time it helped feed an excessive supply of people toward the civil service.

Finally, in law, teaching, and to an extent medicine, professional modernization had broken down. Provision of elaborate training and state licenses was supposed to prevent oversupply. It still did in newer areas such as engineering; French and German engineers prospered during this very period on the basis of their training, which was increasingly suited to the managerial and research needs of modern industry. But, lacking the traditional cachet, they drew fewer recruits than there were jobs. Professional modernization still worked in England, and the crisis of the professionals did not reach there, although only expansion of jobs in the Empire prevented unemployment. On the Continent, more people could acquire training than the old professions could accommodate. Secondary school teachers grew fearful of new competition; this was one source, in Germany, of opposition of women's entry into teaching careers. Primary school teachers were unable to professionalize at all, because of oversupply. Entry into the ranks of university professors was difficult, for their number did not expand rapidly; the average German professor was fifty-four in 1907. Lawyers, with their largely classical training, did well on civil service examinations, but there were not enough posts. So many, as in Germany, served as mere file clerks. They also, of course, played a disproportionate role among parliamentary politicians, but this provided relatively few jobs overall.

And lawyers lacked the specialized training that might make them useful in business management, which is where the newer opportunities lay.

The case of doctors is still more interesting. Here was a profession that seemed able to modernize successfully. It had its associations, licensing, and professional journals. It developed one specialization after another: surgeons, gynecologists, obstetricians, and by the end of the century specialists in pediatrics and geriatrics. But all of this rested on a very shaky base in terms of knowledge. Two kinds of medical knowledge advanced particularly in the nineteenth century. The germ theory, developed first by Pasteur in the 1860s, was vital for improvements in public health; it also helped cut deaths on the operating table or in the delivery room, always assuming that the doctor believed the theory and remembered to wash his hands. The other main advance came in pathology; there was a real gain in knowledge of what diseased organs looked like, through discoveries in autopsies. But none of this helped treat sick people very much. There were some gains, of course. Gynecological surgeons were able, by the 1890s, to operate successfully on ovarian cysts and other problems that previously would have killed their victims. The growing use of obstetricians instead of midwives did reduce both infant death and death in childbirth, though mainly toward the end of the nineteenth century. But the simple fact was that doctors were not responsible for most of the health gains that occurred during the nineteenth century, which resulted more from changes in diet and improvements in public sanitation—like the purification of water that spread in cities during the second half of the century and gradually eliminated typhoid. The further fact was that adult health did not really improve very much. Life expectancy at age twenty was little better in 1900 than it had been in 1800 and a host of adults, even in the middle classes, endured unpleasant chronic illnesses, even when nonfatal, like the 80 per cent of all French women who suffered from leucorrhea in 1865. And the final fact was that doctors really did not have very much special knowledge to offer their patients before the 1930s, unless of course the patient died, when they became increasingly adept at identifying the causes. Professionalization had outstripped knowledge. Doctors themselves often doubted their own training. As late as the 1930s many French doctors returned to Neo-Hippocratism, attacking official medicine and claiming that the real causes of many diseases were still unknown and that the doctor should stress an appreciation of the individual temperament of each patient. Homeopathy continued to win converts among trained doctors. From the standpoint of potential patients, there was little to distinguish the professional doctor from the charlatan. Even with the successful professionalization of medicine in England, quacks were still listed, as an occupational category, through the 1880s. The situation was worse on the Continent. Not only did peasants resist new medicine in favor of traditional cures, but urban residents often went to magnetisers, hypnotists, or herbalists, for these were in fact little different from the doctors who, around 1900, were still advocating cancer cures through living on a boat in the Rhone River and playing music during meals.

Most people went to doctors only in the late stage of an illness, if at all. Only the few doctors with a clientele among the upper classes, who had been more fully converted to medicine, made much money, along with some who offered consultations by correspondence. There were more trained doctors than could find even a marginal medical practice, almost 8 per cent more in France. Still larger numbers found their income and prestige well under their expectations; in 1901 it was estimated that only half the doctors in France considered themselves prosperous.

A large segment of lawyers, teachers, and doctors was thus alienated from the modern world. They could ally with some other professions or near professions that were also in trouble. Priests and pastors lamented the decline of religion in the modern world, which meant a decline in their own prestige. More directly, the rise of the state school system, with its symbol, the secular school teacher, reduced the local prestige of clerics. Journalists, though not professionals, in that anyone could try his hand at the game, were badly paid and irregularly employed in the larger cities.

Finally, professionals bordered on a final group that almost defies definition as part of modern society: the intellectuals, many of whom had professional training or came from professional families. There had been intellectuals throughout recorded history, of course, but until the eighteenth century most had been part of the priesthood or under noble patronage. The disappearance of estate society did not initially bother intellectuals, who could support themselves by writing for a middle-class audience. But this happy marriage ended after the mid-nineteenth century. The leading poets and artists became increasingly recondite, writing and drawing more for each other's appreciation than for the general public. For their part the middle-class public became increasingly convinced of the Bohemian immorality of the artists. Here, clearly, was a vicious circle. By the later nineteenth century many intellectuals, apart from the scientists who were in the mainstream of middle-class esteem, defined themselves apart from modern society. The fact is that they did not have a clear function. Most were inspired by styles emanating from romanticism that called one artistic convention after another into question, and they left any substantial public behind. They had largely abandoned politics after the disappointing failures of intellectuals' participation in the revolutions of 1848; earlier, intellectuals had served as middle-class political spokesmen. Not a class, not an occupational group, they were united by distrust or outright hatred of the modern world. The works they produced could find a considerable audience among the highly literate, highly troubled ranks of the failed professionals.

The Middling Class

The horizons of many shopkeepers and master artisans were little changed in the mature industrial period. The owner of a German barbershop expected his worker to live in his home, and work fifteen hours a day seven days a week, uncomplainingly. He would join with other owners in a voluntary guild to lament, still, the disrespect that was spreading among the lower classes. Parisian shopkeepers and artisans liked to think of themselves as the "little people" of society; one of their favorite newspapers was appropriately called *Le Petit Parisien*. As we have seen, the ranks of the small property owners expanded gradually but steadily during these decades. Their average incomes did not improve, but they were not bent on maximizing their earnings anyway. They continued to build their life around the shop, putting in long hours, with their wives serving as their cashiers and accountants.

What was changing was the world around these traditional operations. Although some workers might be content with the traditional bed and board, others wanted more independence. Small bakers and barbers even faced unionization among their employees, which infuriated them, although they often had to make concessions. Most notably, competition from department stores and other large commercial units reduced the significance of the small shop in the cities. Shops continued to handle most foods and many other goods. But the middling class, both retailers and master artisans, were driven out of the clothing industry except for the luxury trade. They could see they were losing ground relatively even when they were not displaced, and the threat of displacement was always there.

Signs of Discontent

Manifestations of anxiety among the middling class and the disgruntled middle class were rather scattered before 1914. Some, in both groups, became socialists, for the early socialist parties drew much support from the middle ranks of society. Here was even a chance for some intellectuals to seek a new political role, although as theoreticians they were usually shunted aside somewhat when the parties gained a mass base. A small-town socialist meeting in France would often be attended by a doctor, a journalist, a teacher, two grocers—and one worker. Even aside from support for socialism, professional people and shopkeepers might help in workers' strikes, for they saw big business as their enemy too. Many a French strike received some guidance from a liberal newspaper editor and food and credit from local shopkeepers.

This movement toward the political left should not be minimized, but the more typical expression of the same anxieties came in support for nationalist causes and anti-Semitism that had rightist implications. Nationalism was respectable. It associated people who felt lost in the modern world with a larger cause. News of imperialistic victories in Africa and Asia gave excitement to otherwise drab lives. Extending the doctrines of racial nationalism, anti-Semitism provided an outlet for some of the specific grievances of shopkeepers and professional people. Jews could be blamed for much that was disturbing in the modern world. The prominence of Jews in finance and as owners of department stores made them a target for the growing hostility to big business. Many shopkeepers in Paris, for example, belonged to the Merchants' Antisemite Leagues, which worked to limit the commercial competition of Jews. Similarly, students in the professional schools, particularly the law and medical faculties, often joined nationalist and anti-Semitic groups.

Intense nationalism generally and anti-Semitism in particular occasionally led elements of these groups to precipitate disorder. A number of riots occurred over imperialist crises, such as those in London in 1898 over Fashoda and Rome in 1911 over the issue of conquering Tripoli. These riots were stirred up by the excitement of the popular press and were often led by professional nationalist agitators; but they attracted a certain number of shopkeepers, master artisans like butchers and their young assistants, who provided the bulk of the popular support for the agitation. The large riots over the Dreyfus case in Paris in 1898 drew participation directly from the lower middle class and students. The initial riots over Zola's letter claiming that Dreyfus was innocent were spurred by the desire to protect the honor of the national army against an officer assumed to be traitorous partly because he was a Jew. The popular press was uniformly hostile to Dreyfus, and some anti-Semitic papers, such as Drumont's *La France Juive,* called for riots. Students answered this call first, but they were not alone. Riots in January and again in October called forth many grocers, pastry-shop owners, waiters, and small investors in stocks and bonds. Along with medical and law students, these groups provided most of the participants in the riots and drew most of the arrests. This sort of nationalist and anti-Semitic agitation was not typical. Only a minority of the middling class participated, largely in capital cities, and only infrequently. Political parties organized on anti-Semitic lines, such as the group organized by a Lutheran pastor, Adolf Stöcker, in Germany during the 1890s, attracted only a small number of votes. (Stöcker's party drew about 400,000 at its peak.) Only in Vienna did a Christian Socialist party draw mass support from the shopkeeping element; yet despite an anti-Semitic platform the party in power concentrated on improving urban transportation facilities and municipal insurance programs, suggesting that had governments given more attention to the material problems of the middling class they might have won them from extremism altogether.

For what was a slender current before World War I became a massive tide of discontent thereafter. During the 1920s the formation of small firms slowed notably under the pressure of large commercial and industrial combines and the low rate of economic growth. The unemployment of professional people reached new heights. In 1926, 14,000 of 48,000 trained physicians in Germany were not able to practice medicine and were engaged in clerical jobs instead. In Germany, where the problems of these elements of the middle class were greatest, it was not uncommon by 1929 to see newspaper advertisements proclaiming personal misery: "30 years old, married, 3 children. Nothing earned for 3 years. Future: Poor house, madhouse, or the gas jet." In many European countries rising rates of suicide reflected the extremes of despair.

Most important was the damage caused by inflation and subsequent depression. In Germany inflation destroyed over 50 per cent of the capital of the middling class by 1925. The whole notion of the value of savings and prosperity was undermined. Pensions were reduced and many retired bureaucrats lived in near misery and some actually starved. Even such an eminent professor as Ernst Troeltsch subsisted in retirement only on aid from friends. The government prohibited the raising of rents during inflation, so many small property owners saw their incomes lag behind prices. Half a million people were forced into factory work during the 1920s as a result of economic pressure. And all the while the incomes of the wealthy capitalists were visibly increasing. A hatred of big business and of labor, already evident before the war, inevitably increased.

The depression heightened this distress. Many shopkeepers suffered as their clients' purchasing power declined. Increased taxes on small business, as in Germany, added to the problem. Professional people had difficulty finding work. In Germany 7,000 engineers lost their jobs, and by 1930, 300,000 German university graduates were competing for 130,-000 positions. European governments fired literally hundreds of thousands of bureaucrats and clerks as tax revenues declined during the crisis. Thousands of teachers were unemployed (40,000 in Germany alone). Furthermore, unemployed members of the middle class did not receive the social insurance benefits and union protection accorded to the workers, and their resentment of the working class increased as a result.

In general, important segments of the middle ranks met economic disaster during the period, particularly during the depression. Some were entirely out of work; others had to accept jobs beneath their levels of training and their social status. An even larger segment suffered from the decline in economic growth during the period. A class that had based its position on professional training or property ownership now found both eroded by apparently uncontrollable trends in the economy, even though recovery after the trough of the depression brought renewed profits to many shopkeepers and restored employment for numerous professional people.

Here was the background to a mighty explosion of protest. Still loath to engage directly in violence, discontented artisans, shopkeepers, and professionals supported political parties whose mission was violence. What they sought from Nazism and other rightist movements, and what many of these movements seemed to promise, was a return to an older economy, in which the family firm would have its due. The promises to attack big banks and department stores were never really kept, though for a time guilds were revived in Nazi Germany. But from the standpoint of the supporters involved, not only of Nazism but of radical rightist movements like the *Croix de feu* in France, the promises were long believed. Under pressure of unprecedented economic shock, the middling class and many professionals turned against the modern world, almost everywhere save in countries like England, where the liberal impulse was strong and the guild tradition unusually weak. Ironically these rightist movements attacked not only modern economic forms but also important elements of the new middle-class culture, such as changing roles for women.

The Middle Class and Its Values

For certainly before World War I, and to an important degree between the wars, the bulk of the middle class remained thoroughly committed to modernity. It had few political grievances, for civil liberties seemed adequately protected while the parliamentary form prevailed. It had faith in modern science; it believed in advancing prosperity. And although the middle class might not actively oppose anti-Semitism it was not sympathetic to it. The tone of general middle-class culture was thus little changed from the previous period. The magazines most popular among the class, such as the durable *Gartenlaube* in Germany, preached the ethic of liberal humanitarianism and progress. Even socialism was not viewed as a total threat, for it proved compatible with the parliamentary system and many middle-class politicians could easily cooperate with socialist representatives on specific projects of reform at the national level and even more in municipal government, where both were interested in improving the physical facilities of the cities.

The optimism of the middle class was captured in 1900, when newspapers and other publications, looking back on the developments of the past century, could only be impressed with the progress that had been achieved. The economic situation had been transformed by the revolution in technology and the massive increase in production. New products were available to almost everyone. Advances in health and increases in population were evident. Political changes had brought new liberties and opportunities for participation to the middle class and even to the masses. Knowledge had advanced as education spread, and scientific discoveries challenged the forces of ignorance and superstition. In terms of the values held by most of the middle class, progress seemed undeniable, and there was little doubt that further advance would come.

Who was in the middle class? Successful lawyers and doctors, middle-level industrialists, and other independent businessmen—all the groups that had been represented before in middle-class ranks. Increasingly, however, the middle class was expanding on the basis of specialized training and managerial skills rather than property ownership. Giant corporations required a complex layer of managers, beginning with the director of the individual plant or mine. Their research needs created the technician, who could apply scientific training to industrial products; hence the industrial chemist, alongside the engineer. This kind of expansion meant upward mobility for many. Forty-three per cent of new British managers, for example, had improved their status. New educational opportunities allowed many to rise through technical training. Not a few shopkeepers' and artisans' sons took advantage of these opportunities to enter the middle class, for small owners were alert to educational advantages in a period when their own economy seemed shaky. Here was an important junction between old and new groups. Mobility into the middle class slowed during the 1920s, given reduced economic growth. A large number of managers now came from established managerial families. In Britain the result was a decline of almost 50 per cent in the number of managers who had risen from the lower classes, whereas in Germany there were many complaints that the few new positions available were given to outsiders, sometimes relatives of the owner, instead of being used as channels for promotion from within. The advent of the depression brought outright unemployment to technical personnel, such as 7,000 German engineers. The middle class was thus far from being immune to difficulties. On the whole, however, the mature industrial period saw the chance for considerable expansion and redefinition.

The Lower Middle Class

Paralleling these developments was the immense expansion of white-collar employment, creating an essentially new lower middle class that was the most rapidly growing segment of society.

There were several major sources of white-collar employment. The the new wealth of upper and lower classes alike increased the demand for services not connected with manufacturing or with manual labor. Services such as teaching, the staffing of hotels and resorts, and banking expanded rapidly in the period and played a major role in the extension of lower-middle-class jobs.

The expansion of large organizations required an array of lower-level bureaucratic personnel. Huge corporations needed quantities of secretaries, clerks, and other white-collar workers. The spread of large factories increased the demand for foremen to supervise and direct the labor force. In earlier industry many of these tasks had been handled by employers and their families. Wives had often done accounting and secretarial work for their husbands, and manufacturers had supervised workers directly in many small plants. With the expansion of firms, bureaucratic personnel became absolutely essential. Furthermore, this new bureaucracy was not confined to private enterprise alone. Governments also expanded their administrations during the period; they too participated in the movement to develop more massive organization, particularly in the economy. Expansion of government functions created thousands of new jobs. New taxing powers, including tariffs and even income tax, required massive paper work and the clerks to handle it. Government education systems demanded teachers. New factory inspection laws called for inspectors and their clerks to execute them. Postal services expanded. By 1900 at least 5 per cent of the labor force in France was employed by the government in white-collar jobs. The expansion of bureaucracy, both public and private, was the most important single source of the growth of the lower middle class.

The expansion of white-collar employment was extremely rapid. Britain had 7,000 female secretaries in 1881, 22,200 in 1891, and 90,000 in 1901. By 1871 the lower middle class constituted about 10 per cent of the British population, up from roughly 7 per cent in 1850. By 1900 the British lower middle class was a full 20 per cent of the population. Comparable development took place in other industrialized countries. A significant clerical class began to rise with the spread of corporate bureaucracies even in countries such as Russia, where 3.5 per cent of factory employment was in the white-collar category by 1900.

The lower middle class drew its new numbers from several social groups. To sons of beleaguered displaced businessmen and artisans white-collar positions seemed relatively attractive alternatives, befitting their educational levels and sense of respectability. People from craft backgrounds were particularly numerous and welcomed the chance to avoid factory work; in one survey over half the sons of German printers had entered the lower middle class. The thousands of women who found white-collar employment came from a wide variety of social groups, including factory workers, for clerical positions were far less demanding physically and far more respectable socially than factory labor. On the whole, more white-collar women than men came from working-class backgrounds, which suggests the importance of these jobs for female mobility. This was one reason servanthood declined, as better education and the white-collar jobs opened new opportunity for working-class girls. But certain white-collar positions were filled by male members of the working class; foremen, particularly, usually rose from the ranks. Sometimes they retained the attitudes and interests of the labor force, but more commonly they assumed a lower-middle-class orientation. Very few lower-middle-class jobs were filled by people of rural origin. This was an urban class, as its culture was to indicate.

As with the middle class, the lower middle class declined somewhat as a source of mobility between the wars. Large numbers of workers still sought to switch; half a million German workers moved into lower middle class ranks right after 1918. But this new supply tended to reduce wages; by 1929 at least a million white-collar workers earned no more than a skilled factory hand. Moreover, the depression brought considerable unemployment. Again in Germany 600,000 of 4 million salaried employees were out of work by 1933, almost as high a proportion as in the working class. It was tempting to respond along with disgruntled shopkeepers or professional people, and some clerks and technicians undoubtedly swelled the ranks of supporters for Nazism or other radical causes.

Economic Values and Social Status

Even before this there had been links between white-collar workers and the shopkeeping element. Some stemmed from the fact that many white-collar workers, particularly males, came from a middling-class background. This was a distinct group, in that its position was not based on property ownership. But it valued the idea of ownership and tended to distrust people, such as socialists, who advocated its destruction. In addition, it was slightly harder to unionize white-collar workers than to unionize their factory counterparts. Some of the unions that were formed were unusually conservative. The German Federation of Salaried Commercial Employees, formed in 1893, attracted a quarter of all private salaried personnel by 1914 and actively sought favorable legislation on hours and wages for white-collar work. It was not a working-class type of union, however, and was hostile to the socialist labor movement. It shunned strikes, issued anti-Semitic propaganda, and sought above all to promote its members' sense of status. This sort of development has led some observers to lump white-collar workers with shopkeepers in a single large, potentially fascist, lower middle class. But this is not really accurate. White-collar workers often organized in radical unions. This was true of postal workers and primary school teachers in France; the former even conducted a major strike before 1914. British white-collar workers unionized rapidly around the turn of the century. Unionization spread still farther in Germany during the 1920s, and although the biggest groupings were nonsocialist, a large socialist union found favor with many.

The lower middle class is best understood as a new group, separate from older propertied groups. It was distinctly not working class, either in conditions or aspirations, though individuals and groups, as in France, might sympathize with the labor movement. White-collar work appealed to the age-old distinction between manual and nonmanual labor. Clerks were able to dress well on the job, indeed they were typically required to dress rather formally. This set them off from workers. They were paid by the month and had more job security; this set them apart economically even when their listed wage rates were no higher than those of workers. Some, undoubtedly, treated workers with scant respect. Foremen were often peremptory, pay clerks sometimes insulting. Many workers had ambivalent feelings about the lower middle class, hating their social pretensions but unable to deny that they were indeed a socially superior group.

Much of the distinctiveness of the lower middle class came from its origins. In the early industrial revolution and before, business clerks had considerable prestige. Many, indeed, were the sons of owners and would rise to a managerial position with age. This gave clerks a sense of participation in management that a manual worker could not have. As bureaucracies expanded the literal association of clerks with managers largely disappeared, but a sense of contact remained. At least this was the case for male employees; female secretaries were separate and unequal. But even the female might have dreams of marrying the boss, and a romantic, largely inaccurate, literature quickly developed around this theme. For males, separation from management in terms of dress and friendly greetings in the morning was far less sharp than for the working class. Big companies carefully preserved this linkage, setting up special benefit programs for office personnel. In Germany, even national insurance schemes were segregated, which suited the aspirations of the clerks admirably. By their own choice they were middle class, not workers.

That there was a great deal of bluff in all this is obvious. Working conditions in the offices, and still more for female department store clerks, were often similar to those in the early industrial factories. Long hours combined with harsh shop rules that dictated dress and behavior. One German office manager installed a steam jet in the employee's toilet, timed to go off every three minutes, to prevent idling. New technology became more and more routinized. Many clerks resented the intrusion of typewriters. Here was a precious opportunity for women, who, not having had secretarial positions before, had less reason for concern; women monopolized typing from the first. Complaints about the routinization of office work became still sharper in the 1920s. This was a potent cause of the unionization movements. Yet still the lower middle class found its work situation distinctive, and self-delusion was only part of this. Speed-up efforts and time clocks could never eliminate the possibility of socializing on these jobs. Clerical work retained a slower pace than manufacturing. Moreover, the fervent belief in middle-class status could be translated into reality. A substantial minority moved further upward in society. Thirty-five per cent of the managers of British industry named between

1900 and 1920 came from the lower middle class, but only 25 per cent from the far larger laboring classes.

By the 1920s, in fact, if not before, the lower middle class was beginning to define a new relationship of work to life. Legislation and unionization efforts pushed hours of work down. The continued sense of responsibility on the job, plus the relatively relaxed pace and social contacts, made the work seem pleasant; almost certainly far more clerks than workers would have defined their jobs as satisfying. But clerks were also bent on making work only one segment of their lives. One sign of this was in the growing interest in formal retirement plans, particularly of course among government employees such as postal workers and teachers. Far earlier than businessmen or workers, the lower middle class pushed for formal retirement, with pension plans to make this possible. In France some groups won a retirement age of fifty-five, by the 1930s; in Britain and elsewhere sixty-five was more common. An old age free from work was just one aspect of the life style this class sought. More than the middle class, which was still more likely to be wrapped up in the job, the lower middle class sought a pleasant life in and around home and family. Earnings did not yet extend to massive consumer purchases, only about half of this group even owned a radio in the 1920s. But there were suggestions of a new consumer style.

The lower middle class was distinctly more concerned about good housing and furnishings than workers. They could devote more of their budget to rents even when their earnings were no higher than those of the workers. Their housing interest was thus distinctly middle class, and clerks imitated middle-class taste in furniture and home decoration when possible. To make sure they could afford good housing as well as to promote their children's mobility opportunities, the lower middle class reduced its birth rate notably below middle-class levels. They also purchased large amounts of life insurance, to assure security. But this was not a conservative group, clinging defensively to a dated respectability. The lower middle class not only spent more heavily on recreation than the middle class but also spent more for it than workers. Members of the lower middle class led in the rising interest in motion pictures and radio, whereas the middle class was longer attached to older entertainment forms such as concerts. They also led in the growing expenditures on tobacco. They were, in sum, at the forefront of a new definition of middle-class, off-the-job culture by the 1920s.

The Leisure Ethic

Well before this, the middle class had begun to relax. As industrial pioneers were replaced by managerial bureaucracies the hours of work went down. New leisure, plus at least a modest affluence, permitted the development of new interests. At first this was rather tentative, for the hold of the work ethic was strong. English recreational magazines, which began to appear in the 1850s, urged sports and vacations because of their role in improving work performance. A man who exercised and got out into the pure country air would be able to do his job better. But gradually leisure was recommended for its own sake.

Middle-class recreational interests took many forms, with a strong element of faddism apparent in most. The class believed in change; the new leisure had scant traditional base. So one enthusiasm followed another. One channel was dancing. As early as 1860 there were sixty-eight dance halls in Paris. This was a new kind of dancing. Couples held each other closely and one style followed the other: the *maxixe,* the cakewalk, and then in the 1920s the Charleston. Sports formed another interest, with England leading the way. Horse racing drew new crowds. The first adult soccer football club was formed in 1858. Rugby grew more popular. Croquet had its day during the 1860s, tennis and rollar skating came in during the next decade. By the 1880s bicycling was the reigning passion, and the automobile craze soon followed. In the 1920s boxing and car racing were added to the list of spectator sports. In yet another development seaside resorts drew new numbers of people.

These new leisure interests cut middle-class devotion to religion; church attendance began to fall in this group too. Some pastors, eager to keep up with the times, suggested drive-in services for bicyclists, but there was really no remedy. Middle-class leisure was a big business, and followed some clear commercial patterns. Codification was one: old sports, like rugby and soccer, were given clear rules for the first time. Advertising was another. Specialized magazines grew up around every new interest, and notices in the general press were urging Europeans, by 1900, to smoke cigarettes, drink *apéritifs,* go to the beach, build muscles, or buy a newer-model bicycle.

The new leisure activities tended to loosen the public attitude of the middle class toward sex. The plays and, a bit later, the movies that the class helped patronize grew franker in their discussions of sexual matters; a popular play in Paris in the early 1900s stressed the desirability of premarital intercourse. The bicycle and the automobile helped change courtship patterns. An older chaperone might try to keep pace with a courting couple on bicycle, but it was a losing battle. Women's costumes changed, becoming looser and more revealing; the short skirts of the 1920s culminated a long trend here. For the new dances, for bicycling, the restrictive costumes of the early industrial middle class simply would not do. Indeed the whole notion of what a woman should look like evolved as part of the leisured life style. The woman should be slender, a bit athletic though not heavily muscled. Imperfections in face or hair should be modified by cosmetics; older women should take care, using similar products, to look as young as possible. The battle against graying and fat had begun.

There were areas of the new leisure from which women were long excluded. Only in the 1920s, after World War I had further loosened traditional standards, was it good form for them to smoke and drink. Overall, however, the middle-class recreational patterns were notable for their inclusion of women.

The Middle-Class Family

Many features of the middle-class family had been launched in the previous period; they were now consolidated. Limitation of the birth rate became steadily more pronounced, aided by improvements in the quality of birth control devices. By the 1930s the single-child family was a commonplace. There was still a tension between the discipline regarded as desirable in dealing with children, particularly on the Continent, and a growing affection. Parents wanted to be honored and loved at the same time. But the general trend was toward ever-growing affection and attention, and the leading child-rearing manuals urged parents (fathers as well as mothers) to have fun with their offspring: "How simple it is to be happy . . . to be loved all one's life by a being one loves."

In this context the middle class discovered a new problem by the 1890s: adolescence. Never before defined as a particularly remarkable period of life, adolescence was now seen as fraught with untold problems and tensions. This was a leading theme in the psychology of the day, but in actual family behavior as well. Improvements in education extended schooling into adolescence; this was new for the bulk of the middle class. It kept the teen-aged child out of the work force; it also made him, or her, more knowledgeable than his parents. Here was a built-in generational tension as part of educational modernization. Much of the new leisured culture gave special opportunities to teenagers: the dance crazes, and looser courtship patterns affected them particularly. It was easy for parents to disapprove, again a tension that has continued to be part of modern life. Finally, the age of puberty kept declining, yet the middle class did not clearly redefine its premarital sexual ethic. Premarital sex was in fact becoming more common, at least for boys. In France secondary school students regularly patronized brothels, which helped support the tens of thousand of prostitutes in Paris by the end of the nineteenth century. Others took working-class or servant girls as mistresses during their years before marriage. But it was still widely believed that sexual intercourse too early in life, or too frequently indulged in, was harmful to health, and masturbation and homosexuality were held in horror, though undoubtedly widespread in boys' schools. Some adolescents, particularly girls, were kept in sexual ignorance as a result; one girl believed she had become pregnant after a man put his arm around her on a train. Generally, however, the sexual problems of adolescence, as seen by parents, seemed acute. At the same time the definition of adolescence as a difficult age actually helped parents cope with some fears that before had been hard to understand; hence fulminations against masturbation, which had gone so far as morning checks of sheets to make sure a youth had not offended, declined by 1900.

The development of the concept of adolescence had a number of more general results. Schools and other institutions, even in dealing with lower-class youths, tried to stress conformity and discipline. Fear of adolescent wildness led to new preoccupation with juvenile delinquency, the rates of which rose in part because definitions of improper behavior became more rigorous. A variety of movements were developed to channel adolescent energies. The youth group became an obligatory branch of institutions ranging from churches to socialist parties, while the Boy Scouts emerged as a distinct organization. Adolescents themselves began to see themselves as a group apart. Many hiking and athletic organizations arose after 1900, for in general the emphasis on adolescence related to a stress on action over thought. Finally, thanks in part to dissemination of the concepts of Freudian psychology, the repressive approach toward adolescence eased further by the 1930s. Adolescent sex, even homosexuality, were viewed with less rigor.

Through most of the mature industrial period, adolescence loomed large as a family problem for the middle class, however. In a sense it was the counterpart to the growing affection lavished on children in typically small families. With few brothers or sisters to deal with, the child was in rather constant contact with doting parents, whose love, by the time the teen-age years were reached, could seem cloying. The problem of relating the family as a unit of affection to the need for individual independence was severe.

The middle class faced a related concern about old age, although this was far less clearly articulated. With some improvements in health, there was growing realization that survival into one's sixties or seventies was likely. Yet age was conventionally seen as a time of debility. There were some erroneous cultural impressions involved in the view of old age; for example, it was almost universally believed that sexual intercourse was likely to be fatal for anyone over fifty-five or so. In other words old age was assumed to be a period of more rapid and complete physical deterioration than was in fact necessarily the case. But this view encouraged important segments of the middle class to develop the notion of retirement; in addition, of course, bureaucratic managers were eager to get rid of older employees because they were believed to be inefficient. So the older parent, living on an often rather meager pension, became an increasingly common family problem. Contact between adults and their parents developed widely in the middle class, at least loosely reproducing an extended family network. With the telephone and the automobile the contact was facilitated.

Between husband and wife a final set of ambiguous developments occurred. Marriage age declined slightly, which was the reflection of new courtship patterns. But in the middle class the husband was usually considerably older than the wife and, as already suggested, more likely to be sexually experienced. Furthermore the business aspect of marriage remained important, particularly on the Continent. Dowries and formal marriage contracts were regular practice in France. As one observer noted, "For the great majority of the bourgeoisie, marriage is the greatest financial transaction of their lives." This led to continuing tension in some families, as the male sought sexual enjoyment with a mistress rather than with his own wife. Some wives were frightened by sexuality, which they endured only to have a child or two. Others might be frigid with their husbands, when marriage seemed merely a business arrangement, but sought affairs of their own; a few even worked secretly as part-time prostitutes, to supplement their household budgets. So there were problems in integrating the growing recognition of the importance of sex into middle-class marriage. But marriage manuals increasingly urged the importance of sexual compatibility in marriage, stressing the need for mutual orgasm. Better birth control information and the growing emphasis on romance in courtship could facilitate ties of affection in many families.

Certainly divorce, which was legalized or, if already legal, made easier during this period in most countries, did not significantly dent the middle-class family. In France the divorce rate rose until 1920, then stabilized; during the 1920s and 1930s, 5 per cent of all marriages ended in divorce, but more commonly in the working class than the middle class. It was also notable that formal marriage contracts declined in France, as the link between family and property loosened. The mixture of affection and financial arrangements, whatever the proportions of each, gave middle-class marriage a continuing vitality. The growing connection of the family with new recreational outlets provide an additional focus.

Middle-Class Women

The family remained the center of most women's lives. The wife increased her importance as a consumer agent, for the decline of servants was matched by new purchases such as vacuum clearners and washing machines. Housework was still a major challenge, for standards of cleanliness became even more demanding, bolstered now by the germ theory as well as the desire for a respectable home. Good appearance was another challenge, and housewives paid growing attention to diet as well as to fashionable clothing and cosmetics. There were ambiguities in this situation. With fewer children, who were in turn more often in school, the maternal role lessened somewhat. Movement to the suburbs left many housewives alone during much of the day, although their visits or calls to relatives might compensate somewhat. A traditional crutch was removed as growing restrictions on drugs reduced the availability of opiates. New forms of recreation helped, as attendance at the movies suggested, but some pastimes, such as dancing, were more accessible to girls before marriage than to housewives. Married women rarely worked in the middle class, so this was not an available outlet; even the impact of inflation and depression did not force many middle-class wives to defy family respectability by taking a job.

More dramatic developments occurred for single women in the middle class, though it must be remembered that these were a minority as marriage continued to dominate the goals of most women. Better education and legal reforms opened professional careers to some middle-class women. Able to obtain a university education (by the 1900s about 12 per cent of all university students were female in France), some pushed for admittance to law, medicine, and the civil service. Numbers here were still small, and far more women were channeled into only semiprofessional jobs, such as primary school teaching, regarded as appropriate for their maternal qualities. Where relatively large numbers were concerned with careers of this sort, a new feminist movement arose around 1900. Britain led the way here, for by this time there were almost 200,000 professional women. The feminists called for equal pay for equal work and insisted on gaining the vote. They obtained hundreds of thousands of signatures on their petitions and shortly before World War I conducted a number of massive demonstrations and acts of violence. The movement did not address itself to the concerns of the housewife, nor was it particularly successful in attracting working-class support. This helps explain why, after the right to vote was granted, feminism subsided rather quickly. On the Continent individual feminists were active during this same period, and socialist parties advocated a number of new rights for women, but nowhere did the current match the outburst in England. As with so many of the changes in middle-class culture, the most basic developments were occurring beneath the political surface.

The new culture did have an indirect political effect, however. More relaxed behavior and new women's roles roused the ire of the disgruntled segments of the middle class. Some professionals feared women as possible competitors. Many lamented the moral decay that, to them, the leisure ethic represented. When life was filled with games and movies displaced concerts, civilization was sorely threatened. Themes of this sort were visible before 1914; a number of anti-Semitic movements, for example, included blasts at women's rights. With the shock of World War I, followed by the further elaboration of the leisure ethic during the 1920s, traditionalist outrage mounted. One of the appeals of the Nazi movement was to return women to the home and curb modern fashions. The peasant *Dirndl* was to replace the flapper's outfit, as the middle classes continued to be divided on their basic orientation toward life.

The Working Classes

The working classes remained extremely diversified during the mature industrial period, though the balance among the major elements was shifting. The artisanal element remained strong. Large numbers of bakers and metalworkers still lived with their masters. Although sorely pressed by the spread of factories even the domestic manufacturing system hung on; almost 5 per cent of all German manufacturing workers still labored at home in 1907. The growth of the working class was concentrated, however, in three major segments.

1. *The urban crafts: woodworking, many kinds of metalwork, printing, and so on.* These were increasingly centered in units of about fifty workers, well above traditional artisanal size. This meant that journeymen shared some of the problems factory workers had, in terms of more impersonal organization and the introduction of new technology. We will see, however, that the journeymen's situation remained distinctive. Except for construction, where the number of workers increased rapidly, this was the slowest-growing section of the working class, but it retained considerable importance.

2. *Factory work and mining.* Here growth was more rapid. But some sectors stagnated, such as textiles before World War I and both textiles and mining afterward. This meant that many workers, or their children, had to shift into the expanding industries—machine tools, electrical equipment, for example—or face unemployment. Reshuffling, rather than rapid growth, now characterized this central segment of the working classes.

3. *The unskilled.* This category embraced some factory workers, who simply moved goods, but it was particularly important in construction and transportation work. This group of workers faced some of the greatest changes of any working-class element during the period. Indeed they increasingly moved from the category of faceless, transient poor into the mainstream of working-class life. They had some new job opportunities. New equipment allowed untrained personnel to move into positions in metalworking or the manufacture of furniture. Wherever they worked they were now in contact with machines: loading cranes, trucks, taxicabs. And their units of employment grew more structured. The development of big shipping companies most obviously put the unskilled on the docks and on board ship in contact with big business for the first time. Many resented change. This was the only group that now produced any direct attacks on machinery, which was feared as a threat to jobs. In reaction to new

business organization the unskilled became increasingly sensitive about their dignity; as some French sailors proclaimed, "We are not pariahs, and we have the same right as any man to aspire to improve our lot." From the unskilled, then, came bursts of anger that were more profound than those of other sections of the working class. But the very ability to react showed that the unskilled were moving from their transient, impoverished life to a position similar to that of other workers. They still suffered problems unknown to other groups. On a normal day before World War I, 36 per cent of all London dockers would be out of work; for factory workers the rate was nearer 2 per cent, for artisans nearer 5 per cent, except in depressions. But the rate of unemployment among the unskilled tended to decline, with the expansion of shipping and trucking and the other new jobs available. And the unskilled themselves were more settled, less likely to move about from one season to the next and more likely to form families.

One final group of workers requires discussion. The job situation of women workers changed more dramatically in the mature industrial period than ever before. During early industrialization women workers had essentially tried, or been forced, to concentrate on the same kinds of jobs they had always done. Large numbers still worked at home; the manufacture of clothing, for example, remained a predominantly home industry well into the late nineteenth century. Other women continued to manufacture textiles, even specializing in spinning just as they had before (for men quickly resumed their positions as weavers). They had to move into factories to do this, which was a big change, but as we have seen they continued to function as part of a family economy. Finally the largest group of women went into domestic service, again changing locations, by moving into the cities, but retaining a traditional role in many respects. This pattern of adaptation was now disrupted. The stagnation of the textile industry (which remained heavily feminized) meant that new numbers of women had to seek work elsewhere. Some home dressmakers held out but the industry was increasingly moved into shops. Above all, servanthood began to decline or at least stabilize. Millions of women still worked as servants; one of Adolf Hitler's more interesting and unsound moves during World War II was to retain a large number of women servants despite a desperate labor shortage in the factories. But nowhere did the female servant population keep pace with overall urban growth, in the mature industrial countries, and in France it began an absolute decline as early as the 1890s. With new household appliances middle-class families needed servants less. Wages tended to stagnate, making domestic service less attractive than factory work from a sheer economic standpoint. Furthermore young girls, now accustomed to the city, began to prefer the independence other kinds of work could give them. Former servants in England reported they found "more life" in the factories, whereas comparable

German girls noted, "the foremen were not nearly so coarse as the gracious ladies."

Whether prodded by economic change or attracted by new opportunities, women began to push into new branches of work, outside the domestic setting. Many moved into clerical jobs, as we have seen. But others took work in printing, machine building, and many other factory industries. Like the unskilled generally they benefited from the new machines that reduced the skill levels in such industries, forming an important part of the new semiskilled category. In some countries, such as Germany, even married working-class women took factory jobs in increasing numbers. World War I temporarily increased opportunities for women's work everywhere, though in the 1920s levels fell back again somewhat. All in all, however, many working-class girls and some wives were gaining more diverse and independent work experiences than ever before.

The overall expansion of the working classes was now slowing up. They constituted 30 to 40 per cent of the population of the mature industrial countries, but they were no longer the most rapidly growing segment. This meant that changes in the situation of one group might seem newly menacing to another, for not only craftsmen but also many skilled factory workers were accustomed to their jobs and their position in society. They wanted to pass their work on to their sons. The association of family and factory work had been consolidated over the early generations and many workers took a proprietory interest in their jobs. All this reflects a natural maturing of the working classes. But it gave workers a somewhat conservative caste, because change could only threaten the accommodations that had been made. So skilled workers resented the unskilled. Women's entry was particularly feared. A French printer noted: "They're too impulsive. One day they are enthusiastic for our work, the next day they've changed their minds. The only way perhaps to resolve the problem would perhaps be by absorption. Each male typographer would marry a female typographer. That would be a solution." We have seen that, in the early industrial period, the working class survived its first exposure to the factories by adaptation of many key traditions. These traditions, including that of women's proper role, were now challenged.

A New Security

Obviously many of the worst problems of industrial life were ended or at least modified by the late nineteenth century, thanks to the adjustment that had already taken place plus greater prosperity. Many workers were still badly fed. Low wages plus traditional diets, which neglected fruits and vegetables in favor of meats and starches, caused much poor nutrition. But the food situation was obviously improved. This, along with better housing and clothing, meant better average health; infants were less likely to die, adult workers more likely to live into their sixties. Average unemployment declined in years of normal prosperity, at least until after World War I and the growing economic dislocation. New machines and methods frightened workers who were more conscious of their need for stable employment than ever before, but they displaced few workers directly. More common was an intergenerational change, in which the son or daughter of a weaver might have to decide to go into another line of work. This caused tension, but the fact remained that more workers had more regular work, year in and year out, than had been the case since the population boom of the eighteenth century. Child labor declined to almost nothing, if only because of legislation. Working-class children might resent the rigors of school, but overall they benefited from not having to start work until they were fourteen or so. And this helped release jobs for adults.

The picture of change should not be overdrawn. Less unemployment still meant that about a fifth of the skilled segment of the working class, not to mention the unskilled, were unemployed for part of each year, and rarely by their own choice. Illness or recessions made a mockery of any effort at complete stability, and the sense of unpredictability continued to be an important part of working-class culture. Child mortality declined but as late as 1900 the average working-class family would have to mourn at least one infant death. Workers themselves perceived their tantilizing position between a really new level of security and subjection to traditional, hardships. Some mothers took the risk of loving their babies more fiercely than before, only to be plunged into sorrow when one died; others played it safer, finding death inevitable and a proper funeral adequate solace. Workers might talk in one breath about their aspirations for better jobs and more training, and then in another admit that life was out of their control and that they would end "where the wind blows me." In one case their hesitation to risk a change in outlook was positively damaging. Most workers refused to recognize that they were living longer, at least until they reached their fifties. They expected to die young and they associated old age, naturally enough, only with illness and suffering. They thus made little effort to push for pension plans or formal retirement programs, arguing that any pension that began at age sixty-five would come too late: "pensions for dead people," as the French trade unions proclaimed. Only with the depression did the retirement rate of workers pick up, out of necessity. Until then older workers had to continue work or, if disabled, take advantage of the meager benefit programs available through state or company plans while hoping that their children would care for them. Important improvements in the workers' lot should not, then, be equated with genuine affluence.

Furthermore workers' previous adaptation to industrial work removed some traditional remedies for dissatisfaction. It was harder to think about changing jobs or moving from one area to the next. New workers faithfully reproduced the traditional pattern. Many unskilled factory workers were now recruited from foreign laborers, another sign that traditional unskilled workers were finding new options. Italians who flocked to the mines and metallurgical factories of France and Germany and the Poles who poured into the Ruhr changed jobs frequently, often returned home for harvest work, and displayed a high rate of absenteeism. Women workers, as they entered new fields, were more likely to change jobs than men and of course still typically left the factories altogether when they married. For most factory workers, absenteeism and particularly job changing were less attractive than before. They had become attached to their jobs and they were conscious of their need to support their families. Most did not drift into factory work accidentally. Although their range of choice was limited, most skilled workers at least could give a reason for their work, citing the guidance or example of their parents or the interest they expected to take in their jobs. This kind of attachment could be immensely satisfying, for it meant that a worker saw a purpose in his factory labor and could hope to pass this same sense on to his sons. But it left workers vulnerable as well. Skilled workers increasingly refused to take other work even when unemployed, for this would be beneath their professional dignity. Sons could not always follow their fathers. Some undoubtedly enjoyed the chance to strike out on their own, particularly when they could earn a higher wage. But parents were upset, and laments about the decline of the trade and the heedlessness of the young reflected this common generation gap in the working class. Many young workers were in fact confused by the need for choice. Their conservatism was tragically revealed after World War I, when masses of miners and textile workers resisted retraining and relocation, preferring to hold out in hope that their own industry would revive. Even before this, the growing sense of attachment to work was challenged by the changing nature of work itself.

A New Kind of Work

Most workers entered the mature industrial period preserving something like a traditional pace of work. This was least true in England, where per worker productivity was highest. It obviously applied more to journeymen than to factory workers, and to the unskilled most of all. Dockers, for example, alternated periods of intense labor, up to thirty-six hours at a stretch, with days in which they would not even bother to seek work, preferring to rest instead. But the notion of long periods of work, punctuated by rests, applied in most factories as well. British machine builders could take naps on the job as late as the 1870s. Many German metalworkers stayed twelve or fourteen hours at the factory in the 1890s, but had over three hours in rest periods and managed to limit their pace of work even aside from this; as a result they took work home after hours, turning out wire or simple tools in the evenings and on Sundays. Workers in many factories put on tremendous bursts of energy at the end of a week, hoping to boost their earnings right before payday, and were then so tired they had to sleep all day Sunday; to compensate for their lack of recreation, they would then take Monday off to get drunk, only to return blearily on Tuesday or Wednesday and begin the whole cycle over again. Obviously machines had speeded up the pace of work in the factories already, and the factory whistle was the symbol of the new sense of regularity that work was supposed to involve. But few workers had been forced radically to redefine what work was all about. They still thought in terms of a relatively slow pace combined with long hours in the factory.

Only some big-city craftsmen, such as construction workers, had even pressed for a major reduction in the hours of work before the 1870s, and this not because their pace was being forced but because they wanted to spread the work and limit unemployment. Well into the late nineteenth century workers spent most of their waking hours on the job except for traditional holidays and rest periods, which they might supplement by taking some days off on their own.

Within this context some of the new developments of mature industrial society were not as bothersome as might be imagined. Technological changes might be welcomed. Artisans whose work was being taken over by the factories naturally howled; a Parisian shoemaker proclaimed: "If I want the revolution it's not to do any harm to people but to be able to destroy all these machines." But many workers valued new equipment that reduced physical strain, particularly when they got some of the benefit of increased output in the form of higher wages. English cotton workers actually tried to prod their employers to provide more productive equipment. Even artisans could adapt when direct displacement was not involved. Printers worried about the new composing machines, but mainly in advance of their installation. Once they began work on them they found that they still had a sense of skill, if somewhat reduced, and enjoyed the extra money their higher productivity won. Machines worried most workers, although some were fascinated by them, but they did not make them feel dehumanized. The semiskilled workers who were upgraded by the possibility of machine work, including many women, could gain a new feeling of worth on the job. Skilled workers, whose numbers continued to increase, though more slowly, found their jobs a bit less interesting but were not completely antagonized. As a German machine shop worker noted, "One good thing about machines is that a person can at least think about other things."

Big business forms had a similarly ambiguous impact. Artisans were concerned about their larger units of employment, though some welcomed their freedom from the master's personal supervision. The collective bargaining procedures that spread widely in construction and the crafts partially replaced person-to-person contacts. A printer, for example, could go to his shop representative, called the Chapel Father in England, if he had any grievance, knowing that the representative could take it up directly with the employer. Factory workers were not so lucky. Big companies did develop grievance committees, but usually under strict employer control. Rarely did they let collective bargaining extend to on-the-job complaints, and as we will see, many big industrialists refused to have anything to do with unions at all. So as company size increased, workers might grow restive under the impersonality and remoteness of management. British miners talked of their friendly relations with foremen in the past; but now the foreman, pressed to keep production up, would simply refer them to the branch manager, who put on airs and said, "What the bloody hell do you want?" A German worker phrased his anger rather formally: "The consciousness of dependence on the employer embitters me. A gesture of the director is enough to make my blood boil." So many workers did think in terms of a change in factory organization that would give them greater voice over conditions. But most workers were less directly affected by the rise of big business. If their foreman seemed fair they might find the job pleasant; personal clashes, more than disputes over remote management, were most common on the work site. Some directors were known to be fair, even friendly men. The policies of paternalism continued by most big companies had their predictable effect of contenting some workers, who valued the material benefits of housing programs or hospitalization plans and found it natural to defer to this management approach, while infuriating another group more conscious of personal freedom. Big business encouraged an atmosphere of class strife, particularly after 1900, but it was far from universal.

In combination with changes in organization and technology, a persistent pressure to intensify the pace of work affected a large segment of workers from the 1890s onward. Again, journeymen were largely immune. Their industries were not heavily involved in international competition and their strong craft unions prevented excessive innovation. Hence employers who tried to introduce piecework rather than daily pay, to encourage greater individual effort, were successfully rebuffed. In construction per worker productivity actually declined as workers held their pace down. But in factories and in transportation the pace steadily increased. Machine workers, for example, were pressed to accept the piece rate, which by rewarding higher production with a higher wage stimulated faster work. Their unions objected, but to no avail; and a few workers found piece work more interesting precisely because of the motivation it provided. By the eve of World War I, particularly in the machine shops, time and motion studies were being conducted by outside engineers, to determine how each worker could be compelled to greater efficiency. This was a foretaste of the assembly line system, in which workers in automobile factories and elsewhere repeated small operations on products as they moved past on the conveyor belt, the apotheosis of routinized, semiskilled labor. Spurred by the example of American productivity, the assembly line spread increasingly after World War I.

This kind of forced pace could drive workers to despair. "Why should we be asked to work under a system that indicates every movement of our elbow?" "We are driven like dumb cattle in our folly, until the flesh is off our bones, and the marrow out of them." "It seems to me that we are living to work, and not working to live." Other workers, however, continued to express pleasure in their jobs: "There is no work as interesting as that of a miner." A 1928 poll in Germany showed that 65 per cent of all skilled workers and 44 per cent of all unskilled found more pleasure than distaste in their jobs. But work had changed. It was now intense, not leisurely; driven, not traditional. Even those workers who found pleasure in their work might complain of job tension, headaches, and sleeplessness. Nervousness was replacing physical hardship as the result of work, which is another way of saying that work had become modern.

One other change explains why workers could survive the new work system, even when they found aspects of it objectionable. The hours of work were now significantly reduced. New legislation pushed hours in textiles down to ten a day in most advanced industrial countries by World War I, and for miners the eight-hour day was established. Collective bargaining reduced hours to nine or ten for urban journeymen and had some impact in factory industry. Workers were implicitly agreeing that work might be intense, even abandoning traditional rest periods during the workday and reducing their absenteeism, in return for provision of time for life off the job. The idea of formal annual vacations gained ground from 1900 onward; French workers in the 1930s won a substantial yearly holiday.

Thus the traditional concept of work gave way, if only reluctantly. Workers still could find satisfactions in work but could no longer build their whole lives around it. They adopted, or were forced to adopt, a partially instrumental view toward work; that is, work was valued not only for its own sake but also for what it could provide toward life off the job. With the value of work now challenged, though by no means completely undermined, the quality of a worker's existence depended heavily on what he could do with his new leisure time.

Life Off the Job

In this area adaptation was incomplete. The working class could not, as a whole, seize as completely on a leisure ethic as the lower middle class did. Its resources were more meager; average earnings were lower and job instability greater. Traditional family patterns retarded adaptation as well. And work was hard. Many workers came home too worn out to use their leisure for much but sleep and light reading. Particularly for older workers leisure activities did not diversify greatly; the working-class recreational patterns were mainly for the young. There were important changes in behavior, but not enough, for many, to compensate fully for the alteration of work.

Big-city journeymen made the switch best. For their work was not really more intense, and their hours were shorter than before (though increased commuting time qualified this, as more and more moved to respectable suburbs). Quickly, around 1900, they reduced their family size, almost to middle-class levels. This protected their standard of living while also helping to assure that they could place their children properly now that the crafts were expanding more slowly. Artisans in London joined clerks in going to the new music halls, as well as finding social diversions in pubs. Their recreational life was increasingly dissociated from the job, and music hall humor helped make work and family bearable by poking gentle fun at class divisions, mothers-in-law, and so on.

Workers more generally developed new interests in sports. Young miners played football and saved their money to attend a Saturday match. Belgian workers raced pigeons and bet on the results. Many workers took excursions on the railroads. Some enjoyed trips to the beach, though, in England, it was only in the 1920s that workers normally were able to swim. Movie houses spread widely in working-class towns even before World War I. But there was long a certain tentativeness to this leisure ethic. Many workers, with new leisure time and some new funds, really did not know exactly what to do. Many turned to increasing use of traditional outlets. Drinking went up in France and Germany; Paris, with 30,000 bars, had more than any other city in the world. This reflected job tensions, but also the absence of a diversified recreational tradition to refer to.

German workers polled shortly before World War I listed gardening and walks in the countryside as their favorite pastimes. Sports interests were spreading among the young, but again traditionalism played a continued role. And this in turn qualified the workers' ability to take an instrumental view toward work. Many of their recreational interests were rather inexpensive, particularly after they married. This followed from their modest wages, but it also discouraged elaborate new wage demands. It was not automatic, therefore, for workers to respond to changes on the job with demands for more money. Individuals developed this ability, which is why some liked the piece rate, but collectively workers were slow to convert to a progressive wage mentality, because new uses for money were not clear. They still responded to a windfall wage gain by bringing home a new present for the kids or a bigger piece of meat for Sunday dinner, not by changing their basic pattern of life. The balance between change and tradition thus remained important.

The same was true of family life. The working class began to reduce its birth rate by the 1890s. It still had larger families than the middle class, and some male workers believed that their masculinity required them to sire many children. Many women as a result had to resort to abortion; in Berlin around 1910, a survey showed that 24 per cent of all working-class women had undergone at least one abortion. Women did not otherwise exercise control over the birth rate in this class, for the only control device commonly used was the condom and its employment obviously depended on the cooperation of husband or suitor. With regard to children, the working-class reduction of birth rate constituted a sensible but historically significant realization that children were no longer an economic asset; hence a family should have fewer of them and for different reasons. Mothers began to lavish more affection on their children. But the father's role changed less clearly; many fathers were authoritarian, even brutal, with their children.

And there were some signs of new tension between husband and wife, quite apart from possible arguments over birth control. Working-class women were in an anomalous situation. Their education was improving, their jobs before marriage becoming more diversified. But once married their roles remained rather traditional. They were still responsible for the main consumer expenditures of the family, and when living standards began to stagnate with the inflation after 1900 this could prove a demanding function. They still formed a kinship network with their relatives. A classic theme in music hall comedy was the working man returning home only to find his wife surrounded by her mother and other relatives, from whom he would flee in horror to the nearest pub. But new roles were not available. There was only a slight increase in the percentage of married women working outside the home, for this was still frowned upon in working-class culture. When women took new jobs during World War I they created tensions in the family. A French railwayman wrote: "Women no longer want to obey. . . . We talk about marriage between men and women as people talk of peace between the Germans and the French." For their part most of the new recreations men were developing were exclusively masculine: they played soccer or went to the races alone.

The working-class family was not in serious trouble. Marriage rates remained high and the marriage age relatively young. The working-class girl might enjoy her new independence in a factory or office job, but she busily saved her money to be able to furnish an apartment once married; her work was thus still family-centered. Often she would get pregnant to win her man, and for both sexes courtship was regarded as more fun than marriage. But working-class culture, now respectable, saw to it that the man did marry. A small minority of unions ended in divorce; the rate jumped up after the disruption of World War I but then fell back again. Gardening and excursions allowed the family to serve as a recreational unit. What had not occurred, however, was the kind of qualitative improvement in family relationships that might compensate for new tensions on the job. Indeed strain at work caused many men to come home so nervous and exhausted that they could not treat wives and children with the affection they really intended. Here too the working class was caught in an incomplete adaptation. Traditional relationships were still valid; some new interests were developing; but the mixture was not entirely satisfactory.

Discontent

The situation of workers both on and off the job readily explains the most obvious feature of working-class life during the mature industrial period: the emergence of new protest forms and organizations. It also explains some of the restraints on this protest. Most workers were not thoroughly dissatisfied with their jobs or their lives off the job. They wanted change but most were not in a revolutionary mood. Hence they were not attracted by movements that attacked the industrial system in the name of older values; here was one key difference with the unrest of the previous period. In France and to a lesser degree in Britain, the revolutionary syndicalist movement echoed earlier protest themes. Syndicalists believed that trade unions should work toward a general strike that would overturn the political and economic system alike; they admitted that classic revolution was now impossible because the ruling classes had the strength of a modern military apparatus behind them. But if all workers everywhere stopped work, capitalist society would collapse. Syndicalists looked to a future society in which there would be no government. The economy would be organized on the basis of small, egalitarian units that recalled idealized guilds. Syndicalism did have some attractions for the working class but its greatest gains were in Italy and Spain, where workers were confronting industrial society for the first time. In France the syndicalists won control of the major trade union federation, the *Confédération générale du travail* (C.G.T.); it proved particularly appealing to the revolutionary tradition of Parisian artisans. But most unionized French workers, including craftsmen, were not syndicalists and syndicalism was on the wane by 1910. Distrusting modern organization, the syndicalist unions were weak, underfunded, and lacking in bureaucracy. They could not successfully confront employers. More basically, most workers in the mature industrial countries did not now think in terms of replacing the industrial system; they protested within it.

Mature industrial protest thus differed from its early industrial predecessor in that it was not backward looking. In addition, it produced direct action more in good times rather than in bad. Workers had learned that action during depressions just invited defeat, for employers had no reason to make concessions. So they waited, now able to form demands even in prosperity. The key weapons of mature industrial protest were politics and strikes. Neither necessarily involved violence, although both might bring clashes with police or recalcitrant workers. With strikes, at least, violence tended to decline as workers gained experience and organization. The immediate goals of mature industrial protest, however, had changed less completely than the methods. Protest still focused on consumer problems, on changes in the standard of living, more than on problems at work. It stressed less a radically new set of rights than maintenance of what the workers already had.

Strikes

The modern labor movement took shape in western and central Europe from the late 1880s onward. A rising rate of strikes was one key element, and strikes revealed much about the nature of the new tide of protest.

Organized strikes became easier to conduct in this period. Politicians, eager to win popularity among newly enfranchised workers, loosened the limitations on unions and strikes. France relaxed the restrictions in the 1860s and removed them finally in 1884. In 1874 Britain repealed the laws making strikers liable to arrest. Germany withdrew similar limitations in 1881 and Belgium did so in 1868. There were still some legal barriers; the British courts, for example, attacked the right to picket and the political activities of unions in the 1900s, and only after some difficulty were these rulings overturned through legislation. French and German law forbade any interference with the right of individuals to go to work, which made it difficult for labor leaders to compel obedience to a strike call. The result was frequent arrest of strikers and recurrent conflicts with police. Direct action was no longer illegal, as it had been in the days when the lower classes had to rely on riots to express their goals, but it remained difficult.

In a broader sense the new outburst of protest depended, ironically, on the greater resources, leisure, and education of the labor force. Workers could read propaganda. Perhaps more important, because reading interest was still not widespread, their understanding of standard French or German opened them to the speeches of radical leaders. Higher wages allowed strike funds; greater leisure gave time for planning. This is why protest became more frequent and regular than ever before in history, though these same improvements might limit its goals. On the other hand strikes, more than union membership or protest voting, still involved real hardship. Loss of wages was rarely fully compensated for by strike funds, and there was a real risk of dismissal and even arrest. Strikes were not yet a normal part of the industrial scene. Employers, even governments, viewed them with great fear, and for many workers they expressed profound grievances.

In 1892 French workers struck 261 times against 500 companies. Most of the strikes were small and local, usually affecting only one company; and only 50,000 workers were involved. By 1906, the peak French strike year before the war, there were 1,309 strikes with 438,466 participants. The British strike rate was higher than the French; here a massive wave of agitation brought out over 2 million workers between 1909 and 1913 alone. Although this was unusual, a rising level of strikes developed in all the mature industrial countries. Most major kinds of strikes also appeared in the same period. The average strike was small (in Germany it involved only 119 workers), but industrywide strikes developed in mining, railroads, the merchant marine, and on the docks. National general strikes occurred in Belgium, Holland, and Sweden. Citywide strikes were still more common. Even some of the small strikes were carefully planned, as workers sought to attack one company at a time to break down employer resistance.

Yet most workers struck rarely and many strikes were still quite primitive. Only miners were likely to conduct repeated, massive strikes. The danger of their work and their cohesion in mining villages explain their unusual performance. Most other workers never struck at all before World War I. Journeymen were much more active than factory workers, but even they rose repeatedly only in the biggest cities. Many workers were satisfied with existing improvements in their lot. Others were intimidated by employers, still others too deferential to rise. Many strikes that did occur reflected this tentative consciousness. They often followed from a specific incident, such as an insult from the foreman, that personally angered a group of workers. This is why so many movements were small. Only after World War I did strikes begin, overall, to take on more modern shape. They became less frequent but larger and better organized. In part this occurred because employer resistance stiffened; workers had to be more careful if they were to have any chance of success. But it also followed from the time required for workers to learn to curb spontaneous anger in favor of a more organized approach, for in the mature industrial period protest too had to be bureaucratized.

The most experienced workers conducted careful strikes even before World War I, and their demands reflected similar sophistication. Miners and urban journeymen, particularly printers and skilled construction workers, asked for shorter hours and higher pay. For most factory workers, including miners in their earliest strike activity, demands were more diffuse. There was often an initial impulse to use strikes to protest changes in working conditions. As late as 1897 British machine builders tried to attack the spread of the piece rate and other speed-up measures. On the whole, however, strikes over working conditions became rare if only because they were almost impossible to win; employers simply would not yield on these vital issues. Furthermore workers often disagreed over what conditions were appropriate. But this meant that those workers who found their jobs increasingly dismal could not turn to strikes in direct response. Their only outlet was the strike against a hated foreman or a worker who set too fast a pace, and these strikes, though small and usually abortive, continued at a high rate. The most common strikes related to working conditions more indirectly. Some asked for union recognition, which was designed to give worker representatives some voice; for the journeymen this was a highly successful ploy, but for factory workers union recognition, if won, rarely touched day-to-day working conditions. Other strikes sought a reduction of hours, which was a vital part of the accommodation to the new pace of work. But more than anything else, strikers worked to defend their wages.

Many strikes asked for higher wages than ever before, to compensate for new methods of work. This was the instrumental approach: I'll accept possibly more disagreeable work if I'm paid more. Printers used this approach widely in reaction to the new composing machines. But other workers were not yet ready for this. They undoubtedly wanted higher wages, though their consumption goals were not always clear, but they had much more fundamental concerns. Most wage strikes were designed to protect an established, if rising, standard of living rather than to ask for more. They occurred when prosperity returned following a slump, seeking restoration of wages that had been cut. After 1900 they increasingly reacted to inflation; this was the key cause of the massive British strike wave right before World War I. Workers had to have higher money wages simply to make ends meet.

The immediate demands raised in strikes, along with most of the methods used, reflected a rather moderate labor force. Adaptation to work was sufficient, enjoyment off the job adequate for workers to refrain from rocking the boat too vigorously. Only if their adjustment was seriously threatened, as in the British inflation, would they threaten to turn strikes into massive disruption. This was a far cry from the violent, politically conscious strikes occurring during these same years in Russia and Italy; even the average strike rate was lower in the mature industrial countries, when measured against the total number of workers.

Trade Unions

The development of trade unions followed from many of the impulses that went into the strike movement. Indeed many unions were initially formed as organizations for combat and only gradually developed other functions. Trade unions were not new, of course. Many crafts had formed local unions by the mid-nineteenth century. In France and Germany they were long loosely organized. The German Hirsch-Duncker movement was of national scope, but it had attracted only 66,000 members by 1892. In the 1880s French craft unions linked locally around the labor exchanges (*Bourses du travail*), which briefly formed a national organization. Only in Britain, through the Trades Union Congress, had craft unions developed strong national representation before the end of the nineteenth century.

Some craft unions maintained a radical stance; the French *Bourses du travail* were a major source of syndicalism. But the typical craft union, even in France, worked for pragmatic gains for its members, adapting guild techniques to modern economic life. They usually shunned political activities as irrelevant to their function. The British movement, in the 1860s, even opposed the extension of suffrage to workers. Craft unions stressed large benefit funds to help members in sickness, old age, and unemployment, thus continuing the mutual aid tradition on a larger scale. Many provided travel support for journeymen to move from one area to the next seeking work. Most used strikes only sparingly, preferring calm collective bargaining with employers. Between 1851 and 1889 the British Amalgamated Society of Engineers paid out £3 million in benefit funds, while spending only £88,000 on strikes. Many were successful in getting local collective bargaining agreements that would guarantee a minimum wage for each type of work, a maximum level of hours, and extra pay for overtime and travel. They also restricted the number of apprentices in their craft, to guarantee traditional training and to limit the number of new craftsmen. Finally, craft unions worked for respectability and self-improvement; this was one reason they disliked resorting to strikes. They sponsored union libraries, and urged temperance and good habits on their members. Craft unions reflected the kind of adaptation to industrial society that artisans had been developing even in the first stage of industrialization. The form could be found at the origin of virtually every union movement. When typographers in Bosnia, for example, established the first trade union, in the 1900s, they carefully reproduced the purposes of craft organization, including the cautious approach to strikes.

Until the 1890s craft unions predominated, although in Britain there were important organizations among miners and cotton workers as well. The craft approach deliberately left most workers out, for it relied on exclusive skills for its bargaining power. In the 1890s, however, two related developments occurred. A new kind of industrial union arose, and the craft unions modified their own tactics.

In 1889 the successful London dockers' strike, conducted by thousands of unskilled workers, made it clear that even the poorest elements of the labor force could organize with success, and the union movement caught fire and spread quickly to most types of workers in industry and transport. A similar trend developed soon after this in France and Germany. Not all the new unions were durable; British maritime employers, for example, beat down the dockers' union in 1893, and it revived more durably only in 1911. Many workers themselves, hostile to organizational controls, moved in and out of unions during their first decades. But among miners, factory workers, railroad workers, and ultimately the maritime trades the union movement became a permanent part of working-class life.

Industrial unions were huge. National mining and railroad federations had hundreds of thousands of members. British unions collectively had more than a million members in the 1890s and more than 3 million a decade later. Germany had almost a million and a half members by 1906. France lagged a bit with a smaller labor force and smaller firms, but French unions had half a million members in the 1890s and twice that many a decade later. Nowhere did unions embrace more than a minority of the labor force. Some workers objected to the movement because of its risk; others, who approved of unions but resented their dues, found they could benefit from union action without joining. However, the unions became the largest active organizations ever developed in Europe, and they reflected the attitudes of a large segment of the working class.

The industrial-union movement brought important changes to the organization of unions. Local unions embraced all types of workers in an industry, not just a single skill, and the locals were joined in a strong national federation within the industry. Sheer weight of membership was the key to union power. The industrial federations linked into a national union organization, which brought in many craft unions as well. The German and Austrian movements, influenced by the Marxist stress on organization and by the concentration of industry, were particularly centralized. Links among British unions, which centered on the Trades Union Congress, were looser but still significant, and individual industrial federations had considerable central power. In France the C.G.T. was founded in 1895 and embraced the *Bourses du travail* movement in 1902. It long failed to attract the majority of French unions, and its central powers were relatively weak until after World War I. Many industrial federations in France, however, had effective central organization with substantial funds and strong professional leadership. This was true of the northern miners' group, the railroad union, and the textile federation in the north. In Italy the *Confederazione generale del lavoro,* formed in the image of the C.G.T., was limited in power, but some federations had great central strength. Massive membership and considerable direction from the center characterized the industrial-union movement.

Industrial unions had none of the compunctions about strikes that the earlier craft unions had manifested. They existed above all to improve the wages and working conditions of their members. Hence they formulated general goals, stressing better pay, shorter hours, safer working conditions, and union recognition. Because big industrialists were loath to deal with them, strikes were an essential weapon for the industrial unions. However, the initial combative tone of the industrial unions waned with time. To win durable worker support the unions found that they had to develop benefit programs. They also organized social functions, such as dances and picnics; unions became an important part of the lives of many members. Strikes remained significant but union leaders had to curb any radical enthusiasm; for strikes cost money and, if they lost, they cost members as well. So the industrial unions increasingly preached moderation and careful planning. Ultimately their promptings caused the modernization of strike tactics already discussed, but there was often a disparity between their caution and the anger groups of workers could develop on the job.

During this same period, partly because of the example of the industrial unions, craft unions changed their approach. Individual artisans were vital in providing leadership for the newer efforts: the London dock strike, for example, was led in part by radical dissidents from the Amalgamated Society of Engineers. So there was from the first a link between the craft and industrial approach. Furthermore journeymen now used their unions as a counterweight to the important changes in their own job conditions. As their firms became larger and new machines were introduced, they became quite ready to strike, when necessary, to impose collective bargaining. They also grouped nationally, a logical response to the heightened organization of their employers. By the 1900s the differences between craft and industrial unions had diminished. The crafts still stressed exclusivism and protection of skill. But both movements were well organized, usually linked through a national confederation. And both were relatively moderate.

For the cautiousness of unions was a common theme. Where unions existed as part of a socialist party, they invariably played a moderating role, advising against risky tactics or revolutionary efforts. Workers expected their unions to provide benefits here and now. Rarely were they attracted to unions that advocated political action alone. Hence in Germany initial socialist unions, under firm party control, drew only 350,000 members (in the mid-1890s). Unions had to develop their own goals and methods, and as the German movement escaped political control, a separation formalized by the Mannheim agreement of 1906, they quickly increased their membership. But more often than not the tail could wag the dog. By the 1900s German union leaders played a key role in reducing the revolutionary zeal of the socialist party. Because, with rare exceptions, they won support only through immediate gains within the system, union leaders became naturally cautious. They also had their own position to consider. Most were of working-class origin and could be proud of their rise to power in a mighty bureaucracy. On occasion, at least, their desire to avoid jeopardizing their position antagonized their membership. Workers could find union bureaucrats too remote, too concerned with protecting the organization's treasury, and strikes against union orders became common before World War I. However, although some workers urged a more radical union approach, on the syndicalist model, nothing durable developed.

Socialism

As political rights spread, workers increasingly learned to use their votes to express discontent. Here was an obvious vehicle for workers who found their jobs appalling, for whom unions and ultimately strikes became too tame.

New political doctrines spread to the working class, however, from outside leadership. Socialist parties were almost uniformly founded and long led by members of the middle class, usually people with a professional background who used socialism in part to express their own discontent as well as a genuine ideological fervor. Guesde and Jaurès in France, Liebknecht in Germany, Turati in Italy were all lawyers or journalists with advanced education. So was the initial French syndicalist leader Fernand Pelloutier; even anarchism was founded by a Russian military officer. The Labour party in Britain had genuine working-class leadership, but its ideology, which was adopted only gradually, came from the eminently middle-class Fabian society. Middle-class leaders alone had the understanding of doctrine and organization that could impel a political movement.

Early socialism, in fact, won few workers. Socialism has a rich history before the 1880s, but its membership was limited to a small minority of the working class. Often, in fact, middle-class ideologues were too abstract to catch on at all; hence efforts to establish a Marxist group in Britain failed almost totally, save in London itself. Early socialism helped build up a leadership group, devoted to pure, usually Marxist, socialist doctrine and to preaching the revolution.

By the 1880s socialist parties grew rapidly, mainly on the basis of working-class support. The British Labour party was formed in the 1890s to represent the working class specifically, although it cooperated with the Liberals to fight for welfare legislation and other government assistance to labor. On the Continent socialist parties were larger than in Britain. France had more than a hundred socialist deputies by 1913; the German party was receiving almost a million and a half votes by the mid-1890s and 4 million by 1913. The Austrian socialist part rose to a similar position of strength, and socialist movements in Scandinavia, the Low Countries, and even Italy drew the support of increasing numbers.

Most of the Continental socialist movements were Marxist, although some native traditions, such as the French, did persist. In Germany and Austria the socialists were characterized by tight organization and strict control from the top, after the pattern Marx himself had established in earlier stages of the movement. Elsewhere, in France, for example, there was a constant tendency to splintering within the movement, although a Marxist orientation was accepted by most socialists at least in theory.

Under Marxism the Continental socialist parties rose to great prominence; they were supported by most of the working class and urged the abolition of capitalism by means of revolution and the establishment of a new working-class society. Without doubt, many workers believed the existing economic and political system unacceptable. Many found the idea of a radically new society based on worker rule and on equality of wealth extremely attractive. Most workers had not developed their criticisms and hopes very explicitly, but they were certainly susceptible to conversion by Marxist leaders. However, hopes for revolution and for a future utopia were not dominant in the minds of most working-class supporters of Marxism, though they continued to influence many leaders. For the socialist movement changed significantly as it developed mass support. A German worker expressed his thoughts this way: "You know, I never read a social democratic book and rarely a newspaper. I used not to occupy myself with politics at all. But since I got married and have five eaters at home I have to do it. But I think my own thoughts. I do not go in for red ties, big round hats and other similar things. All that does not amount to much. We really do not want to become like the rich and refined people. There will always have to be rich and poor. We would not think of altering that. But we want a better and more just organization at the factory and in the state. I openly express what I think about that, even though it might not be pleasant. But I do nothing illegal." There were many kinds of working-class socialists, ranging from devoted ideologues to people who looked to socialism simply for specific reforms. On the whole workers wanted direct benefits from the movement. They did not expect to change the whole society, even preserving some idea, as the German worker suggested, that a social hierarchy was natural enough. They might, however, harbor some hopes that socialism would bring them a new voice over job conditions.

Partly in response to this sentiment, most socialist parties began to work for reforms more than for outright revolution by the 1890s; it was no accident that they began picking up mass support at the same time. In the 1880s a Possibilist party split from the Marxist movement in France, specifically renouncing revolution and proclaiming the possibility of reforms through parliamentary means. In Germany a bit later Eduard Bernstein stated that Marxist predictions of increasing poverty under capitalism were not true and that the revolutionary approach in general was inaccurate and needless. He too urged cooperation with middle-class parties for reform.

The socialist movements in general renounced these new doctrines, known formally as revisionism. Both the German and the French movements asserted the continued validity of Marxist teachings. In practice, however, socialist behavior became increasingly revisionist. German socialists worked primarily for new welfare measures and for political reforms, especially in the Prussian voting system, that would increase democracy. They talked of revolutionary Marxism, but they did nothing. In France, similarly, socialists such as Jaurès struggled to defend the republican form of government against attack. French socialists talked of the principles of the new society, but their efforts were increasingly bent toward welfare legislation, laws protecting unions and strikes, and other measures that would aid labor. A similar reformist approach developed in most Continental countries, and in Britain the party was not revolutionary even in theory.

By 1914 the socialist movement, trade unions, and strike activity all presented much the same tone of vigorous moderation. Articulate workers had a firm sense of their rights, though there were still many who found every aspect of the labor movement irrelevant or dangerous. The articulate workers, their numbers growing, wanted their own political representatives, and through them they sought new dignity as well as improved welfare protection. It was socialist pressure above all that encouraged the elaboration of national welfare programs after 1900. Equally important, in many factory centers socialists gained power in urban government and were able to put through improvements for working-class schools and neighborhoods. Workers did not feel fully a part of the existing political and economic system; they did not find their rewards appropriate. But they worked within this very system to improve their situation.

A minority of socialists found this pragmatic approach inadequate. Workers more generally, although only rarely rebelling against party or union directives, might yearn for a protest that would express their resentment at their continued dependence on employers, their lack of voice over conditions basic to their lives. They might thus welcome revolutionary rhetoric even when they had no intention of launching a revolution. Or they might simply hope that someday, somehow conditions more appropriate for revolution might come about.

World War and Depression

The turmoil of the world war and the exciting example of the Russian Revolution briefly opened up a new period of agitation when the fighting ended. Some workers, ironically, were drawn to the labor movement because it had gained new respectability during the war. Union and socialist leaders served in coalition governments after war broke out, proving their own moderation and making them seem less fearsome to more timid segments of the working class. But the tension of wartime existence and deteriorating material conditions at the war's end, which in Germany amounted to near starvation, brought still more workers into the labor movement in a quest for radical changes in their existence. The

French C.G.T. quadrupled its membership by 1920, rising past the 2 million mark. In Britain the Labour party rose for the first time to a position of major importance, displacing the Liberals as one of the two principal parties in the country. Everywhere unions grew and socialist parties received more support, while strike levels reached an all-time high.

Many workers sought new kinds of control over their lot. German workers, imitating the Russian revolutionaries, formed councils, or soviets, in many factories, hoping to take over management directly. Workers in Italy in 1920 conducted sit-down strikes, refusing to work but trying to seize control of their factories. British workers talked of entrusting power in the plant to elected shop stewards, and miners and other groups pressed for nationalization of their industries in hopes of gaining more open and responsible management. At least temporarily, the war brought to the surface the radical impulse harbored by important elements of the working class. This was heightened by the disgust of some socialist and union leaders at the moderation of the main body of labor, particularly after the events in Russia convinced them that revolution was feasible.

Generally, however, the most specific revolutionary efforts did not win wide support. When syndicalist leaders in France, in their last independent gesture, called for a general strike in 1920, hoping to topple the social order, they drew only some railroad workers who were mainly interested in attacking a single company over disciplinary problems. Radical German strikes were put down by the new government, under the direction of the moderate socialists. Everywhere the recession of 1920–1921 dampened workers' ardor. Some were frightened by the outburst that had developed; others were disillusioned that revolution had not come. From this radical period one durable development did emerge: in France, Germany, and some other countries the labor movement split into socialist and communist wings. This confirmed socialist parties and the main union movements in their moderate, nonrevolutionary approach; but now there was a specifically revolutionary movement to their left.

Throughout most of the 1920s, however, the working class reverted to earlier protest patterns. The communist organizations drew only modest support. In Germany they continued to strive directly for revolution until 1923, but their final abortive risings were rather contrived affairs attracting only a handful of party faithful. The advent of communist parties did affect national politics, but more because of their tactics than because of their popularity. Most articulate workers stuck with the moderate socialist approach. Union membership dropped down near prewar levels. Strike activity returned to prewar patterns also, except for the improvement in organization and strategy. Goals focused once again on wage demands, inspired by the intense inflationary pressure. The one major exception occurred in Britain, where miners and others afflicted by significant unemployment and insistent on government support launched the largest strike movement in British history. The 1926 general strike involved 2.5 million workers. But it failed; in fact strike movements generally encountered more resistance from employers and the public. This, plus generally satisfactory economic conditions in most countries, reduced direct action. Political support for socialist or communist movements remained more solid, in part because employers were so intransigent, so the 1920s did produce a tendency toward further politicization of working-class demands. Even the British general strike was really aimed at government action in the mining industry, not the employers directly. To be sure, socialist and labor parties could not win undisputed national political power during the 1920s, but their importance did increase and they often served in coalition governments. Their control of city governments gave them even greater power, for here they could extend direct benefits to their constituents.

The tendency of workers to turn to political action became abundantly clear during the depression, but the mood changed decisively. Only in England, where so many workers were already unemployed and disillusioned and where the Labour party had proved inept, did the depression fail to produce a new surge of protest. Elsewhere the depression, with its searing effect on both incomes and morale, capped the development of mature industrial protest. Workers stepped forward, though impelled by catastrophe, to demand new rights.

The depression challenged much of the adaptation workers had developed during the mature industrial period. Their standard of living was obviously jolted as wages fell. Workers who had learned to enjoy aspects of their jobs and value a certain professional dignity now faced unprecedented crisis. In 1932 a Silesian mine was closed by the state after 300 workers were asphyxiated by gas, but the surviving workers petitioned that it be reopened: they preferred the danger of death to the demoralization of unemployment. In some cases women, with their lower wages, found it easier to keep work than men; this challenged yet another value in working-class culture.

Union membership rose as one expression of the new and vigorous sense of grievance. By 1935 French unions had grown from 785,000 to 4 million members. In 1936 an important series of strikes was conducted for improvements in wages and hours. Factories were occupied, often for several weeks; and the workers won their point. The action had been spurred by the election of a Popular Front government controlled by the socialists, for workers wanted to make sure that the government would take the corrective action they wished.

The principal focus of working-class protest against the depression had to be political. Union action, particularly strikes, was of little avail in this depression, as in any other; what was needed was a new kind of government action. The result was a major increase in support for socialist and, in some areas, communist parties. Elements of the middle class and peasantry, themselves suffering intense economic hardship, also gave some support to these parties, but the major impetus came from the workers. Even in Britain support for the Labour party steadily grew in the later 1930s and the party's victory in 1945 was a continuation of this movement. Scandinavian socialist parties received clear majorities and took control of the governments. Votes for the French socialists increased, but even more notable was the steady rise in communist political power; in the 1936 election the number of communists in the Chamber of Deputies rose from ten to seventy-three, and they had become a major political force for the first time. Spanish socialist parties in the industrial areas of the north steadily increased in strength, and a small communist movement was founded. In Germany the communist party provided a particularly vigorous expression of working-class grievance. German workers had long supported the socialists; to express their new discontent, some of them naturally turned to a more radical movement. By late 1932 the communists had almost 17 per cent of the total vote.

The new political efforts of the working class had varying results. In Germany the Nazi victory decapitated the labor movement. In Scandinavia the socialist parties were able to introduce a variety of social-insurance schemes and increased governmental control of the economy. Political backing was given to cooperatives and to unions; collective bargaining became general in Scandinavian industry. Public housing was developed and greater assistance given to large families, to the aged, and to the sick. Under this administration the effects of the depression on the working class were soon eliminated; production rose and relatively full employment was restored. The working class was more protected and more prosperous than ever before, and the attachment to socialist parties was solidified.

The French labor movement won only limited results. Only in 1936, after the depression had already made major inroads, did the socialists gain control of the government, and that control was extremely shaky. The socialists depended on the cooperation of the middle-class Radical party, and this was soon withdrawn in opposition to the various economic measures that the socialists took. The perpetual division between socialists and communists further weakened the government. Communists supported the government at first but refused to participate in it; and gradually their support became undependable. The Popular Front government was doomed to failure, and many of its measures were subsequently rescinded. It did attempt, however, to counter the effects of depression and to provide an economic structure more favorable to the working class. There was some effort to guide the economy, particularly by government operation of the Bank of France. Most important, the government tried to meet the demands of the workers, expressed in the strikes of 1936, for significant improvements in working conditions. It sponsored a series of compulsory collective bargaining arrangements, the Matignon agreements, between employers and unions. The possibility of providing the workers a greater voice in industry, with government assistance, was a notable feature of the settlement. The agreements set higher wages, established a minimum wage and a forty-hour week, and guaranteed two weeks paid vacation a year. These gains were not well administered, and some, such as the limitation on hours of work, were soon abandoned. The discontent and material hardship of the workers were not eliminated and they were reflected in the steady increase in communist popularity. Nevertheless, the Popular Front had introduced some new principles into French industrial life. It represented the sort of approach workers clearly sought and supported.

The impact of the depression on workers and on their political habits proved enduring. The new voting patterns were maintained well after the peak of the depression and even after World War II, except in countries such as Germany, where the leftist political movements were disbanded by government action. Workers and their leaders continued to seek economic devices, centering around greater government action, that would guarantee full employment.

The importance of protest in working-class life should not be exaggerated. Other kinds of adaptations were just as significant. New attitudes toward work and leisure actually proved more durable than some of the forms of unrest. But the working classes had developed a new kind of protest approach during the mature industrial period, and this was a vital part of the continued modernization of the class. Some disparity remained between what labor leaders professed to want and what workers were willing to strive for through collective action. But mature industrial protest did reveal a solid interest in defending economic conditions above the subsistence level. It periodically suggested, as after World War I, an interest in reshaping the industrial power structure. As its concerns found increasingly political expression, working-class unrest inevitably touched the whole society.

The Peasantry

Despite important new connections to the cities, the peasantry remained rather remote from many key aspects of modern life throughout the mature industrial period. They did accept a formal system of education; the agricultural crises opened them to new interest in technological training. School systems gave them contact with authorities outside home and village, which was particularly novel for peasant women. Their local dialect yielded somewhat to more standardized language, which allowed them to understand urban politicians and other outsiders. But all of this took time, and there were other forces working against change among the peasantry. Emigration damaged them. Though the massive exodus to the cities had now slowed, the more enterprising young peasants were still prone to leave the village. In many areas the peasant population aged rapidly as a result, which reduced their ability to adapt to change. Peasants did alter their methods and their organizational structure to deal with the presistent agricultural crises. In both respects they moved in ways parallel to urban modernization, for their technology became more complex, their economy more impersonal. But there was a defensive element as well, when peasants asked for special favors from the state to reduce their need to change. Similarly, peasants learned the value of politicization, but again they gave it a special form; their most distinctive contributions to politics came through efforts to defend rural tradition, including the small family farm.

There could be no question of the challenge posed by the competition of cheap imported foods. Falling grain prices hit earnings directly and tumbling land values threatened the basis of peasant status. Many had to borrow heavily to survive.

All over western and central Europe peasants tried to counteract the agricultural crisis by improving the efficiency of their methods. Never before had peasants been so eager to try technical innovations. They purchased new tools, including seed drills and even threshing machines. After 1892 most wheat fields in France, large or small, were cultivated and harvested with machines. Danish dairy farmers began to use cream separators after 1870. Everywhere the utilization of fertilizers increased. The result of the quest for efficiency was a general and significant improvement in yields. French production of both wheat and wine increased after 1890 even though the amount of land devoted to each of those crops declined. An interest in technical advances began to penetrate the peasantry, promoted both by education and economic pressure, and the spread of new methods definitely helped the peasants to improve their economic position in the face of falling prices.

Peasants also began to change the crops they raised. They increasingly abandoned grain, in which competition was most intense, in favor of meat, dairy, and truck products. In Germany the raising of animals, particularly hogs, increased rapidly, especially in the small-holding areas. Danish peasants intensified the specialization in dairy farming that they had begun before the crisis. British farmers curtailed the amount of land devoted to arable farming, and their production of wheat actually declined. They concentrated instead on meat and dairy goods, as did farmers in Normandy. The peasants of Brittany and several other regions of France specialized in truck farming, but France as a whole retained a higher level of wheat production than any European country except Russia. Generally, the conversion to more marketable crops was an important result of the agricultural crisis. The growing demand of the urban masses for meats and dairy products assured an excellent market for the new specialties. Peasant attunement to the market, already well developed, was clearly increasing.

Most peasants converting to mechanized farming or to a specialty crop ran into important difficulties. Mechanized equipment was beyond the means of many individuals. Conversion to stock raising or dairy farming required far more capital than was necessary for grain production. The growing dependence on the market posed certain problems in itself. Peasants were economically weak in comparison with the producers of agricultural equipment and fertilizers; they could easily be victimized in their transactions. They were weak also in relation to the wholesalers who bought their crops. Some peasants entered into contracts with breweries, sugar refineries, and canneries in an effort to assure their sales; too often these contracts left the peasants in virtual servitude to the manufacturer. Peasants who borrowed money to buy new equipment or stock were often exploited by the lenders. For a variety of reasons peasants found it difficult to respond to the agricultural crisis and adopted new equipment and crops only hesitantly, despite the great need for change. In France, most notably, peasant agriculture remained extremely inefficient, with inadequate use of fertilizer and modern equipment. Much peasant adaptation simply continued older patterns; a gradual consolidation of plots into slightly larger holdings, which might or might not facilitate new methods, along with a reduction of common lands and of village decisions on how to farm. And even this change was slow; in 1892, 71 per cent of all French farms had five hectares of land or less; by 1929 the figure was still 54 per cent. But change was essential, and it had to go beyond a mere acceleration of earlier modernization. By a new organization of the peasantry, by a combination of peasant resources, capital could be provided, supplies purchased, and even marketing arranged to the advantage of each producer. An extensive cooperative movement arose in direct response to the new economic needs of the peasantry.

Cooperation and Peasant Politics

The first cooperatives were established before 1850 as savings banks and lending agencies for the members. The Raiffeissen banks in Germany, begun in 1846 as a response to the agricultural crisis of that year, and the Schulze-Delitzsch credit cooperatives did a great deal to reduce interest rates on loans and to provide more ample funds for German peasants. Savings and loan organizations were the most popular rural cooperatives, and their membership grew rapidly after 1870 in Germany and elsewhere. Purchasing cooperatives were also formed to buy expensive supplies and even heavy machinery for shared use. After 1870 Danish cooperatives helped purchase cream separators; the first French cooperative was founded in 1881 to buy fertilizers. Other groups in France were established to acquire vines from the United States to replace the diseased French stock. Cooperatives extended their purchasing functions even to such consumer goods as clothing. By grouping the purchasing power of individual peasants, cooperatives lowered prices, assured high quality, and allowed technical improvements impossible to the individual peasant. Finally, some cooperatives developed storage and processing facilities for agricultural goods and served as sales agents for their members. Again, the cooperative organization had far greater power in the market than did individual peasants.

The cooperative movement spread widely; 750,000 French peasants were in cooperatives of some sort by 1910, and over a quarter of the German peasantry was enrolled. In Denmark, which adapted most successfully to the new agricultural situation, cooperatives played a major role. Nevertheless, cooperatives demanded important sacrifices from the peasants. They violated the individualism many peasants had developed during the earlier period of adjustment to market agriculture. Cooperatives also demanded administrative skills that few peasants possessed. The movement, although it spread constantly, did not touch the bulk of the peasantry during the period. In France, where peasant individualism was unusually intense, no more than a tenth of the agricultural population joined cooperatives before World War I, and many who did only joined credit cooperatives, which were in business to finance individual, not collective, effort.

Peasant political consciousness inevitably rose in the period as education and voting rights were extended. In a few cases peasants used their vote to express radical discontent. There were isolated pockets of socialist voting in southwestern Germany. Around Bologna, where large estates were formed in the 1860s on newly drained land, peasant support for socialism developed before 1900. Landless laborers in several industrial countries began, somewhat hesitantly, to strike and unionize. Their position was made ever more desperate by the agricultural crisis, as wages fell and their employers became more demanding. With the richer peasants fighting for more land, more people were forced into this dependent position. One French laborer described how his landlord employer called him "Thing," not bothering to remember his name: "Obey and Work: I ask nothing else of you." Small wonder that major strikes broke out among agricultural laborers in France after 1900. The same impulse carried about 100,000 rural laborers into the French Communist party when it formed in the 1920s.

Generally, however, peasants in industrial countries were not attracted by extremes of this sort. They developed new political interests but remained conservative. In France peasants traditionally had supported monarchist notables and Bonapartists; only in a few areas had they ever developed an interest in republicanism. During the 1870s republican campaigners, led by Léon Gambetta, tried to persuade peasants that a republic could maintain order and protect private property; most French peasants therefore became firm republicans. Elsewhere, traditionalism was not modified even to this extent. Peasant voters in Austria rejected the political control of the landlords by voting for the Christian Socialist party, but they were still supporting a conservative party favorable to religion. Many German peasants still voted as the landlords told them to. Gradually, however, peasants did become aware of the possibility of using their votes, always in a conservative way, to win economic assistance from the government.

Governments offered various assistance to farmers during the period. They extended advanced technical training in agriculture. German universities offered night courses to peasants, in the villages, on the principles of scientific agriculture, and the British government established similar training after 1900. In 1900 the British government also allowed county councils to buy land for rental in plots of moderate size in an effort to encourage small farming. The German government promoted consolidation of land and also purchased some estates to assist small farmers. The French government lent money to the cooperatives, and governments generally tried to develop the credit facilities in the countryside.

Of greatest interest to the peasants was the possibility of establishing tariff protection for agricultural goods. Most countries had abandoned significant duties on food prior to 1870. Agricultural producers who depended on exports, such as the Junkers, supported free trade, but the peasants took little interest in the issue. As the crisis in agriculture began, pressure for tariff protection rose. The peasants did not initiate the pressure; issues of this sort were unfamiliar, and peasants were not accustomed to political action of any kind. In Germany the Junkers launched the agitation by forming their Union of Agriculturalists to spread propaganda for tariff protection and to serve as a vigorous lobby. In France not only large landowners but also some industrialists pressed for new agricultural tariffs; the industrialists hoped to promote a general return to protective policies. These various interests began to appeal to the peasants for support in their campaigns. Conservative politicians sought peasant votes by pointing to the need to defend the nation's agriculture against foreign competition. Propagandists from the German Union of Agriculturalists talked to the unity of agricultural interests and the need to defend agriculture as a whole. As we have seen the group persuaded many peasants to urge tariffs that were often against their own economic interest.

More generally, peasants supported tariffs, once the idea was presented to them, as a means of reducing the need for change. With high duties on food imports, old methods and traditional products could still be profitable. In France, Germany, and elsewhere tariffs undeniably protected methods and crops that were economically wasteful. The French tariff of 1892 returned France to a position of almost complete agricultural self-sufficiency, despite the fact that French peasants could not produce grain as economically as farmers in the New World. The main victims of this system were urban buyers of food, however, not the peasants themselves, who saw their incomes and habits alike defended by the tariff system.

Peasant attachment to tariff advocates was intense. Along with continued political traditionalism, it helped maintain the conservative political orientation of most of the class. Peasants in France voted generally for moderate republicans because they offered tariffs, governmental sympathy for the church, and a firm defense of private property. German peasants usually voted either for the Catholic Center party, urged on by their priests, or in Protestant areas for conservative groupings controlled by the Junkers. Both of the parties receiving peasant support in Germany were staunch advocates of agricultural tariffs. The peasantry became accustomed to the idea that their inefficiency should be supported by the rest of the nation. In France peasant interest groups successfully advocated specially low taxes along with other favors. Beyond this, peasants, constantly told by conservatives that their way of life was more moral than that of the cities, were encouraged to believe that the old ways were of benefit to the entire nation.

The defensive adaptation helped keep peasant living standards low. There was some improvement, as more urban products became available. Clothing was usually factory-made now. Bus service allowed peasants to attend movies in the nearby town. But diets and particularly housing remained well below urban standards. This poverty drove some peasants away, for the city was a constant temptation. In France and Britain the absolute number of peasants began to decrease for the first time and some land was taken out of cultivation. The spread of education and military service, which gave peasants dramatic experience of other regions of the country, encouraged this movement. But all this simply enhanced the self-satisfaction of the peasants who remained. Except for the stirrings among landless laborers, the attachment to traditional work and the land, the village festivals and games, and, usually, the continued interest in religion gave sufficient satisfaction.

The peasant way of life thus yielded only reluctantly to the pressures for change. Peasants proved surprisingly resilient in their defense of tradition, and in learning new ways to express older values they had an important impact on European politics and economic life. Their response, and the echo it found in other troubled segments of society, prevented any real solution for the basic difficulties of European agriculture.

World War I

The war and its immediate aftermath heightened the pressures on the peasantry, causing their defensive political stance to alter into positive reaction. The war itself was a great shock. Peasants provided a disproportionate number of infantrymen, for factory workers were too valuable to spare in such numbers. Few peasant families, therefore, would be without a death to mourn, for the slaughter was appalling. Many peasants who did survive chose not to return to the countryside. Some of the land torn up by the war was not returned to use. Disruption of habits showed in the decline of religious practice in German villages, long bastions of traditional ways.

Ironically the war briefly interrupted the basic economic crisis of agriculture. A period of prosperity continued during the first years after the war before production was fully restored. Many peasants managed to pay off their debts and raise their personal consumption. French peasants borrowed to buy more land, Germans to buy new equipment. But by 1923 or 1924 pressure on agricultural prices returned, and the new debts became a great burden. The depression made matters worse by reducing agricultural prices up to 50 per cent. In France peasant buying power compared to 1913 was down 10 per cent by 1930, 28 per cent by 1933. Peasants continued to introduce some technical improvements in an effort to meet this pressure. Still, material levels remained low. In France the average peasant's house was at least a hundred years old. Government programs allowed some improvements, particularly by extending electricity to most villages. But only a minority of peasants had indoor plumbing facilities.

During the 1920s there were few signs of increased peasant discontent. Political patterns remained largely traditional and conservative. French peasants often elected conservative estate owners, the traditional notables, to newly created agricultural bureaus. Some new farmers' lobbying groups were formed in both Germany and France, but there was little significant change. With the advent of depression and the new political movements in the cities, peasant political patterns began to alter somewhat. Leaders of both left and right began to solicit peasant support more actively. And peasants themselves had a greater desire to express their material discontent and, often, their distrust of the growing power of urban workers.

In France communism made some headway among peasants and the C.G.T. had 180,000 peasant members by 1936; in 1937 many farm workers struck for collective bargaining. More important were the gains of agricultural parties and groupings on the right. A Peasant Front was formed in 1934 that stressed the need for a political system more attuned to the needs of agriculture. The Front was soon split, but important currents of activity in defense of specifically peasant movements remained. There were also some cases of direct action. Demonstrations occurred in several areas, and in 1934 a peasant group marched to Paris. A milk strike occurred in the same period, the first time that peasant owners, as opposed to agricultural workers, had banded together for protest action. Cooperative movements continued to gain. Whereas before the war only a tenth of the French peasantry had belonged to cooperative groups, by the 1920s a full third of the class was enrolled. The cooperative movements continued to provide important assistance in matters of credit, purchasing, and processing; they also reflected the new willingness and ability of peasants to join together in matters of mutual concern. Finally, a new Catholic youth group developed, urging better technology and a new outlook, and thus helped train the new kind of peasant who came into prominence after World War II. The various efforts by peasants to better their lot had only limited success. Material conditions remained poor. Governments offered some new technical assistance, and in 1936 the Popular Front ministry established a Wheat Office to support wheat prices and improve peasant incomes. Various other subsidies were extended. For the most part, these measures relieved but did not remove the major economic difficulties. Increasing peasant activity was not yet sufficient to win substantial material improvements.

German peasants also developed some distinctive political expressions during this period, particularly after the depression brought new and widespread hardship. As in France, the basic grievances concerned falling prices and lack of capital. There was also some general resentment over the declining status of the peasantry in society as a whole, the growing dominance of big business, and the rise of communist and socialist movements that threatened private property and seemed to give the workers undue influence. As a result of these various sources of discontent, many peasants proved vulnerable to Nazi propaganda. The first areas to offer majorities to the Nazis were regions such as Thuringia, which lacked a substantial industrial population and were dominated by peasant small holding. Traditional, tightly organized villages were particularly liable to turn to the Nazis.

To many peasants the Nazis offered protection against change. They promised to support peasant tenure. They praised the peasantry as the true bearer of German tradition and promised to promote peasant traditions of dress and behavior in an effort to return to the essence of German culture. To be sure, peasants did not win what they wanted; the Nazi regime, once in office, continued to pay lip-service to a peasant ideal, but in the interests of efficiency it busily furthered consolidation of agricultural holdings and the displacement of the smaller peasants.

Mature Industrial Society and Eastern Europe

During most of the period in which mature industrial society took hold in western and central Europe, the east and south were experiencing their own version of an early industrial revolution. The most obvious result was a pattern of agitation far more pervasive than that of mature industrial society, an exacerbated version of the early industrial upheavals that had occurred a century before in the west. A small middle class, composed primarily of professional people, espoused liberal and nationalist goals, sparking insurrections from the Bosnian and Bulgarian risings of 1875 through the Russian revolution of 1905. In 1904, as Russia suffered from its war losses to Japan, groups of teachers, lawyers, and doctors formed unions to work for liberal political reform, ultimately creating the Kadet party to push for effective parliamentary government.

But the middle class was too weak to control agitation in these areas; hence, in Russia, the short-lived liberal phase of the 1917 revolution. More serious was peasant grievance, which continued into the post-World War I years in the form of peasant parties in eastern Europe, persistent anarchist agitation in southern Spain, (including attempts to seize estates when Civil War broke out in 1936), and rising rural crime in many areas and even endemic banditry in the Balkans. The massive political and economic power of the landlords, except in Russia, combined with low agricultural prices and economic pressure to maintain the tensions typical of an early industrial society. In Hungary 0.7 per cent of the population owned 48.3 per cent of the land; in Poland, 0.6 per cent owned 43 per cent. Overall, 70 per cent of the peasants in eastern Europe possessed less than twelve and a half acres of land, enough for a bare subsistence at best. In Rumania, the one non-communist country where land reform did occur (only 7 per cent of the land remained in large holdings), 50 per cent of the peasantry held less than seven and a half acres. Without capital or education, Rumanian peasants were unable to produce for the market and returned to a near subsistence economy. Here and elsewhere up to a third of all children still died before reaching two years of age, reflecting the impoverished housing and diet available.

Added to rural unrest was the unusual agitation of early factory workers. Russian workers conducted thousands of strikes between 1895 and 1914. Various socialist doctrines spread there and among workers in Poland, southern Italy, and many parts of Spain.

All of this again serves as a reminder of the major differences in stages of development between the two principal zones of Europe. But something of a mature industrial society was to develop in these areas, and although its nature can be pursued in a final assessment of contemporary Europe an outline can usefully be suggested now. In eastern Europe, initially in Russia, mature industrialization arose under the guidance of communist regimes. This altered some of its basic aspects. Most obviously the upper-class amalgam of big businessmen and aristocrats so important in the west was absent, for the new regimes gave primary power to dedicated communists drawn from diverse social origins but including a substantial segment from working-class and peasant backgrounds. By reforming higher educational facilities, using scholarship funds to open them to talented students from various classes, and spreading primary and secondary schools widely, the communist regimes long kept the ruling class open to accessions from below.

But as Russia neared industrial maturity, in terms of the several generations of experience involved, by the 1930s and certainly after World War II, it repeated some aspects of the social characteristics developed earlier in the west. The same was true of other communist countries after World War II, where rapid efforts at industrialization or, as in Czechoslovakia and East Germany, consolidation of earlier industrial progress created a new society. A managerial and professional class obviously developed. Like its counterpart in western Europe earlier it restricted its birth rate to protect its own standard of living and to maximize opportunities for the children born. This class made strenuous efforts to place its children well in school in order to launch them on appropriate professional careers.

The entry of women into key professions was more significant than in western mature industrial society, but there were some comparable problems of status. Although fields such as medicine were dominated by women, they were less prestigious and lower-paying than their western counterparts.

The professional–managerial class in eastern Europe, although requiring many of the same planning skills and manifesting many of the same personal traits as its western counterpart, could not develop along exactly similar lines. It was not distracted by the anxieties of an anarchronistic shopkeeping element. State controls over most retailing, although painfully imposed by the communist regimes (in Russia Lenin had to allow some reversion to private ownership during the 1920s, but this was reversed under Stalin), eliminated what had always been a small urban middling class. At the same time opportunities for development of a leisure ethic were limited. The managerial class could enjoy small country homes and regular vacations, but a work ethic, sedulously fostered by communist states bent on rapid industrialization, continued to hold away. Costumes and cultural activities remained, by western standards, rather traditional and somber.

For the working class the communist regimes provided a more successful adaptation to mature industrial structures than had been true in the west, in certain respects at least. Communist parties and unions gave individual worker representatives a voice in management decisions; they also prevented the development of spontaneous protest outlets, for independent organizations were forbidden. Workers were constantly told of their importance to society; they could not feel as isolated as some of their western counterparts. They were required, however, to adapt to rapidly changing technology and consistent pressure to speed up their pace of work. Prizes given to unusually productive workers in Russia during the 1930s, modified piece rate systems and differential pay for differential skills, careful supervision by foremen, all reproduced the apparently inevitable trappings of advanced factory production. Provision of recreational facilities, usually at communist party headquarters, and annual vacations compensated workers somewhat. So did pension plans and other social security benefits that were more comprehensive than their western analogues during the mature industrial period. On the other hand limitations on the production of consumer goods, including very restricted housing facilities, prevented some of the individual work compensations workers in the west came to know. This was long a function of the greater traditional poverty of these regions, as well as the more collectivist impulses of the communist system. Along with the absence of protest outlets it did raise questions about the ability of these societies to transcend the earlier phases of industrial maturation. By the mid-twentieth century, persistent signs of worker alienation and a stagnation of per-worker productivity harked back to the problems faced in western Europe around 1914.

For the peasantry, the communist version of transition to a mature industrial society was decidedly different than that of the west, and on the whole less successful. Some traditional problems were removed; notably, advancing industry reduced population pressure on the land. The spread of education brought peasants closer to urban attitudes in other respects. The new regimes made concerted efforts to disseminate more advanced agricultural technology. But traditional peasant adaptation possibilities were cut off by the collectivization of land ownership. There was every sign that peasants wanted their own control of the land and might best have adapted at their own slow pace, once this was achieved, as western peasants had earlier. This had already been suggested, in Russia, by the favorable reception given the Stolypin reforms. Under the impact of the 1917 revolution Russian peasants seized more land from the large estates, and some of the poorer peasants attacked the richer ones. But the Russian peasants kept their individual holdings only briefly. By 1918 the Soviet government attempted to press for greater collectivization of agriculture and particularly for new state controls over output and distribution. The peasants resisted, largely by restricting their production to their own needs. In 1921 the government, as part of Lenin's New Economic Policy, relaxed its pressures, and the peasants enjoyed a new period of private individual holdings. Earlier trends toward the concentration of land in the hands of a minority of wealthy kulaks continued, and agricultural production rose once again. At the end of the decade, however, renewed repression, including the extermination of the kulaks, attacked the peasant agricultural system, and collectivization was fully imposed. Again, some poorer peasants joined the attack on the kulaks but only in the interest of acquiring land themselves; the policy of collectivization thwarted them just as it did the more substantial farmers. Overt resistance to the new system was limited, but in the early 1930s many peasants destroyed their livestock and smashed equipment before entering the unwelcome collectives. Although the government imposed its will by military force, the peasants' traditional desire for individual holdings remained unquenched.

Similar tensions developed with the imposition of communist regimes in the smaller eastern European countries after World War II. Everywhere the conflict between official policy and peasant interest was reflected in low rates of agricultural productivity that kept a far higher percentage of the population on the land, in order to assure food for the cities, than was true of contemporary western European society.

But even this fact recalls the applicability of some aspects of a mature industrial model to both the principal zones of Europe. In both cases, despite the radically different forms involved, there was a disparity between peasant values and those of the urban world. Peasant agriculture in France remained unnecessarily inefficient. Nowhere, save where a peasant mentality had never really developed (as in the United States) or where the peasantry had essentially been eliminated (as in England) did mature industrial society successfully deal with the problem of agriculture. None of this is to argue that eastern Europe toward mid-century can be interpreted in the same terms as the mature industrial society we have more fully outlined for western and central Europe. Some key problems were avoided, notably through the more thorough, if sometimes brutal, elimination of traditionalist urban and upper-class elements. Some important advantages were also missed, some of which must be raised again in the final section on contemporary European society. Most notably the outline of a new leisure ethic was far different. Urban groups in eastern Europe did develop something of the same separation between work and leisure that came to prevail elsewhere; this included some similar interests, as in mass sports. But the impulse was more collectively controlled and far more somber than western Europe had developed by the 1920s. A youth culture was frowned upon, in favor of youth groups organized for disciplined exercises and marches. Women, although given important new job and educational opportunities, did not play the same role in a consumer society; not for them, to the same degree, the bright dresses, cosmetics, and faddish dances of England or Germany. The difference in tone affected part of the working class, though the middle class more obviously; it raised questions about the ability of communist society to maintain the personal motivations that advanced industrialization required, and to this we will return. But the difference may have been to the credit of the communist version of mature industrialization; the word *advantage,* used deliberately above in describing the west, is open to debate.

Mass Culture and the Leisure Ethic

The most durable innovation of the mature industrial phase in western and central Europe, along with the suggestions of a new, nonpropertied class structure, was the new definition of life off the job and what to do with it. Contemporary observers, most of them disgruntled intellectuals, saw the rise of a new mass culture. The term is acceptable if we make several obvious qualifications. Although "the masses" had vast new opportunities, from politics through spending money, they were not homogeneous. Quite apart from the rather recalcitrant peasantry, urban groups differed widely in their definition of leisure time or politics. The most obvious new culture was in fact a mutation of middle-class values, in which the new lower middle class and the upper segments of the working class played a key role. Mass culture reflected a reshuffling of class lines, but not their obliteration. Traditional leaders, bemoaning their loss of political influence or the decline of the classics, undoubtedly had the impression of a barbaric, undifferentiated mass, but they exaggerated its unity and ignored the extent to which their own sons and daughters, newly interested in pleasure, shared some of the new cultural values.

The rising urban culture involved two elements: a decline in traditional systems of belief and their possible replacement by new ones, and a change in personal values. Organized religion tried to adjust to mature industrial society but on the whole it was unsuccessful. Many people still went to church, but in the cities this was now part of individual choice, not an overarching community of belief; and in fact church attendance declined steadily among middle and working classes alike.

Many Protestant organizations tried to react by establishing settlement-house facilities to aid the urban poor. They sponsored scouting groups and various efforts in social work to offer recreational facilities and material assistance to the lower classes. In Britain a new Protestant movement, the Salvation Army, was founded in 1880 to provide material as well as spiritual solace to the poor and downtrodden.

Catholic programs were also developed to promote material well-being and thereby attract working-class groups to the Church. Many Catholic unions were founded in Germany, France, and elsewhere. Far more moderate than other union movements, they stressed mutual aid and bargaining without strikes. They won only modest membership but they revealed the new level of Catholic interest in the needs and demands of workers. More generally, Pope Leo XIII tried to modify the Church's earlier opposition to modern political and social movements. He admitted the acceptability of democratic and even republican regimes, urging French Catholics, for example, to rally to the support of the French republic. Further, while attacking socialism and insisting on the importance of private property, he urged greater attention to social justice. In the encyclical *Rerum novarum,* issued in 1891, he approved of the union movement and of government welfare programs and recommended that employers better the conditions of their workers.

On the whole, however, the churches had begun effective adjustment to the new position of the lower classes too late. Some few workers were attached more firmly to the church by the new programs, but far more were left untouched. Important rural and aristocratic elements in the churches resisted many of the programs of modernization, so efforts to woo the masses were small and were often contradicted by conservative action by Christian leaders. Many French Catholics, for example, ignored the pope's appeal to support the republic and seized on the Dreyfus affair as an excuse to attack republican principles. Catholic army officers, aristocrats, some members of the upper middle class, and certainly many members of the hierarchy continued to view religion as a force for social conservatism. It was significant, nevertheless, that the efforts by both Protestant and Catholic churches to woo the masses were based on recognition of the need to combine religion with social reform. The working of religion in the world, beyond mere charity, became an increasingly important part of church activity.

The hold of religion on the urban lower classes was weakened by developments in church–state relations and in intellectual life. The middle-class political attack on church privileges continued, and middle-class parties had greater power than ever before because of the rise of parliamentary structures. And they were aided by the new socialist parties, which were almost uniformly hostile to Christianity. Together the parties launched a major attack on the churches, especially the Catholic Church, in most countries. The German *Kulturkampf* of the 1870s suppressed many religious orders, secularized much of the educational system, and established civil instead of religious marriage. In Italy and France the government and the liberal parties were in a virtual state of war against the Church; many religious orders were suppressed, and the Church's role in education was curtailed. After the Dreyfus affair the attack was renewed in France, for the Church seemed attached to the enemies of the republic. Religious orders and schools were weakened further, and in 1905 the Church was separated from the state; state funds and protection were entirely withdrawn.

The political clashes weakened the churches in several ways. The churches lost institutional power and many traditional functions. Their educational role was reduced; traditional charity was diminished by the advance of secular welfare efforts. The Christian marriage ethic and influence over the family were hampered by new laws permitting divorce and civil marriage. Furthermore, the political disputes distracted many Christian leaders from the pressing problems of dealing with the newly awakened lower classes. The continued concern with defending institutional privilege often furthered the impression that the churches were conservative, out of date.

This impression was heightened, finally, by the spread of new scientific doctrines, such as the theory of evolution, and the popularization of attacks on the historical veracity of the Bible. These new doctrines were published widely in the press and were often taught in the school systems;

they confirmed many members of the middle and working classes in their view of religion as superstitious and irrelevant.

Despite the decline of religious interest, the churches showed considerable vitality during the period. The new scientific doctrines were answered by a revival and revision of Christian theology. The churches gradually accepted new political regimes; Catholics adjusted to the new German state after the 1870s and even to the separation of church and state in France. There was a huge burst of missionary activity from Catholics and Protestants alike. Many churches were gaining in wealth; the Irish and Spanish churches, particularly, were richer than ever before. The decline of religion was thus ambiguous; the churches were still receiving support and seemed to be gaining in vigor despite growing indifference among major groups.

The power of the churches came largely from nonindustrial classes, many of whom turned to religion with renewed interest, in reaction to hostile modern trends. Peasants remained loyal to the faith and were often guided politically by local priests. The churches were vital to aristocratic conservatism and, in most countries, to shopkeepers and other elements of the middling class. Missionaries, for example, were recruited from small-town elements that found it easier to preach the faith to heathen than to adjust to what was, to them, the strange new society around them. Largely nonindustrial regions, like southern Germany, or whole countries, such as Ireland, were the bastions of religious fervor. Religion was increasingly a refuge for people who were being reduced in status by the classes most directly associated with the leading economic forms. Where anti-modern political movements developed, they usually had Christian overtones and appealed to many Christians. The conversion of many French priests to anti-Semitic movements and the association of many German Protestants with anti-Semitism, were extreme forms of Christian protest against the modern world.

Of course sincere religious belief was found among individuals in every part of society, and the association of religion with traditionalist elements was incomplete. But the churches were declining and, although this was not entirely new, their decline raised important questions of alternatives for the leading urban groups. Some people sought an alternate, encompassing loyalty. It has often been pointed out that socialism provided religiouslike values for certain of its adherents: it had a Bible (Marxism), martyrs, a heaven to come in the future, and often important rituals. A German miner, describing the role of socialism in his life, proclaimed religious fervor: "What is my meaning in this great world plan where brutal physical and psychological forces feast themselves in orgies? Nothing! Only Social Democratic activities could give me goals . . . , so that I may attempt my plans. I therefore adhere to socialism with every fiber of courage and idealism." In eastern Europe, the later rise of communist loyalties could replace religion. Everywhere some individuals made the transfer quite directly, abandoning traditional churches as irrelevant but switching their entire devotion to socialism or communism.

Nationalism might serve something of the same purpose. It was more likely to be combined with religion, as conservative leaders came to support both loyalties by the end of the nineteenth century. But workers might unite nationalism with socialism, like the German who declared himself "a good socialist and a good soldier of the Fatherland, both at the same time." Some intellectuals certainly attributed religiouslike importance to their devotion to the nation; this was particularly true in multi-ethnic areas where one's nationality could so easily seem oppressed by others, as in the Habsburg monarchy where Slavs resisted the dominance of Germans and Magyars.

Critics of mass culture noted the rise of new loyalties with disfavor. Both socialism and nationalism were manipulable by calculating leaders. Both could rouse masses to blind, sometimes violent enthusiasms. Roaring mobs, shouting obedience to a rabble-rousing speaker skilled in playing on their emotions, vowing death to an enemy class or race, were not one of the most attractive features of mature industrial society, though they played an important role. Again one might question how new this kind of loyalty was, for its resemblance to religious enthusiasms was considerable. More important, it was not the most pervasive expression of the new kind of popular culture that was taking shape.

For most people replaced religion (and popular religion had never been primarily a question of encompassing dogma or even, save for brief periods, wild emotion) with a more informal set of values. Most socialist workers really wanted a new society but they did not see socialism as a religion; hence, among other things, they were mildly nationalistic too, as their loyal performance during the first years of World War I was to indicate. Most middle-class people, although believing in nationalism, also believed in science and material progress and a host of other values. For the majority of all urban groups the culture that really replaced religion was hedonistic, a commitment to a range of individual choices about what pleasures to seek when work was done.

Nothing more clearly mirrored and shaped the new popular culture than the mass press that developed at the end of the nineteenth century. Working-class literacy of course attracted a variety of socialist newspapers that provided political information and guidance to their members and maintained a high level of excitement about current problems. Though significant, these were not the papers that gained a really mass following, their circulations being limited to a small number of the faithful.

The truly mass press had a twofold basis. First, it was able to lower prices drastically. This was due partly to major improvements in printing, but particularly to the development of huge advertising revenues. Second, the new press catered to people whose reading habits were not sophisticated and who sought entertainment in what they read. In both respects the press reflected the new search for pleasure. Older journals of course continued, appealing to the upper classes with their serious accounts of political and cultural events; but their readership was limited. By 1900, however, *Le Petit Journal* in Paris sold 2 million copies a day. The Berlin *Lokal-Anzeiger* had a million readers, as did both the *Daily Mail* and the *Daily Express* in London. The size of these giants allowed steady reductions in cost and development of various new features to keep the readers entertained; both tended to increase the readership even further.

The entertainment function of the mass press was expressed in many ways. Stories of crimes and of personal melodrama proved increasingly popular. This contrasted with the older middle-class press, which had devoted space to short stories with a moral message and to comments on theater, music, and the like. Special features were developed to appeal to the interests of various groups. Women's sections discussed social news and other matters of concern to female readers. Accounts of sporting events were greatly expanded. And in all the features of the paper, writing was simplified, headlines made more sensational.

The political content of the new papers differed from the older middle-class press and from the working-class press. Little attention was given to internal politics. The great interest in editorializing, which typified older middle-class papers, declined as the enlarged reading public showed little concern for elaborate discussions of issues. However, the papers did have a political tone, almost uniformly conservative. The publishers and the advertisers were businessmen; they had a definite interest in turning the masses away from social discontent. And they discovered quite quickly that appeals to national loyalty, particularly in accounts of imperial ventures, appealed to readers. Stories of national empire could be filled with excitement and the lure of the strange and they promoted a comforting sense of importance among readers who saw their nations dominating inferior peoples.

After World War I the entertainment functions of the mass press became still more prominent. Newspapers found that only their frivolous articles attracted readers. They provided intensive coverage of particularly interesting crimes, the activities of the socially fashionable (including the affairs and divorces of film stars and aristocrats, whose amusement value almost gave the class a new function) and other phenomena that were diverting in their peculiarity, such as nudist movements or the tales of the Loch Ness monster. Sports sections were expanded, covering the new range of athletics and also expanded betting possibilities, for gambling on horse racing and football games won growing popularity.

In addition to the mass press, music halls and, after 1900, films provided new entertainment outlets. The radio, available in bars if not in all private homes, offered yet another set of standardized entertainment fare. All in all a formidable array of diversions was available. Bars retained popularity, though the level of public drinking now declined in places like France, as earlier in Britain. Dancing, sports, shows, gambling, light reading, and excursions all contributed to the pleasure-seeking culture of the 1920s.

It is easy to criticize this new culture. It was highly commercialized, for the leisure industry was big business. It was sensationalist in many respects. The main organs of mass entertainment were highly standardized. It was a passive culture in most of its manifestations, involving watching other people perform or hearing about disasters that occurred someplace else. But this was not really the deterioration of some glorious tradition of popular entertainment, for leisure was itself a new development. Older popular festivals were unusual occurrences, not regular chances for enjoyment, and they themselves were highly stylized and custombound, leaving little room for individual initiative on the part of participants. Many of the weaknesses of the leisure culture derived from the inevitable fumbling that occurred as people adjusted to the use of unaccustomed funds and free time. Although standardization and control by rapacious businessmen trying to play on poor taste in order to make money were legitimate targets of criticism, from the viewpoint of the masses the culture provided unprecedented scope for choice. Not everyone read newspapers; some preferred the radio. Although some thronged to soccer games others preferred bicycling. Nor, finally, should the passive element be overplayed. The new culture for youth, at least, involved active participation in dancing and games. For older people the passivity was greater, a weakness that is only now receiving attention in modern society. Even the 1920s constituted the merest beginning in the new popular culture. This was more than enough for the traditionalists, who wanted the masses to behave either like idealized peasants or like budding classical scholars. For large elements of the lower classes, the problem was rather an inadequacy of means and energy to take full advantage of the conversion to leisure values.

World War I and the Collapse of Industrial Society

Although it suggested a popular culture that has received much fuller development in recent decades, the period of industrial maturation had a number of inherent weaknesses. We have already sketched the serious structural imbalances of the economy that led to recurrent crisis well before World War I; we have dealt with the incomplete adaptation of the upper class and of tensions within as well as between the middle and lower classes. Where this would have led without the catastrophe of World War I is anybody's guess. Advanced industrial countries that were not involved in the war, such as Sweden, made the transition toward yet another stage of modernization relatively smoothly; without great tension, Sweden moved quickly toward a welfare state in response to the economic problems of the 1930s. Possibly, then, the malaise of the 1920s and 1930s was not inevitable. On the other hand, the World War itself arose in part from social tensions. This was obviously the case in Russia and the Habsburg monarchy, where the initiative for war first rested. Social tensions in both countries had reached such heights that statesmen were vowed to use diplomacy to distract from the dislocations of early industrialization; if this meant war, so be it. But even in Germany and Britain, upper-class leaders, frightened by the belligerence of the working classes, had become partial victims of their own nationalism. They too had used diplomacy as a political panacea, first through imperialist ventures and more recently through internal military buildups. Many German officers, dissatisfied with their position in modern society, wanted war. British statesmen who used the threat of war to stop strikes, claiming that agitation would damage the nation, were milder but perhaps almost as unsure of their position in a changing economy and a changing culture. At the very least they were guilty of leaving the diplomatic initiative to unstable states such as Russia. Ironically, important elements of the middle and lower classes also welcomed war at first. Youth responded to the idea of adventure and action; soldiers left eagerly for the front, convinced that this would be a fun war of short duration. Socialists loyally entered wartime governments, abandoning all pretense of protest.

Aspects of mature industrial society thus promoted war, though it is hard to argue that it was an inevitable product of this stage of industrialization. In any event the results of the war transformed the necessity for change, to deal with the weaknesses of industrial maturation, into catastrophe, and another bloody purging was needed before Europe could move beyond the tensions of incomplete modernization.

The war proved to be one of the most frustrating and certainly one of the most brutal encounters in European history. It killed millions and sapped the morale of millions more. On the western front battlelines established within the first few months shifted only slightly during the next four years. Day-long battles could result in the loss of ten of thousands of lives. New war machines were introduced that were unprecedented in their destructive power. Submarine warfare attacked even civilian shipping. The use of gas, tanks, and flame throwers provided awesome proof of the power of technology to injure and destroy. Airplane warfare, including some bombing of major cities, brought the horrors of war directly to some civilians. Destruction seemed endless and without clear purpose.

The total death rate was staggering. Germany lost 2 million people; France lost 1.7 million, a full 5 per cent of her total population. Italy and Britain lost a million each, and Russia was to lose a full 17 million in war and the revolutions and famines that followed. In all, 16 million men died or were lost during the war and 20 million more were wounded. Most families had to mourn the death of at least one close relative. Much of a whole generation was wiped out, which would long reduce the vitality of European leaders by limiting the competition of able young men for established positions in society. Above all the very fact of such wanton slaughter made a mockery of the optimistic tone of Europe's popular culture just a few years before.

The people most affected by the shock of the war were, of course, the fighting men themselves. The armies on both sides embraced millions of men; in war as in other activities the age of the masses had clearly arrived. These millions were directly faced with the daily pressures of shelling and with the frequent anguish of bloody but inconclusive battle. Soldiers felt that their efforts deserved some sort of special recognition from society, that their hardships should result in a changed world and a better life. During the war itself many troops believed that civilians, particularly politicians and war profiteers, were not responding properly to the situation at the front. Important mutinies by troops, from 1917 until well after the war's end, indicated the discontent of the fighting men.

After the war troops returning to civilian society continued to feel abused and somewhat separate. They faced inevitable problems of adjustment to civilian life after the bloody stress of war. Many were wounded, others psychologically marred. Veterans also faced economic difficulties, for the national economies adapted only slowly to the influx of returning workers and peasants. The problems of veterans were heightened in some countries, notably in Germany, by the reduction even of professional military ranks, in which officers as well as troops were thrown out of their accustomed positions. Again, it proved easy to focus the frustrations of peacetime on civilian society, on the politicians, on the capitalists.

Some of these frustrations very early assumed a political form; veterans formed organizations designed to remake society. Many supporters of communist groups in the postwar years were veterans, and the massive strikes and attempted revolution were sparked by returning troops. At the other extreme the founders and followers of rightist movements were veterans who could not find a suitable place in civilian life. More general veterans' organizations such as the German *Stahlhelm* or the French *Croix de feu* became active proponents of radical and nationalist conservatism.

The shock of the war affected civilian populations as well as fighting men. Civilians in front-line areas, such as Serbia, Belgium, and Poland, were subject to the same pressures of bombardment and attack as soldiers themselves. Civilians everywhere were actively involved in the war effort. The economies of Europe had to convert almost totally to wartime production. Rationing of foods and some other products was introduced. Most countries suffered from a lack of consumer goods, particularly food. In

Germany and eastern Europe the conscription of peasants into the armies and the difficulty of importing food led to real hardship for most civilians by 1916. Diets were reduced to subsistence levels, with primary dependence on potatoes and other starches. In Russia outright famine reappeared in some areas. These reductions in standards, coming after a period of rising material expectations, produced a psychological as well as material shock to the millions affected.

Involvement in war economy was not confined to consumption patterns. More and more people were drawn and even forced into war industries. Many countries, including Britain and Germany, set up compulsory labor procedures to channel workers into the most vital branches of production. This brought new experiences to many people, including large numbers of women who found jobs of unprecedented importance open to them. It also brought a sense of involvement in the war itself and in its frustrations. Moreover, governments were not content with requiring economic participation of civilian populations; they insisted on moral participation as well. War in industrial Europe brought not only the creation of armies of unprecedented size but also the subjection of civilians to centrally directed propaganda designed to instill uniform and active loyalty to the war effort. Censorship of all forms of publication and arrests of dissidents became commonplace. Governments also planted news in various media, without particular regard for truth. The German government tried to instill firm belief in German victory and war aims and in the evils of the opposing powers, with such success that many Germans were unaware that the tide had turned against them in 1918. British and French propaganda painted the Germans as barbaric Huns whose defeat was essential to western civilization. All governments tried to promote a constant sense of excitement and tension that would lead to more vigorous support of their cause. The propaganda efforts were not totally successful. Particularly among the working classes, partially hostile to the established order before the war, movements of protest developed as material conditions deteriorated. On the whole, however, extraordinary loyalty was maintained. After the conflict was over, the emotional and economic involvement with the war brought to civilian elements some of the frustrations that afflicted veterans.

Partly because of the tension and expectations promoted during the war, the aftermath disillusioned most people everywhere. Some had put faith in Wilsonian principles of a democratic society free from war. They were quickly disillusioned, because Wilson's efforts were partially thwarted. Far more people, spurred by government propaganda, had expected massive national gains. Frenchmen hoped not only for the return of Alsace-Lorraine but also for permanent protection from Germany; they were disappointed. Italians dreamed of great acquisitions in the Balkans and the Near East; they were frustrated. Germans had expected huge gains in both east and west; instead they lost much of their own land in both areas. Newly created states in eastern Europe, though excited by their existence, were almost uniformly discontented about territory that they did not receive.

For various reasons, then, there was a widespread feeling that the war and all the strain it involved had led to failure. Radical socialists gained mass support by pointing to capitalists as the scapegoats. German nationalists began to preach that revenge was necessary, that Germany had lost only because of the disloyalty of politicians or labor leaders or Jews. Italian groups, including the new fascist party, made rapid gains by citing the failures of the parliamentary government to win significant new territory. Even in a less agitated nation like Britain many leaders urged that the war had been a mistake and that Britain should pull out of its Continental involvements; again, these views corresponded to sentiments held by a wide public.

To the horror of the war itself, then, was added a widespread disillusionment about the peace. It became more difficult to maintain the confidence and optimism that had dominated much of the prewar mood. The bloodshed and the apparent futility of the war efforts helped to change the tone of European thinking. Some groups, particularly in the defeated countries, preached the need for revolutionary change to right the wrongs of the war. Far more people, in most social classes, were vaguely bitter and confused as a result of the shattering conflict, and their uncertainty about traditional goals and principles dominated much of the behavior of the interwar period.

Economic Effects

Europeans might have recovered from the shock of war itself. Pessimistic intellectuals found a new audience for their predictions of doom, for it was plausible to believe that civilization had come to an end. Books like Oswald's Spengler's *Decline of the West,* if not widely read, were at least widely known. On the surface, however, after a few important years of disruption, popular culture regained a certain equilibrium. Workers protested violently for two or three years after the war, revealing new aspirations plus their discontentment with wartime privations, but then they returned to calmer protest patterns. Elements of both middle and working classes seemed satisfied by the new pleasures open to them. The 1920s was not simply a restoration of prewar Europe, though many people wanted nothing better. There were new, enduring tensions. The rise of communist parties reflected the politicization of important lower-class grievances, just as the advent of rightist groups played on the frustrations of former military men or the disgruntled middling class. Even the popular culture of the decade, with its heightened faddism and pleasure seeking, can be judged a superficial, really frenzied effort to conceal the inevitable collapse of European society.

Probably Europe could have recovered from the shock of war itself. The extreme right and extreme left in Germany, for example, remained minority phenomena and even receded after 1924, and Germany was the country hardest hit by defeat. But to the shock of war was added economic catastrophe, for the war exacerbated virtually all the structural weaknesses of the economy. Serious economic problems were inevitable anyway; the war seemed to make them virtually insoluble.

Population growth had been slowing; the war brought it to a virtual standstill in western Europe. This reduced the market for goods. Actual devastation in the war was considerable, for approximately one thirtieth of Europe's assets were destroyed. Physical damage was greatest in France, Belgium, Serbia, and eastern Europe. The worst damage could be made good, for reparation payments plus government aid allowed actual modernization of equipment in France and Belgium. There were, however, other points of weakness. Wartime demand for food stimulated production elsewhere, in the United States, for instance, and even in combatant nations such as Britain, which reversed its earlier tendency to abandon farming. By the mid-1920s, however, traditional producers had for the most part returned to their earlier levels of production. There was a greater surplus of agricultural goods than ever before, and farming income suffered accordingly; here was another market damaged.

The war also drastically altered the economic position of Europe in the world. The diversion of production and shipping to war needs made it impossible for European industry to supply its export markets. Non-European powers, led by the United States and Japan, entered these markets and retained part of their hold on them after the war. To these material difficulties was added a blow to morale as traditional views of European superiority were weakened.

Europe's credit position was also drastically altered. The need for foreign supplies, especially from the United States, compelled many countries to abandon their investments abroad in order to pay for needed materials. Foreign investments were also lost, particularly by France, when the Russian revolutionaries renounced their foreign debts. For both Britain and France the loss of these investments was accompanied by new borrowing. Germany also borrowed significantly during and after the war; her debts also were increasingly owed outside Europe, especially to the United States. Thus Europe was transformed from a creditor continent to a continent considerably in debt.

Finally, the peace settlement was economically disruptive. A few nations profited economically from the settlement, notably France, which gained the remainder of the iron ore resources of Lorraine. Even for the victors, however, the new boundaries were drawn on the basis of nationalist impulse rather than economic reality. The new states in eastern Europe were for the most part economically weak. They were too small, and they quickly increased their economic isolation by a nationalistic policy of high tariffs. Russia lost Polish industry and the oil resources of Bessarabia. Germany lost part of her coal resources in Upper Silesia and was deprived of the coal fields of the Saar for fifteen years; and she lost three quarters of her iron reserves as well as merchant shipping, railroad rolling stock, and cash in the various reparation exactions imposed upon her. The various deprivations of markets and resources, heightened by the protective tariffs adopted by all European states immediately after the war, decreased the economic possibilities for mature and emerging industrial nations alike.

All of this meant that economic crisis was not only inevitable, short of new govenment policies that no state aside from communist Russia was able to take, but that it would be far more extensive than its prewar counterparts. As we have seen, large sections of Europe, from the outdated industrial regions of Britain to the agricultural nations of the Balkans, were in severe depression by the mid-1920s. Unemployment was rising in Germany early in 1928, and of course inflation had earlier taken its toll. The Great Depression, stemming directly from the collapse of American finance, massively heightened Europe's economic problems, but it did not create them.

Social Chaos

From depression, in turn, came an almost complete polarization of European society. Lines had been hardening during the 1920s. The middle classes and upper class, their morale damaged by the war, were frightened by the Russian Revolution and rise of communist movements in most European countries. Here seemed proof that the workers could take over. Accounts of Russian communist atrocities appeared quite frequently, and conservative parties played on the communist threat; in France rightist groups during the early 1920s had great success with a poster showing, without comment, a red hand holding a dagger dripping with blood. In the context of growing class war, businessmen became more resistant to workers' strikes, so despite the improved organization of many unions the rate of strike victories and compromises declined. In Britain the general strike of 1926 provided a clear illustration of hostility to the demands of labor, for it was marked by willingness of members of the middle class, including students at Oxford and Cambridge, to replace workers in loading jobs, in the running of trains, and in other functions. There was a clear desire to keep the economy operating sufficiently to defeat the strike; and the middle class won its victory. In the following year legislation was passed forbidding sympathetic strikes and weakening the general bargaining power of labor. Class interest was now predominant.

The active defensiveness of the middle class was clearest, of course, in the political field. From the early postwar period middle- and middling-class voting patterns displayed greater conservatism than had been typical of the prewar period. Traditional middle-class political vehicles such as the British Liberal party declined rapidly, as the class switched its votes to the Conservatives. The French Radical party retained substantial middle-class support only because of its resistance to any real social reforms. Furthermore, under stress major segments of the middle ranks of society turned to other political movements. In Italy after 1919 certain middle-class elements joined with other groups in support of the fascist party. To the middle class fascism offered an acceptable defense against working-class revolution, in the name of national unity; the Italian middle class was interested in nationalist causes anyway and had been disappointed by the lack of gains from the peace settlement. Fascism also proclaimed a need to protect small business against large stores and industries. It promised an end to antagonistic labor unions and parties and a solution to economic difficulties. Italy was wracked by the postwar depression, the rise of a militant socialist party, and a wave of strikes. These developments induced some members of the middle class to support fascism directly and others to acquiesce in the fascist takeover. Crucial to the fascist government was an arrangement with big businessmen whereby the control and profits of industry remained in the hands of the upper middle class, despite the earlier anticapitalist talk of the party.

In Germany the Nazi party was formed in the years following the war. It attracted little initial support. Only in 1924, at the peak of resentment over the inflation, did a coalition of which the Nazis were a part poll nearly 2 million votes. With the onset of depression, however, Nazi power rose rapidly, and the party achieved far more massive direct support than the Italian fascists ever knew. The party polled 37.3 per cent of the vote in 1932, largely at the expense of traditional middle-class parties. It attracted many members of the middling class by its promises of full employment and welfare aid and its attacks on communism and big business alike. Even more than Italian fascism, the movement appealed to the middling-class desire to protect the small firm against modern capitalism as well as against the power of organized labor. It was particularly popular, therefore, in the smaller towns. At the same time, as in Italy, the party depended for its final seizure of power on an agreement with business leaders in which protection for business was promised in exchange for financial support. The upper middle class was not committed to Nazism, but it saw in the movement a chance to defeat the rising threat of communism. Thus, for various reasons, by 1933 many elements of the German middle classes had turned to Nazism.

Elsewhere in Europe, of course, middle-class support for fascist movements was more limited; conservatism remained more powerful. And a minority of the class turned left to protest; by 1936 some of the most ardent supporters of the French socialist party were clerks and teachers. On balance, however, the rightist impulse predominated. In France violent rightist groups such as the *Jeunesses patriotes* attracted some middle-class support even before the depression. As the economic crisis deepened and as socialist and communist parties grew in strength, semifascist groups like the *Croix de feu* and, after 1936, the *Parti populaire français,* obtained the backing of hundreds of thousands of members of the middle classes. These groups appealed to the new desire for economic protection against both depression and the leftist threat to private property and cited the need for attention to the nation instead of to the divisive elements of class warfare.

The new reactionary parties, drawing from small property owners (including peasants in the more traditional villages) above all, also could attract support from some professional people, students and other youth eager for action, even some workers who were disappointed with the political left. In Germany Nazism drew more votes from women, who perhaps saw in it a protection for their traditional roles, than from men; it also attracted more new voters than experienced voters. The new parties were thus socially complex. All in all they did primarily appeal to a desire to go back to a simpler but more structured society, free from advanced capitalism, organized labor, and the new fads and fashions. Spurred by their own suffering during the depression, the propertied elements could turn against even the remnants of a liberal political tradition, denying the virtues of liberty and the parliamentary system, denying even the rationality of men in favor of leaders who stressed the need for physical activity, violence, and war.

For its part the left, drawing mainly from the working classes but with some agricultural and middle-class support, added to what became a political vicious circle. Even relatively small leftist groups, by using new political tactics, stimulated the fascist or semifascist response, and vice versa. The agitation of maximalist socialists in Italy right after the war really created the basis for fascism, though unintentionally, by rallying the forces of order around Mussolini's claim to be able to restore social harmony. Communist demonstrations and strong-arm tactics in France in the 1920s helped create the first paramilitary organizations on the right. In Germany and France the increase in communist voting strength resulting from the depression stimulated fascist gains, which in turn brought new vigor to the left; the French Popular Front was a direct response to rightist agitation in 1934–1935.

Class warfare involved a cerain amount of violence. Communists and even socialist groups occasionally broke up political meetings. In Spain the perpetuation of the anarchist tradition among many workers and peasants led to even greater violence, including murders, during the republican period. On the whole, the methods of the left were not so violent as those of the right. Worker parties and unions relied on their increasing strength of organization and growth in numbers to win their purposes. Major strikes, such as the British general strike or the French sit-ins in 1936, involved almost no violence at all. Workers and their leaders were also afraid of the repressive power of the troops and the police, whose officials were usually conservative in inclination and notoriously more ready to repress workers than to attack rightist demonstrations. Working-class protest, therefore, was limited primarily to the polls, to strikes, and to many gigantic but calm street demonstrations.

The right was more unruly, particularly in Spain, Italy, Germany, and France, where significant fascist movements arose. Fascist rioting, beatings, and murders were common during the period of greatest social tension. Fascists themselves praised violence as a true expression of the human spirit, and they tried to attract attention to themselves by its use. They hoped to create sufficient chaos to provide an opportunity for the seizure of power and recruited large, uniformed forces to stimulate such chaos. Brownshirts in Germany, blackshirts in Italy, and several different colors in France did create considerable disorder. The fascist shock troops were drawn from young unemployed professional people, unemployed workers, clerks, and the like. In Spain, of course, massive participation of the military in the conservative cause brought about a bloody civil war, the extreme expression of the class conflict that had developed. In Germany and Italy considerable fascist rioting and demonstrations preceded the actual takeover. France saw large demonstrations and some rioting early in 1934, which culminated on February 6, when thousands of Parisians rioted against the parliamentary regime, attacked policemen and deputies, and stormed government buildings. Labor groups responded with counterdemonstrations, and France came close to civil war. This was the worst outburst in France during the decade, but demonstrations and beatings continued even later.

It was in the political arena proper that the principal manifestations of class conflict took place. Only a minority was involved in violence on either side. Fascist leaders themselves recognized, except in Spain, that they could not take power by force alone. In many countries leading elements on both left and right refused to accept the existing regime and took all possible measures to bring about its downfall. In Germany massive communist and fascist parties in the early 1930s helped paralyze the government. Similar chaos existed in Italy in the early 1920s and in France during much of the 1930s. Everywhere a dynamic political center was missing. The middle class and its allies largely withdrew allegiance from parties that were interested in bridging the social gap between them and the workers. Workers, for their part, supported either socialist parties, which were reluctant to become too involved with the existing regime, or communist parties, which rejected the regime altogether. Even in England, where political extremes were less marked, there was a tendency toward polarization of parties on a class basis. In the major Continental countries the polarization threatened to become total. The only link between left and right was a common hostility to the existing situation.

In most countries extreme social chaos lasted for only a few years. The Scandinavian nations, which, like Britain, were not afflicted by the most radical political hostilities and in which, furthermore, the depression was not severe, resolved many of the tensions by the welfare policies. These policies were sufficiently effective to alleviate workers' grievances and to prevent their recourse to more vigorous action. At the same time, the measures were mild enough not to provoke the hostility of the middle class. Conservative elements were distressed by most of the new programs, but their resistance was expressed only through the normal channels of parliamentary action.

In other European countries, however, social tensions were relieved most clearly by the total victory of the extreme right. This was the pattern in Italy, Germany, Austria, Spain, and to an extent the authoritarian states of eastern Europe. The new fascist or semifascist regimes obviously protected the interests of large landowners and the leaders of industry. Despite the anticapitalist elements of fascist doctrine, little was done to control industry or profits; landed estates were left untouched. Only in Germany were certain limitations placed on private industry, in the interest of increasing the economic power of the state; but even there private ownership and substantial profits were not affected. For the lower classes, even those that had opposed fascism, the new regimes offered numerous benefits, though they never won wholehearted working-class support. Full employment was restored in Germany, and public works in Italy improved the economic position of many workers, although the depression did cause some unemployment. The governments of both countries offered subsidies to large families in the interest of promoting demographic growth, and in Germany an increase in population growth rate resulted. Organizations such as the "Strength Through Joy" movement in Germany tried to fulfill the workers' desire for leisure and recreation by promoting hikes and outings. New state unions gave some workers a sense of participation in decisions about labor conditions, although in fact the interests of management remained dominant. Beyond this, the fascist state organized an elaborate propaganda and police apparatus that actively promoted public satisfaction with and loyalty to the regime. Educational systems were altered to stress fascist principles. A state of national tension was maintained through the many news media under government control, which induced even greater attachment to fascist leaders. Finally, organizations with a potential for protest were quickly and completely eliminated. This affected the working class particularly, for workers represented the class most hostile to fascism before the takeover. Communist and socialist parties were outlawed, and many labor leaders were arrested. In Spain the execution and exile of thousands of leftists removed the possibility of worker protest in a similar, if bloodier, manner. Unions were disbanded and replaced by the state organizations.

Thus the new regimes stifled protest by a combination of benefits and repression. Almost no active resistance to the fascists developed. Class warfare had been ended by an alliance of the upper classes and dynamic lower-class leaders. The resulting regimes proved impossible to dislodge except by war.

In Britain and especially in France hardly any solution to social conflict was discovered during the interwar period. The British government, under Conservative party control, did take steps to alleviate social and economic distress. Increased government economic activity was developed to retrain workers, to channel investments, and to promote exports. The extension of earlier social insurance programs, notably unemployment insurance, did allow some redistribution of income. Before World War I workers had paid more in dues and taxes than they had received in government aid. By 1935 the working class paid in only about 80 per cent of the money it received in benefits. British suffering from the depression, though intense, was alleviated by an economic boomlet during the later 1930s. Renewed attention to new industries, such as the production of automobiles, refrigerators, and even a modest number of television sets, brought new prosperity to southern England; there was also a housing boom, as suburban development resumed. But in other areas there was much unemployment still. England's moderate political traditions, plus the partial recovery, kept class tensions within bounds, but rising support for the Labour party on the local level, before World War II, showed that class antagonisms might yet affect the state.

In France the government was far more completely paralyzed by a network of political and social divisions. The promising measures of the Popular Front did not relieve working-class grievances, for economic conditions continued to deteriorate. Communist strength mounted steadily. At the same time, larger elements of the middle class were attracted to radical conservative movements; by 1938 the *Croix de feu* claimed 2 million members, and several other groups had formed on the extreme right. Economic difficulty and the perpetual conflict between right and left made it impossible to undertake any significant action or reform after the failure of the Popular Front.

Furthermore, internal social conflicts affected diplomatic policies. Social divisions in Britain and France paralyzed both countries internationally during the 1930s. The rise of Nazi Germany was recognized as an international threat, but the western nations lacked the will to act.

288 EUROPEAN SOCIETY IN UPHEAVAL

The political right, although not for the most part favorable to the Nazi regime, feared communist Russia as the primary enemy. The political left was willing to take action against fascism but was not strong enough to impose its will. Divisions over foreign policy first became clear during the Spanish Civil War, when the French Popular Front was forced to remain idle while its Spanish counterpart was gradually crushed. Powerful conservative movements opposed action in coordination with Russia and against the advocates of private property and religion, and they could not be overcome. From that point onward, the governments of France and Britain worked for peace at almost any price, for they lacked the internal strength to do otherwise. The results of their efforts, the Munich agreements of 1938, were hailed by large elements of the citizenry.

When war did come, it caught Europeans in a far different mood from that of 1914. There was no confidence, no belief that the war would be easy or pleasant. At best, there was a grim determination to see it through; at worst, the alienation of important groups from the established order hampered the war effort itself. In contrast to 1914, important segments of the labor movement resisted participation in the war, for the communists regarded Germany, however temporarily, as an ally because of the Nazi–Soviet pact. The social conflicts of the period were carried over into the war itself in France, where the Vichy regime drew much support from traditionalist elements despite its acceptance of France's defeat. Yet, curiously, the developments during and after the war solved or alleviated many of the social and economic problems of the preceding period. The mood of hopelessness so clearly apparent in western Europe before the war receded, and a new period of social development began.

6

THE CONSUMER
SOCIETY

After a brief though important period of dislocation following World
War II, Europe began to reverse many of the most disheartening trends of
the interwar years. Twenty years after World War I Europe had undergone
disastrous inflation. New, warlike regimes had been installed in Germany
and Italy. Class tension, reflected in politics, seemed to paralyze the western countries. Twenty years after World War II, on the other hand,
Europe had undergone an unprecedented economic rise. Class tensions
were reduced and some of the most bitter opposition to change was eliminated. Nationalism declined and with it the likelihood of European war.
New movements of cooperation, most notably the Common Market, reflected a desire to innovate, departing from a background of economic
and military rivalry, and promoted a growing sense of confidence. Europe
largely divested itself of colonies. Whole civilizations, including the Greek
and the Roman, had foundered on the corruption of internal society
through a desire to cling to colonies when their age had past. Postwar
Europe was perhaps fortunate in being too weak to make the effort,
although decolonization was resisted even so, particularly in France. From
a larger perspective, however, the decolonization movement reflected
the willingness to concentrate on building a strong domestic society that
had been wanting during the mature industrial period. And although
some members of the upper classes grumbled at the undeniable loss of

world stature the former colonial powers suffered, few people cared much about empire by this point.

World War II and its aftermath took an important toll, but they were not as devastating as the results of World War I had been. Population losses in Germany and eastern Europe were higher than before, and although considerable demographic vitality compensated within a decade, the shock was long felt. Mortality rates in western Europe were far more modest. Bombings created great tension within the civilian population, but were not as murderous as the trench warfare of 1914–1918. Economic damage was substantial. But here too the claims of air forces were exaggerated. Only a tenth of Germany's productive capacity was destroyed; bombers proved much more adept at hitting houses. Destruction of bridges and rail lines helped create temporary chaos. For three or four years after 1945 Germany was reduced to a near subsistence economy, as even food supplies were deficient and unbelievable inflation reduced the value of money to almost nothing. Nonmonetary units of exchange, such as cigarettes, replaced normal currency. France and England faced immense postwar hardship, and in eastern Europe the devastation was far greater. Confusion was enhanced by a tragic movement of millions of people made homeless by the war and later territorial changes. More than a million people from eastern Europe refused to return, because of their hatred of Soviet domination. Millions of Germans fled from the eastern part of Prussia, now given over to Poland, and millions more from the subsequent communist government of East Germany. All these refugees had lost property; many were ill and weak, and their psychological and economic integration into the countries where they sought new homes was extremely difficult.

And postwar Europe was soon caught up in a struggle between the two superpowers, the United States and Russia. Russia gripped eastern Europe, initially taking resources and equipment from this area to help rebuild her own shattered economy; only later was there attention to reconstruction. The United States, wealthier, turned more quickly to a policy of assistance, but this barely veiled a desire for dominance. Diplomatically, most European countries were powerless, and through the mid-1950s many people expected yet another world war, over which they would have no control but which would threaten them with atomic obliteration.

The war and its aftermath left their mark. Divorces increased, the inevitable result of years of separation and tension. Crime rates rose in many areas, and this proved to be a more durable trend (for the divorce rate descended again after 1950). Many penniless German girls had to resort to prostitution, and juvenile crime and crimes of violence began a gradual increase everywhere. Postwar hardship increased labor unrest in many countries. Workers in France and Italy turned to communism in growing numbers, and again this proved a durable trend. More briefly, strike waves mounted throughout western Europe, though German workers were too demoralized to attempt even this. The harrowing experience of war and the subsequent feeling of Europe's impotence helped produce a hedonist ethic: eat, drink, and be merry, for tomorrow heaven knows what. For some observers, this gave a frenzied, superficial quality to the values that developed even after prosperity returned.

Yet the fact is that prosperity did return and Europe did not collapse in a morass of self-pity. By 1948 the peak of postwar unrest had passed. By 1952 the worst threat of new war was over, for Russia and the United States began to balance each other out, and under this fragile umbrella the European countries could stake out their own existence. Ironically, in some ways western Europe became freer to adapt to a new level of modernization than did her American ally. Between the wars it was America that led the way toward a new culture: American dances, American films, American music. By the 1960s the tide had partially turned, and the United States was busily importing European miniskirts, the Beatles from Liverpool, and what Americans were wont to call pornography from Scandinavia. Superficial symptoms, perhaps, but ones that suggest a new turn in the modernization process. Europe, far from successful in meeting the demands of mature industrialization, was open to the opportunities of a consumer society.

The main theme of postwar social history is not simply Europe's recovery, though this seemed miraculous to anyone who examined the Continent's gloomy prospects as late as 1950. Rather, industrial societies toward the mid-twentieth century entered a new phase of development, which in fact created a new set of tensions that Europe's prosperity could only partially conceal. Its wheels now greased by unprecedented affluence, Europe (and North America) sketched out a fourth phase of modernization.

Some have described the society that emerged by the 1960s as "post-industrial" or even "postmodern." These terms, though clumsily dramatic, are out of place, for the new society was in most respects a logical outgrowth of the previous stage of modernization. It involved a reshuffling of class structure and social values, but not a decisive new course. The development of a consumer society was thus comparable to the earlier advent of mature industrial society. But the basic causes of change were different and, if anything, less comprehensive. Here again, consumer society was in considerable measure the product of trends visible long before: increasing organization of the economy and social position based on bureaucratic standing, plus growing wealth and the need to assure its regular consumption.

Hence two traditional indexes of a major break in social development did not take a totally new turn in contemporary society. Technology evolved but did not radically change. Computers altered office work; automation affected some new industries, such as petrochemicals; atomic power seemed, by the 1970s, a possible replacement for fossil fuels. But although all these developments suggested possible technological revolutions for the future, none had yet caused one. Most people's work was not dramatically changed, and despite scare stories, few workers were even terribly burdened with a threat of technological displacement.

Contemporary society also did not usher in a new stage of demography, at least in any obvious way. There was a change from the doldrums of the 1920s and 1930s, and this had brief significance. Eastern European countries, particularly Poland, continued to have a higher birth rate than western Europe, though their growth steadily slowed after the typical recovery from wartime losses. West Germany's population increased more rapidly than it had during the interwar decades. The same reversal was even more dramatic in Britain and France. Britain's population grew from 45 million to 47 million during the war itself, and by 1960 had passed 52 million; the rate of expansion was a steady 0.5 per cent a year. Scandinavian population rose in similar fashion, and the Netherlands, another highly organized country, jumped to first place in demographic vitality in western Europe. But the greatest surprise was France, Europe's traditional laggard. Between 1945 and 1954 French population grew by 3 million, the fastest growth rate the country had enjoyed since the early nineteenth century.

This population spurt reflected a new confidence in Europe's economic prospects. It was the direct result of new welfare systems that provided state payments to support larger families. The population boom encouraged economic revival by providing new markets for goods, though it caused obvious problems of housing and the provision of new school facilities. But although all of this formed an important backdrop for Europe's social history through the mid-1960s, it did not reflect a permanent change in demographic structure. By the early 1960s birth rates began dropping sharply, returning most European countries toward demographic stability, though overall growth continued as the result of previous expansion. It was clear that the advanced industrial societies tend toward zero population growth, though they are capable of moderate increase on occasion. The east European countries had obviously entered the same stage.

The more durable demographic development concerned the population's age structure. Advanced industrial societies had produced the oldest population known in human history. This followed in large part from the birth rate pattern that had developed by the 1930s, though it was not widely recognized until after World War II. With few babies being born, the average age of the population automatically went up. The postwar population spurt modified this trend but did not supersede it. In addition, the life expectancy of adults was now rising. In 1900 a man fifty years old could expect to live another twenty-one years; by 1950 he could expect another twenty-three years, and the trend was steadily upward. Developments in medicine, notably antibiotics, were at last having a measurable effect on traditional killers, such as pneumonia. Improvements in nutrition and reductions in hours of work played a role as well. No industrial society has fully come to terms with this massive change in the balance among ages. An older society might turn out to be less innovative, more stiffly resistant to change; it certainly could be costly to maintain large numbers of retirees. These problems have been discussed but little action taken, beyond provision of minimal pension plans that are an important part of the welfare state. Much depends on the nature of aging in the consumer society, and this remains to be fully determined.

If neither demography nor technology marked off a new stage of modernization in the conventional manner, though the trend of aging may turn out to have fundamental significance, two or three factors do define something of a watershed. Key traditional social groups were essentially eliminated, giving pride of place to more fully modernized elements; the rise of the welfare state furthered this change and created a new relationship between state and economy; and this in turn helps explain the new affluence of European society, which created a host of opportunities and some nagging problems.

Toward a New Social Structure

The changes in social structure can be simply put. The upper class was altered as the aristocracy to all intents and purposes disappeared while the old industrial barons gave way to new managers. The middling class of shopkeepers and master artisans, though by no means wiped out, lost so much ground that it was incapable of decisive reactionary activity. Along with this, as we shall see, the peasantry changed; it continued to decrease as a percentage of the overall population but it also developed a new, more progressive spirit. All of this means that society at large was freed from defense of older kinds of property and prestige. Social classes remained, and their differences were reflected in quite varied average earnings. But their basis rested less on ownership than on educational levels and position in a bureaucratic hierarchy. The upper class held men of great wealth, but their power lay less in their investments than in their bureaucratic leadership. The middle class consisted more of technicians and middle-level managers than of middling property owners.

The decline of the traditional classes followed in large part from the steady advance of industrialization and corporate ownership; it was inevitable. Hitler's regime in Germany ironically advanced the modernization of German society by encouraging big industry; by the late 1930s there were few independent artisans left, and shopkeepers were to a lesser degree challenged by new marketing forms. The upper class was less affected, but new groups were able to take advantage of higher education, which suggested a future shift at the top of society. In wartime Britain new people rose to leadership ranks and the upper classes, mindful of the need to conciliate the lower classes to assure their loyalty after the disastrous depression, made serious concessions to a more democratic spirit. Among other things stiffly progressive taxes cut into the fortunes of many landed proprietors. In several countries, particularly France, the Resistance movements during the war attacked the traditional upper class. They sought a new society, purged from the control of the landlords and big businessmen, with their conservative allies in the state bureaucracy, that had led Europe into such a morass. Their policies received some execution after the war, as nationalization of railroads, mines, and some automobile companies reduced the power of big business families.

Certainly the aristocracy was eliminated in its main bastions of power, for the advance of communism across eastern Europe brought the confiscation of the large estates and stripped the class of its titles. New educational opportunities here, but also in western Europe, filled the state civil service increasingly with people of middle- and sometimes working-class origin. High property taxes imposed by postwar welfare states hit hard at landed holdings. Some aristocrats ingeniously hung on, opening their homes to gawking, but paying, tourists or even converting ancestral grounds into open-air zoos. Titles remained in western Europe and had a certain prestige in the popular press. The aristocracy in Spain and Portugal alone had real power, however; elsewhere the class, if identifiable at all, was little more than a museum piece.

The transformation of the great industrialists was less decisive. Some, like the car manufacturer Renault, having supported the fascist regimes, were stripped of power. Others died out or lost interest in business control. The giant Krupp concern, for example, revived after the war, but direction was in the hands of a new manager, Berthold Beitz. The managers, both in state and private industry, were not only new men. They had received more explicit technical training. Even lawyers were now given education in economics and business management. Hence the top economic planners were labeled technocrats, because of their devotion to economic growth, efficiency, and long-term development.

The changes at the top of society should not be exaggerated. An upper class, in terms of property ownership, could still be identified in western Europe. In 1954, 68 per cent of the earnings from private property in Britain went to the top 5 per cent of the population; this was down from 79 per cent two decades before and, given nationalization, private property loomed less large overall. But the figure has significance. Nevertheless the upper class was partially renewed by new blood and a new attitude. Most important it contained no major element that, like the aristocracy as late as the 1930s, felt threatened by modern society. The new upper class had many faults. Its planning mania could cause it to lose any human touch, which contributed to a sense of impersonal rule in state and economy. Political changes added to this weakness. With state functions becoming increasingly complex, parliaments, whose members alone were directly elected by the people, lost much power. The executive branch, filled with these eager bureaucrats, ruled the roost. Furthermore parliamentary deputies themselves were far more commonly middle class than lower class; this was a shift from earlier decades, though the lower classes had never predominated. Parliamentary members of the British Labour party, for example, were increasingly middle class or, if rarely working class, had received the same kind of university training as their Conservative colleagues. It could be argued that the political establishment was becoming closed off, that the new upper class was really too successful in taking over the main centers of power. With its rationalizing outlook and its freedom from the need to defend traditional kinds of status and ownership, the upper class did seem more in tune with the demands of modernization than its predecessors had been.

The demise of the middling class was long overdue. New chain stores and supermarkets attacked even small grocers and bakers. In France, particularly, the shopkeepers fought back, demanding special tax concessions from the state in order to survive. They wanted nothing more than to continue their traditional business, arguing that they alone gave a personal touch to commerce. And enough customers agreed to allow small shops to survive in some number. But the class was fading. Its one effort, in France, to mount a distinctive political party failed rather quickly. In the 1950s Pierre Poujade, himself the owner of a small paper goods shop, formed a party designed to attack big business and give special state protection to small property. Though it briefly won some voting support and drew attention by rowdy political tactics, the party quickly died off. More fundamentally the importance of self-employed people of middling levels of ownership declined steadily in the population as a whole. In 1968 self-employed people constituted 24 per cent of the economically active population in France, and this of course included many professional people as well as shopkeepers and farmers; in 1973 the proportion was down to 20 per cent. The farming sector alone declined almost 5 per cent a year, constituting less than 9 per cent of the total French population.

The Welfare State

The shift in class structure, along with the shock of the war itself, helps explain the rise of new state functions. Europe's political spectrum swung to the left. Fascism was discredited by its excesses and defeat; only in southern Italy, still in the early throes of modernization, were neo-fascist parties able to gain significant support. Elsewhere their social base had been eroded, for there were not enough shopkeepers and middling peasants left to revive the movement even after the wartime stigma had waned. Western European countries, though quite varied politically, generally developed a new, more flexible conservatism, often in the form of Christian Democratic parties, that was willing to see the state take on new functions. At the same time strong socialist and, sometimes, communist parties pressed for reform. Broadly speaking, this meant that the working class, particularly right after the war, became more insistent than ever on state action to prevent repetition of the hardships of the depression. This was the culmination of the politicization of working-class protest. At the same time the middle class became willing to see changes in the state's role, partly to reduce class tensions and partly to provide benefits for the middle class itself.

The process was clearest and most immediate in Great Britain, a country untouched by direct invasion and one in which social tensions had been relatively moderate before. The war immediately reduced party frictions in Britain, and all major political elements were represented in the wartime cabinet. The inclusion of the Labour party promoted a belief in its respectability among many elements of society. At the same time, the war provided greater opportunities for contacts among members of different social classes. There was a sense of unity against the enemy, forged through the realization of the tremendous danger Britain faced. Military service and war work offered common experiences that reduced, although they did not eliminate, class barriers.

The war modified the privileges of the upper class. Rationing of essential consumer goods allocated scarce products on a basis of per capita need, not per capita income, so that the gap in standard of living between rich and poor was narrowed. The wealthy accepted these measures in the interest of national defense. Many people realized that new policies were needed to cure the unhealthy social situation of the interwar period; British manufacturers, for example, were willing to grant labor a greater voice in industry by 1949. The wartime loyalty of the working classes stimulated the conviction that the poor should be rewarded in some way for their sacrifices.

Concrete measures during the war itself were intended to aid the lower classes. Rationing procedures assured supplies of milk and meat for all; for many of the poor this meant better diets than ever before. The war also provided full employment for the first time since the previous conflict, and wages rose in most essential industries. Finally, the government began to plan for further social gains after the war. The Beveridge plan, drawn essentially in the spirit of middle-class humanitarianism, suggested the expansion of social-insurance measures to prevent unemployment and even to redistribute income. Other plans urged extension of education facilities for the poor. These programs reflected new social concern on the part of governing groups. They also stimulated the expectations of the lower classes.

The altered social attitudes were expressed most clearly in the first postwar election in 1945. The principal issues in the election were economic, with the problem of housing heading the list. Not only the working class but also large sections of the middle class felt that government action was essential. The result was a clear majority for the Labour party for the first time in British history. The party received the vast majority of the working-class vote but also, crucially, a full third of the middle-class vote. This partial transfer of middle-class support was not permanent, for by 1951 only a quarter of the class voted Labour; but the vote in 1945 was a vital sign of the new needs of the class itself and the new realization of general social problems.

The Labour government's attention between 1945 and 1951 was primarily devoted to providing greater material protection for all citizens. Existing social insurance schemes were elaborated, and the unemployment insurance program was extended; for the first time in British history no unemployed person would have to rely on a dole. In addition, a national system of health care was instituted, giving virtually free medical attention to all citizens, with the bulk of the funds coming from tax sources. This measure obviously increased the medical facilities of the poorer classes. It was also, in its reliance on tax support, a major means of redistributing income.

Other programs were adopted that combined direct aid to the lower classes with a certain reallocation of income through taxation. Housing programs were greatly expanded. They were designed partly to compensate for wartime damage and neglect; but they resulted in the provision of better housing than ever before for many citizens. By 1960 more than a quarter of the entire population resided in government-built housing. Direct financial aid to large families was also established by the government.

Finally, two of the principal programs of the Labour government were intended to raise economic levels and to alter the existing system of class relationships. First, educational facilities were greatly expanded. Particular attention was given to the secondary schools; the school-leaving age was raised to fifteen years, then to sixteen. At the same time, university scholarships were greatly increased, and many new university facilities were created. Only a small minority of the population could go to the universities even now, and university students were still drawn primarily from the upper classes, but the earlier stratification of education was considerably modified. Working-class youths, a rarity at universities before the war, now passed unnoticed. Even larger segments of the working class were given new opportunities in some of the major industries. The Labour government brought mining, the railroads, and the steel industry under state ownership, and worker groups were given a voice in the direction of those industries. It was hoped that such basic industries could be more efficiently run, in the interests of the economy as a whole.

Eastern and Western Europe

On the Continent, under the heel of Nazi occupation, wartime conditions were obviously far different from the British situation, but attitudes and programs were being shaped that were not very different from those in Britain. They resulted in the years immediately after the war in the elaboration of welfare systems quite similar to the one being created in Britain at the same time.

Continental wartime governments themselves introduced certain measures that were to endure as part of a more general welfare program. The Nazi government had already developed a commitment to full employment. In France the wartime Vichy regime attempted to encourage consultation between workers and industrial managers, and it extended a system of financial aid to families that was to become a major element of the French postwar welfare program. Family aid had already been developed in Germany and Italy as part of the fascist encouragement to population growth. However, it was not from the fascist governments but rather in resistance to them that the impulse to postwar welfare measures really arose. In every occupied area significant resistance movements developed at some point during the war; those movements dominated the national governments in the three years immediately after the war. In all cases, they used their period of dominance to elaborate a series of major reforms. For the resistance movements, despite considerable diversity in social composition, were not simply hostile to fascism; they also wanted to create a new Europe free from the national and social conflicts of the past. They hoped to develop some new comity among nations, perhaps even a real unity within Europe. Internally, they intended to modify the capitalist system in the interest of social justice; they wanted to use the government to introduce greater economic equality and security. Much of the idealism of the movement was to be disappointed, but it provided a stimulus to change that could not be totally denied.

The Resistance movements, though small in size at least until victory was in sight, were supported by elements of several social classes. Working-class movements were well represented in the Resistance through socialist and particularly communist participation. After Hitler's attack on Russia, communists provided the major force for resistance in many areas. They had the organization and the experience in subversive activity required for resistance work. And from the Resistance the communists derived new support, funds, and even respectability, which were to prove invaluable after the war. In Yugoslavia they were able to seize power directly. In the remainder of eastern Europe they seized power with Russian support. In France and Italy they took over the principal union movements and became the primary political representatives of the working class. And in all these cases communists participated in postwar governments and in the development of programs to aid the lower classes.

In western Europe elements of the peasantry and the middle class also participated in the Resistance movement. For some young peasants activity in the Resistance encouraged a desire for reform, which was reflected in higher levels of voting for communists after the war in France and Italy and in new efforts at technical change and a general pressure on governments for greater attention to the problems of agriculture.

The involvement of a minority of the middle class in the Resistance was to have even greater political effects. The most important middle-class resistance groups were formed under the banners of Christian democracy. This was not a totally new movement; it had been suggested in France before the war and had arisen briefly in Italy prior to the fascist takeover. The Christian Democrats tried to allay middle-class hostility to sweeping change by a definite recognition of social problems and by advocacy of greater social justice. After the war the new Christian democratic parties of France and Italy actively participated in the elaboration of new welfare programs. As in Britain, then, an element of the middle class was now willing to join with the working class in developing significant social reform.

Governments in eastern Europe, both before and after the communist takeover, were active in creating welfare programs. Social insurance for workers protected them in illness, accidents, old age, and unemployment. Only Czechoslovakia had developed such programs before the war. A variety of state-sponsored vacation schemes supplemented the benefits to workers. Government housing programs gradually repaired wartime damage in the cities, although the growth of cities continued to limit the housing opportunities for most workers. Generally, the workers were not allowed much independent participation in welfare plans and in industry; this was a major distinction of the east European systems. Unions were under state control. In Yugoslavia, however, a program of factory councils was developed in the 1950s and provided a real voice for the workers in the determination of work conditions and even in investment and production plans. Eastern European governments were active also in the spread of educational reforms. Many peasants received education for the first time, and opportunities for able people from the lower classes to advance to secondary and university training were greatly increased.

Immediately after the war peasants also received a large number of individual land holdings, as large estates were conclusively eliminated in all eastern countries. In Poland and Yugoslavia peasants were allowed to retain the bulk of these small holdings. Elsewhere a program of collectivization began late in 1948 that was over 80 per cent complete by 1960. This program was designed to carry out communist principles of collective ownership and to promote agricultural efficiency by destroying small units and allowing a higher level of agricultural technology. The program proved to have grave drawbacks. There was little direct resistance, but many peasants lost their motivation for vigorous production. The old peasant yearning for private holdings clearly remained: it was this that had dictated a general renunciation of collectivization in Poland and Yugoslavia. Nevertheless, the collectives did provide peasants with certain facilities for education, medical care, and the like, which they had not previously possessed. And peasants benefited from many of the same social insurance plans that protected the workers.

Finally, government programs of industrial investment tried, with more success, to alleviate the pressure of people on the land. Factory industry grew everywhere, and a major movement to the cities naturally resulted. Eastern Europe remained heavily rural. In the late 1950s Yugoslavia was still 70 per cent rural, Rumania 65 per cent, Hungary 60 per cent, and Poland 54 per cent. The industrial levels of the west had not been attained. Nevertheless, change was clearly underway. Population pressure was relieved in the countryside, but at the same time peasants were faced with new requirements for market production and better agricultural technology. All of this, in general outline, resembled earlier developments in western Europe, but the movement in eastern Europe was conditioned by a combination of state control, imposed even on peasants through the collectives, and of state protection, which differed substantially from earlier patterns. Some of the earlier dislocation and hardship were avoided by the protective measures; and certainly much of the possibility for active discontent was repressed.

In western Europe the welfare programs established after the war were obviously less novel than those of eastern Europe, and they involved far less complete government control. The Italian government, for example, divided some of the large estates in the south, but not all. It encouraged industrialization in the south by state investment and tax privileges to private entrepreneurs, but progress was not so rapid as in eastern Europe. Nevertheless, there and elsewhere the reforms induced by governments had extensive social effects.

Government control of industry increased. In Italy and Germany the government already owned facilities such as the railroads; the postwar period saw some extension of government ownership, as in the Italian takeover of electric utilities in the 1960s. Everywhere government aid to housing grew. This was made vital by wartime destruction (40 per cent of German housing had been ruined) and by the growth in population; only gradually did building programs begin to catch up with need. Everywhere there was a vast extension of social insurance programs. Unemployment insurance and medical programs received the greatest attention. In Sweden, for example, a program of ninety days of free medical care was established after the war. Greater material security, new educational opportunity, and more extensive government economic encouragement and control were provided quite generally in western Europe.

The most complete new welfare program was developed in France, particularly in the years 1945–1946. France had long lagged in this area; in a sense, it was now catching up with leaders such as Germany and the Scandinavian countries. And it was in France that the political effects of Resistance movements were most keenly felt. The French government in the immediate postwar years was directed by a coalition of communists, socialists, and Christian Democrats, all of which were interested in social reform.

A real social security program was established for the first time. Hospital costs were insured, and coverage was provided for old age and unemployment. Workers, both in industry and agriculture, were compelled to participate in the programs. They paid a part of the cost, but employers paid 30 to 40 per cent of the cost and the state also contributed. Supplementing these measures was a large program of family aid; families received annual payments from the state for each child, the aid increasing with the size of the family. These payments were given to any family, regardless of income. Drawn from tax funds, these payments allowed some redistribution of income in favor of the poor. (And because it remained true that poorer families had more children, their benefits increased on this basis as well.) A laborer with low earnings and a large family could increase his income by as much as 40 per cent by the family aid he received. The program provided a minimum of material well-being for most families and promoted population growth as well. All in all, about 16 per cent of the French national income was being devoted to the various social security programs. In addition, the French state participated actively in educational reform. The school-leaving age was raised from fourteen to sixteen, and the curriculum of secondary schools was altered to meet the needs of a larger segment of society. Classical subjects, though still important, gave ground to science, modern languages, and social studies. Attendance at the most advanced secondary schools, the *lycées,* increased markedly. In the 1930s only 15 per cent of French children had attended these schools. By the 1950s this had grown to 20 per cent, and the *lycées* included all strata of the middle class and some children from the lower classes as well.

Finally, the French government introduced several measures to alter the control of industry. Experiments were made with a system of *comités d'entreprise,* joint labor–management councils, that would rule on working conditions and on general industrial policy. These experiments were not fully successful, partly because the unions resisted involvement with management, preferring to remain independent and free to protest. At the same time, the French government attempted to encourage worker participation in more traditional ways. Collective bargaining was facilitated, and the government extended direct aid to unions for training programs, including training in union management. Most important, of course, was the government's direct role in the economy. Several industries were nationalized. Railroads were taken over entirely; in Europe generally it was felt that transportation links were too vital to the economy to be left in private hands. Coal mines were nationalized because of their economic importance and the hardships of mine labor. The government also developed a general agency, the *Office du plan,* to set basic standards for economic development. By a combination of direct government allocation of funds and tax benefits and a program of persuasion, this office tried to encourage the economy and maintain full employment.

Characteristics of the Welfare State

The welfare systems that had been developed in western and central Europe varied considerably in details. Britain possessed the most complete medical program, France the most extensive program of family aid. One of the keynotes of the welfare state was a certain pragmatism and flexibility, but certain common ideals did operate in the various programs.

There was a belief in the responsibility of society to banish poverty. A clear effort was made to set minimal conditions for factory work, for the incomes of the lower classes in both industry and agriculture, and for the whole society in such matters as medical care. There was a desire to limit, though not to eliminate, inequalities of wealth by funding the welfare programs by graduated taxes. The state was to serve as a redistributive agent.

The material goals were the most obvious and, in many ways, the most fully successful aspects of the welfare state. Beyond them, however, was an interest in eliminating class barriers to opportunity by extending educational facilities. There was a hope, finally, of giving the lower classes, particularly the workers, greater participation in their own governance. Nationalization was undertaken in part to allow workers more voice in crucial industries previously dominated by large firms. The nationalized industries tried to involve their own workers in decisions by creating mixed governing boards within the industry. The French *comités d'entreprise* represented a similar attempt in private industry to allow worker participation. In 1951 Germany set up supervisory boards in the iron, steel, and coal industries; heavy worker representation on these boards was designed to provide greater social control of vital industries. State encouragement of collective bargaining and of recognition of unions obviously promoted a bilateral determination of conditions of work. In Scandinavia particularly, but elsewhere to a great degree, collective bargaining represented an important part of the welfare state. It helped raise wages, improve material conditions, and moderate class hostility and the sense of isolation of workers in industry.

The welfare programs obviously represented a great extension of the power of the state to compel for the public good. The size of government bureaucracies increased substantially. Regulatory action was extended from traditional fields to cover minimum wages and even the conditions under which workers could be dismissed. Direct government action in matters such as housing and industrial ownership was vastly increased. Compulsion was extended to participation in the new insurance programs and to the fees doctors could charge, as in the British health scheme. At the same time, compulsion was not total in the welfare states; there was still great stress on persuasion and substantial reliance on private initiative. The new attention to worker participation in decisions extended some initiative to wider groups than ever before. After setting certain minimum standards of material conditions and some guidelines for general economic development, the welfare state intended to leave society with more opportunities for effective initiative than ever before.

The benefits as well as the controls of the welfare state penetrated the whole society, for welfare principles were extended to groups beyond factory labor. Insurance programs were fully applied to clerical and agricultural workers and even to many of the self-employed. Medical plans and new educational facilities affected society generally. Protective legislation covering matters of hours, vacations, and wages applied to almost all categories of employees. The intensification of welfare measures brought the state more clearly into the normal lives of most people than ever before. Earlier programs, aside from general regulation of working conditions, had tended to concentrate on disasters—unemployment, illness, old age. These programs were increased after the war; there was unprecedented security from risk. Even farmers received greater protection from the hazards of weather and blight by systems of income support. Beyond this, however, welfare programs extended assistance to daily life. Measures such as family aid and medical care were of far more constant benefit than many of the earlier insurance schemes. The extension of benefits to all groups in society and their application to more aspects of material life were leading characteristics of the welfare states.

The establishment of the welfare state both annoyed and disappointed many people. Its controls offended some traditional liberals and certain elements of the upper class; its failure to effect a profound social revolution dismayed those on the far left; and its materialism and pragmatism repelled many intellectuals. Yet the welfare state drew on many political traditions in Europe, embodying elements of both liberalism and socialism. It went some way to fulfilling traditional lower-class beliefs that the state should protect them from disaster, beliefs that in primitive form were visible even in the preindustrial tradition of bread riots. The welfare state also met middle-class interests. The middle class had never been comfortable with poverty; now it could claim that poverty had been banished. By providing new jobs for professionals and new educational opportunities the welfare state helped the middle class directly. And although it relied in part on graduated taxes, these were not confiscatory. Although Sweden and Britain had fairly steeply graduated income taxes their levels were actually a bit milder than those of the United States, where a full welfare state had not developed in terms of new state functions. France relied even less on income taxes, deriving much tax money from concealed sales taxes. Particularly in France but to a degree everywhere the welfare state proved quite consistent with a substantial range of economic inequality. Thus the welfare state had wide appeal, although almost every group could find something to object to in it. The welfare state faced no serious challenge as Europe entered the mid-1970s. Most political debate centered around modifying it or extending it; few people clearly proposed an alternate definition of state functions.

The welfare state was capped, in the eyes of its designers, by unprecedentedly steady economic growth. Protection of the lower-income groups was among other things intended to assure their purchasing power. And the welfare state was committed to full employment and economic growth. Government funds were poured into industrial investment. France had the most elaborate planning of the western countries, but Scandinavian states were active in the field, and all governments exerted some control. Italian and French governments tried to bring industry to backward regions such as southern Italy and western France by subsidies and tax credits. These programs gradually reduced some economic gaps within the countries. At least partly because of state policy, Europe entered a period of genuine affluence following three or four years of confusion after 1945. This affluence was vital to the favorable reception the welfare state encountered.

Economic Development

It would have been difficult, as late as 1950, to predict a major economic advance. Wartime dislocation kept production levels down; disruption of transportation facilities was particularly damaging. With production low and governments attempting to increase industrial investment, massive inflation developed, for demand inevitably exceeded the supply of goods. Germany stabilized its currency only in 1948; Italy did so in 1952, but only by pegging the lira at one fiftieth of its previous value. French inflation ultimately reduced the franc to one twenty-fifth of its postwar level. Britain, too, suffered a substantial devaluation. All of this discontented workers, when wages lagged behind prices and wiped out savings: many entrepreneurs also questioned the future of the economy. Inflation plus the need for foreign, particularly American, food and industrial equipment left the European countries in perpetual deficit in their balance of payments; observers predicted that the "dollar gap" would reduce Europe to permanent economic dependence on the United States.

But in 1947 the United States launched the Marshall Plan program to provide funds for redevelopment, hoping not only to aid Europe but to stem the growth of communist movements of protest. This was the first step toward rapid recovery. But it was also apparent that much of the wartime damage and confusion could be quickly repaired. Once its transportation network was rebuilt and its currency stabilized, for example, Germany was ready to move ahead in what Germans rather ostentatiously proclaimed an "economic miracle." Postwar economic advance was not simply the result of American aid or the resumption of earlier growth. Something new was afoot, a more vigorous desire for economic change. Government planning and assistance aided the movement but so did new expectations of business managers and workers alike. Germany's miracle was soon matched and even eclipsed by the rapid development of French and Italian industry. Only Britain, of the major noncommunist countries, expanded at a modest pace.

Beginning in Germany in 1948, and in France and Italy in the early 1950s, an economic advance of vast proportions began that continued through the 1960s. It was not completely uninterrupted and there were years of reduced growth. But in contrast to previous industrial history there were no real recessions. Even recessions in the United States merely resulted in a slower pace of growth, not in a cessation. State guidance helped channel resources to points of actual need and prevented speculative over-development. The provision of minimal standards for all classes and the maintenance of full employment opened a new mass market for many goods. Thus economic growth was unprecedentedly steady as wartime damage was repaired and production soared to new heights.

Growth was also rapid in most countries, exceding the rates of the interwar years and also the decades before World War I. It also surpassed the rates of the more troubled American economy from the mid-1950s onward. The German economy expanded at an annual rate of 6 per cent during much of the 1950s. During the early part of the decade significant unemployment persisted, tolerated by the trade unions in the interest of using resources for new investment. But by the end of the 1950s German industry was crying out for more workers and growth continued at a high rate during most of the 1960s. In 1973 expansion had returned to a 6 per cent level.

France attained an 8 per cent annual growth by the end of the 1950s. Expansion continued at a somewhat slower pace during the 1960s, rising again in the early 1970s to over 7 per cent a year. By 1959 the Italian economy expanded at the rate of 11 per cent a year, propelling Italy into the ranks of advanced industrial nations, though serious labor troubles reduced expansion again by the 1970s. Growth rates in Scandinavia and particularly in Britain were somewhat lower. The British economy grew at a rate of about 4 per cent a year in the 1950s. British workers and entrepreneurs both seemed more resistant to technological change than their counterparts on the Continent; as a result, the British standard of living declined in relation to France and Germany. But even in Britain there was significant advance, in contrast to the stagnation of the interwar years.

Certain traditional industries continued to decline throughout western Europe. Textiles and particularly mining suffered. Some mines were completely closed, unable to compete with petroleum fuels. On the whole, however, this decline was more than balanced by the advance of petrochemicals, electronics, and heavy consumer goods such as automobiles and appliances. There was a marked increase as well in the service sector of the economy, as the need for teachers, sales personnel, and the like expanded. Indeed the growth of the service sector rapidly outstripped that of the classic working class. In France in 1968 half of all salaried workers were in the service sector; by 1973 this proportion had risen to 53 per cent. An affluent society needed new services. Bureaucratization demanded educated, nonmanual personnel. Improved technology in manufacturing allowed production advances without a rapid increase in the size of the working class. All of this of course involved substantial social mobility. It was estimated that 30 per cent of the French working class had moved into white-collar jobs in the twenty years after World War II.

These shifts in turn altered the regional balance of national economies. Italian industry continued to be centered in the north, despite the location of a few important firms elsewhere. In France and Britain, however, the coal regions, the traditional centers of manufacturing, declined. Many of the newer industries preferred to locate in regions free from the grime of the mining areas. Service industries, such as insurance, and many company bureaucracies tended to settle in the capital cities or other financial centers. Paris, London, and Frankfurt, and the regions around them, expanded rapidly. Southern England, long eclipsed by the industrial north, was now reversing the process. A few traditional factory areas in Britain and the coal districts of Belgium were afflicted with noticeable levels of unemployment. But generally the expansion of the economy more than sufficed to compensate for lagging areas and industries. All this meant greater geographical as well as social mobility.

Agriculture participated strongly in economic growth. Increasing numbers of peasants abandoned the countryside for the city, where industrial growth assured them of jobs. The result was less rural poverty and more efficient farm units. Governments encouraged more productive methods on the farms, providing better training and information on new techniques. They promoted the consolidation of small plots into larger, more efficient holdings and they actively backed the cooperative movement. Improved equipment, including tractors and other agricultural machines, spread widely, resulting in a sharp increase in crop yields. West Germany, cut off from the agricultural east, raised agricultural productivity rapidly; by 1952 West German wheat yield per acre was 1.2 tons, compared to 0.4 in the United States. French agricultural gains were in many ways still more dramatic, and output rose rapidly. European farmers were not as efficient on a per-worker basis as those of North America, where farming was far more mechanized. Their increased output added to the problem of excessive agricultural production in the industrial nations of the world and this output could be maintained only by tariff protection and subsidies. Nevertheless agriculture was not the invalid it had been during the previous half century. It was less of a drain on the economy as a whole and provided better-quality food to Europe's cities.

Rising Standards and New Problems

Growth in most major sectors of the economy rapidly advanced general prosperity. The European middle classes enjoyed high rates of profits and salaries. Continuing a well-established trend, the size of businesses grew steadily. The establishment of the Common Market encouraged the formation of international business combines. Small wonder then that earnings rose, sometimes more rapidly than wages. Because of government encouragement to private enterprise and labor's surprising acquiescence in modest earnings, German profits climbed faster than wages until the late 1950s. French government programs of anti-inflationary wage restraint in 1958–1959 allowed profits to rise more rapidly than working-class income. But the earnings of the lower classes increased overall, and this was one of the key results of the new economic setting.

Unemployment was virtually eliminated after the economic boom began, though there was a lag in Germany, where more than 2 million workers were out of work as late as February, 1954. After the mid-1950s, rates of no more than 2 per cent unemployment were maintained in France and Germany, which meant that most of the unemployed were simply in transition from one job to the next. Both countries, along with Switzerland, Belgium, and other areas, relied extensively on immigration to fill the soaring demand for workers created by economic growth. Large numbers of Italians, Spaniards, and Turks were brought in to work in Germany; several hundred thousand Algerians found employment in France; close to 2 million Pakistanis and West Indians poured into Britain. Many of the new workers were badly treated, if only because they filled the most unskilled positions. In Britain, where unemployment (at about 3 per cent) was higher than on the Continent (though far lower than it had been in the 1920s), serious racial hostilities developed. But some of the immigrants benefited from their work and there were other, clearer gains as well. Emigration, along with rapid industrialization, significantly reduced Italy's traditional pool of unemployment; by the 1970s Italian unemployment was little over 3 per cent. Immigration combined with full employment also allowed growing numbers of workers to rise to higher-paying jobs in the most prosperous countries. Finally, growing numbers of women found employment, which boosted family income. In Britain the number of working-class women with jobs rose two times over the level of the 1930s. By 1973 women constituted 39 per cent of the employment population in France. And this was not a traditional kind of advance. Employment of teen-aged girls fell steadily, because more and more were prolonging their schooling. It was adult women, many of them married, who were entering the labor force; in France the employment of women aged twenty-five to fifty-four, 52 per cent in 1972, had risen past 53 per cent in 1973, a rate of growth far higher than that of the labor force as a whole. Women played an important role in the factories but they were particularly concentrated in the ranks of employees. Never, in fact, since the population explosion of the eighteenth century had such a high percentage of the adult population been regularly employed over such an extended period of time.

Full employment and the steadily rising demand for workers naturally produced a rise in wages. Demands by individuals and unions for new raises met little resistance. By the early 1960s wage rates were rising fast, which helped ultimately to create a renewed threat of inflation. Before this point, wage rises brought the urban lower classes in western and central Europe unprecedented affluence. This was not mass consumption of the limited sort developed before World War I; rather it involved not only improvement in diet and clothing but also mass purchase of large and expensive consumer goods. Television sets and refrigerators were now normal household items for the majority of the people, and the average family in the wealthy countries possessed a motor vehicle, either a scooter or an automobile. Recreational opportunities increased as work hours were lowered and most workers were legally guaranteed two or three weeks of paid vacation.

Despite the remarkable economic advances, there were weaknesses in Europe's new economic structure. Because of its slower growth rate and dependence on massive imports of food and other goods, Britain faced a chronic balance of payments problem that dominated national policy by the 1960s. The British, bent on improving their consumption levels, bought more imported goods but did not export enough to earn the necessary foreign exchange. In order to produce more for export and adjust the payments' balance, the government periodically imposed restrictions not only on imports and travel abroad but on consumer spending at home. France more briefly faced a similar problem after the social unrest of 1968. Both Britain and France undertook another devaluation at the end of the decade in order to improve the payments situation. Germany, on the other hand, regularly exported more than was imported and so faced periodic pressure to revalue the mark upward. In general, however, European currencies remained strong and relatively stable into the early 1970s.

In 1969 a French politician and journalist, Jacques Servan-Schreiber, published a book called *The American Challenge,* which quickly won wide attention. Though directed primarily toward France, he pointed to problems that affected other countries as well. His claim was that despite impressive economic gains, including a growth rate far more rapid than that of the United States, Europe had not achieved a level of technology or of business organization comparable to American standards. European firms were too small, their willingness to innovate still too limited.

The argument was difficult to assess. It was true that large American firms had moved into the prosperous European market in increasing numbers, setting up subsidiaries and buying European firms outright. This development disturbed many Europeans and some halting limitations were imposed, particularly by the French government. Yet it was hard to resist the ample investment funds and the technical expertise the Americans could provide. Undoubtedly something of a "lag" existed, though it was exaggerated by the peculiar position of the dollar as a world currency, which European governments had to defend in order to protect their own currencies, despite the weak balance of payments situation of the United States. In effect American businessmen could invest vast sums abroad because the European governments would underwrite the value of the currency. But to the extent that a real lag existed, its economic significance remained unclear. American penetration worried Europeans politically, but it helped spur further economic advance. In terms of employment and economic growth levels, Europe remained in considerably better shape than the United States by the early 1970s. Most European countries were also more successful in export sales than their American rival. One wondered who was lagging behind whom.

The most important problem in the European economy by the late 1960s and early 1970s was a renewed bout of inflation that affected even stable, secure Germany. Some blamed the flood of unwanted dollars from American investors and speculators, which increased the money supply and contributed to price rises. Other factors were also involved. Food prices were pushed up in part because tariffs and subsidy programs limited agricultural competition. Big business manipulated the price of manufactured goods. Consumer expectations were rising steadily, despite continuing income inequality and some outright poverty. It was not so easy to expand production in order to meet these demands. France and Germany already suffered from a shortage of labor, which limited production gains. Workers there and also in Britain resisted undue pressures to step up the pace of work or introduce rapid technological change. At the same time many groups of workers and others pressed for massive wage increases. When they won, they contributed to the formula for inflation. Price increases did not get totally out of hand, but wages and earnings for many groups failed to keep pace between 1965 and 1970. By the early 1970s prices were rising up to 10 per cent a year in several countries. Governments, particularly in England, attempted a variety of controls to limit inflation, sometimes jeopardizing economic growth in the process, but nothing seemed to work.

Somehow inflation seemed to have become the endemic weakness of advanced industrial economies, the counterpart of recessions in the earlier stages of development. Damage was muted by the fact that most elements of the population were wage earners and not dependent on fixed income such as rents. Their wages were normally flexible, though they might not always match the price changes and some confusion was inevitable. Despite inflation real wages rose at least 4 per cent in the main European countries in 1972–1973. In this sense inflation could be endured because of the decline of property ownership as an element of economic and social structure, and certainly it encouraged a further decline. But groups of the population on fixed incomes, such as many pensioners, suffered greatly.

In 1973 a more ominous development clouded the European economic scene. The shortage and rapidly rising cost of fuel threatened Europe particularly, because of heavy dependence on oil imports from the Middle East. Economic advance would almost certainly slow as costs increased and Europe's competitive position worsened. In the short run, rising unemployment was forecast, particularly in fuel-using industries such as automobile production. Some European governments took immediate steps to provide alternate sources of energy. In both Italy and France atomic energy facilities, already fairly widely developed, were to be expanded. Whether this crisis could reverse the tide of economic modernization was unclear, although initial reactions indicated that the European economies could weather the storm.

For until this threat, the tide of economic advance had prevailed for twenty years. Economic problems and imbalances must not be minimized, but the development of European society was based above all on new affluence. Almost all major groups had come to depend on economic change; for the first time since industrialization began there was no serious popular cry for a return to some older economic order. This obviously heightened the importance of a successful response to the new energy crisis.

The Vanishing Peasantry

The peasantry, as a distinct social class, came close to extinction as the consumer society took shape. This was not simply a question of dwindling numbers, although in western Europe the farming population now constituted a small minority, its size shrinking steadily as migration to the cities continued. In eastern Europe, and even in Spain and Portugal, the new wave of industrialization reduced peasant numbers as well, although not yet to the same extent. Except in southern Europe, and particularly the Iberian peninsula, changes in values made even remaining peasants more urban in outlook. In the south, continued poverty and the power of the landlords kept many peasants in the grip of tradition, unable even to continue the unrest that had rocked the countryside into the twentieth century. In southern Italy, for example, extensive devotion to the Church and conservative voting patterns were the surface signs of a still-isolated peasant culture. Even here, however, migration of workers back and forth from the cities of the north gradually brought some changes in behavior. A minority of younger peasants, for example, began to defy traditions of arranged marriage.

Elsewhere the hold of peasant customs was still visible but no longer dominant. Peasants were still more likely to be religious than other elements of the population. They still had larger families; they had the lowest divorce rates of any social group. A French survey in 1970 showed that only peasants continued to define a successful family in terms of the number of children it had. Peasants in many areas remained attached to age-old but now inefficient economic habits, such as the scattering of small plots of land around a village. Vigorous encouragement by postwar governments to consolidate family holdings made only slow headway. So peasants continued to travel from one little field to another, sometimes unable to use farm machinery efficiently on any one plot. On the whole peasants also continued to accept a standard of living that fell below urban standards, although not without some protest. Housing, diet, and clothing were still limited, along with opportunities for holidays and other recreation. Peasant traditionalism was maintained by the continued departure of many younger, ambitious peasants to the cities; as before, the rural population was older than the national average.

However, continuity was beginning to be overshadowed by change. The peasant situation shifted most dramatically in eastern Europe, with the communist attack on the large estates and the collectivization of agriculture. Even in Yugoslavia, where small holdings were permitted to remain, peasant life changed with the spread of a vigorously antireligious education and new contacts with the cities. Rapidly declining rural birth rates were one sign of the new rural life that was developing.

In western Europe conditions changed almost as rapidly. The welfare state provided new material benefits for the peasants, as in family assistance and medical care programs. It gave novel political experience as well, for peasants were called upon to participate in a host of government-sponsored committees. Although peasant incomes did not reach urban levels, the peasantry was touched by affluence. New consumer items such as radios and television spread widely in peasant homes, and this would only heighten the conversion to an urban value system.

With government encouragement, peasants showed a growing interest in economic change. Observers noted a virtual revolution in the attitudes of younger French peasants. Their interest in technological improvement was most striking, and tractors became a more important status symbol than land itself. Some peasants bought them even when their plots were too small to permit their use, letting them sit in the front yard as a sign that they had arrived socially. The cooperative movement continued to spread, aided by government subsidies. This too brought new organizational experience, and elections for the leadership of cooperatives and of local state agencies altered the nature of village politics. Political contests became a subject of lively, even bitter debate, as traditional village leaders were pushed aside by younger, more forward-looking ones. Peasants' understanding of national politics also changed and their voting rates increased markedly.

Peasant modernization was not without some tragic irony. Interest in new methods helped increase agricultural production, but it did not yet make European agriculture as efficient as that of North America. So peasants had to continue to use their political voice to seek special protection; French peasants were particularly successful in asking not only for high tariffs on food products but also for special subsidies from their own government and from the Common Market.

In combination with the constant threat of falling agricultural prices, the new peasant outlook was extremely conducive to protest. In France and Italy a minority of peasants voted communist. Some were expressing resentments against the remote, big-city governments of Paris or Rome and were often located in regions that had long been hostile to the central state. Others used communism to protest the dominant leadership group in the village, and some agricultural laborers sought to attack their employers. In the early 1960s a more direct protest movement developed in France, led by peasants who had adopted the most advanced new techniques. Many of the protesters were conservative politically, even active in the Catholic Church; this was not a fully politicized movement and the protesters were partly asking for more under the existing system. But they were aware that their conditions did not meet urban standards and they looked to the government for remedies. They repeatedly demonstrated to call the attention of government and the urban public to their hardships. A favorite tactic was an invasion of a provincial administrative center by thousands of tractor-driving peasants or the use of tractors to block highways during the vacation period; urban motorists were sometimes led, gently but firmly, into the peasant home to see how poor conditions were.

These protests had limited success, though they undoubtedly helped maintain government agricultural support.

The tensions of a peasantry-becoming-modern-farmers remain acute, and they are spreading beyond France. In 1970 almost 100,000 peasants from all the Common Market countries conducted a vigorous demonstration in Brussels, the Market capital; considerable violence occurred. The solution, as seen by the major governments, is to continue phasing out the agricultural population, and so far, given full employment in the cities, this has worked without great hardship. For the peasantry is already sufficiently urban in outlook that movement to the city no longer occasions great stress. Those who remain in the countryside will be free to improve their economic efficiency and, assuming continued income support, their standard of living. The most ancient of all European classes has been absorbed by modernization, its distinctiveness perceivable but no longer significant. European society is increasingly dominated by the various levels of the middle and working classes, all solidly urban.

The Middle Class

The new structure of the middle class brought its problems. Rapid growth meant new competition. Bureaucratization entailed a loss of independence for some. Doctors, for example, were more fully employed than before with the spread of prosperity, the state support of medical payments, and their own increased professional skill, which made them more widely attractive to people seeking better health. But some resented the control of their fees by government bureaucrats, believing that precious professional freedom had been lost. More than one doctors' strike occurred over efforts to prod the state into granting higher incomes.

For clerks and lower-level managers, bureaucratization could frustrate aspirations for mobility. A special ability was not necessarily recognized; personal contacts more than talent might push one up the organizational ladder. And the sheer weight of detailed promotion procedures could disgust someone who, in the classic middle-class manner, wanted to get to the top. Along with potential frustration came the routinization of many office jobs. Personnel managers and office supervisers kept careful tabs over employees, and new office machinery made some former clerical skills redundant. It was not hard to feel a kinship with ordinary workers in this situation. This was one reason that many middle-class people developed a new sympathy for labor and socialist parties; the bulk of the class did not vote for these parties but most found them an appropriate part of the political system and some turned to them directly at times. More concretely, unions spread increasingly among office personnel and a growing number of strikes were conducted. Usually this agitation concerned specific issues of pay or work conditions and was kept separate from workers' unrest. But occasionally there were hints of unity. In the May, 1968, general strike in France many clerks and technicians joined workers in the rising. Here was a possible theme for the future. The fact that most middle-class people were not salaried employees, dependent on impersonal upper management, might drive them toward the working class in protest.

However, apart from the fact that the working class itself was not massively aggrieved, a persistent middle-class protest against dependence and the frustrations of bureaucracy had not clearly developed by the mid-1970s. Mobility was by no means gone. The upper managers were recruited heavily from below; in one large Italian company only 13 per cent of the directors were sons of industrialists, the rest coming from families of professional and white-collar workers. Furthermore, even below this level, the work ethic had not lost its validity. Middle-level managers gave themselves extensively to their jobs. Professional people did the same. Benefiting from improved specialized training in medical and law schools, even the older professionals found satisfaction in their work. University professors for the most part abandoned their nostalgia for the good old days of classical education, for the majority were now engaged in scientific or social scientific research and teaching. All the professionals found new job opportunities with the expansion of state functions. One sign of work satisfaction on the part of professionals and the higher managers was a relatively late retirement age.

The lower middle-class pattern was somewhat different, as had been suggested even in the previous period. More attention was given to life off the job. Retirement age was relatively low, and this group devoted a great deal of attention to assuring appropriate pensions; far more than workers, for example, clerks were likely to subscribe to supplementary pension plans beyond the system provided by the welfare state. But there was job satisfaction for this group too. Most polls suggested that 70 to 80 per cent of the clerks enjoyed their work. They still benefited from the contact they had with higher levels of the bureaucracy. Some could move up the ladder. The expansion of state educational systems, particularly at the secondary school and university level, gave many sons and daughters a real chance to gain higher status through training. Many developed social contacts with friends on the job. The work situation of the middle class at most levels thus did not completely interrupt the traditions of the class, even though a minority might regret the loss of older criteria of status such as property ownership. And of course job satisfaction was facilitated by the steady advance of middle-class earnings.

Furthermore the middle class retained decisive advantages over the working class, and those who depended on a sense of superiority could take satisfaction in this. Despite new working-class prosperity the average salary level of the middle class was distinctly higher. More important, their pay was in the form of salary, not wage. They were paid a monthly or yearly rate and had more job security, more freedom from temporary layoffs, than workers whose earnings were based on hourly or daily performance. Their educational advantages were pronounced. Most European systems based entry into the most prestigious secondary schools, those that would allow later advancement into universities for the ablest students, on an examination to be taken around the age of eleven. Success in this early testing depended heavily on home environment, the encouragement parents could give their children to do well in school. And here the middle class, again taking advantage of its traditional ethic, continued to thrive.

Along with these important contacts with class tradition, however, came an elaboration of the newer leisure ethic. Far more clearly than before, the middle class learned to have fun. Ample leisure time and regular annual vacations of at least three weeks created a new life style. Clerks as well as bankers became continental travelers, for the middle class had discovered the sun. Every year millions of middle-class Germans, Britons, Scandinavians, and Frenchmen poured into the south of France, into Italy, and into Spain. The bronzed body became an important status symbol, now that more people worked indoors, in contrast to the nineteenth century, when fashionable women strove to preserve the whiteness of their skin. New attention to leisure activities altered middle-class spending patterns. No longer did house and furnishings loom so large. These were still considered important, but growing numbers could accept pleasant but not showy row houses and apartments, if only because they planned to escape them frequently. Not only formal vacations but also weekend drives to the country, which packed the roads around every major city, became a regular part of middle-class life.

More tentatively a new attitude toward retirement developed. Europeans were urged to think of their later years as a "third age," in which they could expect to be healthy and to engage in a host of activities they had been too busy to enjoy during their adult, working years. The middle class was particularly able to take some advantage of this advice, and more than was the case with the working class its members professed to find retirement enjoyable.

The new outlook of the middle class carried over into family relationships, for the family was the key recreational unit. Continuing an earlier trend, marriage was increasingly based on romance, at least in theory. In fact, polls suggested that middle-class marriage, although by no means guaranteeing romantic fulfillment, had a better chance than that of other groups: in a French survey twice as many middle-class as peasant women claimed they had achieved a "great love." Other surveys indicated that the middle class was now decidedly freer than the working class in sexual practices, both before and after marriage. For the first time old people were encouraged to enjoy sex, contrary to a centuries-old culture that warned against anything but platonic love after fifty-five or so. Certainly the sexual tolerance of the class increased, for there was little outcry against the growing permissiveness of films and the theater. There was significant change also in the general attitude of husbands toward wives. As more and more women gained advanced education and took jobs, their role in the family economy and family decision making was strengthened. Middle-class families also relaxed their discipline of children. Fathers became less severe and remote, and were more inclined to play with children and take an active role in their care. The middle class eased its rigorous toilet training of young children. Teen-agers were allowed as never before to socialize with people of their own age and enjoy a specific youth culture in terms of songs and dances. This was widely claimed to have eased parent–adolescent tensions. The European middle-class family remained more disciplined than its American counterpart, partly because more crowded housing required stricter regulation and more parent–child contact. But the authoritarian middle-class family, never entirely a reality, was gone.

Indeed most of the middle-class family and recreational patterns constituted elaborations on trends visible earlier, although now greatly heightened by affluence. In certain respects the European middle class had moved farther toward an enjoyment of a society of abundance than its counterpart in America. It had more seriously reduced its commitment to work; it took longer vacations on the average. Less tied to an expensive, individual house in the suburbs, the class had more means to enjoy other aspects of life. Perhaps this was why it produced fewer outcries against sexual permissiveness or the dangers of communism. Certainly the European middle class had developed a new kind of adaptation to modernization.

The Working Class

Throughout most of the years since World War II the working classes have seemed relatively calm and contented. The immediate postwar agitation gave way to a moderate level of protest. Voter support for the Italian and French communist parties receded only slightly but it never advanced above the 1948 level (which was a quarter of the total vote in France and a third in Italy). Union membership remained high but again no massive gains were made. The strike rate varied from one country to the next during the 1950s and early 1960s. It was extremely low in the Scandinavian countries, where collective bargaining between union and employer, with government sponsorship, seemed to settle most problems peacefully. It was low also in Germany, as workers seemed content to take advantage of rising prosperity after the horror of war, despite the fact that profits outstripped wages, and their leaders wanted to cooperate in postwar rebuilding. Strikes were more frequent in Britain and particularly in France and Italy. Here workers in state-run enterprises, such as French miners or British railway labor, were most energetic. This showed that nationalization had not met one key working-class demand for a more effective voice in the running of industry; workers did not find state directors more sensitive to their needs than private employers. More important, many of these industries were in economic difficulty, mining being the clearest example; the state tried to keep wages down in order to make ends meet. Thus most strikes were efforts to catch up with the wage gains of workers in private industry. Workers showed a new determination to insist on steady improvements in the standard of living, which was significant; no longer were they simply fighting to maintain existing gains. But the strikes did not challenge the established order.

Beneath the surface the moderation of the working class showed through even more clearly. Votes for the French communist party were undeniably significant; they expressed the sense of separation many workers felt from the ruling classes of society, although of course not all workers voted communist (some voted socialist, others for the Christian Democrats), and not all communists were workers. But the interest workers took in communist activities declined. Party membership, as opposed to votes, fell off; the leadership began to age. Attendance at party meetings went down. Other labor movements had the same experience. In Britain and elsewhere, the percentage of workers who even bothered to vote in national elections went down. Union leaders bemoaned the lack of interest their members took in organizational activities. Certainly the unions no longer served as a social center; workers had other things to do with their time.

There were three reasons for this change in protest patterns, which many observers took, rather prematurely, to signify the decline of traditional class hostilities in industrial society. The first concerned the composition of the working class. There was an impoverished, unskilled element still. In 1949, 18 per cent of the British population was listed as near subsistence. Some of these were pensioners, for old people continued to have trouble keeping their incomes up. But some were also unskilled workers. Prosperity reduced the subsistence figure to 12 per cent by 1963, but this was still substantial. Yet the poor rarely figured in protest. In addition to all the traditional limitations on mobilizing the poor, the unskilled element of the labor force, not all of them impoverished, was now filled increasingly by immigrants. In Switzerland in 1960, 23 per cent of all immigrants were unskilled (compared to 7 per cent of the native Swiss) and 37 per cent more semiskilled. Pakistani bus drivers in Britain, Algerians serving as unskilled workers in the Renault auto works, these were but two typical situations elsewhere. Many were disoriented by their sudden exposure to industrial society. Others intended to go home, and some did; this kept them away from protest. Discriminated against by native workers and employers, often not citizens, divided by language and custom, the unskilled immigrants kept the lower, most desperate segment of the working class quiet. Only in the 1970s, in France, did foreign workers show some signs of being able to demand incomes and opportunities comparable to those of native workers, as a strike by Renault labor raised these issues quite clearly.

At the other extreme the flood of the unskilled helped native workers advance their own position. With the worst jobs handled by foreigners they could rise easily into skilled occupations, which, with modern technology, increased more rapidly than unskilled jobs; in 1973, for example, 66 per cent of all French male workers were skilled, as against 54 per cent in 1968. With foreign workers largely excluded from skilled ranks, mobility for many natives was almost automatic. Small wonder that over half of all chemical workers in West Germany rated their promotion chances as good or fair. These people might be loyal union members and labor or socialist voters, but their zeal was not likely to be great.

The second reason for the waning of interest in traditional vehicles for class conflict was at least as disturbing as the first. Many workers, intensely aggrieved, no longer found the main unions or parties relevant to their needs. Labor organization had become too big, too remote, and possibly too tame. Many Labour voters in Britain really did not believe that their party's victory would help them much. For some workers a sense of deep discontent combined with the absence of an adequate outlet created a truly tragic situation. Other workers shared some of this feeling: the government was too remote, job conditions not really in their own control, but they did not carry things so far.

The third reason for the decline of workers' interest in active protest was the society of affluence itself. Relatively stable employment removed one long-standing concern, which as we have seen antedated the beginnings of industrialization. Protection in case of sickness or accident alleviated other disasters. Pensions helped, too, though many workers still did not really think about retirement. Affluence was probably more important than the welfare state in changing workers' outlook. This was qualified affluence; workers constituted a group able to afford spending well above subsistence, but not free from worry. Hence a dual reason for reducing interest in attending union meetings or communist or labor party functions: workers were either busy working overtime to earn enough money for their car payments or out with the family enjoying the car itself.

Workers were becoming increasingly privatized, turning to family and personal enjoyments. Not only unions but also bars declined as centers of working-class society. Dependence on sweeping ideologies, such as

Marxism, waned as individual enjoyments became more diverse. Some observers claimed that workers were undergoing *embourgeoisement,* becoming similar to the middle class. Except for some individuals who were trying to move up in society this was not the case. But it was true that workers were developing some behavior patterns and attitudes similar to those of the middle class; for them too this constituted a further stage of modernization.

.Workers retained the ambiguous work ethic they had developed as industrial society matured; they did not take the same pleasure in their jobs that managers or even clerks did. If asked directly most said they found some pleasure in their work. Skilled workers particularly believed they could create satisfaction on their job. As a British factory electrician said, "I always *make* it interesting. I like to do a good job." Some workers claimed they chose their jobs only for money, hating the work all the while, but this was not the normal situation. Workers expected and normally received rising pay on their job, but they did not operate on this basis alone.

Yet they often felt mistreated. Many found their supervisors unsympathetic to their suggestions, which wounded their professional pride. "I have to go and tell the foreman all the time and then wait two days for his decision." Hence most workers, when asked, said if they had it to do all over again they would choose another line of work. Many had adopted a middle-class sense of social status. They talked of wanting their children to become doctors or civil servants. But again the ambiguity, which was by no means new: they did not really expect to be able to rise in society or to see their children do so. Hence they talked of their jobs as all right "for the likes of us." Or for their children: the same workers who said they wanted their son to be a doctor provided little encouragement for special success in the early school years, which remain so crucial in Europe. What this added up to was a continuation of a hierarchical view of society: it might be nice to achieve a higher level but few really could. Along with this, there was a certain satisfaction in the job being done. Middle-class pollsters who tried to get the majority of workers to say they hated their factory positions failed, though they could easily elicit resentments against an unsympathetic management.

Workers' life off the job harbored similar ambiguities. The family focus remained intense. Even when workers moved to new areas to seek high-paying jobs they relied heavily on the extended family for social contacts. With more mothers working up to a third of all families in the class depended on grandparents for child care. The automobile and new leisure time allowed them to see even distant parents and relatives with some frequency. On the other hand the traditional working-class neighborhood was often disrupted by new housing projects. Thanks to the welfare state the European city was less segregated by class than it had been in earlier stages of industrialization. The worker might live next to the clerk in a government housing project, both recently moved in. Workers took greater pride in housing than before too. But their social contacts were often more limited than those of the middle class, which was where the family came in again.

Within the family some traditional tensions undoubtedly relaxed. The authoritarian husband and father began to fade here as in the middle class. With most working-class wives now working to supplement the family budget, they found a useful outlet apart from the home and at the same time gained new voice in family decisions. Many British workers claimed equal status with their wives: "Full partners: we must agree together in everything." Although some still complained that they came home from the job too exhausted to behave decently to their families, more judged the family their main focus in life: "That's my life, wife and children." Again this was not an entirely new sentiment, but it was one that workers had increasing time and money to develop. For working-class recreation was more and more a family matter. Television played an important role here, but so did other hobbies at home.

A new attitude toward children followed the same pattern. The stern, sometimes brutal father became a loving dad. Working-class children were still subjected to greater discipline than those of the middle class, if only because their parents had less free time and patience to coddle. Toilet training, for example, occurred at a younger age. Cramped housing, more limited laundry facilities, and the fact that the working-class family was still larger on the average than that in the middle class accounted for this sort of difference. But mothers and fathers alike tried to devote new affection to their children. Indeed one of the motives some workers cited for their lack of interest in trying to rise to a better-paying job was the preservation of home life. New love for children was in part a substitute for the fact that, in modern factories and with the new school-leaving age, few men could expect to work alongside their sons. And it had its ambiguities, for the working class now encountered the tensions of an explicitly defined adolescence. Many teen-aged sons, even when recognizing how different their fathers were, in their affectionate attitude, from their fathers' fathers, stated their dilemma: it might be harder to free oneself from a loving parent than from a taskmaster.

Despite limitations, working-class family life clearly served as a vital counterpart to work. Hence many men refused to discuss their jobs at home, for family was intended for relaxation: "I never mention work at home; otherwise I would never relax." "Home should give you strength for the next day." Indeed, in contrast to the traditional ethic of the lower classes, it was the family that governed the quality of work. Workers' performance varied radically with the problems or satisfactions they encountered at home, for jobs were not the center of their lives.

Workers had thus achieved their own version of modernization. They expected a rising standard of living and protested when this was interrupted; conditions on the job, though not entirely satisfactory, were less important. Their use of leisure was necessarily less diverse than that of the middle class. Only when single could a male worker afford a vacation abroad. Workers were still less likely than the middle class to save, for they preserved their traditional culture of uncertainty. They were less likely to be ready for retirement as well, in terms of plans for other activities as well as the pensions they had accumulated. A woman worker in Paris expressed a very common sentiment: "I never thought of stopping work; I thought I'd be dead before, I was so tired." Hence workers who did retire were more likely to feel sick or bored: "While I was working it was hard, but at least I felt like other people." As we have seen, their mobility aspirations were limited; hence, particularly in France and Germany, few tried to send their children on to universities. In France by 1965 only 4 per cent of all university students came from below the middle classes. In a variety of ways, then, workers preserved the culture they had formed in response to initial industrialization, simply taking advantage of new affluence to add to their family enjoyments and personal hobbies. Their life off the job, though far from perfect, was better than before; whether it had improved enough to compensate for continued work tensions was a matter of individual reaction.

Mature Industrial Societies

Neither Spain nor the eastern European countries had achieved a consumer society by the 1970s. Spanish industrialization advanced. A dynamic element developed within the middle class, seeking economic progress. Cities expanded, the economic growth rate stepped up, and there was greater prosperity for the urban population. Spain's rulers were more ambiguous in their reaction to modernization than the governments of northwestern Europe had been a century before. Certainly workers were denied the outlets their counterparts had had. Forbidden to join independent unions, they conducted periodic and bitter strikes to protest government repression. Spain was thus not a typical mature industrial society, and her ability to develop the political and social forms typical of the consumer society was not clear.

The same was true of the communist states of eastern Europe. Most maintained high economic growth rates, with industrialization advancing steadily. Here the leadership was firmly committed to industrial expansion. Agriculture remained a problem, for the gap between peasant motivation and the organizational framework of the collective farms had not closed.

Peasants were not so much neo-capitalists as traditionalists; they adapted readily to increasing output only when they could claim their own plot of land. Harsh weather and inconsistent production of advanced agricultural equipment added to the problem. To assure food supplies a large farming population had to be retained.

In the cities, however, communist societies had at least one advantage over the earlier mature industrial stage in the west: there was no substantial middling class to fight the modernization process. Urban society was roughly divided between a managerial class and workers. Managers and professional people received relatively high incomes. They worked to advance their children, using educational opportunities to try to assure their careers. Their family structure closely resembled that of the west, with birth control playing an important role. Here, too, ties of affection between husband and wife and parents and children developed increasing significance. But the work ethic remained strong; leisure outlets were far less diverse than in western Europe. There were signs of discontent with the limitations on consumer pleasures. A number of young people became attached to western fashions, insofar as they could learn of them. Styles of dress, dances, and music popular among western youth had a devoted eastern audience, despite official denunciations of bourgeois decadence.

The working class lacked independent outlets for protest, again differing from its western analogue in the mature stage of industrialization. Advanced social security protection and the constant assurance of workers' importance to society may have made protest less necessary. But there was little indication that factory labor was either more or less pleasant under communism than under capitalism. Hence scattered signs developed that indicated that workers sought individual remedies for tensions on the job. High rates of drinking, absenteeism, theft from the plant, and above all a deliberate preservation of a slow work pace suggested serious problems of motivation. Occasionally these burst forth directly. Czech workers, taking advantage of a liberal atmosphere during 1968, eagerly participated in new factory councils, seeking more direct voice over their conditions. A Polish rising in 1970 protested food shortages and high food prices. But it began in port cities when workers rebelled against more stringent production requirements unless they were paid more. Straws in the wind, given the inadequate information available about social conditions: but workers seemed to be moving toward a semi-instrumental approach to their work, like their western counterparts earlier, in which higher production had to be motivated by better conditions off the job. One result was a marked reduction in the industrial growth rates of most communist countries, including Russia, by the late 1960s.

It is difficult to avoid the impression that workers, and perhaps important elements of the managerial class, were moving toward the kind of expectations that had ultimately produced the consumer society in western Europe. Whether this would force a reluctant and powerful leadership into major concessions was unclear; it was also possible that some other successful advance on mature industrial society could be made. In any case, eastern Europe had not made the turn and some tension was beginning to tell.

A New Tide of Protest?

In western Europe a different kind of unrest developed. It was more open, if only because protest outlets were more accessible. More important, in the view of some observers it already called the consumer society itself into question. Beginning in the mid-1960s a new tone could be discerned in important segments of the working class. Along with new grievances on the part of some white-collar employees and particularly with rising unrest among university students, it seemed that industrial society was in for another, possibly decisive, stage of unrest.

The most distinctive new element came from university students. Agitation first broke out in 1967, at the Free University of Berlin, where students and some of the younger faculty attacked inadequate facilities and impersonal university organization. In the following months Italian students conducted sit-in strikes at several universities; Spanish students forced the temporary closing of the University of Madrid; and uprisings occurred in other German universities, in Czechoslovakia, and in Yugoslavia. A student revolt in Paris precipitated near revolution in May, 1968.

The wave of protest had direct roots in the universities themselves. It signalled a recrudescence of student problems that had occurred in earlier stages of the modernization process. University organization had not changed with the times. Facilities were overcrowded, given the growth in student populations; here was an older theme now repeated. Interestingly, little unrest developed in British universities, where teacher–student contact was more personal and informal. On the Continent most classes were conducted in large lecture halls and examinations occurred only infrequently, with high rates of failure. Some students also feared for their professional future; agitators were drawn particularly from departments such as sociology, where jobs did not keep pace with student interest. Young instructors in many fields resented a rigid university hierarchy that subordinated them to older professors. And students were acting on a general belief in the power and purity of youth, another motif that had cropped up before in the modernization process.

Student protest was not simply selfish, however; although no clear ideology was put forward, students complained about the basic nature of the consumer society. Universities typified a bureaucratized, impersonal structure. They ignored the needs of the lower classes. As a French student

proclaimed: "We believe that the university is an essential element supporting society. We are convinced that the sole way of solving the problems
at all levels is to take part in the destruction of the system."

After an important wave of unrest, student agitation subsided. No
one could predict that it would not revive, but by the early 1970s the peak
of ferment seemed to have passed. The most concerned students had perhaps tried to confront the principles of modern society too directly. They
fought organization but did not develop strong organizations of their own;
without a single ideology they tended to divide into small groups, each
with their own slogans. Their attack on materialism did not find wide
popular support. Many workers indeed regarded students as privileged
in their own right, with their wealthy parents and state scholarships. This
was a dramatic episode, but it produced more catchy phrases than results:
"Imagination has seized power"; "Be realistic, demand the impossible."
Furthermore some university reforms did result from the agitation. New
funds and self-government powers were given in the French system, and
in Germany students and younger faculty gained unprecedented voice in
university decisions. Students—an age group, not a permanent social class
—calmed down. Some might be contented with reforms; far more, as
suggested by the low rates of participation in the new university voting
systems, simply turned their attention elsewhere.

But students did not constitute the only group where there was unrest.
The Parisian rising of 1968 not only sparked a response in other French
universities, but also triggered a massive general strike of several million
factory and office workers. Indeed from 1965 onward the strike rate
had increased in most advanced industrial countries. Workers in Germany
and Sweden, breaking their long silence, began to conduct vigorous strikes
for higher wages. They resisted government conciliation procedures and
also the restraint urged by their own unions. British workers staged a
number of large strikes for higher wages and also a bewildering series
of wildcat strikes, often directed against moderate unions as well as management. French strikes soared, and Italy was repeatedly paralyzed, to
the point that economic growth declined and the country was threatened
with chaos.

The most general cause of the new unrest was the mounting inflation.
Wages at first failed to keep pace with prices, and workers rose in anger.
Hence in the 1968 general strike French workers, after several years
of decline in real wages, initially rejected a settlement offering raises of
10 to 35 per cent. New unrest thus may have reflected less new goals than
a new situation. Workers since the early 1950s had demanded regular
improvements in the standard of living; now they resorted to protest for
this same purpose. By the early 1970s, when real wages began to rise again
despite continued inflation, the strike rate generally leveled off or declined. And even in the France of 1968, workers followed their strike

with a rather conservative vote, in which they confirmed the existing regime; this suggested that they were not revolutionary in intent.

Yet more, possibly, was involved. Working-class organizations demonstrably tried to hold their constituents back. The leading French unions and the communist party urged restraint in 1968, among other things trying to keep radical students away from their clientele. This played a major role in the workers' ultimate willingness to settle. Agitation has continued in Italy, where despite rapid economic development since the 1950s worker gains have not kept pace. But again this could be taken as a special case, not typical of the consumer society, for Italian workers (and also clerical groups such as postal employees) were really asking for a fairer share in national wealth that would allow them to enjoy relative affluence for the first time.

Some workers everywhere were seeking more than material gains in their protest. Many of the British wildcat strikes, for example, dealt with human relations on the job. Companies in Scandinavia and elsewhere found that to attract workers they had to modify assembly-line procedures. They began to let teams of workers decide on work methods and trade off specific jobs to provide more variety. The German trade unions embarked on a major campaign to win co-determination between workers and management in making important industrial decisions, and not just those that affected working conditions. In other words some workers were thinking about new kinds of participation in their own governance. On the same basis during the Czechoslovak rising of 1968, worker councils quickly formed and asked for a direct voice in management. This revived the interest workers had periodically shown in new control systems. Even more novel was the suggestion that workers, individually or in protest, could seek more enjoyment from work itself.

All this fell short of a major challenge by the mid-1970s. Many employers proved willing to experiment with new work methods, although results are not yet clear. Welfare-state governments did not attempt a mindless repression of the new unrest. They responded partially to students and they answered workers as well. Not only did real wages resume their increase. The French government began to encourage monthly payment rates for workers, called *mensualisation,* which would make them more like white-collar employees and increase their job security and ability to plan ahead. Profit-sharing plans were also promoted.

Utopia had not been reached. The very fact the workers could be contented only with wages that rose faster than productivity and prices suggested interesting problems for the future. Implicitly, at least, a new kind of pressure had developed in which workers could be satisfied only through an increasing share of the national income. This obviously fed inflation and might at some point antagonize other elements of society whose position was improving less rapidly; a new round of class warfare, based on new worker expectations, was conceivable. In Britain, where the government tried to control both prices and wages during the early 1970s, the fuel crisis of 1973–1974 semed to set off exactly this kind of confrontation. Coal miners, their product newly valuable as oil became costlier, voted a general strike in support of substantial wage demands; their vote, 80 per cent in approval, was unprecedented, and so was their refusal to make any concessions in negotiation with an anguished government.

Some younger workers undoubtedly wanted more humane work systems and a new voice in management decisions. Far more had developed expectations about wages that demanded satisfaction; and here, for all that the workers struggled within the industrial system, the new challenge should not be minimized, for never before had large groups asked for so much. Through the early 1970s the most advanced industrial economies seemed to be able to answer this kind of demand, though Italy's recent advent to the consumer society caused special tensions while Britain's slow growth reduced the flexibility of response. As the energy crisis of 1973–1974 brought predictions of economic stagnation, the response of workers became increasingly problematic.

Other Tensions

Until the energy crisis, however, the advanced industrial nations had succeeded in muting class antagonisms. Changes in both working-class and middle-class outlook played a role in this, although the classes did not fuse. Certainly rates of serious collective violence and disruption were less in Europe than in other advanced industrial areas, such as the United States, where racial clash loomed larger than a direct class struggle. Indeed some of the worst tensions in Europe concerned religious or ethnic divisions; the frictions between Catholics and Protestants in Northern Ireland and between Walloons and Flemings in Belgium caused more violence and political disruption than class antagonisms in the same area. There was no guarantee that serious class conflict would not resume or that some other divisions, as between employees and decision makers in a bureaucracy, would not take its place. But there were other problem areas at least as interesting as conventional class antagonisms as consumer society developed.

Crime

Rates of crime increased in most advanced industrial countries after World War II. They had risen in Britain since 1920 and then were aggravated by the war. On the Continent they had increased more steadily with industrialization. Prostitution actually dropped off a bit, for working-class use of prostitutes declined. But luxury prostitutes, operating discreetly for the benefit of businessmen, gained ground. Some more definite crimes, such as theft and fraud, seemed to mount naturally with affluence, for have-nots might see an easy way to become haves. In England, for example, forgeries increased sevenfold between 1938 and 1963, and shopbreaking quintupled. But although most of the crime increase concerned property, there was a disturbing trend toward greater violence, which called into the question the earlier industrial pattern in which the incidence of attacks against persons declined as a proportion of all crimes committed. The murder rate did not rise, and here Europe differed decisively from the United States; the whole of England could not produce as many murders per year as a single enterprising American city such as Houston, Texas. And indeed European crime rates overall were far below American levels. But crime categories such as what the British call "malicious wounding" rose as rapidly as thefts.

In early industrial society high crime rates reflected serious social malaise in both city and countryside. The meaning of contemporary crime trends is less clear, but obviously they deserve attention.

Adolescence

A large part of the crime increase stemmed from a rise in juvenile delinquency. New terms—Teddy boys, *blousons noirs, Halbstärke*—designated the teen-age gangs that formed after the war and included many delinquent elements. In Britain 1,663 male offenders per 10,000 males in the fourteen-to-seventeen age group were recorded in 1953; by 1960 this figure had risen to 2,436. Most delinquents were of working-class origin, and many were the product of broken homes. Their crimes were often minor. The place of adolescents in society had not been resolved, however, though only a minority of teen-agers were delinquents of any sort. Now compelled to remain in school, barred from earning an income, and dependent on parental support longer than ever before in urban society, many teen-agers grew restive. The fact that they were better educated than their parents created obvious friction in many working-class homes. Sexual tensions added to their problems, for though the old hostility to teen-aged sexuality declined (the fear of masturbation waned, for example), the fact was that adolescent puberty occurred at a younger average age each year. Approved sexual outlets did not keep pace. By the 1960s illegitimacy rates began to increase once more, for the first time over an extended period since 1870. Here was another trend whose meaning was not yet clear.

Women

The legal position of women improved in most countries after World War II, though situations varied. French women got the vote; German women had the constitutional right to full legal equality, including equal pay for equal work. Yet those women who did work faced obstacles their male counterparts could avoid, and this was despite the fact that their role in the labor force became steadily more important. An employed woman was only a third as likely as an employed man to be a member of the professions, in France. Educational differences between the sexes prepared different performance at work. German girls seeking vocational training concentrate in a few "female" trades, such as nursing. Fewer girls than boys receive vocational training at all, so that the bulk of the female labor is semiskilled, whereas among German men a full half is skilled. Though the number of women in universities increased (to 23 per cent in Germany in 1964) very few went into "male" subjects such as science, economics, or law (where only 8 per cent of all students were female). With this background it was not surprising that most women saw work as a supplement to the family income, not as a source of professional pride and independence; their job ethic thus differed somewhat from that of men.

In some countries women faced other special problems. Many, ignorant of birth control measures or unwilling to use them, had unwanted pregnancies, in or out of marriage. The abortion rate remained high. Many countries liberalized abortion laws by the 1960s, which made the procedure easier and safer, but this was not universally the case. France, for example, maintained strict prohibitions. This worked no great hardship on the wealthier classes, for women here could go to Switzerland or England for the operation; but working-class women had to resort to clandestine, often unqualified, practitioners. Yet even a modest liberalization measure was shunted aside by the male-dominated parliament in 1973, though under a new regime the question was to be reconsidered in 1974 and birth control efforts were given new legal sanction.

The position of women should not necessarily be interpreted as distinctively tragic. Europe did not develop a significant new feminist movement to match that of the United States by the 1970s, which suggests that many women were content with their roles. Their position in the family had improved. Many did not want a professional career, at least at the expense of their role in the home; two thirds of all German women, for example, favored a law that would prohibit any mother from working until her children had passed ten years of age. But it seemed unlikely that society's adjustment to the modern situation of women had been completed. Better educated, more likely to work, less burdened with frequent child birth, women might think about further change. Few established political parties were ready to give them much encouragement; many of the radical groups were in fact most eager to confirm women in their domestic roles.

Old People

The situation of the elderly also improved in many ways in the consumer society. A smaller percentage were institutionalized than earlier in the twentieth century (only 8 per cent, in England). This reflected better health and better pensions. Most lived separate from their adult children and preferred their independence, but most also visited their children regularly and drew satisfaction from these family ties. But few were fully satisfied with their retirement. Pensions were low, though material concerns were no longer predominant. Old people felt out of place in a youth-oriented society, useless, even scorned. Some regretted that they had chosen or been required to retire. Few were able to develop new leisure interests, though many continued pastimes established earlier. The place of old people in modern society, indeed the view that the elderly had of themselves, had not changed as rapidly as the number and health of people over sixty-five. Here was another novel problem just beginning to receive attention.

The Family

Many of the problems beneath the surface of class and political relations touched closely upon the family—adolescence, women's roles, the personal contacts so important to the elderly. On the whole the family was in good shape in postwar Europe. Marriage rates were high and rising; the marriage age in fact tended to decline with affluence. Divorce rates declined in the 1950s, after the inevitable postwar surge. They rose again in the 1960s, though not to American levels. In 1961, 9 per cent of all British marriages would end in divorce; by 1965 the figure was 16 per cent, with the most common incidence of divorce falling between the tenth and the twentieth year of marriage. Yet even the divorce rate did not fully call the family into question, quite apart from the fact that most marriages still lasted. For most divorced people remarried, usually rather quickly. And as we have seen, family relationships seemed to improve in both the middle and working classes. Extended family ties remained important, and husband–wife and parent–child contacts became more mutual, less stiff. Here clearly was a major reason that most people got through their lives without intense despair. Women could avoid the kind of commitment to work that would drive them to anger against job discrimination because they had a dual role, with the family interest predominating. But men's views were not necessarily completely different, despite a greater preoccupation with their jobs. As one worker said: "A loving family is the finest thing; something to work for, to look to and to look after."

And yet the family was carrying a precarious burden. Modern society preached romance. Modern people sought romance (over 70 per cent of all French people agreed that love marriages were the best kind). Yet often modern people had to settle for companionship. As yet another British worker noted, "The process of cooling off is a natural thing." The companionship was vital; family stability remained essentially intact. Nevertheless, for many, there were expectations not fulfilled.

Conclusion

Each stage of modernization brought its own problems, but those of the consumer society are unique in one respect. In all previous stages the dominant tensions involved clash between groups rooted in the past, their social position depending on maintenance of older criteria of worth, and the modernization process itself. In the consumer society the preindustrial classes have been virtually eliminated. Social stratification remains important, but the leading groups accept modernization in one fashion or another. Even the classic confrontation between workers and owners has taken on a new shape as a result. But the political process and political parties have not changed accordingly; both are rooted in earlier stages of industrialization. This is why some leading problem areas have barely surfaced at the political level; there is no predicting their impact when and if they do. It is possible, of course, that the consumer society has so raped the world of its natural resources that its doom is sealed. But if this is the history of the future it cannot yet be written, for industrial societies have been ingenious in the past about finding new sources of energy and supply. The possibility of catastrophe aside, it is clear that modernized society is for the first time free to shape itself, defining its own problems apart from the legacy of a preindustrial past.

7

CONCLUSION: MODERNIZATION REVISITED

How different are modern people from their premodern ancestors of just two centuries ago? They are larger, sexier, and longer-lived. They are far less religious. It is popular to add that they are more materialistic, but premodern man was of necessity dominated by material concerns; modern men differ in their acquisitiveness and dependence on material progress. Modern people are more individualistic. They face a wider variety of personal choices. They are less controlled or protected by small groups such as village or guild, which formed such a closely knit framework for life before the disruptions of industrialization. They are at the same time exposed to more massive, impersonal organizations than had ever developed before; the ability to deal with bureaucratic procedures has proved a vital part of modernization, though it coexists uneasily with the assertion of individual choice.

The modernization process must of course be qualified by a number of factors. Geography may be one. Although key aspects of behavior, including family relationships, seem to develop along similar lines in any modernization process, it is possible that different political systems may produce distinctive variants. Communist societies in eastern Europe may be able to continue modernization without the specific trappings of the consumer society. It must be remembered that eastern Europe began to modernize from a distinctive kind of preindustrial base; this too could channel the transformation in different directions. In any given area modernization varies with social class. Peasants remain notable for their blend of traditional and modern values. They have changed greatly, but they are less secular, less hedonistic, less fully converted to a belief in science than their urban counterparts. Within the cities working-class modernization has not involved exactly the same outlook as that of the middle class. Male–female differences must also be considered. The modernization of women has taken place more fully within a home and family environment. Initially this sheltered some women from certain kinds of change, for in the working classes at least they were supposed to maintain a host of traditional values. But ultimately women helped transform the home, and began to move outside a strictly domestic setting; the changes they experienced, though different in specifics, were no less great than those encountered by men who were earlier exposed to modern systems of work. Distinctions of this sort are vital in any summary of the modernization process. Yet they do not call into question the idea of a fundamental transformation operating in a coherent general direction.

Yet not all is change. One of the ways people survived successive waves of innovation was to adapt traditional institutions. The family has been utilized as never before. It is still popular to talk about a clear-cut modernization of the family: the preindustrial family was extended, the modern family became nuclear and gradually lost its economic functions, and the contemporary family is near collapse. This, as we have seen, is almost completely inaccurate. Preindustrial families were not rigidly extended. Modern people have relaxed extended family contacts somewhat but rely on them extensively. The modern family has changed its economic functions, moving toward behavior as a consumer unit, and it has decidedly not collapsed. Some students of the family assert that family relationships have not really changed at all. They point to cycles in child-raising concepts, moving from authoritarian to relaxed and back again, that they find in preindustrial as well as industrial generations. It seems likely that the family has become steadily more important as a unit of affection, which was only an accidental purpose before modernization began. But the persistence of traditional elements cannot be denied. Even apparently modern phenomena partially reproduce older kinds of behavior. Birth control, the hallmark of modernity, actually restored the number of children surviving to adulthood that characterized the premodern family; the new method, involving far less childbirth, represented a decisive change for women, but the purpose was not entirely new. One of the most common ages of divorce, the early fifties, in part reproduces the age at which, in preindustrial society, one mate would have been likely to die, leaving the other free to remarry.

Certain other changes may be more superficial than real. Modern people are far less exposed to the sight of death and agony than their premodern counterparts. They are more squeamish about bloodshed, less likely to engage in personal violence. They beat wives and children less often, fight with neighbors less than villagers did. Of course these changes are incomplete, for childbeating and fights continue. But they are important nevertheless. Yet if modern people see death rarely and have abandoned cockfights and public executions, they have not proved reluctant to administer death at longer range. The bombardier or artilleryman may blithely kill people so long as they are spared the sight of the grisly results. Violent sports provide another surrogate for a traditional impulse. So, perhaps, does automobile driving. The European highway death rate is considerably higher than the American, despite the lesser violence of European life in other respects. One reason is prosaic; there are more motorcycles on the road, whose drivers are more vulnerable. But it is not fanciful to note also a mania for speed, on the part of some drivers, that barely disguises an instinct for destruction. How much has really changed? A great deal, but perhaps not nearly enough, given the new technology at the ordinary person's disposal.

The theme of death raises another problem in any simple interpretation of the modernization process. Modernization has reduced the acceptability of death without removing its inevitability. Believing in progress, seeing death less regularly, modern people became increasingly unwilling to receive death calmly. Their battle against death, beginning with the nineteenth-century fight against infant mortality, has won some important gains. Yet the problem remains. Some observers have argued that modern man is less able to cope with the prospect of death than premodern people were, with their greater fatalism and religious belief. One symptom of this is the persistent modern impulse to return to a traditional ceremony to remove some of the stigma of death. The contemporary European is far more likely to have a funeral ceremony than he is to have any particular ritual for birth or marriage. Yet it is doubtful that the ceremony avails much when other social attitudes have changed so greatly.

And from this it is but a step to argue that modernization has taken man away from his true nature, so that he is unable to handle not only death but many other inevitable aspects of life. It has been argued that an undercurrent of madness runs through modern society. Certainly the theme of nervousness and anxiety is inseparable from modern life. And every stage of modernization has taken some toll in terms of insanity and suicide. Other destructive behavior—the barbaric acts of concentration camp guards, for example—suggests deep-seated tensions. These are not entirely new; we do not know how much more insanity or suicide there is in modern Europe than in premodern Europe, and in all probability the incidence of physical cruelty has declined. But it cannot be denied that there are extremes of nonadaptability. Possibly the unquestionable modern impulse carefully to define insanity and deviant behavior and shut their victims off from society reveals a fragile claim to rationality on the part of sane and orderly citizens, such that they must remove expressions of impulses they can barely control and try to remold the "deviant" perpetrators back into their own image.

Without claiming some generalized madness, other observers, as early as the mid-nineteenth century, talked about alienation as an inevitable part of modern life. Karl Marx saw the alienation of workers consisting of their inability to control the results of their labors, for the profits went to the capitalists, and their subjection in the factories to processes that deprived them of a sense of skill and a capacity to create a whole product. Later sociologists have added to the alienation concept, noting the isolation of the individual in modern society, the difficulty of finding self-identity and of relating to other people given the collapse of protective institutions such as village, church, or guild.

In terms of the actual history of modernization the alienation concept is most applicable not to the newer social and occupational groups, but to those being displaced. Each successive stage of modernization redefined the social structure and threatened to leave important categories out. The abolition of legal estates obviously jeopardized the aristocracy. Many were able to adapt, for a group with established wealth and prestige has automatic advantages in dealing with change. But many aristocrats, huddled grimly on their beleaguered estates, were truly isolated from modern life. Early industrialization challenged the middling peasant and the traditional craftsmen, because no one could now retain traditional social status while clinging to a nonmarket mentality. Mature industrialization went further in attacking small property ownership as a guarantee of secure social place. In each case the groups involved showed signs of alienation from modern life. At an extreme they attacked modernity directly: hence artisanal Luddism or the anti-Semitism of elements of the middling class. The stress was greatest in places like central Europe, where industrialization was not spontaneous and there was a highly entrenched middling group before machines began their challenge. Even here the worst problem was usually over in a generation or two; individual journeymen or shopkeepers began to convert to new ways quite early, and their children, thanks to the possibility of change from one generation to the next, were still more open to innovation, whether they remained at their parents' social level or strove for upward mobility.

One group has perhaps been less fortunate. The problem of intellectuals' self-definition remains crucial to modern society. Here too the group is divided. Any characterization of intellectuals will include many people, particularly but not exclusively scientists, who accept the premises of modern life. But others have not, for the intellectual has no inherent position in modern social structure—unlike their ancestors, the priests— or any assured institutional slot. Universities provide a home for some, although this does not assure contentment, for many intellectuals dislike the organizational aspects of modern university structure; and some intellectuals want no part of university life at all. The alienated intellectual remains an important modern phenomenon, and from some intellectuals have come some of the most sweeping generalizations about the alienation of the whole of modern society.

Extreme claims of modern madness or alienation, though they deserve consideration against a more optimistic interpretation, miss the mark in two essential respects. First, they implicitly exaggerate the virtues of preindustrial society. No pollster visited a village in 1700 to ask its inhabitants if they were happy and blessed with integrated personalities. Admittedly some such questions would have had no meaning, for the villager had little sense of alternatives. But his poverty, his routinized approach to work, his subjection to collective controls lead to some rather harsh judgments. There is no need to dismiss all the values of preindustrial society or to deny that modernization brought new tensions, but many people were glad to escape the preindustrial framework, not only because they found some material improvements but because they gained new measures of self-control and new freedom from personal dependence. Too many of the alienation models depend on the idea of a past golden age. Except for key groups caught in a sudden erosion of status, few people undergoing the modernization process would have agreed.

All the studies of the modernizing classes suggest that simple alienation theses do not fit. Research on contemporary workers, often conducted by pollsters eager to find any sign of discontent, uniformly reveal a majority who claim considerable satisfaction with their jobs. And this adaptation to industrial work, a blend of traditional expecations and a modern, instrumental view, began quite early in the industrialization process. This is not, as we have seen, complete bliss. Many workers would prefer to be doing something else, though this thought does not haunt them. And a minority may remain truly alienated. For most, however, a certain tension between pleasures desired and pleasures discovered more accurately conveys modern life than a notion of sweeping antagonism. Sensibly enough, most people from the early stages of modernization onward actively tried to find satisfactions in novelty. New sexual pleasures, new leisure activities at least compensated for, and might improve upon, more traditional comforts. And the modern person did not in fact undergo the strain of industrialization alone, making agonizing decisions as an isolated individual. Typically he or she quickly and deliberately formed a family and used this as a buffer against too much strangeness. Hence modern protest, as it developed among the working classes with mature industrialization, was designed to enhance adaptation rather than to attack industrial life. It expressed frustration at the gap between expectations and reality, but it sought to spur further change, not stop the clock.

Modernized society remains very new in many respects. Mass literacy is barely a century old. A culture of leisure is more novel still. It is impossible to predict the future course of modernization exactly, because the results of past change have yet to be solidified. Modern Europeans themselves, for all their adaptations, remain somewhat tentative about the future, for even the belief in progress is still new and often enough contradicted by events to be incompletely accepted. In December, 1973, as the shortage and rising cost of fuel became evident to all, a variety of intellectuals published articles in France's most prestigious newspaper announcing the end of the consumer society. They spoke with some glee, accusing Europe of having indulged in an orgy of greed in its addiction to affluence; the intellectual hostile to modernity remains ready to speak or write at a moment's notice. At the same time an opinion poll indicated that over 73 per cent of all Frenchmen were basically happy with their life. Yet another poll, focusing on the energy shortage, revealed that 69 per cent anticipated a profound economic crisis that might require a new political system for its solution. Fairly happy now, worried about the future; this is another way to characterize modern man. The same outlook lies behind the oft-repeated assertion that the pace of change is becoming ever faster. This is almost certainly untrue, for the earlier stages of modernization caused far greater shock when measured against preindustrial society's zeal for stability. But the perception of speeding change remains interesting, for it follows from the sense that the ride has, on the whole, been fun up to now but that maybe the merry-go-round should stop.

Yet the history of modernization suggests that further change is inevitable. Short of overturning the basic technical and organizational structure of society, which is not now on the horizon, the development of modern society will probably continue within the recent framework. Modern culture, which is a new creation despite important continuities with the past, shows no sign of giving way to a fundamentally different set of values. This means that despite concern for the future, expectations will continue to depend on change—on new knowledge, new recreational fads, new chances for mobility as well as greater affluence. How much strain this process will produce cannot be anticipated. But one keynote of the modern mentality has been a nervous adaptability. Admittedly not shared by all the groups threatened by change, and certainly dependent on an advancing standard of living to cushion anxiety, adaptation thus far has broken down only once, under the impact of an unprecedented war. With this important but brief exception, Europeans have moved through three major phases of modernization and into a fourth. They may move further still, as the implications of modernization continue to work themselves out. Certainly the process persists.

Appendix. Class Structure, a Chart of Major Changes

Premodern Society	Early Industrial Society	Mature Industrial Society	Consumer Society
Aristocracy gentry magnates	Aristocracy gentry magnates	Upper Class aristocracy big business	Managerial upper class
Peasantry farmers middling owners near-landless laborers Rural merchants and professionals	Peasantry farmers middling (being squeezed) laborers: agricultural and manufacturing	Peasant-farmers Agricultural laborers	Farmers
Rural artisans Bourgeoisie Artisans Servants	Middling Class Middle Class Master Artisans Journeymen Working Class (including female servants)	Middling Class Disgruntled Middle Class (older professions) Middle Class Lower Middle Class	Middle class: Middle mangers, technicians Lower Middle Class
Urban poor	Urban Poor	Working Classes journeymen factory workers unskilled	Working Classes skilled semiskilled unskilled

BIBLIOGRAPHY

The following bibliography is intended to fulfill a dual purpose. It provides a basis for further reading in the major topics of modern European social history, where such reading is available. In this category preference has been given to studies of broad geographical or chronological scope and, where possible, to work in English. At the same time, there is some indication of the most important monographic material. These studies can offer insight into subjects and methods far beyond the limits of the topic itself; they provide important guidelines for further efforts. Certainly much exciting work has recently been done in a variety of aspects of modern European society.

At the same time many of the major subjects of modern European social history remain almost untouched. In a few cases an excellent study can be cited for one small area and time period, but no general work has been done. In other instances, central problems have scarcely been treated at all. Only a few topics, such as labor organization, can offer a really full bibliography. Leading categories, such as the peasantry and the artisan class, have received only scattered treatment; even the middle class, so often cited, has rarely been studied. The social history of women is just beginning to receive attention. The bibliography offered here is not of course an exhaustive list. But it inevitably reflects gaps in our present knowledge. The openness of modern social history, the prospect of vital works yet to come, enhance the basic excitement of the field.

I. Journals

Much of the most exciting work in social history appears as journal articles rather than books. The following journals are particularly important for the field: *Journal of Social History; Comparative Studies in Society and History; International Review of Social History; Past and Present.*

Among foreign language journals see: *Annales, Economies, Sociétés, Civilisations; Mouvement social; Revue d'histoire économique et sociale; Vierteljahrschrift für Sozial—und Wirschaftsgeschichte;* and *Zeitschrift für Geschichtswissenschaft.*

II. General Works

Barrington Moore, *The Social Origins of Dictatorship and Democracy* (Boston, 1966) is an important comparative study. Several national surveys are useful. On Britain, Harold Perkin, *The Origins of Modern English Society 1780–1880* (London, 1969) and Eric Hobsbawm, *Industry and Empire* (New York, 1968) are particularly good. See also Pauline Gregg, *A Social and Economic History of Britain, 1760–1960* (London, 1962); David C. Marsh, *The Changing Social Structure of England and Wales, 1871–1951* (London, 1958) and G. D. H. Cole and Raymond Postgate, *The British Common People 1744–1946* (London, 1961). Two studies of the Victorian period provide good social analyses: Geoffrey Best, *Mid-Victorian Britain 1851–1875* (London, 1971) and J. F. C. Harrison, *The Early Victorians 1832–1851* (London, 1971).

On France, George Dupeux, *La Société française, 1789–1960* (Paris, 1964) is a brief sketch; more imaginative is Theodore Zeldin, *France, 1848–1945: Ambition, Love and Politics* (Oxford, 1973).

On the Mediterranean, J. G. Peristiany, ed., *Honour and Silence: The Values of Mediterranean Society* (Chicago, 1968). On Italy, Carrado Barbagallo, *Cento anni di vita Italiana, 1848–1938* (Cardiff, 1938) contains some helpful insights. Traian Stoianovich, *A Study in Balkan Civilization* (New York, 1967) is a fine essay. On Russia, Cyril Black, ed., *The Transformation of Russian Society: Aspects of Social Change Since 1861* (Cambridge, Mass., 1960).

Several books on daily life can be of value: Maurice Allem, *La Vie quotidienne sous le Second Empire* (Paris, 1944); Pierre F. Bertaux, *La Vie quotidienne en Allemagne au temps de Guillaume II en 1900* (Paris, 1962); G. Blanquis, *La Vie quotidienne en Allemagne à l'époque romantique* (Paris, 1958); Robert Burnand, *La Vie quotidienne en France de 1830* (Paris, 1943) and *La Vie quotidienne en France de 1870 à 1900* (Paris, 1947).

III. Population Change and Urbanization

On demography the most readable sketch is E. A. Wrigley, *Population and History* (New York, 1969). The most comprehensive study is Marcel Reinhard and André Armengaud, *Histoire de la population mondiale* (Paris, 1961). See also Carlo Cipolla, *The Economic History of World Population* (Baltimore, 1962); Herbert Moller, *Population Movements in Modern Europe; A History* (New York, 1964); J. W. Innes, *Class Fertility Trends in England and Wales 1876–1934* (Princeton, 1938) and Charles Morazé, *La France bourgeoise* (Paris, 1952). Michael Drake, ed., *Population in Industrialization* (New York, 1969) contains essays on a number of key problems. The most general survey of urbanization is Adna Weber, *The Growth of Cities in the Nineteenth Century* (Cambridge, England, 1961) and Arthur Redford, *Labour Migration in England, 1800–1850* (London, 1926). Louis Chevalier, *La Formation de la population parisienne au XIX siècle* (Paris, 1950) provides a more specific case study. See also Robert E. Dickinson, *The West European City: A Geographical Interpretation* (London, 1951) and Lewis Mumford, *The City in History* (New York, 1961). On particular cities the following are particularly useful as social history: Asa Briggs, *Victorian Cities* (London, 1953);Hans Bobek and Elisabeth Lichtenberger, *Wien: Bauliche Gestalt und Entwicklung seit der Mitte des 19 Jahrhunderts* (Graz, 1966); Wolfgang Köllman, *Sozialgeschichte der Stadt Barmen im 19. Jahrhundert* (Tubingen, 1960); and Harold J. Dyos, *Victorian Suburb: A Study of the Growth of Camberwell* (Leicester, 1961).

IV. Economic History

The best survey is David Landes, *The Unbound Prometheus: Technological Change and Industrial Development in Western Europe from 1850 to the Present* (Cambridge, England, 1969). For more on technology see Kingston Derry and T. I. Williams, *A Short History of Technology* (Oxford, 1961). W. W. Rostow, *The Process of Economic Growth* (Oxford, 1960) sketches a general theory of industrialization. For eastern and southern Europe, see Alexander Gerschenkron, *Economic Backwardness in Historical Perspective* (Cambridge, Mass., 1962).

On the twentieth century, Paul Alpert, *Twentieth Century Economic History of Europe* (New York, 1951) and M. M. Postan, *An Economic History of Western Europe 1945–1955* (New York, 1957).

William O. Henderson has written three books that provide some comparative perspective: *Britain and Industrial Europe, 1750–1870* (Liverpool, 1954); *The Industrial Revolution on the Continent* (London, 1961); and *The State and the Industrial Revolution in Prussia* (Liverpool, 1958). See also Charles Kindleberger, *Economic Growth of France and Britain 1851–1951* (Cambridge, Mass., 1964).

On Britain see T. S. Ashton, *The Industrial Revolution, 1760–1830* (London, 1948) and particularly Phyllis Deane, *The First Industrial Revolution* (Cambridge, England, 1965); for more detail see J. H. Clapham, *An Economic History of Modern Britain, 1820–1929* (3 vols., Cambridge, England, 1930–1938).

On France, Arthur L. Dunham, *The Industrial Revolution in France, 1815–1848* (New York, 1955) and Rondo Cameron, *France and the Economic Development of Europe, 1800–1914* (Princeton, 1961).

On Germany see Heinrich Bechtel, *Wirtschaftsgeschichte Deutschlands* (Munich, 1956) and Richard Tilly, *Financial Institutions and Industrialization in the Rhineland* (Madison, 1966).

On other cases see S. B. Clough, *A History of Modern Italy* (New York, 1968); Eli Filip Hecksher, *An Economic History of Sweden*, G. Ohlin, tr. (Cambridge, Mass., 1954); John McKay, *Pioneer for Profit: Foreign Entrepreneurship and Russian Industrialization* (Chicago, 1970), and finally, Hans Rosenberg, *Grosse Depression und Bismark* (Berlin, 1967).

V. Preindustrial Society

The best general survey, though specifically British, is Peter Laslett, *The World We Have Lost* (London, 1965); see also Pierre Goubert, *Louis XIV and Twenty Million Frenchmen*, A. Carter, tr. (New York, 1969).

On the aristocracy and the bourgeoisie see Eliner Barber, *The Bourgeoisie in Eighteenth Century France* (Princeton, 1955); Edward Bevill, *English Country Life, 1780–1830* (London, 1962); Peter Feldbauer, *Herrschaftsstruktur und Ständebildung: Herren und Ritter* (Vienna, 1973) (on Austria); Jeffrey Kaplow, *Elbeuf During the Revolutionary Period* (Baltimore, 1964); Franklin Ford, *The Sword and the Robe* (Cambridge, Mass., 1953); G. R. Mingay, *English Landed Society in the Eighteenth Century* (Toronto, 1963); Hans Rosenberg, *Bureaucracy, Aristocracy and Autocracy; the Prussian Experience, 1660–1815* (Cambridge, Mass., 1958); Mack Walker, *The German Home Towns: Community, State and General Estate* (Ithaca, 1971).

On the urban poor and the lower classes: Emile Coornaert, *Les Compagnonnages en France du Moyen âge à nos jours* (Paris, 1966); J. Jean Hecht, *Continental and Colonial Servants in Eighteenth Century England* (Northhampton, Mass., 1954).

On the peasantry see B. H. Slicher van Bath, *The Agrarian History of Western Europe, 500–1840*, O. Ordish, tr. (London, 1963); Thomas Sheppard, *Lourmarin in the Eighteenth Century; a Study of a French Village* (Baltimore, 1971); Patrice Higonnet, *Pont-de-Montvert; Social Structure and Politics in a French Village, 1700–1914* (Cambridge, Mass., 1971); Gérard Bouchard, *La Village immobile; Sennely-en Sologne au XVIIIe siècle* (Paris, 1972); Charles Tilly, *The Vendée* (New York, 1967).

On family life, Philippe Ariès, *Centuries of Childhood: A Social History of Family Life* (New York, 1962); Christina Hole, *English Home Life, 1500–1800* (London, 1947); David Hunt, *Parents and Children in History: The Psychology of Family Life in Early Modern France* (New York, 1970); Peter Laslett, ed. *Household and Family in Past Time* (Cambridge, England, 1972); and Helmut Muller, *Die kleinbürgerliche Familie im 18. Jahrhundert* (Berlin, 1969).

For social interpretations of the French Revolution see Georges Lefebvre, *The Coming of the French Revolution* (Cambridge, England, 1964) and G. A. Williams, *Artisans and Sans Culottes* (New York, 1969).

VI. The Aristocracy and Bureaucracy

Germany is best covered on this topic: in addition to Rosenberg (see preceding section) see Alexander Gerschenkron, *Bread and Democracy in Germany* (Berkeley, 1943), a stinging indictment of the Junkers; Ernst Bramstedt, *Aristocracy and the Middle Classes in Germany* (Chicago, 1964). On the related subject of the German civil service see John Gillis, *The Prussian Bureaucracy in Crisis, 1840–1860* (Stanford, 1971) and Lysbeth Muncy, *The Junkers in the Prussian Administration under William II, 1888–1914* (New York, 1944).

There is nothing specific on France: see Nicholas Richardson, *The French Perfectoral Corps, 1814–1830* (London, 1966) and René Rémond, *The Right Wing in France from 1815 to de Gaulle,* J. Laux, tr. (Philadelphia, 1966).

On eastern Europe see Jerome Blum, *Lord and Peasant in Russia from the Ninth to the Nineteenth Century* (Princeton, 1961) and *Noble Landowners and Agriculture in Austria, 1818–1848* (Baltimore, 1948); Anatole G. Mazour, *The First Russian Revolution, 1825: The Decembrist Movement, Its Origins, Development and Significance* (Berkeley, 1937); G. H. Schlingensiepen, *Der Strukturwandel des baltischen adels vor dem ersen Weltkrieg* (Marburg, 1959); Hannes Stekl, *Osterreichs Aristokratie im Vormärz* (Munich, 1973).

On England see Roger Kelsall, *Higher Civil Servants in Britain from 1870 to the Present Day* (London, 1955); Arthur Ponsonby, *The Decline of the Aristocracy* (London, 1912); and F. M. L. Thompson, *English Landed Society in the Nineteenth Century* (London, 1963).

Frederic C. Jaher, ed. *The Rich, the Well-Born and the Powerful* (Urbana, 1973) contains essays on the upper classes of several countries.

VII. Agriculture and the Peasant

Southern Europe has been extensively studied, mainly in terms of rural unrest. For an overview see Eric Hobsbawm, *Primitive Rebels: Studies in Archaic Forms of Social Movement in the Nineteenth and Twentieth Centuries* (New York, 1957); see also, on Italy, Antonio Lucarelli, *Il Brigantaggio politico del mezzogiorno d'Italia dopo la seconda restaurazione borbonica (1815–1818)* (Bari, 1948) and *Il Brigantaggio politico dopo il 1860: il sergente romano* (Bari-1946). On Spain, Gerald Brenan, *The Spanish Lubyrinth: An Account of the Social und Political Background of the Civil War* (Cambridge, England, 1950) and Juan Diaz del Moral, *Historia de las agitaciones compesinas andaluzas Córdoba (antecendentes para una reforma agraria)* (Madrid, 1959). Julian Pitt-Rivers, *The People of the Sierra* (Chicago, 1961), is an anthropological study of a Spanish rural region; leading developments in the twentieth century are discussed in Edward Malefakis, *Agrarian Reform and Peasant Revolution in Spain: Origins of the Civil War* (New Haven, 1970).

General studies of the nineteenth-century French peasantry are few: Michel Augé-Laribé, *L'Evolution de la France agricole* (Paris, 1912) and *La Révolution agricole* (Paris, 1955) and Gérard Walter, *Histoire des paysans de*

France (Paris, 1963). More penetrating are regional studies, of which the best are Emmanuel Le Roy Ladurie, *Les Paysans de Languadoc* (2v., Paris, 1966); André Armengaud, *Les Populations de l'Est; Aquitaine au debut de l'époque contemporaine* (Paris, 1961); Georges Dupeux, *Aspects de l'histoire sociale et politique du Loir-et-Cher, 1848–1914* (Paris, 1962); and André Fel, *Les Hautes terres du Massif central; tradition paysanne et économie agricole* (Paris, 1962).

On central Europe Rudolf Braun, *Industrielisierung und Volksleben* (Winterthur, 1960) is unusually important as a study of the impact of domestic manufacturing. For Germany, Theodore Hamerow, *Restoration, Revolution, Reaction: Economics and Politics in Germany, 1815–1871* (Princeton, 1958). Heinz Haushofer, *Die deutsche Landwirtschaft im technischen Zeitalter* (Stuttgart, 1963) provides an overview; see also Werner Conze, ed., *Quellen zur Gerschichte der deutschen Bauernbefreiung* (Gottingen, 1957) and G. F. Knapp, *Bauernbefreiung und der Ursprung der Landarbeiter in den älteren Theilen Preussens* (2 vols., Munich, 1927).

For Russia see Geroid T. Robinson, *Rural Russia under the Old Regime* (New York, 1932); Wayne Vucinich, ed., *The Peasant in Nineteenth Century Russia* (Stanford, 1968); and Nicholas Vakar, *The Taproot of Soviet Society* (New York, 1961).

The standard survey of English agriculture is Lord Prothero (Rowland Ernle), *English Farming, Past and Present* (London, 1961). For more specialized studies see W. G. Hoskins, *The Midland Peasant: The Economic and Social History of a Leicestershire Village* (London, 1957); J. L. and Barbara Hammond, *The Village Labourer, 1760–1832* (London, 1911); plus two studies of protest: David Williams, *The Rebecca Riots: A Study in Agrarian Discontent* (Cardiff, 1955) and Eric Hobsbawm and George Rudé, *Captain Swing* (New York, 1968).

On Ireland see T. W. Freeman, *Pre-Famine Ireland: A Study in Historical Geography* (Manchester, 1957); E. E. Evans, *Irish Folk Ways* (London, 1957); and Cecil Woodham-Smith, *The Great Hunger* (New York, 1963).

A number of twentieth-century studies cover land reform in Eastern Europe, for example, David Mitrany, *The Land and the Peasant in Rumania* (London, 1950); Andrzei Korbonski, *Politics and Social Agriculture in Poland* (New York, 1965); Jozo Tomasević, *Peasants, Politics and Economic Change in Yugoslavia* (Stanford, 1955).

There are a number of anthropological studies of Balkan villages, which provide insight into peasant tradition despite their recent vintage: E. Friedl, *Vasilika: A Village in Modern Greece* (New York, 1962); J. T. Sanders, *Balkan Village* (Lexington, 1949) and *Rainbow in the Rocks: The People of Rural Greece* (Cambridge, Mass., 1926); Irene Winter, *A Slovenian Village* (Providence, 1971); and Vera St Erlich, *Family in Transition: A Study of 200 Yugoslav Villages* (Princeton, 1966). A related memoir is Mahmut Makal, *Village in Anatolia* (London: 1954).

Other twentieth-century studies have focused mainly on France: on the interwar period, Neil Hunter, *Peasantry and Crisis in France* (London, 1938); more generally, Gordon Wright, *Rural Revolutions in France: The Peasantry in the Twentieth Century* (Stanford, 1964) and Jean Meynaud, *La Révolte paysanne* (Pais, 1963). A fundamental analysis is provided by Henri Mendras,

The Vanishing Peasant: Innovation and Change in French Agriculture, J. Lerner, tr. (Cambridge, Mass., 1970).

Important specific studies are R. T. and B. G. Anderson, *Bus Stop For Paris* (New York, 1966) and Lawrence Wylie, *Chanzeaux: A Village in Anjou* (Cambridge, Mass., 1966) and *Village in the Vaucluse* (New York, 1957).

VIII. The Middle Classes

A few general surveys are useful: Charles Morazé, *The Triumph of the Middle Classes: A Study of European Values in the Nineteenth Century* (London, 1966), see also section III; Roy Lewis and Angus Maude, *The English Middle Classes* (London, 1950); Jean Lhomme, *La Grande bourgeoisie au pouvoir, 1830–1870* (Paris, 1960); see also Bramsted, section VI.

For England G. M. Young, ed., *Early Victorian England* (2 vols., Oxford, 1934) provides some good insights into middle-class taste. Three books deal with the formation of middle-class social policies: Reinhard Bendix, *Work and Authority in Industry: Ideologies of Management in the Course of Industrialization* (New York, 1956); Ludwig Puppke, *Sozialpolitik und soziale Anschauungen frühindustrieller Unternehmer in Rheinland-Westfalen* (Cologne, 1966); and Sidney Pollard, *The Genesis of Modern Management* (Cambridge, Mass., 1965).

Adeline Daumard, *La Bourgeoisie parisienne de 1815 à 1848* (Paris, 1963) offers one of the most intensive studies to date. See also, on France, Claude Fohlen, *L'Industrie textile au temps du Second Empire* (Paris, 1956); Jean Lambert-Dansette, *Quelques familles du patronat textile de Lille-Armentières* (Lille, 1954); Henri Laufenburger and P. Pflimlin, *Cours d'économie alsacienne* (2v., Paris, 1930–32); and Marguerite Perrot, *Le Mode de vie des familles bourgeoises, 1873–1953* (Paris, 1961).

Theodore Hamerow, *Social Foundations of German Unification* (Princeton, 1969) offers an overview for the middle class in Germany. Recent specific studies are more interesting: Hartmut Kaelble, *Berliner Unternehmer während der fruhen Industrialisierung. Herkunft, sozialer Status und politischer Einfluss* (Berlin, 1972); Rolf Engelsing, *Zur Sozialgeschichte deutscher Mittel—und Unterschichten* (Gottingen, 1973); Hansjoachim Henning, *Das westdeutsche Bürgertum in der Epoche der Hochindustrialisierung, 1860–1914: Soziales Verhalten und Soziale Struktur* (Wiesbaden, 1972). England is not well served by specific studies in this area, but R. S. Neale, *Class and Ideology in the Nineteenth Century* (London, 1972), provides a useful conceptual framework.

For Russia see George Fischer, *Russian Liberalism from Gentry to Intelligentsia* (Cambridge, Mass., 1958).

There are only two good studies of the nineteenth-century lower middle class: David Lockwood, *The Blackcoated Worker: A Study in Class Consciousness* (London, 1958); and Jürgen Kocka, *Unternehmensverwaltung und Angestelltenschaft am Beispiel Siemens, 1849–1914* (Stuttgart, 1969).

Two studies of anti-Semitism provide insight into the middle class, though they tend to exaggerate the impulse they study: P. G. J. Pulzer, *Rise of Political*

Anti-Semitism in Germany and Austria (New York, 1964) and Robert F. Byrne, *Anti-Semitism in Modern France* (New Brunswick, 1950).

On professionals see W. J. Reader, *Professional Men* (London, 1966) and A. M. Carr-Saunders and P. A. Wilson, *The Professionals* (Oxford, 1933). Two studies of universities link professionals to intellectual discontents: F. K. Ringer, *The Decline of the German Mandarins* (Cambridge, Mass., 1969) and Sheldon Rothblatt, *Revolution of the Dons: Cambridge and Society in Victorian England* (New York, 1968).

On intellectuals, Fritz Stern, *Politics of Cultural Despair* (New York, 1965); H. Stuart Hughes, *Consciousness and Society: The Reorientation of European Social Thought* (New York, 1958); and Richard Pipes, ed., *The Russian Intelligentsia* (New York, 1961). Finally, there is Cesar Grana, *Bohemian Versus Bourgeois* (New York, 1964).

Twentieth-century studies deal with the middling and the lower middle class particularly: on Germany, Heinrich Winkler, *Mittelstand, Demokratie und Nationalsozialismus* (Cologne, 1972). S. Kracauer, *Die Angestellten* (Frankfurt, 1930); and to a lesser extent Herman Lebovics, *Social Conservatism and the Middle Classes in Germany, 1914–1933* (Princeton, 1969) are important studies. On another group, see R. V. Clements, *Managers, A Study of Their Careers in Industry* (London, 1958). See also the section entitled "The Family," p. 349.

IX. Social Protest and Crisis

Several studies of nineteenth-century revolutions provide insight into broader social history, dealing with the full spectrum of society.

An overview is provided by Eric Hobsbawm, *The Age of Revolution, 1789–1948* (Cleveland, 1962). On 1848, a survey, with extensive bibliography, is Peter N. Stearns, *1848: The Revolutionary Tide in Europe* (New York, 1974). Useful special studies include Domenica Demarco, *Una Rivoluzione soziale, la reppublica romana del 1848* (Naples, 1944); K. Griewach, *Deutsche Studenten und Universitäten in der Revolution von 1848* (Weimar, 1949); Georges Duveau, *1848: The Making of a Revolution*, tr. A. Carter (New York, 1967); Roger Price, *The French Second Republic* (Ithaca, 1972); and Karl Obermann, *Die deutschen Arbeiter in der ersten bürgerlichen Revolution* (Berlin, 1950). On the Paris Commune, Edward Mason, *The Paris Commune* (New York, 1930). The nature of lower-class unrest before the mid-nineteenth century has been analyzed by George Rudé, *The Crowd in History, 1730–1848* (New York, 1964). See also Hobsbawm and Hobsbawm and Rudé, Section VII. Important specialized studies of early industrial protest include J. P. Aguet, *Les Grèves sous la monarchie de juillet* (Geneva, 1954); Wolfgang Köllman, *Wuppertaler Färbergesellen-Innung und Färbergesellen-Streiks, 1848–1857* (Weisbaden, 1962); and Malcolm Thomis, *The Luddites: Machine-breaking in Regency England* (Newton Abbot, England, 1970). Two books provide a model for mature industrial protest: K. G. J. C. Knowles, *Strikes: A Study in Industrial Conflict* (Oxford, 1952) and Charles Tilly and Edward Shorter, *Strikes in France, 1830–1848* (Cambridge, 1974).

See also Eduarde Comîn Colomer, *Historia del anarquismo español* (Barcelona, 1956); Hugh A. Clegg and others, *A History of British Trade Unions Since 1889* (New York, 1964); and Peter N. Stearns, *Revolutionary Syndicalism and French Labor* (New Brunswick, 1971).

For the social basis of socialism and communism: Guenther Roth, *The Social Democrats in Imperial Germany; A Study in Working Class Isolation and National Integration* (Totowa, N.J., 1963); Gerhard Ritter, *Die Arbeiterbewegung in wilhelminischen Reich* (Berlin, 1959); Claude Willard, *Les Guesdistes: Le Mouvement socialiste en France, 1893–1905* (Paris, 1965); Annie Kriegel, *Aux Origines du communisme Français, 1914–1920* (Paris, 1964) and *The French Communists: Profile of a People* (Chicago, 1972).

For a short sketch of the labor movement before World War I, with extensive bibliography, see Harvey Mitchell and Peter N. Stearns, *Workers and Protest* (Itasca, Ill., 1971).

Crime is just beginning to receive attention from historians. See Louis Chevalier, *Dangerous Classes and Laboring Classes* (New York, 1967), a rather impressionistic work; also see J. J. Tobias, *Crime and Industrial Society in the Nineteenth Century* (New York, 1967), T. A. Critchley, *The Conquest of Violence: Order and Liberty in Britain* (New York, 1970), and J. V. M. Shields and J. A. Duncan, *The State of Crime in Scotland* (London, 1967). More recent trends are discussed in F. H. McClintock and N. H. Avison, *Crime in England and Wales* (New York, 1969).

X. The Working Classes

There is very little work on artisans. See Hamerow, in the section on "Agriculture and the Peasants," and Paul Noyes, *Organization and Revolution: Working Class Association in the German Revolution of 1848–1849* (Princeton, 1966). J. L. and Barbara Hammond, *The Skilled Labourer, 1760–1832* (London, 1919) and *The Town Labourer, 1760–1832* (London, 1917) are classics. E. P. Thompson, *The Making of the English Working Class* (New York, 1964) deals mainly with the crafts. See also Rudolf Brauns, *Sozialer und Kultureller Wandel in einem landlichen Industriegebiet* (Zurich, 1965).

Three essay collections contain material both on artisans and factory workers: Stephen Thernstrom and Richard Sennett, *Yale Conference on the Nineteenth Century Industrial City* (New Haven, 1968); Peter N. Stearns and Daniel Walkowitz, *Workers in the Industrial Revolution* (New Brunswick, 1974); and Eric Hobsbawm, *Labouring Men* (London, 1964).

There is almost no treatment of the urban poor. See Chevalier, in the section on "Social Protest and Crisis," and especially Gareth Stedman Jones, *Outcast London: A Study in the Relationship Between Classes in Victorian Society* (Oxford, 1971), and Brian Inglis, *Poverty and the Industrial Revolution* (London, 1971).

On factory workers, Friedrich Engels, *The Condition of the Working Class in England,* Henderson and Chaloner, eds. (London, 1958), remains a classic. See also Neil J. Smelser, *Social Change in the Industrial Revolution: An Application of Theory to the Lanchashire Cotton Industry, 1770–1840* (London, 1960) and John Foster, *Class Struggle in the Industrial Revolution* (London, 1974); for a later period, A. L. Levine, *Industrial Retardation in Britain* (London, 1967); and Sidney Pollard, *History of Labour in Sheffield* (Liverpool, 1959).

On France, Georges Duveau, *La Vie ouvrière en France sous le Second Empire* (Paris, 1946); Pierre Pierrard, *La Vie ouvrière à Lille sous le Second Empire* (Paris, 1969); Maurice Halbwachs, *L'Evolution des besoins dans les classes ouvrières* (Paris, 1933) and André Lasserre, *La Situation des ouvriers de l'industrie textile dans la region lilloise sous la monarchie de juillet* (Lausanne, 1952).

The social history of the early working class elsewhere has often been neglected in favor of the study of organized labor, but there are exceptions. See Leo Uhen, *Gruppenbewusstsein und informelle Gruppenbildungen bei deutschen Arbeitern im Zt. der Industrielisierung* (Berlin, 1963) and Reginald Zelnik, *Labor and Society in Tsarist Russia* (Stanford, 1971). Social studies in the twentieth century have developed mainly since World War II, but there are many good ones. Ferdynand Zweig, *The British Worker* (Harmondsworth, 1952) and *The Worker in an Affluent Society: Family Life and Industry* (New York, 1962); J. H. Goldthorpe et al., *The Affluent Worker in the Class Structure* (Cambridge, England, 1969); Dorthy Wedderburn and Rosemary Crompton, *Workers' Attitudes and Technology* (Cambridge, England, 1972); Marcel David, *Les Travailleurs et le sens de leur histoire* (Paris, 1967); T. Parker et al., *Arbeiter, Management, Mitbetimmung* (Stuttgart, 1955); Heinrich Popitz, *Das Gesellschaftsbild des Arbeiters* (Tubingen, 1957); Georges Friedmann, *Le Travail en Mettes* (Paris, 1969). On a vital new topic, Stephen Castles and Godule Kosack, *Immigrant Workers and the Class Structure in Western Europe* (London, 1973).

XI. Women

Most studies of women, and they are too few in social history, deal with work roles. For a more general overview, see Patricia Branca and Peter N. Stearns, *Impact of Modernization on the History of Women* (St. Louis, 1973). On birth control see J. A. Banks, *Prosperity and Parenthood* (London, 1954) and, with Olive Banks, *Feminism and Family Planning in Victorian England* (New York, 1964); Shirley Green, *The Curious History of Contraception* (London, 1971); Norman E. Himes, *Medical History of Contraception* (New York, 1936).

On agricultural work, G. E. and K. R. Fussell, *The English Countrywomen, A Farm-House Social History, 1500–1900* (London, 1953).

On the factories see Margaret Hewitt, *Wives and Mothers in Victorian Industry* (London, 1958); Wanda F. Nef, *Victorian Working Women* (London, 1929); Ivy Pinchbeck, *Women Workers in the Industrial Revolution* (London, 1930). On white-collar jobs see Lee Holcombe, *Victorian Ladies at Work* (Hamden, 1973).

Several essay collections deal with a variety of aspects of women's history: Martha Vicinus, ed., *Suffer and Be Still* (Bloomington, 1972); Mary Hartman and Lois Banner, eds. *Clio's Consciousness Raised: New Perspectives on the History of Women* (New York, 1974); Renate Bridenthal and Claudia Koonz, *Becoming Visible: The History of Women in Europe* (New York, 1974).

On the twentieth century: Evelyne Sullerot, *Women, Society and Change* (New York, 1971) and *Histoire et sociologie du travail feminin* (Paris, 1969); R. Patai, ed., *Women in the Modern World* (New York, 1967); Joseph Schoonbroodt, *Les Femmes et le travail* (Brussels, 1973).

Feminism has not been studied from the standpoint of social history; for an introduction, William L. O'Neill, *Woman Movement: Feminism in the United States and England* (Chicago, 1969).

XII. The Family

The nineteenth-century family has received little attention, but one study is excellent: Michael Anderson, *Family Structure in Nineteenth Century Lancashire* (Cambridge, England). See also André Toledano, *La Vie de famille sous la restauration et la monarchie de juillet* (Paris, 1943).

On age structure see Ivy Pinchbeck and Margaret Hewitt *Children in English Society* (Vol. 2, London, 1973); John Gillis, *Youth and History: Tradition and Change in European Age Relations, 1770–Present* (New York, 1974); On old age see Simone de Beauvoir, *The Coming of Age* (New York, 1972), a gloomy and impressionistic study and, for the more recent period, Ethel Shanas et al., *Old People in Three Industrial Societies* (New York, 1968).

There are a number of good studies of the twentieth-century English family, including Colin Rosser and Christopher Harris, *The Family and Social Change* (New York, 1965); P. Willmott and M. Young, *Family and Class in a London Suburb* (New York, 1960) *Family and Kinship in East London* (London, 1957) and *The Symmetrical Family* (London, 1973); Peter Townshend, *Family Life of Old People* (London, 1970); Ronald Fletcher, *Britain in the Sixties: The Family and Marriage* (Baltimore, 1962); O. R. McGregor, *Divorce in England: A Centenary Study* (London, 1947); Simon Yudkin and Anthea Holme, *Working Mothers and Their Children* (London, 1963).

XIII. Popular Culture

The most important interpretations of changes in popular culture are Raymond Williams, *Culture and Society, 1780–1950* (New York, 1958) and *The Long Revolution* (New York, 1961); Philippe Ariès, *Les Populations françaises et leurs attitudes devant la vie depuis le 18e siècle* (Paris, 1971); and Rudolf Schenda, *Volk ohne Buch: Studien zur Sozialgeschichte der populären Lesestoffe 1770–1910* (Frankfurt, 1970). See also Richard Hoggart, *The Uses of Literacy* (Oxford, 1957); Bernard Rosenberg and D. M. White, eds., *Mass Culture* (New York, 1957) and Carlo Cipolla, *Literacy and Development in the West* (London, 1969).

More specific studies of the uses of reading are Lee Lowenthal, *Literature,*

Popular Culture, and Society (Los Angeles, 1961); Henry N. Smith, *Popular Culture and Industrialism 1865–1890* (New York, 1967); R. O. Altick, *The English Common Reader: A Social History of the Mass Reading Public* (New York, 1957); Edna Sagarra, *Tradition and Revolution: German Literature and Society, 1830–1890* (London, 1963). On sports, Peter McIntosh, *Sport in Society* (New York, 1963) and *Physical Education in England Since 1800* (London, 1969); Philip Goodhart and Christopher Chataway, *War Without Weapons* (London, 1968); Robert Daley, *The Bizarre World of European Sports* (New York, 1963).

On the leisure ethic: Michael Marrus, *The Rise of Leisure in Industrial Society* (St. Louis, 1974). See also Michael Smith and others, eds., *Leisure and Society in Britain* (London, 1973). Drinking and its opponents are discussed in Brian Howard Harrison, *Drink and the Victorians: The Temperance Question in England* (Pittsburgh, 1971).

On education, for an overview see William Boyd, *The History of Western Education* (New York, 1967); Brian Simon, *Studies in the History of Education, 1780–1870* (London, 1960); H. C. Barnard, *Short History of English Education* (London, 1960); E. H. Reisner, *Nationalism and Education Since 1789* (New York, 1923); Michalina Baughan and M. S. Archer, *Social Conflict and Educational Change in England and France, 1798–1848* (New York, 1971); F. Ponteil, *Histoire de l'Enseignement en France* (Paris, 1966); S. C. Engelmann, *German Education and Re-education* (New York, 1945).

On the press see C. F. Carr and Frederick Stevens, *Modern Journalism* (London, 1931); Charles Ledré, *Histoire de la presse* (Paris, 1958).

On religion see Adrien Dansette, *Religious History of Modern France* (London, 1961); J. B. Duroselle, *Les Débuts du Catholicisme social en France, 1822–1870* (Paris, 1951); K. S. Inglis, *Churches and the Working Class in Victorian England* (Toronto, 1963); J. H. Moody, ed., *Church and Society: Catholic Social and Political Thought and Movements, 1789–1950* (New York, 1953); Erich Schmidt Volkmar, *Der Kulturkampf in Deutschland, 1871–1890* (Gottingen, 1962); Serge Bonnet, *Sociologie politique et religieuse de la Lorraine* (Paris, 1972).

On insanity and suicide see Herbert Hendin, *Suicide and Scandinavia* (New York, 1964); Michel Foucault, *Madness and Civilization*, R. Howard, tr. (New York, 1965); George Rosen, *Madness in Society: Chapters in the Historical Sociology of Mental Illness* (New York, 1968). Finally, Jack D. Douglas, *The Social Meaning of Suicide* (Princeton, 1967).

XIV. The Twentieth Century

On the social bases and impact of fascism: Karl D. Bracher, *Die Auflösung der Weimarer Republik* (Stuttgart, 1957) and David Schoenbaum, *Hitler's Social Revolution: Class and Status in Nazi Germany* (New York, 1966); C. W. Guillebaud, *The Social Policy of Nazi Germany* (Cambridge, England, 1941); Louis Rosenstock-Franck, *L'Economie corporative fasciste en doctrine et en fait* (Paris, 1934).

On class structure and culture between the wars see Theodor Geiger, *Soziale Schichtung des deutschen Volkes* (Stuttgart, 1932); Carlile Macartney, *The Social Revolution in Austria* (Cambridge, England, 1926); L. M. Ferré, *Les Classes sociales dans la France contemporaine* (Paris, 1934); E. N. Earle, ed., *Modern France: Problems of the Third and Fourth Republics* (Princeton, 1951); Charles L. Mowat, *Britain Between the Wars, 1918–1940* (Chicago, 1955); Robert Graves and Alan Hodges, *The Long Weekend: A British Social History, 1918–1939* (New York, 1941).

On postwar Europe see Stephen Graubard, ed., *A New Europe?* (Boston, 1963), which offers a series of essays on social and technological change. On demography see Geory Frumkin, *Population Changes in Europe Since 1939* (New York, 1951).

On the welfare state see Wilfred Fleisher, *Sweden, The Welfare State* (New York, 1956); Richard M. Titmuss, *Essays on "The Welfare State"* (London, 1958).

On the major countries see Maurice Bouvier-Ajam, *Les Classes sociales en France* (Paris, 1963); Stanley Hoffman, ed., *In Search of France* (Cambridge, Mass., 1963); John Ardagh, *The New French Revolution* (New York, 1969); Julian Park, *The Culture of France in Our Time* (Ithaca, 1954). Ralf Dahrendorf, *Society and Democracy in Germany* (Garden City, 1968). Milovan Djilas, *Land Without Justice* (New York, 1958) and *The New Class* (New York, 1957) writes on communist society.

On Italy see Joseph A. Martellaro, *Economic Development in Southern Italy 1950–1960* (Washington, 1965).

On Britain see Judith Ryder and Harold Silver, *Modern English Society, History, and Structure, 1850–1970* (London, 1970); A. Shonfield, *British Economic Policy Since the War* (London, 1958); Thomas Stark, *The Distribution of Personal Income In the United Kingdom 1949–1963* (Cambridge, England, 1972); Anthony Sampson, *Anatomy of Britain Today* (New York, 1965); A. H. Halsey, ed., *Trends in British Society Since 1900* (New York, 1972).

On youth revolt see Tarig Ali, ed., *New Revolutionaries: Left Opposition* (New York, 1965). H. Bourges, ed., *The Student Revolt* (New York, 1968) deals with the May uprising in France.

INDEX

Adolescence
  in mature industrial society, 232–33
  after World War II, 327
  See also Children
Aged. *See* Elderly
Agriculture
  by 1800, 71–72
  after 1890s, 260–61, 263, 265
  enclosure movement and, 69–70
  estate, 22
    See also Estates
  family responsibilities in, 35
  market, 90–92, 94
  in 1700s, 14–23
  village, 20–22
  after World War II, 306–307, 312
Agricultural classes, in industrial revolution, 90–93
Agricultural society, in 1700s, 14–23
Alienation concept, 334, 335
Anti-Semitism, 18, 223
Apprenticeship, 49, 149, 150
Architecture, 138
Aristocracy
  in early industrial society, 93–99
  as no longer upper class, 212–16
  population growth and, in eighteenth century, 68–69

Aristocracy (*cont.*)
  preindustrial, 23–31
    east and west, 31
    power of, 27–29
    as ruling class, 29–31
    structure of, 26–27
Artisans, 17, 32, 47–52, 70, 75, 222, 244
  See also Craftsmen
Artists, 136
Arts, patronizing of, 137–38
Assembly line, 183
Assembly of Notables of 1787, 28

Baby farms, 74
Balance of payments, 308–309
Balkans, riots in, 105–106
Banking, 185
Big business. *See* Business
Birth control, 36, 41, 142, 245
Blanc, Louis, 156
Boulton, Matthew, 62
Bourgeoisie, 44–47, 70–71
Brotherton, Joseph, 121
Bureaucracy, 213–15, 313
Business
  big, 86, 241–42
    in mature industrial society, 183–88

353